Advances in Spatial and Network Economics

Titles in the Series

Martin J. Beckmann and *Tönu Puu*
Spatial Structures

Aisling J. Reynolds-Feighan
The Effects of Deregulation on U.S. Air Networks

Åke E. Andersson, David F. Batten
Kiyoshi Kobayashi and *Kazuhiro Yoshikawa (Eds.)*
The Cosmo-Creative Society

Börje Johansson, Charlie Karlsson,
and *Lars Westin (Eds.)*
Patterns of a Network Economy

Bertrand M. Roehner

Theory of Markets

Trade and Space-time Patterns of Price Fluctuations
A Study in Analytical Economics

With 149 Figures

Springer-Verlag
Berlin Heidelberg New York
London Paris Tokyo
Hong Kong Barcelona
Budapest

Professor Bertrand M. Roehner
L.P.T.H.E.
University Paris VII
2 place Jussieu
75251 Paris Cedex 05
France

ISBN-13:978-3-642-79481-0 e-ISBN-13:978-3-642-79479-7
DOI: 10.1007/978-3-642-79479-7

Softcover reprint of the hardcover 1st edition 1995

42/2202-5 4 3 2 1 0 - Printed on acid-free paper

The earth is often in astronomical calculations considered as a point and with substantially accurate results. But the precession of the equinoxes becomes explicable only when account is taken of the ellipsoidal bulge of the earth. So in the theory of value a market is usually considered as a point in which only one price can obtain; but for some purposes it is better to consider a market as an extended region.

Harold HOTELLING
Stability in competition (Economic Journal 1929)

"Data! data! data!" he cried impatiently. "I can't make bricks without clay."

Sir Arthur Conan DOYLE
The Adventure of the Copper Beeches.

Preface

Book titles, because they are compromises between concision and precision, provide but an approximate description of real content. For this book an alternative and more comprehensive title would be: *An investigation of spatial arbitrage as an introduction to the theory of commodity markets: trade and space-time patterns of price fluctuations.* In this title, both the specificities and the limitations of our approach are emphasized. Firstly, our approach concentrates on the basic mechanisms of spatial arbitrage, leaving aside a number of accessory facets of international trade such as the impact of quotas or of exchange rates. Secondly, for the sake of simplicity we restrict ourselves to single commodity markets; the interrelationship of different goods on multi-commodity markets are only occasionally mentioned. The previous restrictions, however drastic they may at first appear delimit and define what can be considered as the core of the process of trade and of spatial transactions. Having thus simplified the object of our study, we are able to tackle the problem in a systematic way and to model spatial differentials along with their relationships to the volume of trade both in equilibrium and in non-equilibrium situations. As far as the subtitle of the book is concerned, we shall postpone the discussion of what is meant by the expression "analytical economics" until the concluding chapter.

The starting point of our inquiry was a simple yet basic problem in economic history: a great number of price records have been collected and published during the last fifty years; they constitute a set of time series characterized both by good resolution in time and by rather long time spans of two or even three centuries. Yet in spite of a number of attempts going back to Beveridge (1921,1922), Labrousse (1932), Abel (1935) or Kendall (1953) the question of their economic significance is still largely unanswered, especially as far as short-term price fluctuations are concerned. Is it possible to uncover the mechanisms of market integration from an analysis of price series? What is the relationship between the volume of trade and the level of transport rates? How are arbitrage policies actually implemented? In which ways is the exchange pattern between markets modified during price peak periods? In the process of analysing such issues, some definite spatial price patterns showed up; this was all the more surprising in view of the chaotic behaviour of short-term prices. Furthermore, growing evidence gradually accumulated showing that the validity of those patterns actually extends to modern commodity markets as well.

While investigating the aforementioned issues, we were led to address a number of related econometric questions. What are the distinctive features of *spatial* autoregressive processes? Could multiple price series adequately be described within the framework of space-time autoregressive processes? What are the characteristic properties of space-time propagation models?

What we believe to be one of the most interesting features of our empirical findings is the *stability* of emerging price patterns; they may provide firm points of reference in the ever changing economic world. The first chapters will probably be more appealing to economists and economic historians, while econometricians will rather focus on the last ones.

This book relates an inquiry which has been in progress for a number of years. It is a real pleasure at this point to thank the many people who kindly provided support and advice. I am indebted to Edmond Malinvaud whose initial encouragements were at the starting point of this study. I am grateful to Guy Laroque whose guidance was enlightening on several occasions. By their suggestions Luc Anselin, David Batten, François Bourguignon, Hubert Jayet and Alain Montfort gave me the opportunity of enlarging the scope of my work. Many thanks to them. The American Cliometric Society and the European Cliometric Society welcomed discussion of this work even at an early stage of its development; I am grateful to many of its members for stimulating suggestions and discussions, especially to Donald McCloskey, Larry Neal, Kevin O'Rourke, Gunnar Persson, Pascal Saint Amour, Pierre Sicsic and Jeffrey Williamson.
While writing this book I had the opportunity of teaching statistical and spatial geography and this has been a refreshing experience. Moreover my contacts in the field of geographical analysis always have been a source of stimulation; I am particularly pleased to express my gratitude to Gordon Clark, Peter Haggett, Robert Haining, Denise Pumain and Thérèse Saint Julien.
Finally, I would like to express many thanks to my colleagues at the level of my department and especially to Alain Bouquet, François Delduc, Bernard Diu, Giorgio Giavarini, Jean Kaplan, Jean Letessier and Galliano Valent.

The book is dedicated to my wife Brigitte and to my son Sylvain whose cheerful encouragements and stimulating support have been invaluable.

Bertrand Roehner

Paris, January 1994

Contents

PART III DYNAMIC MODELS

Chapter 1
Introduction

In this opening chapter we would like to put the problem of market interdependence back in the context of free market economy. First we briefly discuss its relevance to price theory. Then we stress a few basic facts concerning commodity markets; we elaborate in particular upon the various stages at which prices may be registered. We sketch the main methodological ideas on which our approach is based. Finally, we present a number of empirical observations regarding both the patterns of price differentials and the historical process of price convergence.

1 Smith's "invisible hand" in commodity markets

In an economy in which markets are permitted to work without outside intervention, the decisions taken by individual buyers and sellers are coordinated and made consistent with each other by movements in prices. This process of coordination is quite decentralized. The mechanism by which movements in prices coordinate individual decisions has been a central concept in economics for more than two centuries, since the times of Bernard de Mandeville (1670-1733) and Adam Smith (1723-1790). In Smith's mind the "hidden hand" was guiding individuals so that, although they were motivated by self-interest, each of them acted for the good of the whole. In this book our purpose is to analyse the function of the "invisible hand " at a more aggregated level, namely at the level of economic links between geographically distant markets, the only level at which price statistics are actually available. Some of these links, namely those provided by transportation networks are obvious; they constitute the visible part of the hand. The ways in which *information* about price changes is taken into account are less apparent, however.

It is often argued that, in contrast to time arbitrage, spatial arbitrage can in principle be carried out without uncertainty and accordingly it has often been considered as being of marginal theoretical interest. This, however, is a rather schematic view for actual spatial arbitrage mechanisms are far more intricate. Firstly, for arbitrage to take place arbitragers must be present and they must be willing to take the risk. Let us leave aside such special circumstances as political instability or insecurity which may keep them out of the market. A more fundamental constraint is the long delay required to build up transportation means (merchant fleets, railroads, etc); as a result there is a great inertia in the availability of such facilities. But the essential risk in the trade business is of course connected with the transportation delay for the trader then has to face the problem of time arbitrage with its intrinsic uncertainty. It is precisely the role of hedging operations to protect the buyer or the seller against a change in prices (Labys and Granger 1970). But hedging has a cost (in which we include transaction costs per se as well as the time it requires for the merchant to carry out these operations) which comes on top of other charges and increases total transfer costs.

2 Spatial interaction in economic theory

Hotelling's pioneering paper on spatial competition appeared in 1929 in the Economic Journal; it opened the way to the development of imperfect competition and spatial price discrimination theories. In the 1950s, the spatial price equilibrium model was formalized and generalized to an arbitrary number of markets by Stephen Enke (1951) and particularly by Paul Samuelson (1952,1954,1957). Spatial price dispersion also has implications in the theory of international trade. In developing the Heckscher-Ohlin principle, Samuelson formulated the factor price equalization theorem (Samuelson 1948, 1949). It states that unless initial factor endowments are too unequal, commodity mobility will always be a perfect substitute for factor mobility. In other words an increased level of market integration for basic commodities is an essential condition for achieving free mobility of factors of production.

Since Hotelling's and Samuelson's pioneering investigations, there have been a number of attempts at modelling the impact of variables such as distance, location and transport cost on the structure of trade. From a theoretical point of view, one should mention the contributions of Beckmann (1952, 1985), Isard (1956), Takayama and Judge (1971), Capozza and Van Order (1977,1978), Batten (1989), Gabszewicz and Thisse (1989), Faden (1991). One of our purposes is to bridge the gap between formal models of spatial competition and statistical evidence from commodity markets. Following the development of the spatial price equilibrium model, there have been a number of attempts at modelling various commodity markets which we shall discuss in chapter 3. Let us here mention two very clear and lucid critical analysis of the spatial price equilibrium model which are provided by Bressler and King (1970) on one hand and by Batten and Westin (1990) on the other.

The economic relevance of space-time models does not exclusively stem from their importance in the theory of commodity markets. Indeed, location problems are related to many other diffusion and propagation phenomena in modern economics. The analysis of unemployment patterns is one such example (Granger 1969a, Bronars and Jansen 1987); the analysis of inflation patterns may be another. More generally, distance may be regarded as a figurative term for a variety of different qualities. Consider for instance two cider merchants located on the same spot but one selling sweeter quality than the other. Suppose moreover that the consumers of cider may be thought of as gradually differing in the sourness they desire. The two sellers then may be considered as representing two geographically separated markets. The measure of sourness replaces distance, while instead of transportation costs there are the degrees of disutility resulting from the diverse tastes of the consumers. This is a classical argument in the theory of imperfect competition (may be it should not be taken too seriously for the range of consumers' tastes is much more difficult to estimate statistically than geographical distance). More generally, in econometrics data sets pooling together time and cross-section data are referred to as *panel data*. Recent overviews of this field can be found in Chamberlain (1984) and Hsiao (1986).

3 Spatial interaction in geographical analysis

> "**A stone is tossed into a pond.** The consequent splash forms a large wave immediately around the entry point. Within a second, waves are starting to move out in a circular pattern across the surface of the water. Some seconds later, very small ripples are disturbing the weeds on the far end of the pound...
> **A virus is tossed into a susceptible population.** Passengers arriving at an Icelandic port from Copenhagen in the early summer of 1907 include a few known to be suffering from measles infection. One escapes the quarantine procedures, and joins the local population, some of whom are off to the capital city, Reykjavík to form the crowds gathering for the visit by the King of Denmark. The virus is transmitted between some neighbours in the crowd. Within 16 months, an epidemic has spread through the whole island infecting over 7000 people and killing 354.
> Although the stone and the epidemic are in many respects wholly dissimilar phenomena, they do share something in common. What they share is the property of spatial diffusion; that is the ability to disperse from one or more limited centres to a wide geographical area."
>
> Cliff et al: Spatial diffusion (1981, p.1)

As a third illustration of the diffusion phenomena, one may contemplate the spatial propagation of a price shock. Such an example has been given in the introductory chapter of Cliff et al (1981). It is illustrated in Fig.1.1 and displays the propagation of the price fall that occurred in Iowa in the aftermath of the Great Depression. According to these data, the propagation is characterized by a surprisingly low speed. When investigating propagation of price shocks in Chapter 9, we shall meet with the same kind of conclusion.

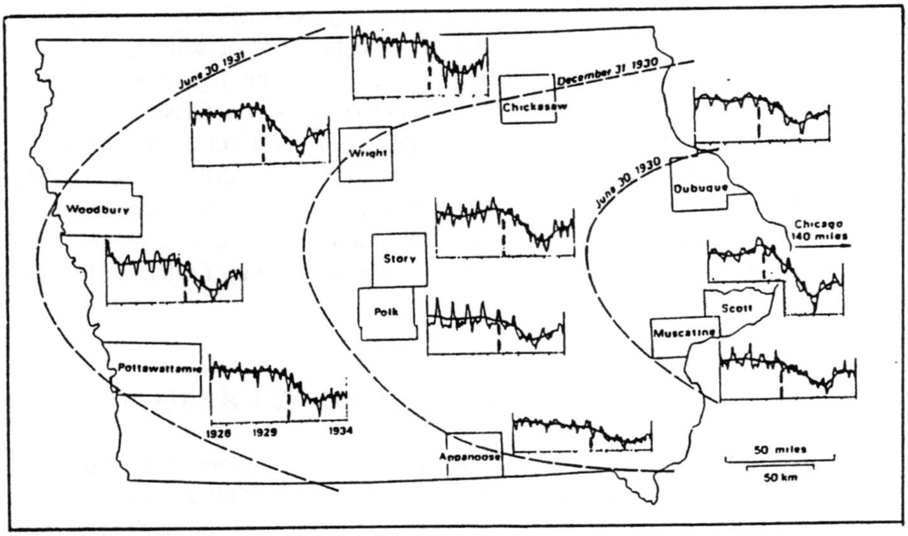

Fig.1.1 Propagation (from East to West) of a decrease in prices in Iowa (USA). *Sources: Cliff et al (1981,p.13), Lösch (1954,p.497).*

In the analysis of spatial interaction, many of the innovative ideas that provided the impetus to develop new techniques came from geographers. Theoretical methods as well as applications may be found in a number of reference books that have appeared in the last twenty years and have much contributed to the vitality of the field: Cliff and Ord (1973,1981), Haining (1978, 1990), Bennet (1979), Paelinck and Klaassen (1979), Upton and Fingleton (1985), Anselin (1988), Griffith (1988), Arbia (1989), Jayet (1994). They include, just to mention a few of them, investigations about the spread of measles epidemics, the spatial patterns of crime, of housing value, of rainfall, or of agricultural production. Furthermore, the significance of spatial interaction in economic problem has been discussed (from the point of view of geographical analysis) in particular by Jones (1983), Clark (1986) and Haining (1984).

4 Regional market integration and famines

Before the twentieth century there have been tremendous price fluctuations in grain markets which resulted in scarcity and in famines for the poorest people. In Western Europe, the last famine can be considered as having occurred in 1817 but even as late as 1847 France, Germany and some regions of the United Kingdom (especially Ireland and Wales) have been hit by a severe dearth which caused great social unrest. Numerous bakeries, grain reserves or goods trains were attacked by hungry people and the army had to be called in. In France, the "Gazette des Tribunaux" reports about thirty cases which came before the courts: three death sentences and many sentences to hard labor were pronounced. In the second half of the nineteenth century after railroads had extended their networks all over Europe, dearths were virtually eliminated, except perhaps under war circumstances. In contrast, even after 1860, India experienced sharp rises in food prices which, by rendering food beyond the reach of the poor, lead to a great number of famines; the most dramatic of them were (Bhatia 1967, Ravallion 1987):

1865	:	Province of Madras
1868 – 1869	:	Rajputana (NW of India)
1873 – 1874	:	Bengal
1876	:	Province of Bombay
1896 – 1897	:	Central provinces, Deccan districts
1899 – 1900	:	Central provinces, Rajputana
1943	:	Bengal
1974	:	Bangladesh

China too was struk by severe famines the last of which occurred in 1960-1961. Adverse climatic conditions are often held responsible for famines. This is only part of the truth however. For instance, Bhatia shows convincingly that in the period 1867-1880, in spite of the high frequency of famines, exports of foodgrains (mainly rice and wheat) have more than doubled. Moreover, many sources report the emergence of feverish speculation in foodgrains in times of famines (see for instance Nash 1900).

Let us briefly examine what is the role played in the occurrence of famines by the low integration level of regional food markets. This question will be at the background of many investigations conducted in this book. For the time being let us be content with the following empirical observations:

1) Obviously, fairly large inter-regional price differentials favoured speculation and consequently also hoarding.

2) During the eighteenth and early nineteenth century there is a marked difference in the frequency of famines between Britain and the Netherlands on one side and continental countries such as France or Germany on the other

side which (among other possible reasons) can be related to differences in transportation conditions. In fact, in Britain or in the Netherlands almost all cities of some importance are within easy reach of ports and usually they are connected to them by waterways. In France on the contrary, the food supply was imperiled by two adverse circumstances: the relatively large size of its population (it was about two to three times larger than the population of Britain) and a rather sparse network of waterways (except in the North). To some extent the same remarks apply to Germany.

3) In India, although the railway network did come into operation between 1865 and 1875 (3200 km in 1871)[1] it was beset by many deficiencies, most of which were related to the fact that it was established at a rather low cost.

4) Ravallion (1987, p.95) shows convincingly that the price instability during the famine of 1974 in Bangladesh is *not* attributable to conditions in the world market.

Before closing this section let us make a few comments about the problem of speculative trading during periods of scarcity. It seems to be a recurrent circumstance that in periods of dearth speculators are accused of aggravating the situation. There are innumerable examples of such accusations either in European countries (before 1850), in India or even during the 1974 famine in Bangladesh. From the point of view of economic rationality this argument hardly makes sense for by hoarding grains and selling them subsequently when prices have reached a high level, the speculators actually have a beneficial effect: the utility of grains is highest at the moment when they are most needed and by selling them at this moment the stockholders increase social utility. However, economic rationality can be deceived by secondary phenomena. For instance, the fact that grain exports from India have been raising throughout periods of famine clearly shows that some extra form of rationality (based for instance on biased exchange rates) was at work. Similarly, during the 1974 famine in Bangladesh there were many reports of rice smuggling, and anti-smuggling operations have been launched by the army on the borders (Ravallion 1987, p.91). In short, to make a sound distinction between "normal" speculative trading and "destructive" speculation (in the words of Bhatia 1967) requires very detailed data about prices, stocks levels (both private and public) and the available information on which price expectations may be based. Ravallion (1987) makes a very interesting investigation of this kind; he comes to the conclusion that rice hoarding was excessive in comparison with what would have been required by rational anticipation. He interprets this behaviour as based on the stockholders' belief that the government would be unable to implement suitable stabilizing responses.

[1]As a matter of comparison one should note that in Britain the railway density still was about 40 times larger.

5 Organization of commodity markets

It is not our intention in this short section to provide an overall view of the structure and working rules of commodity markets; we shall rather focus on a few items which are of special significance for the study of spatial arbitrage. More general accounts of the subject can for instance be found in the books by Badillo and Dalloz (1985), Charvet (1990), Labys (1973), Weymar (1988). Since in the rest of the book we shall have a special concern for wheat prices, we firstly describe the organization of twentieth century wheat markets; then we emphasize that in the long chain that extents from the producer to the consumer commodity prices can be recorded at a number of different levels. Finally, we examine the long term evolution of transport costs, a matter of crucial importance in connection with spatial arbitrage.

5.1 The twentieth century wheat market

By 1990 the world trade volume in wheat amounted to about 100 millions tons; this represents a sizable fraction (about 20%) of the world production; in contrast, world trade in rice represented only 4% of its production (Charvet 1990). A substantial part of wheat grain contracts are on a bilateral basis at the level of the governments. Examples of such agreements are listed in Table 1.1. Overseas transportation and distributions to wholesale dealers are in the hand of a few major firms; some of the most important grain companies are listed in Table 1.2. Similar information can be found for other commodities in Chalmin (1983,1991). Figure 1.2 schematically describes the various stages in the commercialization of wheat. An econometric description of wheat markets in the period 1970-1977 can be found in Grennes et al (1978) and in Mjelde and Paggi (1989).

5.2 Which prices?

In economics there are two kinds of variables: extensive variables such as for instance production data or national income, and intensive variables such as prices, freight rates, interest rates and so on. Since the values of intensive variables usually reflect an equilibrium (or quasi-equilibrium) between offer and supply, they gather information about the respective strength of various economic forces. Thus, they constitute essential bench-marks figures in economic processes.

Among prices, it is useful to distinguish between long term, medium term and short term prices. The long term evolution of *relative* prices can be interpreted as revealing changes in economic productivity. On the other hand, long- and medium-term evolution of the *general price level* is known to be related to

Seller	Buyer	Quantity millions tons	Price $/ton	Contract signed
Argentina	Brazil	1.3-1.5	n.a.	Dec 1972
Australia	China People's Rep	1.	60	Sept 1971
Australia	Egypt	0.5	80	Aug 1971
Canada	Algeria	2.5	n.a.	Aug 1972
Canada	China People's Rep	2.5	63	Sept 1970
Canada	China People's Rep	3.	n.a.	Dec 1971
Canada	China People's Rep	1.5	66	July 1972
Canada	USSR	1.0	66	June 1971
France	USSR	0.5	n.a.	Aug 1972
USA	China People's Rep	0.4	n.a.	Mar 1972

Table 1.1 Major wheat grain contracts during 1971-1972. China was the main importing country during these two years. The terms of the contract also specified dates and conditions of delivery, credit terms,etc ; whenever it is released the price should therefore rather be considered as an approximate indication. *Source: FAO World Grain Statistics 1971/1972.*

changes in the supply of money. This relationship has been postulated for a long time by the so-called quantitative school; in recent years it has been proved quite convincingly by M.Friedman and his co-workers (Friedman and Schwartz 1963,1982). In contrast, less attention has so far been given to short-term price fluctuations.

From producer to consumer there is a long chain of transactions each of which corresponds to a different intermediary price. In the case of a commodity such as wheat or cocoa for instance one may distinguish between prices paid to the producer, cash price quotations at major spot markets, price and option quotations at future markets, export prices, import prices and prices paid by the consumer. Let us elaborate somewhat further on some of the items in the aforementioned classification. First, one should note that export prices are often biased by government subsidies. This is true for the wheat market in the EEC as well as in the US. As far as import prices are concerned their connection with

Name	**Country**	**Part in world trade**	**Other activities, comments**
Cargill	USA	17-25%	poultry industry, steel and barges industry
Continental Grain	USA	13-25%	a specialist of the trade with Russia
Louis Dreyfus	France	13-25%	alcohol, dairy industry
Bunge and Borne	Argentina	8-12%	cotton, fertilizer industry
André and Co	Switzerland	8-10%	textile industry, machine tool industry
Toepfer	Germany	8-10%	fleet

Table 1.2 Major international grain companies in the 1980's. It appears that more than 50% of the world trade is in the hand of three companies. This is much higher a proportion than for instance in the oil industry where less than 45% of the sales of petroleum products was at that time in the hands of the Seven Sisters: Exxon, Texaco, Gulf, Socal, Mobil, Royal Dutch Shell, BP (The Oil Industry in the World DAFSA 1983, p175). *Source: Le commerce de gros des matières premières agricoles DAFSA 1985.*

consumer prices is illustrated in Fig.1.3 for the case of cocoa. Not surprisingly, the fluctuations of import prices are somewhat dampened out in the course of consumer prices.

In order to emphasize the marked differences which show up in the dynamics of various commodity markets we have displayed in Fig.1.4 price series for bananas, for wheat and for sugar. Bananas are one of the products with lowest price volatility; sugar, on the contrary, exhibits huge price peaks and its standard deviation therefore is both high and strongly non-stationary. In terms of volatility, present-day wheat markets have a behaviour which is somewhat in between low productivity products such as bananas and high volatility commodities such as sugar or cocoa. As a matter of comparison, the fluctuations of wheat prices are of the same order of magnitude as those of cotton, lead, rubber or wool. Needless to say, wheat prices exhibited much larger fluctuations before 1860.

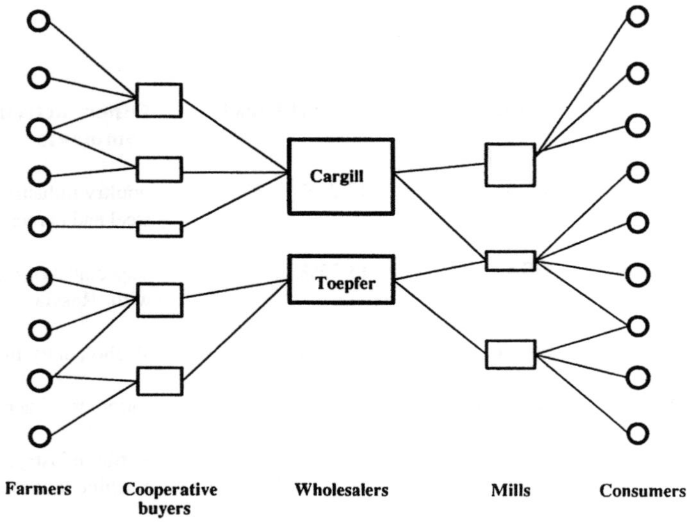

Fig.1.2 From farmers to consumers. The Figure provides a schematic picture of the commercialization network for wheat. Local buyers, whether it may be cooperatives or private firms, collect grains. Foreign trade business and overseas transportation are in the hands of a few major traders (see Table 1.1). The distribution to consumers may take different forms depending on final usage: flour, animal feeding, etc.

5.3 Long term evolution of ocean freight rates

It could appear somewhat inappropriate to undertake an analysis of spatial price patterns at a time when all markets become electronically interconnected so that distance seems to drop out as a significant variable. This would be a misplaced view however. Indeed, the fact that information can travel with the speed of light is not new; it goes back to Morse invention in 1843. Furthermore as far as bulk transportation is concerned, overseas freight still represents about 10% to 30% of total prices; see for instance Table 1.3.

In short, unless goods can one day be transferred through computer networks, one should, as far as market integration is concerned, make a clear distinction between financial markets on one hand and commodity markets on the other. In this respect, it is enlightening to examine the long term evolution of ocean freight rates shown in Fig.1.5 a,b. The main point of significance in these charts is that freight rates did not significantly decrease after the period of the transportation revolution (1870-1913). Such an evolution is probably largely to be attributed to the fact that the world shipping industry managed to keep competition at a rather low level (Alexandersson and Norström 1963).

For a better understanding of this feature a few words are in order regarding the organization of the shipping industry. Merchant vessels are described as liners,

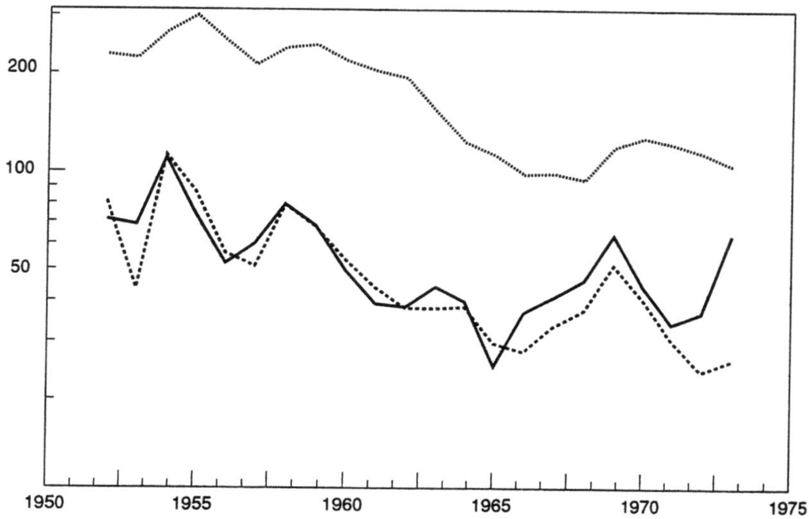

Fig.1.3 Export and import prices versus consumer prices for cocoa. All prices are expressed in US cents (of 1952) /kg. Solid line: exportation price (Brazil); broken line: importation price (Denmark); dotted line: consumer retail price (Denmark). *Source: FAO, Statistiques du Cacao; different years up to 1975 when the publication ceased to appear.*

tramps or industrial carriers. The latter are vessels owned by manufacturing firms for the transport of their raw materials. The tramp is a freight vessel that does not run in any regular line and can be hired either on trip charter for one or several voyages or on time charter for a given period. Liners on the contrary, run on regular lines; they hold an important share in the business; for instance, about 50% of the foreign maritime trade of Germany is carried out by liners. Since a large proportion of the total costs in liner shipping are fixed costs, unlimited price competition is likely to lead to freight rates far below average operation costs. The shipping industry has therefore developed means of reducing the competition, partly by concentration through mergers, partly by gentlemen's agreements or formal shipping conferences. These agreements can be summarized under the following headings.

1) rate agreements
2) pooling of the available traffic
3) control of sailing schedules
4) subventions to "fighting ships" which are operated by a conference at below-normal rates to compete with outsiders.

Is is hardly surprising that rates failed to decrease in such a regulated industry. Furthermore, there can be little doubt that even tramp rates have been pushed up by the high levels of liner rates. Freight rates, it may be noticed, are not the

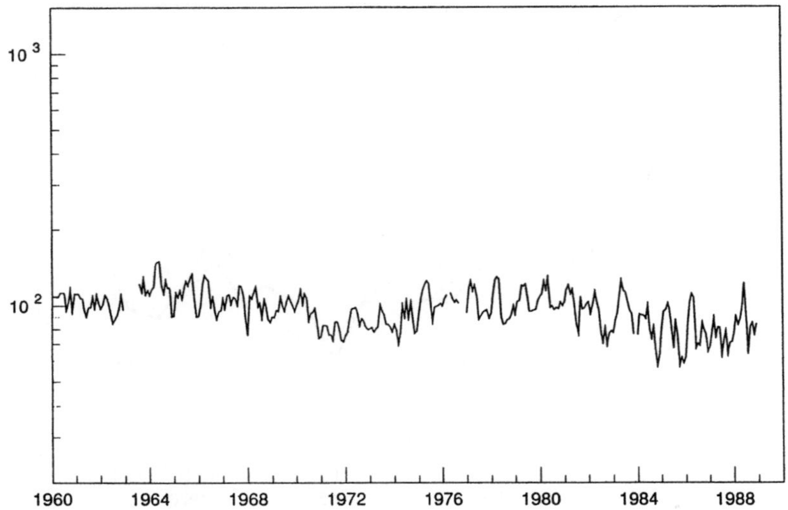

Fig.1.4 a Monthly prices of bananas. The prices are expressed in US cents/lb and are deflated by the US consumer price index. Apart from seasonal fluctuations, the price remains almost constant. The production and distribution of bananas are in the hand of a small number of firms: United Brands, Castle and Cooke, Del Monte. *Source: Monthly commodity prices. Bulletin UNCTAD 1960-1984, 1970-1989.*

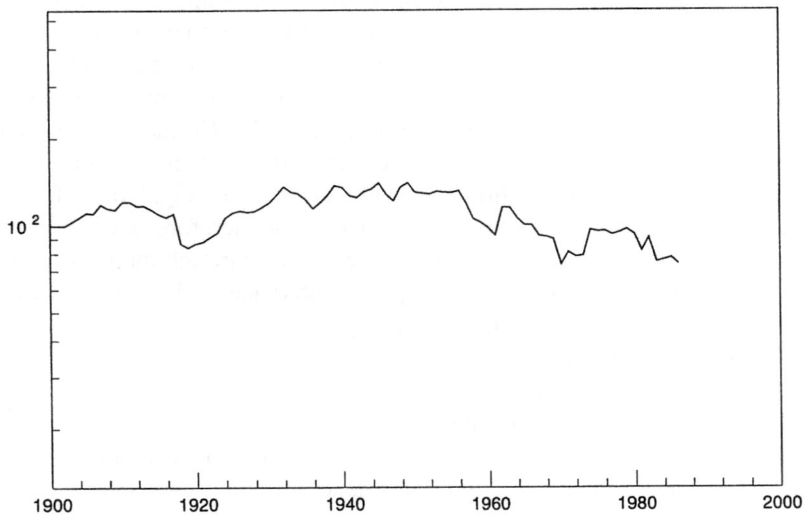

Fig.1.4 a' Annual prices of bananas. Same specifications as for the monthly series. *Source: World Bank (private communication).*

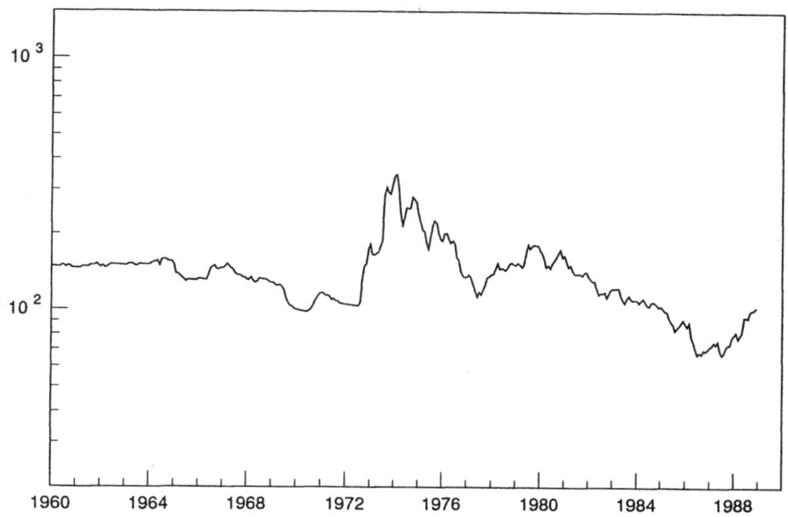

Fig.1.4 b Monthly prices of wheat. The prices are expressed in US dollars/ton and are deflated by the US consumer price index. The figures 1.4 a,b,c are drawn with the same vertical scale in order to make the amplitude of fluctuations comparable; it can be seen that in terms of volatility wheat ranges between bananas and sugar. *Source: Monthly commodity prices. Bulletin UNCTAD 1960-1984, 1970-1989.*

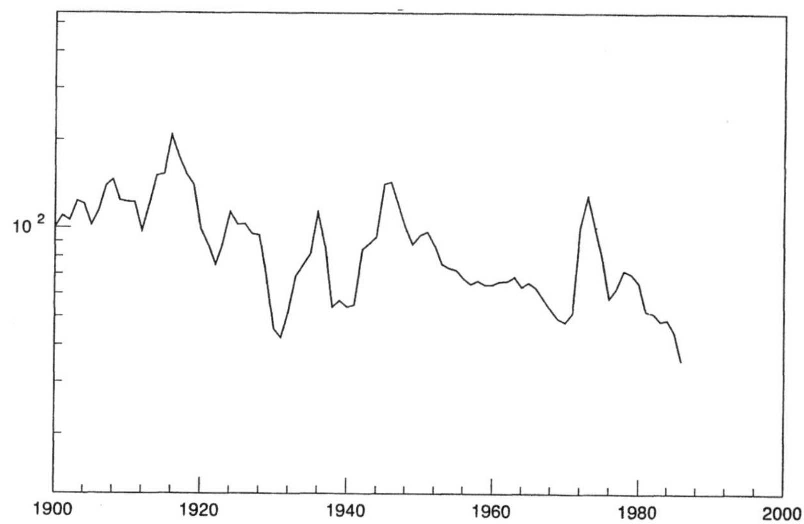

Fig.1.4 b' Annual prices of wheat. Same specifications as for the monthly series. *Source: World Bank (private communication)*

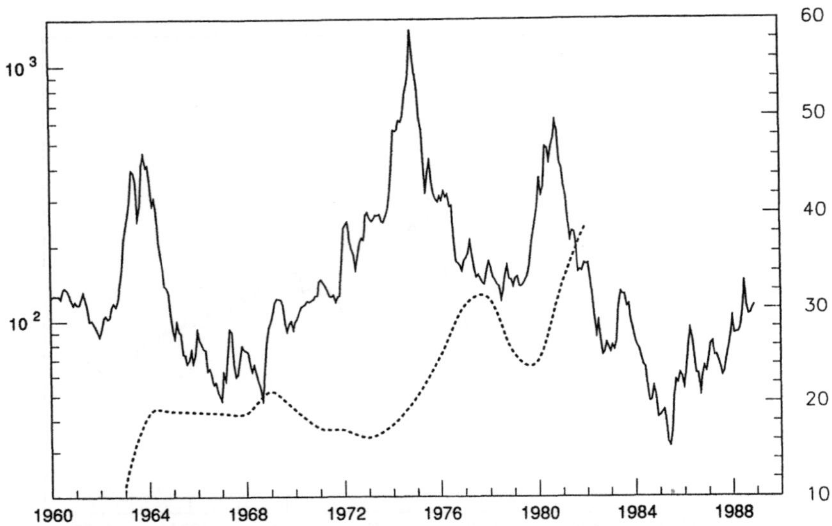

Fig.1.4 c Monthly prices of sugar. The prices are expressed in US cents/lb and are deflated by the US consumer price index. The course of sugar prices displays a number of huge peaks whose duration is of the order of three years. The broken line shows the evolution of world closing-stocks. *Sources: Monthly commodity prices. Bulletin UNCTAD 1960-1984,1970-1989; The McGraw Hill Handbook of commodities trend futures (1985).*

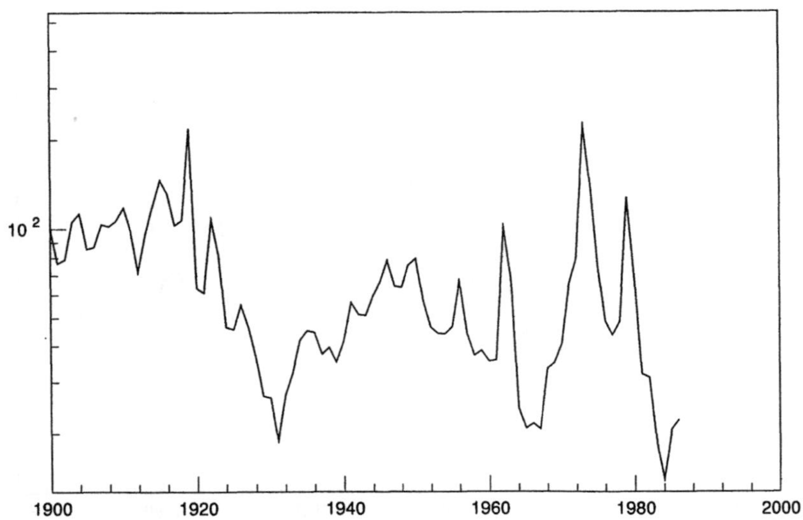

Fig.1.4 c' Annual prices of sugar. Same specifications as for the monthly series. *Source: World Bank (private communication).*

		1978/79		1985/86	
From	**To**	**Freight** US $ / ton	**Freight / Price**	**Freight** US $ / ton	**Freight / Price**
US Gulf	Africa East	21.3	14%	37.8	30%
	Japan	23.0	15%	24.6	20%
	China	24.0	16%	29.0	23%
	Black Sea Ports	16.0	10%	18.0	14%
Argentina	China	30.4	20%	31.7	25%
	Pakistan	22.5	15%	34.1	27%
	Siberia	28.6	19%	37.1	30%

Table 1.3 Freight rates for wheat. In 1978/79 the price of wheat (FOB, US Gulf) was about 150 $/ton; by 1985-86 it had decreased to about 125 $/ton. Freight rates on the contrary show a slight increase trend; as a result the part of freight in the total wheat price has increased between 1978-79 and 1985-86. *Source: World Wheat Statistics (International Wheat Council) 1987, p.73.*

only significant parameter for the trader; the transportation time is an important parameter too; unfortunately, no statistical data seem to be available to measure its long term evolution.

6 Spatial price differentials

Any theory of spatial arbitrage eventually hinges on the analysis of spatial price differentials and of trade statistics. For that reason, we shall in this section examine the first of these issues in some detail. Firstly, we give three examples of price differentials arranged by order of increasing complexity. Secondly, we examine the long term evolution of price differentials and we provide orders of magnitude of price differentials in present-day markets.

6.1 Three examples of spatial price differentials

The first example is about an industrial product not an agricultural commodity. It illustrates the case of a good that is produced in a single city and sold out

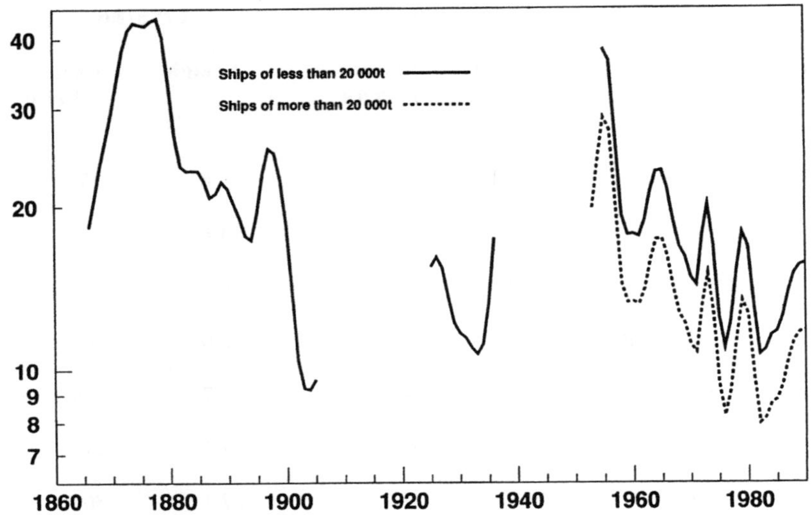

Fig.1.5 a Freight rates for wheat on North Atlantic routes (in 1980 dollar/ton). *Sources: 1866-1907: Das Getreide im Weltverkehr (1900) p.770, Statistical Abstract of the US (1907); 1924-1938: Statistisches Jahrbuch für das deutsche Reich; 1953-1985: World Wheat Statistics; 1986-1990: World Grain Statistics (continuation of World Wheat Statistics).*

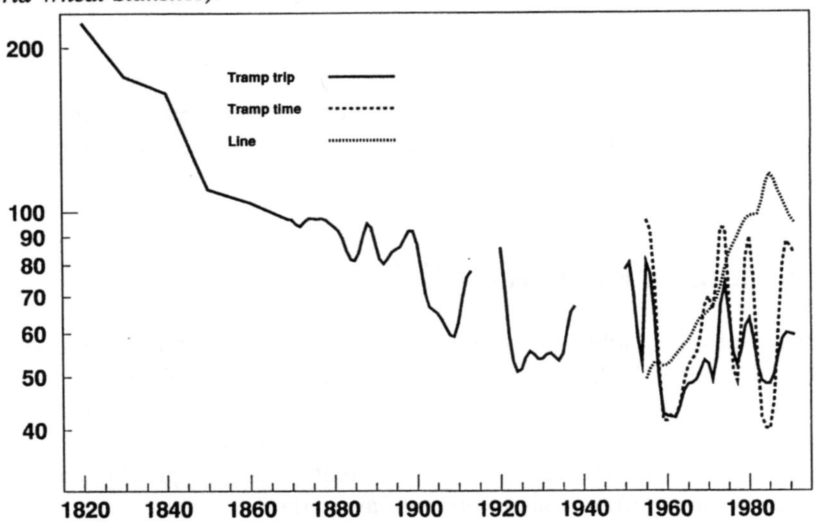

Fig.1.5 b Global ocean freight index. *Sources: 1820-1860: Bairoch (1976, p.36); 1869-1913: Isserlis index, recalculated in deflated form by O'Rourke and Williamson (1992); 1920-1938 and 1950-1954: The Economist freight index (tramp charter); 1955-1990: Review of maritime transport. UNCTAD (1968-1992); this index is compiled by the Ministry of Transport of Germany; for definition and calculation of the index see: Wirtschaft und Statistik 8, p.715-720 (1984).*

all over the country. The data are taken from Lösch (1954,p.483) and concern the prices of a Chevrolet car manufactured in Flint (Michigan) and sold in a number of American cities (in the year 1935). As shown in Fig.1.6a', the price differential increases almost linearly with distance and can therefore be considered as representing the transport cost. Such a conclusion is not surprising in view of the fact that the manufacturer, namely General Motors, was at that time in a situation of quasi-monopoly for this specific type of car.

The second example in order of increasing complexity concerns the case where there are but two productive regions, namely California and Florida. The resulting price distribution is shown in Fig.1.6b'; this time, there is no longer a linear relationship between price and distance.
As a third example, we consider the nineteenth century wheat market in the United States. Although wheat is grown in almost every state, the largest part of the wheat production is concentrated in the wheat belt. Moreover, the main consumption centers (together with exporting ports) are located in the large urbanized areas of the East and West coasts. Therefore, one has in a sense a fairly simple pattern with production concentrated in the center of the country and consumption on the periphery. Let us now consider a specific example, namely the price differential between Kansas and Idaho in the period 1880-1910 (Zapoleon 1918a, p.17). The transport cost from Idaho to New York was about 40 cents/ bushel whereas it was only 15 cents/bushel from Kansas to New York. Now, it is often argued that at that time domestic wheat prices in the US were controlled by export prices (British imports from the US represented about 30% of its total consumption). If this were true, farm prices in Idaho should be lower than in Kansas by about 25 cents. This, however, occurs only once in the four intervals for which data are available (Fig.1.6c). Even more "chaotic" results would obtain when considering annual data instead of five years averages. Thus, even the "simple" American market one may conclude that (Zapoleon 1918, p.19) "no single set of conditions alone determines a price, but each more or less determinable factor is influenced by other elements".

In nineteenth century Europe, production and consumption are not spatially separated. In this respect, the European nineteenth century wheat market compares with the twentieth century wheat market in which almost all major countries are consumers as well as producers (even Britain has become a substantial producer in recent years). As compared to the previous case, this is a situation of greater complexity in the sense that it becomes difficult to guess about price differentials by mere intuitive reasoning. From a mathematical point of view, however, one is in a more favourable position for, with each region both a production area and a consumption center, the model has greater symmetry.

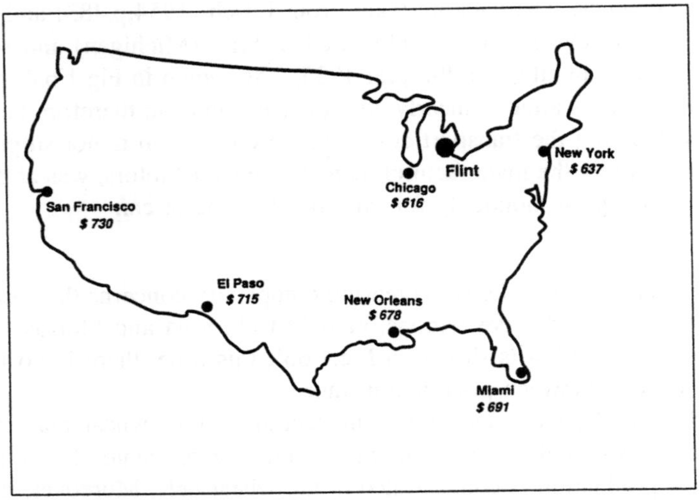

Fig.1.6 a Prices in different American cities of a Chevrolet car manufactured in Flint (Michigan). (January 10, 1935). *Source: Lösch 1954,p.483.*

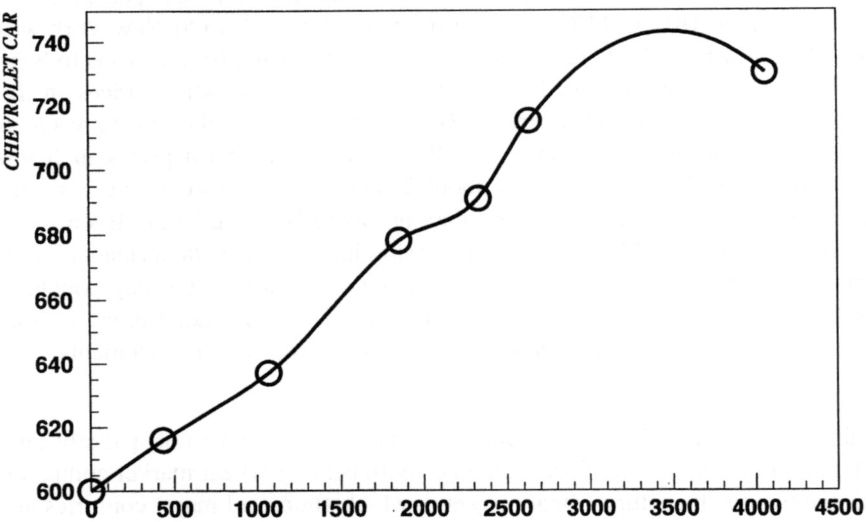

Fig.1.6 a' Price of a Chevrolet car as a function of distance to production area. Horizontal scale: distance in kilometres; vertical scale: price in dollars. As could be expected the relationship between price and distance turns out to be almost linear. Only the last point corresponding to San Francisco is somewhat below the linear prediction; this is quite understandable since San Francisco is on a cheaper route from Flint by sea than by land. *Source: Lösch (1954,p.483)*

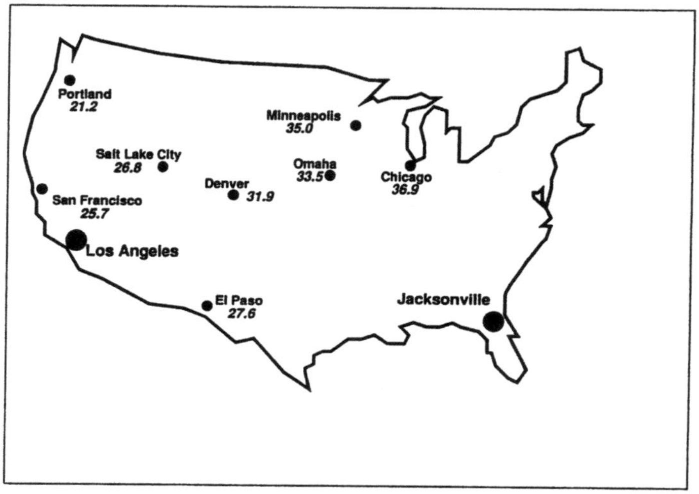

Fig.1.6 b Retail price of a dozen oranges in different American cities (1936). There are two main production areas: California and Florida. Since production prices are lower in California, this region controls about two third of all sales. Chicago is approximately located on the separation line between the market areas of both production centres. *Source: Lösch (1954,p.481).*

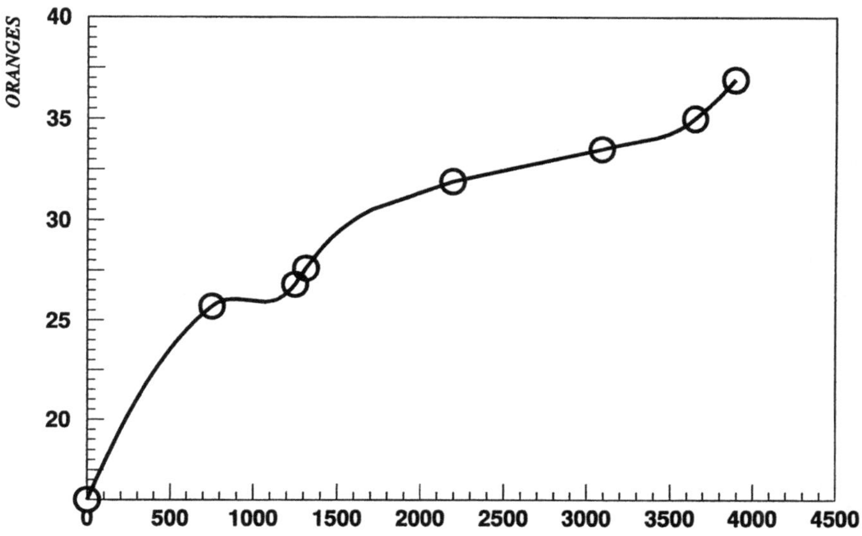

Fig.1.6 b' Retail price of a dozen oranges as a function of distance to production area. Horizontal scale: distance in kilometres; vertical scale: price in cents. The curve is of the logistic (i.e. with saturation) rather than of the linear type. Portland has been left aside for it is "nearer" Los Angeles by sea than by land. *Source: Lösch (1954,p.481)*

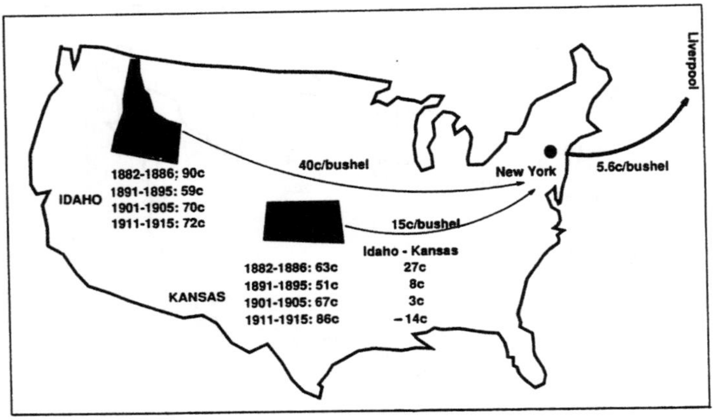

Fig.1.6 c Comparison of wheat prices in Idaho and Kansas. In the United States wheat prices are to some extent expected to be ruled by the export market. From the point of view of transportation costs, Idaho is neutrally located with respect to either routes to Liverpool: 45 (=24+21) cents/bushel via the Pacific; 45.6 (=40+5.6) cents/bushel via the Atlantic. Given the lower transportation costs from Kansas to Liverpool, lower wheat prices would be expected in Idaho. Yet the opposite turns out to be true in three out of four periods; this shows that no single set of conditions alone determines wheat prices. *Source: Zapoleon (1918,p.17,27).*

6.2 Evolution of spatial price differentials

The fact that ocean freight rates failed to decrease in the period after 1918 does not necessarily imply that spatial price differentials did not decrease either. Indeed, it could be argued that improvement in information transmission along with a convergence in national production and consumption patterns may be sufficient to reduce spatial price gaps. In order to investigate this point we examine the long term trend of spatial price differentials. These anyway have an intrinsic interest for they provide a *global* measure of transfer costs which includes all accessory costs (inventory or distribution costs for instance) that are not directly included in freight rates. Fig.1.7a,b shows the long term evolution of the price differential between London and New York respectively for cotton and for zinc. The second case is of particular interest: between 1880 and 1913, the differential has been divided by a factor of 1.5; after World War II, however, it is restored to its pre-World War I level. As this could at first appear to be a rather surprising conclusion, we have taken some care to check it. Thus, in order to eliminate a possible bias due to the deflator factor, we have considered absolute differentials as well as relative ones (broken curves); furthermore, we have considered an agricultural commodity as well as an industrial product; in addition, our conclusions regarding price differentials are consistent with those

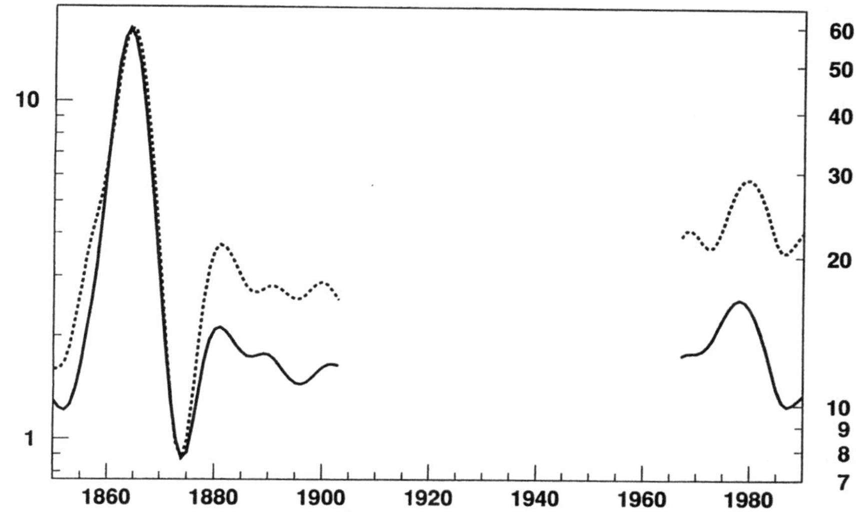

Fig.1.7 a Price differentials for cotton between the United States (New York) and Britain (Liverpool). Solid curve: absolute differentials expressed in tenth of 1900cents/pound and normalized to a distance of 100km; broken curve: relative differentials in per cent. The huge peak around 1865 of course corresponds to the Independence War. *Sources: 1850-1913: O'Rourke and Williamson (1990, personal communication); 1957-1990: International Financial Statistics IMF (1992).*

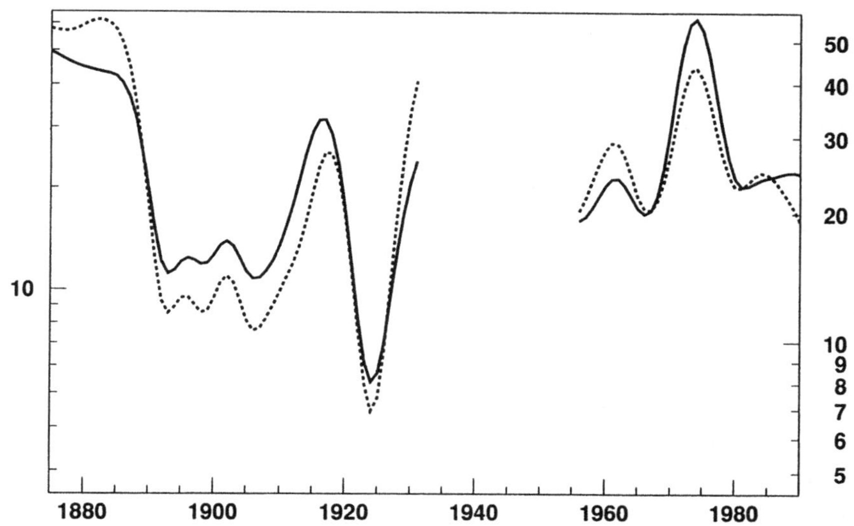

Fig.1.7 b Price differentials for zinc between the United States (New York) and Britain (London). Solid curve: absolute differentials, expressed in 1900cents/ton and normalized to a distance of 100km; broken curve: relative differentials in per cent. *Sources: Schmitz (1979); Metall Statistik (1992).*

already obtained for freight rates on the same route. Finally, these conclusions are confirmed by experts' opinions about specific markets. As an example, let us examine the case of the wheat market. In the 1970s, one could have been tempted to consider the price at the Chicago Board of Trade as a world price. There were several reasons in support of this view. First, the CBT was the largest commodity market in the world; second, the United States were both a major consumer and the first grain exporter; third, the American export price was almost identical with the domestic price and thus could be taken as a reference both within and outside the United States. The introduction of the export enhancement program (E.E.P.) in the 1980s cut off the link between export prices and domestic prices and introduced considerable uncertainty in the market (Charvet 1990, p.63-67). More generally, one should always bear in mind that in the long run the situation of a given market can be subject to considerable changes. For instance, one may recall that by the end of the nineteenth century, Russia was a major grain exporter, while Europe was an important importation center, a situation which is completely reversed nowadays.

Up to now, we have considered overseas price differentials. It could also be instructive to examine the case of regions connected by land trade routes. Figure 1.8 shows such an example; in this case there is a marked decrease trend which is consistent with what is known about the evolution of freight rates (by rail, road or waterways) in the United States (see chapter 4). Figure 1.9 shows a similar example in the case of Europe over the period 1968-1988. For so short a period, one does not expect any definite trend, however it is of some interest to observe that in such a regulated market there still are substantial price differences between various countries. In fact, there are even inter-regional price differentials within each country (crudely speaking EEC agricultural regulations determine a price margin within which prices may move almost freely). Finally, in Table 1.4 we have summarized the orders of magnitude of the price differentials for a number of goods.

7 The concept of market integration

In recent years, the analysis of market integration has raised a strong interest among economic historians; see for instance the proceedings of the European Historical Workshop on Market Integration (Lerici, April 1993) or the session on market integration at the Eleventh International Economic History Congress (Milan, September 1994). Therefore, it may be of interest to recall the definition of this concept. In fact, there are two alternative conceptions.

- In the first one, a region (or a market) is said to be integrated if "enough" arbitragers are present on the markets and if they are acting "efficiently" in a sense which supposes a number of conditions such as for instance the require-

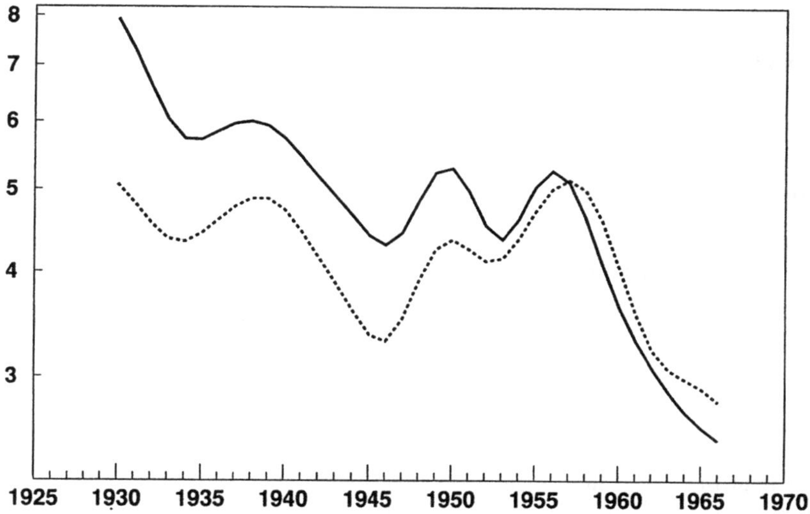

Fig.1.8 Evolution of cotton price differentials. Vertical scale: 1930 cents/pound/-100km; solid line: three markets: Atlanta, Little Rock, Montgomery broken line: four markets: same as above plus Dallas.

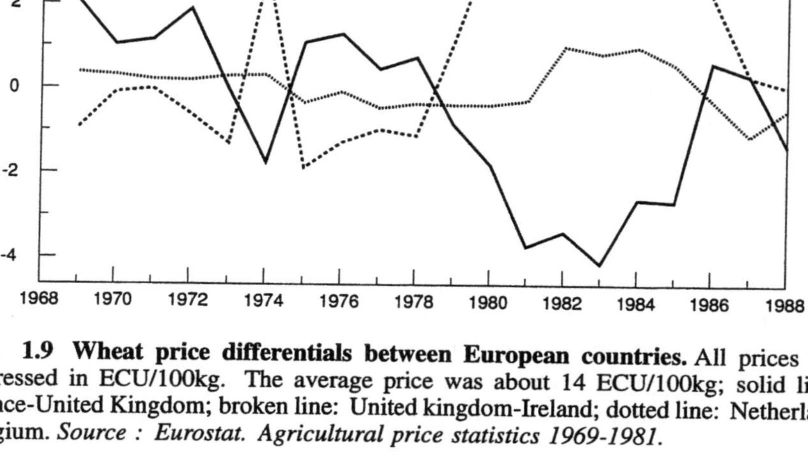

Fig. 1.9 Wheat price differentials between European countries. All prices are expressed in ECU/100kg. The average price was about 14 ECU/100kg; solid line: France-United Kingdom; broken line: United kingdom-Ireland; dotted line: Netherlands-Belgium. *Source : Eurostat. Agricultural price statistics 1969-1981.*

Commodity	Country	Average price	Average absolute price differential	Average percentage price differential
Sugar	USA-EEC	4.1 c/lb	2.4 cents/lb	58%
Cocoa	Brazil-London-NY	56 c/lb	4.4 cents/lb	8%
Wheat	Canada-Argentina	268 c/bushel	42 c/bushel	16%
Copper	London-NY	50 c/lb	6.3 c/lb	13%

Table 1.4 Average absolute cash price differentials. The averages are taken over the period 1949-1990. One must keep in mind that annual price differentials actually are very fluctuating. *Source: International Financial Statistics Annuaires 1979,1991.*

ment of perfect information. In this conception, a market either is integrated or it is not; there is no room for a variable labelled as an integration degree.

- In the second conception, the degree of market integration is identified with the level of intermarket price differentials (or some equivalent variable). If these differentials are large (in relative terms), then the market is said to be poorly integrated; if on the contrary they are small it will be said to be well integrated.

The first conception has its origin in the analysis of financial markets and the question we have to examine is whether this concept of an efficient market can be transposed to commodity markets. If so, one should in particular be able to give an operational meaning to the notion of perfect information. A clear operational criterion of an efficient market would consist in checking that price differentials do not exceed transaction and transport costs. While information on transaction costs is easily available in financial markets, this is no longer true for transportation costs in commodity markets. Indeed, as we shall see in chapter 4, information on freight rates very often is not made public. It is even more difficult to give an operational definition of the notion of perfect information. In contrast to financial markets where only a few variables are required, a commodity contract involves many parameters: quality of the product (within a given grade), specifications regarding hoarding, transportation, loading and discharging, etc. Almost none of these parameters is usually made public. To sum up, in the case of commodity markets it is almost impossible to define market efficiency by a clear operational criterion. Statistical investigation, therefore, has to rely on the second conception[2]

8 Defining and delimiting the problems to be investigated

Related to the study of commodity prices are a number of celebrated issues in macroeconomic trade analysis: the Prebisch-Singer hypothesis[3](Prebisch 1950, Singer 1950, Grilli and Yang 1988, von Hagen 1989), the problem of purchasing power parity[4], the testing of the Heckscher-Ohlin theory[5](Harkness 1978, Deardorff 1984, O'Rourke and Williamson 1992). All these issues have important implications for policy purposes. Yet, because their statistical investigation requires aggregate indexes, the construction of which necessarily relies on specific methodological options, the empirical evidence about their validity remains controversial. This is quite understandable in so far as the tests have to cover rather long time spans (for instance 1900-1990) in the course of which there have been many qualitative changes in the composition of exports and of imports.

As already pointed out in the preface, we shall in this book focus on the microeconomic mechanisms of spatial arbitrage between different markets. In order

[2]One could argue that our previous argument does not apply to future markets. True, transactions on futures very seldom result in an effective exchange of goods. There is a link, however, between future and spot markets because arbitrage is possible between both markets; for instance, the contango cannot in normal conditions become greater than inventory costs.

[3]Basically, the hypothesis says that in the process of industrialization the average price of manufactured goods increases relative to the price of primary commodities, thus leading to a steady decline in the net barter terms of trade (measured by the ratio of export prices to import prices)

[4]The theory of purchasing power parity has its source in the mercantilist writings of the seventeenth century, but it came into prominence about 1915 through the work of the Swedish economist Gustav Cassel. It states that the equilibrium exchange rate between two currencies is such that their domestic purchasing powers (at that rate of exchange) are equivalent. The argument on which the theory is based is best understood on an example. Suppose that the rate of exchange between the dollar and the sterling pound is of one dollar for three pounds; now, if one dollar buys more in the US than three pounds pay in the UK it would pay to convert pounds into dollars and buy from the US rather than in the UK. In that reasoning, transport costs implicitly play a major role. The difficulty of reaching reliable conclusions without taking such costs into account has sometimes been recognized (see for instance the closing remarks in Crouhy-Veyrac et al 1982); more often, however, it has been completely overlooked.

[5]This theory can be considered as a generalization of the law of comparative advantages formulated by Ricardo (1772-1823); it has been put forward by E.F.Heckscher in 1919, it was refined by Ohlin in 1933 and formalized by Samuelson in the 1950s. Basically, it states that a country will export those goods which are intensive in the factor in which it is most well endowed.

to simplify the subject even further, we shall leave aside those aspects of the problem which are not directly related to the existence of a spatial separation between markets; let us for instance mention the existence of quotas, the substitution between similar goods, the influence of exchange rates, the impact of differentials in interest rates. In other words, we shall leave aside the factors which derive from the fact that international trade takes place between *sovereign states*. However important these factors may be for a sound management they are unessential from our point of view. In the aforementioned factors we did not mention tariffs for these can be interpreted as extra-transport costs and can therefore be taken into account in our models.

Of course, it only makes sense to simplify our problem in such a way, if real situations could be found to fit our assumptions. Markets located within one and the same country clearly satisfy our previous requirements. In other words, we shall mainly be concerned with regional rather than with international commerce. Thereby, we trade significance as to policy making for simplicity; in other words we focus on a rather limited question in the hope that we shall be able to settle it once and for all. Let us open a parenthesis to get an idea of how much "economic significance" we have lost in this deal. By consulting the subject classification of the Journal of Economic Literature, it can be observed that a shift from international trade to regional trade means a move in the classification from section F ("International economics") to section R1 ("Urban, rural and regional economics: general spatial economics"), which is the next-to-last section just before section Z ("Other special topics")! Nonetheless, we think our attempt is worth the effort. E.Malinvaud(1990) sets the economic science two assignments, namely "to understand and to advice"; in this study we deliberately restrict ourselves to the first of these objectives.

In the perspective of analysing regional trade, the nineteenth century has decisive advantages over the twentieth century: at that time cereals were products of foremost economic importance (and among them wheat was the most important in Britain, France and South Germany), markets were more isolated, changes in market organization came more slowly, inflation rates and interest rates were more stable and, at least after 1815, no long war disturbed the course of economic development. Moreover, the railroad revolution which occurred between 1845 and 1870 reduced transport costs by a factor of about three, thus providing a unique opportunity to investigate the process of market convergence.

Among European countries, France emerges as a particularly convenient "laboratory" because of a number of specific advantages.

1) Unlike Germany, France had a single currency and a unified system of weights and measure since 1790. In addition, domestic grain trade was almost free of restrictions, except perhaps during some periods of dearth.

2) During the nineteenth century France was by far the most important

wheat producer in Western Europe with a production of 8.5 millions of tons as compared to 4.9 in Russia (but 18 millions tons rye), 3.5 in Germany, 3.0 in Hungary and 2.1 in Britain (Mitchell and Deane 1978, Das Getreide im Weltverkehr 1900,p.783). Furthermore, the importance of French wheat imports remained on average marginal throughout most of the century.

3) As an effect of the centralization of the French nineteenth century state, prices were systematically recorded for about 600 marketplaces. This makes it possible to undertake an accurate analysis of market prices and to describe price variations not only as events in isolated markets but as a quasi-continuum over space and time.

In short, it is for methodological reasons that we shall in this book mainly (but not exclusively) be concerned with French and German nineteenth century markets. We believe that the phenomena regarding trade and spatial patterns of price fluctuations basically remain the same in present day markets. This belief will be checked insofar as permitted by availability of statistical data; in particular, we shall use American state-level wheat statistics.

9 The methodology of our approach: parsimony as a condition of testability

While previously defining the problem to be investigated we have mainly be guided by simplicity requirements. Similarly, our theoretical approach will be guided by a parsimony requirement, i.e. the condition that the number of free parameters in the model be kept at a minimum. Let us briefly develop this point. The more parameters in a model the less convincing its tests on a given set of data, this is known as the parsimony requirement in econometric modelling. Throughout this book we shall adhere to the strategy of parsimonious modelling. Since it is hardly possible to expect good returns from completely "unrealistic" models, we shall usually select the evidence in consistency with the assumptions on which the model is based. For instance, a model that postulates spatial homogeneity cannot be expected to describe the distribution of wheat prices in India because the Ganges basin breaks this homogeneity (Engelbrecht 1908). In contrast, such a model is reasonable for Bavaria or for the center of France.

When an economic interpretation can be given to the parameters in a model, then in addition to standard economic tests, one has the opportunity of a useful plausibility test by checking the parameters to have a "reasonable" order of magnitude.

In designing our models, there is another (rather old-fashioned) notion to which we shall cling, namely the insistence on analytical solutions. Of course, it would be unreasonable to follow this rule too rigidly for complete analytical solutions can be obtained but in the simplest cases. Nonetheless, even in more intricate cases, it may at least be possible to get *asymptotic* solutions (i.e. with one parameter going to infinity); these provide important clues as to model's properties. In chapters 3 and 8 for instance, by working out asymptotic solutions we shall be able to get a better insight into our models.

10 Empirical findings

For the development of a model to be fruitful it has to rely on a set of empirical "regularity statements"[6]. In this section we summarize a number of such statements. The reasons for doing so in this introductory chapter are twofold. Firstly, by describing the phenomena which have to be explained, one points out the relevant objectives for subsequent chapters. Secondly, the statement of these empirical laws may be of interest even to people who might not be interested in the models themselves. More detailed accounts can be found in the chapters indicated in brackets.

10.1 Interdependence between markets [chapter 4,6]

We give here but a rather loose statement; to be more specific, one has to introduce a model and to test it; this will be done in chapter 4.

> **Market interdependence with respect to distance** The strength of the connection between spatially separated markets is inversely proportional to intermarket distance.

Before we present some evidence on which the statement is based, a comment is in order. The above statement could in a sense appear as a trivial consequence of the following commonsense observation (sometimes referred to in geographical analysis as Tobler's rule): "Everything is related to everything else, but near things are more related than distant things." However, the above statement is not as self evident as it could seem; for one thing (as will be shown in chapter 3) it is in disagreement with the standard spatial price equilibrium model; nor is its empirical testing straightforward. Regarding the last point, one is confronted with a variant of Zellner's (1988) "too broad or too narrow" dilemma: if the markets are selected in a rather limited area, there are but small variations in the (pairwise) couplings of markets and these variations then are likely to be screened by statistical fluctuations; if on the other hand the markets are located

[6] It is not easy to make a formal distinction between raw empirical facts and what we call regularity statements; the only thing which can be said is that regularity statements are expected to provide strong guidelines for the definition of a model.

in different countries tariffs and quotas may interfere with distance to the point of obscuring the influence of distance. Good "candidates" for the testing are either regional nineteenth century markets in which the effect of distance is magnified by low efficiency transportation means or American twentieth century markets in which this effect is amplified by the possibility of considerable intermarket distances. Both cases are illustrated in Fig.1.10a,b,c. The Figures 1.10a,b show intermarket correlations while Fig.1.10c displays intermarket price differentials. Theoretically, as will be seen in chapter 3, these two points of view can to some extent be considered as being equivalent. Statistically, however, the analysis of correlations turns out to be much more robust. By comparing Fig.1.10a and 1.10b, we observe that there is a much greater dispersion in the second case than in the first. This is not surprising in so far as the area covered by Fig.1.10b (i.e. the whole territory of the United States) is less homogeneous in terms of climate, wheat grades and production conditions than is the area covered in Fig.1.10a.

10.2 Price intercorrelations [chapter 9]

In the previous paragraph we have considered the variations of price correlations with respect to intermarket distances; here we consider the variations of the intercovariances:

$$c(\delta) = E\left[p_i(t)p_j(t+\delta)\right]$$

$p_i(t), p_j(t)$: prices on market i, j at time t with respect to the delay δ.

Variation of market interdependence with respect to delay The variation of the intercovariance $c(\delta)$ of the prices on two markets i and j a distance d_{ij} apart with respect to the delay δ exhibits a plateau extending from $\delta = 0$ to $\delta = d_{ij}/c$ where c is the velocity of propagation of the price wave.

The statement is illustrated in Fig.1.11a,b.

10.3 Variations in trade with respect to transportation costs [chapter 4]

We consider two fairly distant commodity markets under the assumption that their combined production is on average constant. A decrease in transport rates makes it easier for them to engage into trade relations thereby increasing the trade flow between them. Soon, however, reduced transport costs also bring about a fall in price differentials, thus making trade less profitable. It is not obvious to decide which of these two conflicting effects is to prevail *in the long run*. This question is settled by the following statement.

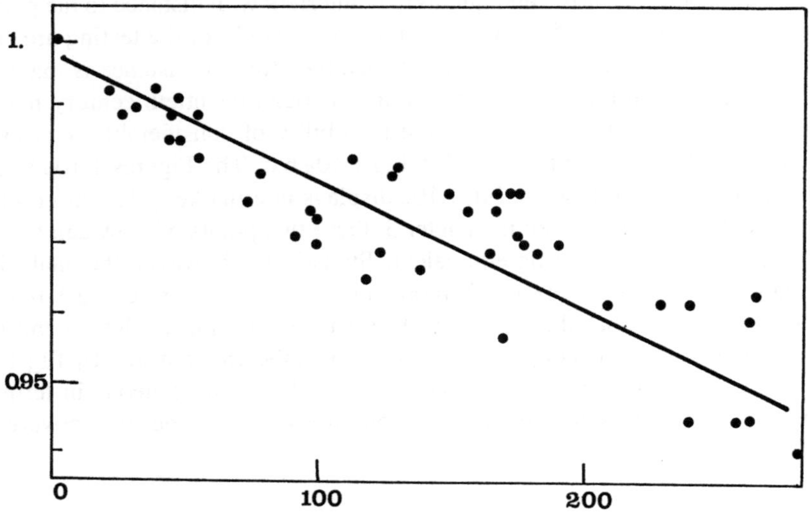

Fig.1.10 a Nineteenth century France: decrease of wheat price correlations with distance. The sample contains 11 markets mainly in the Bassin Parisien and centre. The series are monthly prices 1841-1858. Coefficient of correlation=-0.91. *Source: Drame et al (1991).*

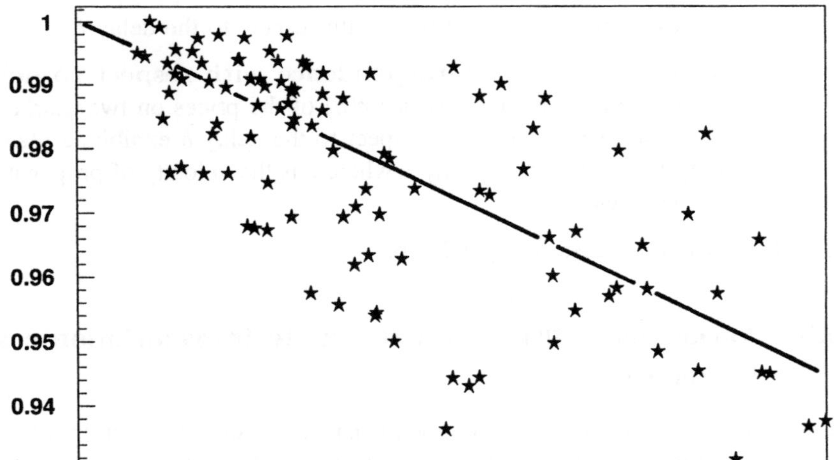

Fig.1.10 b Twentieth century United States: decrease of wheat price correlations with distance. The sample contains 15 states. The series are annual prices 1954-1986. Coefficient of correlation=-0.70. *Source: Langley et al (1989).*

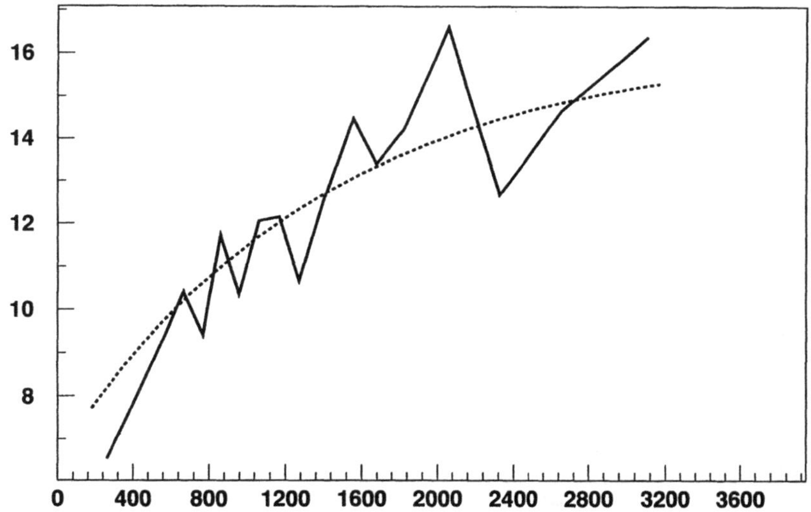

Fig.1.10 c Wheat price differentials as a function of distance in the United States, 1951-1981. Solid line: observations; dashed line: theoretical fit (see chapter 4). Horizontal scale: kilometer. Vertical scale: cent/bushel The sample includes 34 States. Differentials are averaged over 30 market-pairs. The solid curve is an average over the years 1951,1961,1971,1981. *Source: Langley (1989)*

Variation of trade with respect to transport costs In the long run, under the assumption of a stationary production, the trade between a set of distant markets increases along with a decrease in transport costs.

We refer to chapter 4 for the evidence supporting this statement for its test raises a number of difficulties. Firstly, one has to find a way to secure the condition of stationary production (usually production figures exhibits a secular increase trend); secondly, because different transportation means are usually used on a given route, a composite index of transport cost is required.

10.4 The evolution of market integration [chapter 6]

In the three previous paragraphs we have investigated *structural* properties of trade and of price patterns; turning now to the historical evolution of market integration, we leave microeconomics to enter the field of economic history. In section 7 we proposed to measure the degree of market integration by the level of intermarket price differentials (or in a somewhat equivalent way by the level of intermarket price correlations). The historical evolution of market integration has been well documented for the period 1870-1914 corresponding to the transportation revolution (see for instance O'Rourke and Williamson 1992). This however leaves a number of open questions:

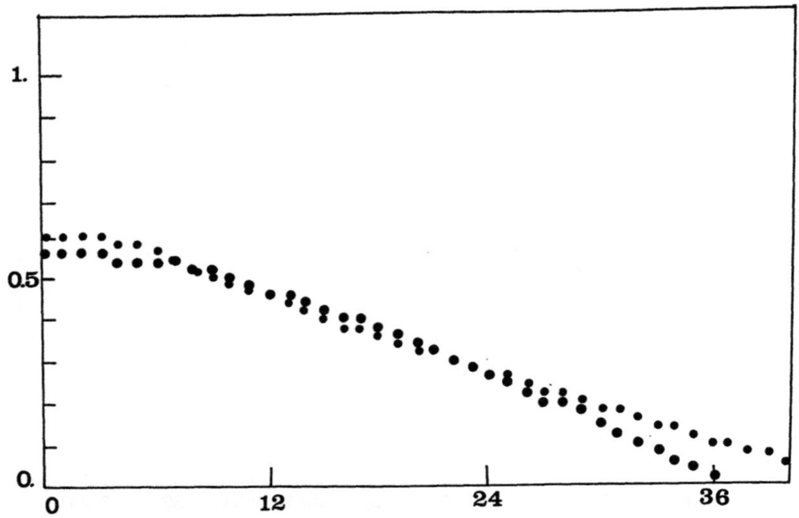

Fig.1.11 a Intercorrelation coefficients between wheat markets. Horizontal scale: delay in fortnights; small dots: Beaugency-Mende (390 km), 1833-1850; large dots: Clermont-Pau (390 km), 1825-1841. *Source: Drame et al (1991).*

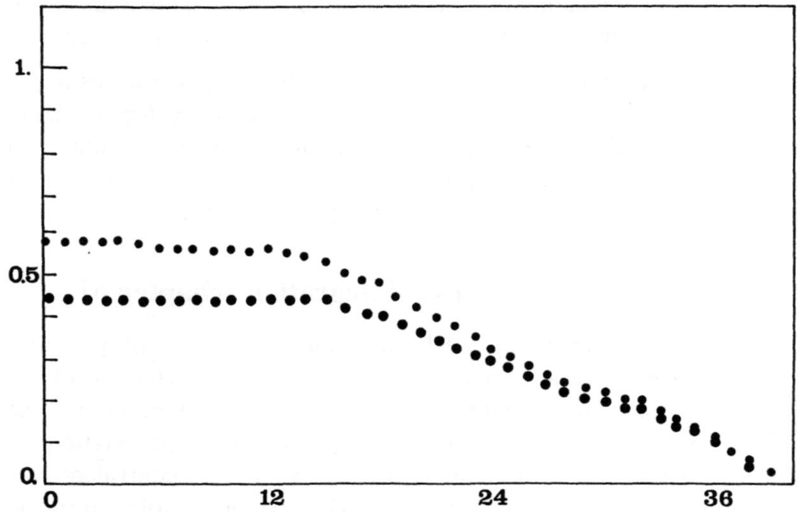

Fig.1.11 b Intercorrelation functions between wheat markets. Horizontal scale: delay in fortnights; Small dots: Douai-Montauban (720km) 1830-1846; Large dots: Arras-Albi (710 km) 1830-1846. *Source: Drame et al (1991).*

1) To what extent did market integration progress *before* and *after* the transportation revolution?

2) Are there significant differences between various commodities with regard to the increase in the degree of market integration?

The "before" part of the first of these questions has in particular been investigated for wheat prices by Granger and Elliot (1967) and Jörberg (1972) with mixed results. Granger and Elliot compared market integration between the periods 1723-1762 and 1754-1793. They concluded to a deterioration in the level of price integration. Subsequently, Chartres (1993) extended their investigation to an earlier period, namely 1693-1700; his result which are based on a rather extensive data set supports the view of a relatively large level of price integration in the period 1690-1760, "which deteriorated in the second half of the eighteenth century and which is not fully restored until perhaps some years after 1810".
The following qualitative statement provides partial answers to the previous questions. Supporting evidence is provided in chapter 6.

> **Evolution of market integration** Before 1825, there has been no significant and permanent improvement in market integration. In the period of the transportation revolution (1825-1914), market integration improved markedly for almost all products with but a few exceptions (such as for instance coffee or sugar). Between 1920 and 1990, there have been further improvements in the integration of continental markets (such as the United States for instance). The evidence of improved price convergence is rather mixed on ocean trade routes (especially in the North Atlantic between the United States and Europe).

10.5 The evolution of price volatility [chapter 4]

One of the features which is of most interest to traders is the volatility of prices in each marketplace. Now, is there a connection between this volatility and the degree of integration of the market? This question is of major importance in the discussion of price stabilization agreements. A number of such agreements have been set up in the last decades for such products as bauxite, cocoa, copper, rubber, sugar, tea or wheat (see for instance McNicol 1978). Surprisingly however, the impact of transport costs is not even mentioned in the study by Newbery and Stiglitz (1981), probably one of the most significant contribution to the theoretical investigation of price stabilization. To our knowledge, the first attempt to question the relationship between market integration and price volatility was conducted by G.Persson (1993). He empirically investigated nineteenth century grain markets and found a significant relationship between price volatilities and the lack of market integration. The stochastic Enke-Samuelson model which we shall develop in chapter 3 confirms this view; furthermore, in chapter 4 additional supporting evidence is presented. The question, however, can hardly be considered as being settled; empirical tests in particular require more long range series both for prices and for transport rates.

11 Outline of the book

In this section we give an outline of the rest of the book along with a few reading suggestions which we hope to be useful. In the second chapter of the prologue we discuss how equilibrium prices are fixed in result of the confrontation of supply and demand. First, we examine the question in the framework of cobweb models; then we introduce the basic ideas on which rational expectations models are based; finally, we discuss spatial price differentials in imperfect competition models.

Throughout the rest of the book, the leading strand is provided by the investigation of the stochastic Enke-Samuelson model in its different settings. In Part II, we focus on the analysis of equilibrium prices. In chapter 3, which is one of the key chapters, we develop the stochastic Enke-Samuelson (thereafter SES) trade model. In chapter 4, we confront the predictions of the SES model with empirical evidence. In chapter 5 which is a digression from the main subject of the book we discuss the implications of decreasing transport costs for the evolution of urban networks and for demographic fluctuations.

Our aim in part III is to develop a full space-time model of spatial price fluctuations. Chapter 6 is a purely empirical introduction to the subject in the sense that whenever autoregressive models are used our objective is to squeeze more detailed information out of our time series; such partial and phenomenological models are not considered as providing an adequate description of a network of markets. First, we discuss the properties of price correlations as a function of distance; this provides a global measure of the level of market integration. In the rest of this chapter we discuss the direction of interaction (or in other words Granger causality) between two or three markets. Because the sample of markets at our disposal contains a variety of marketplaces ranging from large to small ones, we are in a good position to check whether our tests do indeed provide sensible results. In chapter 7 which is a technical preparation for chapter 8 we review spatial autoregressive processes as well as space-time autoregressive processes and we discuss parameter estimation. In chapter 8 we introduce the dynamic SES models. In chapter 9 we consider these models in the framework of *continuous* second order space-time processes; such models are analytically solvable and their intercorrelation functions turn out to exhibit a plateau in the small delay region. Such a feature is bound to occur in any space-time model which is at least of second order in time. This plateau can

be empirically observed in intercorrelation functions provided their sampling period is small enough.
Chapter 10 summarizes some methodological comments and proposes a research agenda for future work.

Here are some suggestions which may be helpful in the reading. The chapters 2,5 and 7 can be omitted in a first approach; those of their results which are required in subsequent chapters usually are recalled before being used and they could therefore just be admitted. The chapters 4,5 and 6 do not require a substantial mathematical background. Chapters 7 and 9 may be of interest even to researchers outside the field of economics; indeed the stochastic space-time propagation model may be useful for instance in describing the propagation of diseases, news, innovations, etc.

Chapter 2
Pricing models

Our aim in this book is to analyse the connections between spatially separated markets. A preliminary step in this direction is to understand how prices are determined in a *single* market. Subsequent chapters (and especially chapter 8) will have to rely on that knowledge. Price theory is a vast subject, however, and this chapter should be seen as an introduction intended for non-specialists rather than a review. Prices are determined by the confrontation of demand and supply; but supply (and also to some extent demand) is adjusted by producers to get the best advantage from the information they have in hand at the time when they plan their future production. In other words, the whole economic environment is likely to play a role in the process. According to these different environments, various kinds of pricing models have been proposed. Our aim in this chapter is to discuss a number of concepts which have been put forward in relation with these topics during the last decades. Many of these concepts have an interest in their own; for instance the rational expectations approach besides being used in price theory has important implications for macroeconomics or for the description of rational learning mechanisms. In section one, we examine cobweb models under various phenomenological (i.e. ad hoc) anticipation assumptions: first we consider models without inventories, then we discuss the role of inventories. In section two, we introduce the concept of rational expectations: first, we review empirical and theoretical motivations for its introduction, then we present the basic results of Muth's original paper. In section three, we discuss how spatial price competition fits into the framework of imperfect competition theories.

1 Dynamic market models with exogenous price expectations

In order to emphasize from the outset the complexities of output and price fixing problems we shall list a number of questions which capture some of the essential economic issues.

a) What is the market environment of the firm? A relatively small number of firms producing nearly equivalent products (e.g. bananas or flat glass); or many producers of equivalent products (e.g. wheat); or a number of firms producing products which are regarded as substitutes by consumers.

b) What economic goals are of importance in the firm's decision-making process? Short-term or long-term profit maximization, market-share maximization and so on.

c) Does the firm generally choose to exercise its market strategy aggressively or does it rather tend to maintain an established price which is considered "normal" in the business?

Expectations are an important concept in economics because what agents expect to happen tomorrow modifies their behaviour today. The psychological nature of expectations, however, has made difficult their mathematical representation. To illustrate the use of various price anticipation assumptions we shall put them to work within the framework of the Cobweb market model for a single commodity. Consider a situation in which the producer's output decision must be made one period in advance of the actual sale such as in agricultural production where sowing must precede by several months the harvesting and sale of the output. Thus we have a "lagged" supply function:

$$S_t = S({}_{t-1}p_t^e) \tag{1.1}$$

where ${}_{t-1}p_t^e$ denotes the value of the price at time t which is expected by individuals forming expectations at the end of time $t-1$. Subsequently, we shall use the simpler notation:

$$p_t^e \equiv {}_{t-1}p_t^e$$

The demand function on the other hand will be supposed to be a function of the current price p_t:

$$D_t = D(p_t) \tag{1.2}$$

The dependence of the supply function on the expected price level highlights the fact that a theory of price fluctuations has to include an explanation of the way expectations are formed. Various "ad hoc" expectations formulas have been proposed. We call them exogenous in contrast to rational expectations which are closely connected to the model itself.

1.1 Cobweb models without inventories

In this section we assume that in each time period the market price is set at a level which clears the market. This market clearing condition is equivalent to the assumption that there are no inventories. The price dynamic will therefore be determined by the equality of demand and supply:

$$S_t = D_t \tag{1.3}$$

Different price patterns will result depending on specific assumptions regarding the price expectation p_t^e.

In the following we shall make the additional assumption of linear demand and supply functions:

$$S_t = -c + \gamma p_t^e \qquad D_t = b - \beta p_t \qquad b, \beta, c, \gamma \geq 0 \tag{1.4}$$

This is a reasonable approximation at least in the vicinity of the equilibrium. The equilibrium condition $S_t = D_t$ then takes the explicit form:

$$\beta p_t + \gamma p_t^e = b + c \tag{1.3b}$$

Although it is somewhat unrealistic to consider models without random shocks, we shall, for the sake of simplicity, begin with deterministic models.
Before proceeding let us briefly present some statistical data about demand functions. The methodology of measuring demand functions has been first discussed by Schultz (1938). Table 2.1 summarizes elasticity results for coffee, cocoa and wheat in a number of different countries. It is interesting to note that, with only a few exceptions, the elasticities of demand with respect to price are rather similar from one country to another; on the contrary, they undergo rather large fluctuations in the course of time (see the results for wheat).

1.1.1 Conservative price anticipation

Let us assume that the output decision in period $t-1$ is merely based on the then prevailing price:$p_t^e = p_{t-1}$. The equilibrium equation $(1.3b)$ between consumption and supply then becomes:

$$\beta p_t + \gamma p_{t-1} = b + c$$

The model is described by a single first-order difference equation which can easily be solved by recurrence. This leads to the following price evolution:

$$p_t = (p_0 - \frac{b+c}{\beta+\gamma})(-\frac{\gamma}{\beta})^t + \frac{b+c}{\beta+\gamma} \tag{1.5}$$

p_t will converge towards the equilibrium price $(b+c)/(\beta+\gamma)$ when $\gamma < \beta$. The parameter γ is related to the response of production to price variations; it is generally small in the case of agricultural production so that the stability condition should, in this highly simplified model, be satisfied.

	Periods considered	Elasticity of demand with respect to price
Coffee		
Argentina	1935-1958	-0.26 ± 0.04
Danemark	1921-38, 1953-58	-0.32 ± 0.06
Finland	1929-39, 1954-58	-0.24 ± 0.05
Greece	1927-38, 1952-58	-0.40 ± 0.11
Switzerland	1924-38, 1950-58	-0.28 ± 0.09
U.S.	1920-41, 1946-58	-0.29 ± 0.05
Cocoa		
Australia	1957-1959	- 0.30
Canada	1957-1959	- 0.25
Japan	1957-1959	- 0.40
New Zealand	1957-1959	- 0.30
South Africa	1957-1959	- 0.40
U.K.	1957-1959	- 0.40
U.S.	1957-1959	- 0.25
Wheat (USA)	1880-1895	-0.02 ± 0.26
	1896-1913	-0.15 ± 0.16
	1921-1929	-0.18 ± 0.03
	1921-1934	-0.21 ± 0.03

Table 2.1 Elasticities of demand with respect to prices for coffee and cocoa. One noteworthy feature is that the elasticities are approximately of the same order of magnitude in all countries. On the contrary, the variability in time is rather large. *Sources: FAO L'économie mondiale du café, Rome 1962. Produits agricoles. Projections 1970, Rome 1962; Schultz (1938).*

Another possible "no anticipation" assumption would be to take the price expectation p_t^e equal to the equilibrium price $(b+c)/(\beta+\gamma)$. This is not an unreasonable assumption as long as the market remains in the vicinity of equilibrium.

Stochastic models will be dealt with in section 2; let us just mention that when γ/β tends toward 1, the price fluctuations may become very large. The stochastic version of the previous model reads:

$$\beta p_t + \gamma p_{t-1} = b + c + \epsilon_t$$

where ϵ_t denotes the random shocks consisting for instance in white noise of zero mean and of variance σ_ϵ^2. Now the variance of p_t as defined by the previous first order autoregressive process turns out to be (Priestley 1981, p.119):

$$\sigma_p^2 = \frac{\sigma_\epsilon^2}{\beta^2 - \gamma^2}$$

1.1.2 Extrapolative price anticipation

Let us now assume that the expected price is an extrapolation of past prices of the last n years. For the sake of simplicity we consider here the case when $n = 2$, i.e.:

$$p_t^e = p_{t-1} + \rho(p_{t-1} - p_{t-2}) \quad 0 \leq \rho \leq 1$$

The dynamic price equation is now a difference equation of second order:

$$p_t + a_1 p_{t-1} + a_2 p_{t_2} = (b + c)/\beta$$

where: $a_1 = (1+\rho)\gamma/\beta \qquad a_2 = -\rho\gamma/\beta$
Not surprisingly, the equilibrium price is the same as before, namely $b+c/\beta+\gamma$; only the trajectory toward equilibrium is modified. The discriminant of the above equation is:

$$\Delta = (\gamma/\beta)^2(1+\rho)^2 + 4\rho\gamma/\beta$$

It is positive for $\rho > 0$; hence deterministic oscillations can be observed only under the counter-extrapolative assumption $\rho < 0$. Let us discuss the stability of the equilibrium. The stability conditions of a second order difference equation are (Priestley 1981, p.127):

$$a_2 \leq 1, \quad a_1 + a_2 \geq -1, \quad a_1 - a_2 \leq 1$$

that is to say:

$$-\gamma\rho/\beta \leq 1, \quad \gamma\beta \geq -1, \quad \gamma(1+2\rho)/\beta \leq 1$$

which leads to:

$$\gamma/\beta \leq \frac{1}{1+2\rho}$$

In the particular case $\rho = 0$, this leads back to the stability condition of the conservative price model; for $\rho > 0$, the stability interval of γ/β is smaller than before.

1.1.3 Adaptative price anticipation

The adaptative expectations hypothesis asserts that having some forecast based on information available at the end of time $t-2$, individuals examine how well that forecast predicted the actual price p_{t-1} and revise their current forecast by some fraction η of the previous forecasting error:

$$p_t^e = p_{t-1}^e + \eta(p_{t-1} - p_{t-1}^e) \quad 0 \leq \eta < 1 \tag{1.6}$$

From the equilibrium equation (1.3*b*), one has:

$$p_t^e = -\beta/\gamma p_t + (b+c)/\gamma$$

substituting this expression in (1.6) leads to a recurrence equation of first order for p_t. But instead of solving this equation let us rather examine the relationship between p_t^e and p_t. Equation (1.6) can be considered as an equation where p_t^e is unknown and p_t a given function; if the process is supposed to start at $t = -\infty$ so that the transient behaviour can be omitted, the solution of (1.6) reads (Priestley 1981, p.123):

$$p_t^e = \eta \sum_{k=0}^{\infty} (1-\eta)^k p_{t-k} \tag{1.7}$$

In other words expectations are primarily based on recent prices.

1.1.4 The problem of mixed time scales

Several kinds of phenomena are intertwined in commodity markets, the response time of which may be greatly different: price adjustments for instance may occur in a couple of months, while crop adjustments may require a delay of at least one year and possibly two or three years. Cobweb models have been developed which take different time scales into account (see for instance Nerlove 1958). In such models, two different supply (resp. demand) functions are introduced, namely a short term supply S_t (resp. D_t and a long run supply $\bar{S}_t$ (resp. $\bar{D}_t$); accordingly *two* market clearing conditions have to be stated:

$$\text{short-term equilibrium:} \quad D_t = S_t$$
$$\text{long-term equilibrium:} \quad \bar{D}_t = \bar{S}_t$$

Regarding the problem of different time-scales one should also mention a pioneering study by P.Samuelson (1957) in which he analyses for instance the following issues:

- The impact of non instantaneous harvests on seasonal price patterns.
- The interplay of long speculators and of short speculators in future markets.

	1986	1987	1988	1989	1990	1991	Average
Wheat							
Closing stocks / Production	24%	29%	27%	20%	18%	17%	**20%**
Corn							
Closing stocks / Production	29%	33%	33%	20%	15%	14%	**24%**
Sugar							
Closing stocks / Production	26%	23%	20%	20%	20%	18%	**21%**
Coffee							
Closing stocks / Production	51%	35%	49%	51%			**46%**
Cocoa							
Closing stocks / Production	27%	26%	33%	41%	49%	54%	**38%**
Cotton							
Closing stocks / Production	59%	50%	40%	39%	33%	31%	**42%**
Copper							
Closing stocks LME / Production	1.9%	1.8%	0.5%	0.6%	1.0%	1.6%	
Lead							
Closing stocks LME / Production	1.7%	1.1%	0.5%	1.8%	0.7%	1.3%	

Table 2.2 Evolution of closing stocks in proportion of production for various commodities. The average ratio is in general well over 20%. Inventories may therefore be expected to play an important role in the process of price fixing. The London Metal Exchange closing stocks do not provide an estimated value of world stocks, but their variations can be considered as being representative. *Source: Chalmin (P.) 1991: Cyclope. Les marchés mondiaux. Economica. Paris.*

1.2 Cobweb models with inventories

In the precedent section prices were assumed to be fixed in such as way as to clear the current output of every time period. This is a rather unrealistic assumption however. Table 2.2 shows that world closing stocks usually represent a substantial amount of world production. Inventory management is therefore an essential issue in modelling commodity prices.

It is useful to distinguish between two kinds of inventories: excess supply inventories on one hand and speculative inventories on the other. In either case the fundamental equation relates current price expectations p_t^e to previous inventory levels I_{t-1} and to previous price levels p_{t-1}. The emphasis however is not on the same variable. In the case of excess supply inventories one may write:

$$p_t^e = f(I_{t-1}, p_{t-1}) \tag{1.8a}$$

implying a causality chain: $I_{t-1} \longrightarrow p_t^e$ while in the second case one may write the demand for speculative inventories as:

$$I_{t-1} = g(p_t^e, p_{t-1}) \tag{1.8b}$$

implying that now the causality chain is : $p_t^e \longrightarrow I_{t-1}$. In this Section we shall give an example of the first kind of models, while the modelling of speculative inventories will be considered in the next Section.

1.2.1 A linear model

Let us make the assumption that the price is set by the seller in a way taking into consideration the inventory situation: if, as a result of the preceding-period price, inventory accumulated, the current-period price expectation is set at a lower level than before; but if inventory decumulated instead, the current price expectation is set higher than before. This is reflected in the following inventory equation:

$$p_t^e = p_{t-1} - \sigma i_{t-1} \quad i_t = S_t - D_t \tag{1.9}$$

with σ being a positive parameter, i_t is the excess supply that is to say the additional inventory for period t. By substituting the expressions (1.4) for S_t and D_t, the equation of the model becomes:

$$p_t^e - (1 - \sigma\beta)p_{t-1} + \sigma\gamma p_{t-1}^e = \sigma(b + c) \tag{1.10}$$

To each different price expectations assumption will correspond a specific inventory model. We note in passing that the crude model $p_t^e = p_{t-1}$ is excluded, since it would imply $\sigma = 0$. On the other hand, the simple, yet rather unrealistic, assumption:

$$p_t^e = p_t \tag{1.11}$$

leads to an inventory model set out in Chiang (1967):

$$p_t - [1 - \sigma(\beta + \gamma)]p_{t-1} = \sigma(b + c) \tag{1.12}$$

Let us summarize the algebraic structure of our inventory models by listing the unknowns together with the model's equations; there are five unknowns:

- the levels of demand, supply and inventories: D_t, S_t, I_t
- the expected price p_t^e and the actual price p_t

On the equation side we have the following five equations:

- the explicit forms of the demand and supply functions
- the market equilibrium condition: $S_t - D_t = I_t - I_{t-1}$

- the control equation of inventories; for instance: $p_t^e = p_{t-1} - \sigma i_{t-1}$
- the price expectation assumption, such as (1.11) for instance.

A serious conceptual objection to linear models arises from the fact that they allow inventories to become negative which is rather unrealistic.

1.2.2 An example: the FAO cocoa price model

As an illustration let us consider a model constructed by the FAO Cocoa Study Group in the early 1960s that is to say before the introduction of the concept of rational expectations. It is summarized by the following equation (Weymar 1988,p.189):

$$\ln p = 2.013 - 0.010\ q + 0.0074\ g - 0.0087\ s + e_t$$

where:

- p is the average monthly spot price of Accra beans in New York (in cents/pound and deflated by the US wholesale price index)
- q is the current forecast of annual world production for the crop year beginning October 1 (in thousands of metric tons)
- g is the current forecast of calendar-year world grindings (in thousands of metric tons)
- s represents the stocks as a percent of grindings during the preceding year.

The comments given in the FAO report (The cocoa situation: recent developments and the outlook for production and demand. FAO, Rome 1961) are almost as interesting as the model itself for they pave the way for the subsequent introduction of rational expectations schemes. "In only 12 of the 28 years that have been analyzed were the year-to-year price changes in the direction to be expected from the changes in production. One of the main reasons for this is that price develop during the year not in relation to the *final* production or grindings outturns (which are of course known only after the end of the period) but in accordance with expectations, foreçasts and market ideas concerning the monthly development of grindings and stocks. For the purpose of this study, the forecasts issued by Gill&Duffus and those issued by the Committee on Statistics of the Cocoa Study Group were used. In reality, however, there are many ideas on these factors in the markets and the ideas change from day to day." The interesting point is that Weymar (1988) was able to show that the completely phenomenological equation set up by the FAO group indeed is consistent with a "rational" pricing model.

1.2.3 Comparison with empirical evidence

Stock-ratios

In specialized business publications the relationship between stock-ratios $R_t = I_t/D_t$ and current prices usually plays a major role. In Fig.2.1 we have summarized the evidence for cocoa, sugar and wheat. For cocoa and sugar there is one important observation to be made. The function $p_t = f(R_t)$ is not single-valued but double-valued: the lowest curve corresponds to "normal" price conditions, while the highest curve corresponds to speculative price peaks, an observation which can be linked up with the non-uniqueness of the solutions of rational expectations models (see section 2.4). The chart for wheat does not display the same feature probably because price peaks are far less pronounced in this case.

As a matter of comparison let us examine the behaviour of the stock-ratio as predicted by our model (1.12). One has:

$$R_t = \frac{I_t}{D_t}, \qquad I_t = i_0 + \ldots + i_t = \frac{p_0 - p_{t+1}}{\sigma}$$

and finally:

$$p_t = \frac{-bR_t + p_0 - \sigma(b+c)}{\beta R_t + 1 - \sigma(\beta + \gamma)}$$

Figure 2.2d shows that there is a qualitative agreement between this simple model and the empirical data at least for moderate prices; the peak-price outliers, however, clearly fall outside the scope of the model.

Predictability powers of price models

Wheat prices Econometric and futures forecasts are confronted with empirical evidence in Table 2.3. It is interesting to note that none of the methods is able to predict substantial price changes and that both methods seem to work or to fail at the same time. The last observation seems to indicate that future prices (which are based on speculator's expectations) partly rely on econometric models.

Hogs prices It has generally been assumed that the cycle of hog prices is one of four years and that it constitutes an almost perfect illustration of the cobweb model. One should therefore be in a good position to obtain an accurate estimate of the producers' price expectations. Several studies have been conducted along these lines (Coase and Fowler 1937, Harlow 1962, Meadows 1970). The results are more intricate than expected however. Firstly, there is substantial a variability in the length of the cycle: actual cycles range between 35 and 50 months. Secondly, there are several kinds of pigs (for instance porkers and bakoners in the U.K.) and it is therefore unclear which demand and supply estimates should be used. Thirdly no single exogenous expectation hypothesis seems to be consistent with observed price fluctuations.

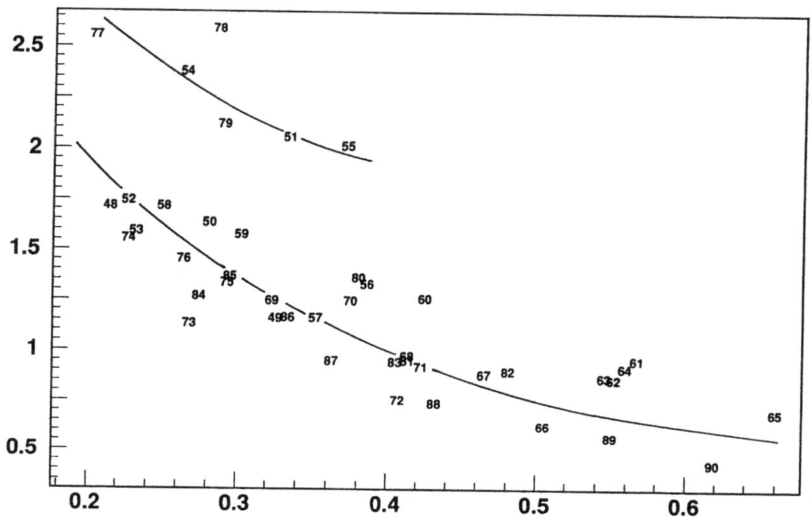

Fig.2.1 a Cocoa: price versus stock-ratio 1948-1990. Prices are deflated unit values of imports in the UK (pounds/ton). Except for the outliers 51,54,55,77,78,79 which correspond to peak prices there is an hyperbolic relationship between prices and stock-ratios. Between 1948 and 1990 demand and production have been multiplied by a factor of 3.5; by considering stock-ratios instead of stocks this trend is ipso facto discarded. *Source: see Appendix B.*

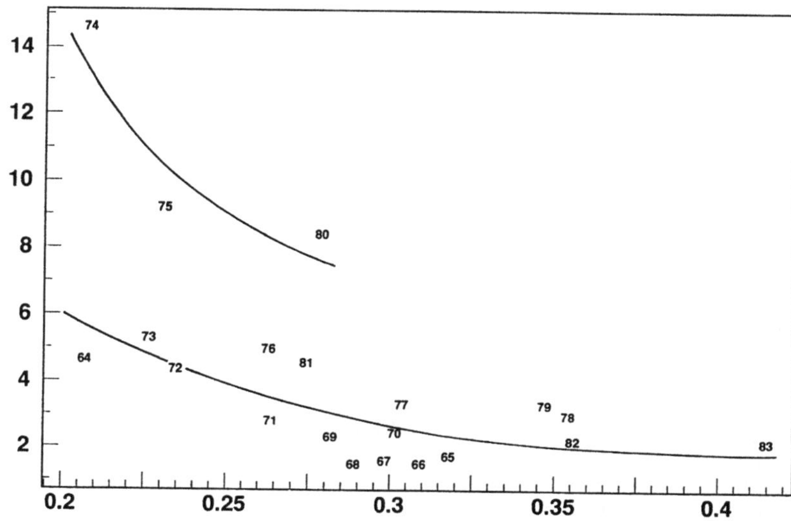

Fig.2.1 b Sugar: price versus stock-ratio 1964-1983. Prices are unit values of imports in the US (cents/lb). Except for the outliers 74,75,80 which correspond to peak prices there is an hyperbolic relationship between prices and stock-ratios. Between 1964 and 1983 demand and production have been multiplied by a factor of 2. *Source: see Appendix B.*

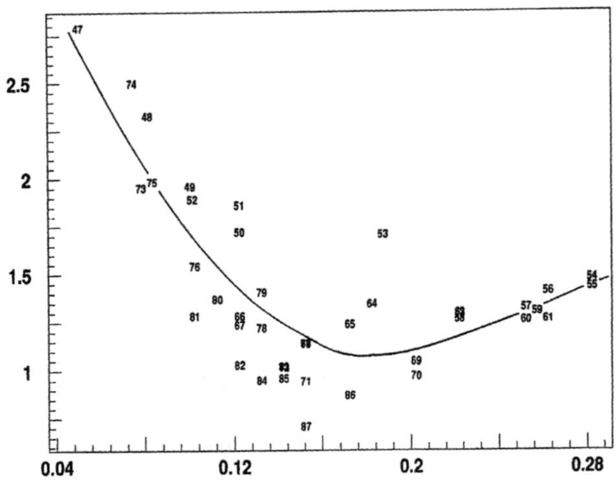

Fig.2.1 c Wheat: price versus stock-ratio 1947-1987. Prices are given by an index of world wheat prices estimated by the World Bank. Between 1947 and 1990 demand and production have been multiplied by a factor of 3.7. *Source: see Appendix B.*

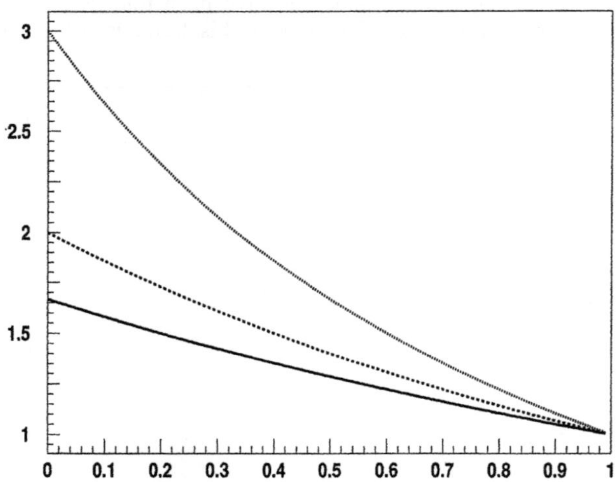

Fig.2.1 d Price versus stock-ratio as given by an elementary inventory model. The model is defined by equation (1.12). The parameters are: $p_0 = 2.; b = \beta = c = \gamma = 0.5$. The three curves correspond to different values of the parameter s which characterizes the relationship between expected price and excess supply (equation 1.9): Solid curve $\sigma = -0.5$; broken curve $\sigma = 0.$; dotted curve $\sigma = 0.5$.

		Season-average farm price $ / bushel	12 months ahead Price $ / bushel	Relative percentage error	6 months ahead Price $ / bushel	Relative percentage error
1986	Actual price	2.42				
	WASDE forec.		2.38	2%	2.30	5%
	Futures forec.		2.42	0%	2.31	5%
1987	Actual	2.57				
	WASDE forec.		2.45	5%	2.50	3%
	Futures forec.		2.76	7%	2.57	0%
1988	Actual	3.72				
	WASDE forec.		3.00	20%	3.63	3%
	Futures forec.		3.05	18%	3.77	1%
1989	Actual	3.72				
	WASDE forec.		4.00	7%	3.93	5%
	Futures forec.		4.25	14%	3.79	2%
1990	Actual	2.61				
	Wasde forec.		3.10	19%	2.65	1%
	Futures forec.		3.42	31%	2.70	3%

Table 2.3 Forecasting wheat prices in the US. Forecasts are made of the monthly average cash price received by farmers throughout the 12 months of the crop year starting with June. "WASDE" (for: World Agricultural Supply and Demand Estimate) is an econometric forecast of the US Department of Agriculture. "Futures" is a forecast based on the current futures prices for the nearest contract maturing after the month being forecast. One can note the great variability of the forecasts errors; both forecasts are inaccurate by a wide margin whenever a substantial change occurs in the actual price. Not surprisingly are the forecasts performed 6 months ahead usually more accurate than those performed 12 months ahead. *Source: Hoffman (1992)*

1.2.4 Nonlinear models

So far we have exclusively been concerned with linear models. There are some features, however, whose description requires nonlinear models; one may mention in this respect the description of limit cycles (see for instance Beckmann and Ryder 1969) or of periodic standard deviations (see for instance Klein and Preston 1969). Let us briefly discuss the second point. In linear stochastic processes the standard deviation of stationary solutions tends to a constant as the transient solution vanishes. On the contrary, in nonlinear systems one may have stationary solutions which are periodic in the mean as well as in the standard deviation. In Klein and Preston (1969) a numerical example illustrating Kaldor's nonlinear trade model is shown to have periodic solutions with the period of the variance being one-half the cyclical duration of the mean series.

2 Rational expectations models

The rational expectations hypothesis assumes that economic agents hold expectations of future variables fully reflecting the structure of the underlying model, i.e. their expectations are formed in the most consistent way according to the known theory[1] . The rational expectations hypothesis is formalized by assuming that individual's probability distributions of expectations coincide with the probability distributions (conditional on the information available at the time expectations are formed) of the variables in the model. In order to keep simple the mathematical techniques most rational expectations models deal with the first moment of the distribution, that is to say the mean. Expectations of the variance are considered only occasionally (see for instance Begg 1984). Thus one has in mathematical terms:

$$p_t^e = E(p_t | I_{t-1})$$

where p_t^e denotes the price expected at time t by individuals forming expectations at time $t-1$; p_t denotes the random variable representing current prices and I_{t-1} stands for the information available at time $t-1$.
It is sometimes stated that the rational expectation hypothesis asserts that individuals do not make systematic mistakes in forecasting the future. This is a consequence of the fact that (proposition 3 in appendix A):

$$E(p_t^e) = E[\ E(p_t | I_{t-1})\ ] = E(p_t)$$

Our subsequent presentation of rational expectations follows the course of its historical development. First, we examine what can be learned from the evidence which was available at the time when the theory emerged. Secondly, we discuss a number of empirical rests which have specifically been conducted in order to test the rational expectations hypothesis. Thirdly, we present the derivation in Muth's (1961) pioneering paper. Finally, we extend our discussion to other classes of expectational equations. For a more complete review, the following books may be helpful: Begg (1982), Pesaran (1987), Broze and Szafarz (1991), Redman (1992).

2.1 Origins of the concept of rational expectations

John Muth's pioneering paper appeared in 1961, while the widespread application of rational expectations ideas has been delayed until the late 1970s (see Fig.2.2). What triggered this renewed interest? Two factors are usually considered as having been determinant in this respect.

[1]Incidentally one may note that on account of this definition, and as noted by Simon 1978, rational expectations would be better labelled consistent expectations.

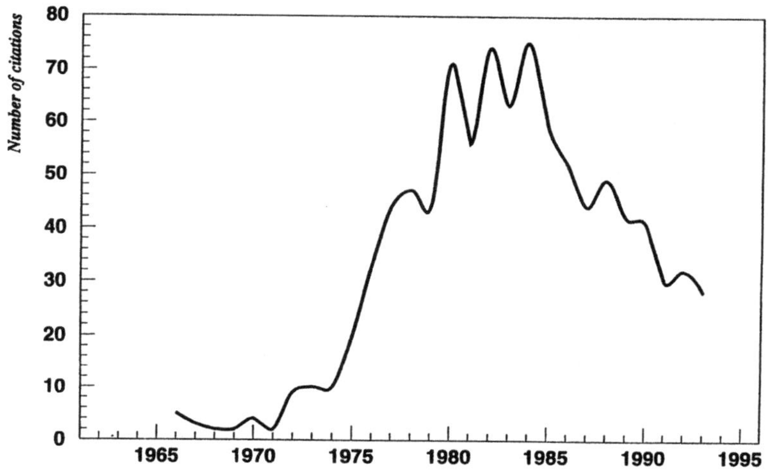

Fig.2.2 Number of annual citations of Muth's 1961 paper.

- The realization that short-run macroeconomic stabilization policies were untenable (Maddock and Carter 1982).
- The accumulation of empirical evidence proving that financial markets are using information efficiently.

Regarding the first point let us merely point out that the idea behind it is that any stabilization policy rule (for instance a fixed growth of the money supply) will be perfectly anticipated and therefore will never cause any deviation from "natural rates". The second point means that the principle of rational behaviour (which is here just another expression for optimal behaviour) can be extended to the acquisition of information and to the formation of expectations. Because information plays a key role in stockmarkets, they constitute an ideal field for testing such an idea. Let us mention two observations of that kind.

1) Ball and Brown (1968) have analysed the effect on stock returns of the publication of operating profits.

2) Fama et al (1969) have examined the process by which common stock prices adjust to the information that is implicit in a stock split. In the past a large fraction of stock splits have been followed closely by dividend increases; they are therefore interpreted by the market in the same way as are publications of increased profits.

These studies show that in both instances the agents correctly anticipated the evolution of the market. Since we are in this book interested in commodity rather than in financial markets we shall examine in more detail the evidence for commodity prices and industrial variables. In such cases the forecasting capabilities of agents generally are much poorer that in finance. We have already seen an example of the inability to predict notable price changes in Table 2.3. Here we shall provide two other examples. The first is about price expectations of farm productions, the second concerns investment expectations in industry.

Errors in forecasting prices. A sample of about two hundred farmers was questioned concerning their price expectations one year ahead for a set of products. The results (Heady and Kaldor 1954) are summarized in Table 2.4. The

	Expected price ($)	Realized price ($)	Relative error	Dispersion of expectations
Corn				26%
Dec.1948	1.51	1.19	27%	
Dec.1947	1.07	1.08	-1%	
Oats				24%
Dec.1948	0.93	0.66	41%	
Dec.1949	0.61	0.54	13%	
Soybeans				19%
Dec.1948	2.71	2.32	17%	
Dec.1949	2.08	2.03	2%	
Eggs				
Dec.1948	0.35	0.36	-2%	
Dec.1949	0.33	0.39	-15%	
Cattle				15%
Dec.1948	30.5	35.2	-13%	
Dec.1949	27.6	25.1	9%	
Calves				
Dec.1948	20.5	25.8	-20%	
Dec.1949	20.9	22.6	-7%	
Hogs				20%
Dec.1948	22.3	20.7	7%	
Dec.1949	17.1	14.7	16%	

Table 2.4 Comparison between expected prices for next year crop and realized prices. In december 1947 and 1948 a sample of 180 farmers of Iowa was asked to indicate what prices they considered most probable during the following year. The effects of price expectations depend not only upon the expected price changes but also upon the degree of confidence which the farmer attaches to his expectation. In this study the degree of confidence is estimated by the relative standard deviation (σ/m) of the expectations. *Source: Heady and Kaldor (1954)*

dispersion of expected prices is seen to be approximately the same for the different products. On the other hand the relative errors of the forecasts vary to a large extent from one product to another. period.

Errors in investments anticipation. The annual surveys conducted by the Securities and Exchange Commission and the Department of Commerce provide investments expectations for a period of nine years; they are summarized in Table 2.5. The time average turns out to be better than individual expectations

Year	Relative forecast error	Relative error of the conservative forecasting model	Relative error of the deflated cons. forecasting model
1948	7.0%	- 4.7%	3.9%
1949	- 0.1%	28.0%	32.0%
1950 (Korean War)	- 18.0%	- 4.6%	-2.6%
1951	0.1%	-31.0%	-25.0%
1952	1.2%	-6.7%	-5.7%
1953	-2.0%	- 2.3%	-0.2%
1954	0.3%	7.9%	8.4%
1955	-6.5%	- 3.5%	- 1.9%
Time average	**- 4.0%**	**- 2.1%**	**1.2%**

Table 2.5 Comparison of anticipated and actual equipment expenditure. The data are based on questionnaires returned to the Securities and Exchange Commission by a sample of firms. In the conservative forecasting model the anticipated investment is merely that of the previous year. In the deflated forecasting model the anticipated investment is that of the previous year ajusted for the variation of the general price level. *Source: Adapted from Modigliani and Weingartner (1958)*

in spite of the 1950 figure which is somewhat out of range because of the beginning of the Korean war. When compared to conservative forecasts (i.e. no anticipation), the firms' expectations appear more realistic.

The two aforementioned tests have been carried out *before* the publication of Muth's paper (1961); in fact, we selected them for this very reason. In the period 1970-1990 a great number of additional tests have been carried out, a review of which has been made in a paper by Lovell (1986). Their results are rather similar to our previous conclusions. In Lovell's words "the weight of empirical evidence is sufficiently strong to compel us to suspend belief in the hypothesis of rational expectations. Instead, it should be recognized that there are competing hypothesis". Two comments are in order:

1) The tests reported in Lovell's paper concern inventory anticipations, inflationary expectations, steel production anticipations, wage expectations, government forecasts, etc but none of them is about expectations in finance.

2) The fact that the rational expectation hypothesis does not seem an adequate description of agents' behaviour does not necessarily preclude its use; indeed, as noted by Lovell, it has long been argued (in particular by M. Friedman) that theories should be judged on their predictive ability rather than on the basis of the validity of their simplifying assumptions. Even if the latter are not fulfilled , it may nevertheless be true that "everything happens as if they were".

To sum up, one may say that in terms of forecasting powers there is a striking contrast between financial and commodity markets. Incidentally, it can be noted that quite a similar conclusion emerged form our discussion of market integration in chapter 1.

2.2 Rational expectations in commodity markets without inventories

In this section, we shall put the ideas of rational expectations to work in constructing a theory of price movements; we shall mainly follow Muth's paper (1961). First of all it must be emphasized that the natural setting for rational expectations is a stochastic framework; in fact the very definition of rational expectation implies the probabilistic concept of conditional expectation (see Appendix A): the price expected to prevail during the period t on the basis of the information available through the period $t-1$ is be defined as the following random variable:

$$p_t^e = E(p_t | I_{t-1}) \tag{2.1}$$

When the available information I_{t-1} reduces to the knowledge of previous prices, equation (2.1) takes the form:

$$p_t^e = E(p_t | p_{t-1}, p_{t-2}, \ldots)$$

Thus the expected price crucially hinges on the dependence between p_t and previous prices as defined by the dynamic equations of the model. This has both advantages and disadvantages: conceptually it is an important gain for it makes expectations endogeneous. On the other hand, price expectations cannot be tested independently of the dynamic structure of the model.

As in Section 1.1 we shall define linear demand and supply functions:

$$D_t = -\beta p_t \quad S_t = \gamma p_t^e + u_t \tag{2.2}$$

The terms b and c are omitted here because the origin has for convenience been transported to the equilibrium point. The stochastic variable u_t is meant to represent fluctuating factors such as for instance changes in climatic conditions. The dynamic behaviour will be ruled by the equilibrium equation $D_t = S_t$ which reads:

$$p_t = aE(p_t|I_{t-1}) + v_t \qquad (2.3)$$

where: $a = -\gamma/\beta, \quad v_t = -u_t/\beta$
Mathematically, (2.3) differs from the recurrence equations we have written in section 1 by the appearance of the conditional expectation term; for that reason it is called an expectational difference equation or (in economic context) a rational expectations equation. In comparison with ordinary difference equations, expectational difference equations have a number of specific properties; some of them are discussed in paragraph 2.4.

In order to solve equation (2.3), let us apply the operator $E(.|I_{t-1})$ to both sides:

$$E(p_t|I_{t-1}) = aE[\ E(p_t|I_{t-1})\ |I_{t-1}] + E(v_t|I_{t-1})$$

Applying the law of iterated expectations (see Appendix A) one has:

$$E[\ E(p_t|I_{t-1})\ |I_{t-1}] = E(p_t|I_{t-1})$$

thus:

$$E(p_t|I_{t-1}) = \frac{1}{1-a}E(v_t|I_{t-1})$$

Substituting this expression in (2.3) one obtains:

$$p_t = \frac{a}{1-a}E(v_t|I_{t-1}) + v_t \qquad (2.4)$$

(2.4) can be considered as a first step towards the solution of equation (2.3): indeed, it contains only expectations of the exogenous variable in contrast to (2.3) which contains expectations of the endogeneous variable p_t; for that reason, (2.4) is called a *reduced form* of the expectational equation (2.3). In paragraph 2.4 we shall see another (and less simple) example of a reduced equation.

In order to obtain an explicit solution from (2.4) one has to specify the stochastic properties of the disturbance term v_t. Following Muth we shall examine two special cases.

- In the first case, we assume that the disturbances u_t have no memory, i.e. they are identified with a white noise ϵ_t, $E(\epsilon_t) = 0$. Thus according to proposition 2a in Appendix A, one obtains:

$$E(u_t|I_{t-1}) = E(\epsilon_t|I_{t-1}) = E(\epsilon_t) = 0$$

thus: $p_t = (-1/\beta)\epsilon_t$

The standard deviation of p_t is given by: $\sigma(p_t) = \sigma/\beta$, where σ is the standard deviation of the disturbances. The price expectation p_t^e is given by:

$$p_t^e = (-1/\beta)E(\epsilon_t|I_{t-1}) = 0$$

in other words, the price expectation is the equilibrium price.

- In the second case, we assume the disturbances to have a fairly long memory, more specifically, we suppose that:

$$u_t = \sum_{i=0}^{\infty} \epsilon_{t-i}$$

Thus:

$$E(v_t|I_{t-1}) = (-1/\beta)E(\epsilon_t|I_{t-1}) - (1/\beta)\sum_{i=1}^{\infty} E(\epsilon_{t-i}|I_{t-1})$$

ϵ_t being independent of I_{t-1}, the first term is again given by $E(\epsilon_t) = 0$; in order to evaluate the terms $E(\epsilon_{t-i}|I_{t-1})$, one has to make more specific assumptions about the information available at the time $t-1$. As stated above, a natural assumption is: $I_{t-1} = \{p_{t-1}, p_{t-2}, \ldots\}$. But this assumption is not sufficient for we do not know the dependence between the prices p_t and the shocks ϵ_t. A stronger assumption is to assume that the available information consists in the knowledge of the previous shocks, i.e.: $I_{t-1} = \{u_{t-1}, u_{t-2}, \ldots\}$. Because of the specific form assumed for u_t this is equivalent to: $I_{t-1} = \{\epsilon_{t-1}, \epsilon_{t-2}, \ldots\}$; thus according to proposition 4b (Appendix A) one has:

$$E(\epsilon_{t-i}|I_{t-1}) = \epsilon_{t-i} \quad i = 1, 2, \ldots \tag{2.5}$$

One obtains finally:

$$p_t = (-\frac{1}{\beta})\epsilon_t - \frac{1}{\beta+\gamma}\sum_{i=1}^{\infty} \epsilon_{t-i} \tag{2.6}$$

The variance of p_t turns out to be infinite, a result which is not surprising as the variance of the shocks u_t is infinite itself. It is more interesting to look at the form of the expected price; it reads:

$$p_t^e = -\frac{1}{\beta+\gamma}\sum_{i=1}^{\infty} \epsilon_{t-i}$$

From: $p_t - p_t^e = (-1/\beta)\epsilon_t$, one sees that there is the following relation between p_t and p_t^e:

$$p_t^e = p_{t-1}^e + \frac{\beta}{\beta+\gamma}(p_{t-1} - p_{t-1}^e)$$

In other words, the expectation is of the adaptative type.

In his paper, instead of first reducing equation (2.3) to its form (2.4) Muth used a moving average method of undetermined coefficients, i.e. he assumed the solution to be of the form:

$$p_t = \sum_{i=0}^{\infty} W_i \epsilon_{t-i}$$

In our method of solution we implicitly had to make a similar assumption. Its main advantage over Muth's derivation is to show by equation (2.4) that the model has a unique solution whatever the stochastic properties of the disturbances.

2.3 Rational expectation with inventories

Muth's approach We shall now examine the effect of inventory speculation by adjoining to our previous equation an inventory demand equation:

$$I_t = \alpha(p^e_{t-1} - p_t)$$

Although the form of this equation is somewhat similar to equation (1.9) in Section 1.3, its interpretation is completely different because here I_t represents a speculative inventory from which the inventory holder expects a profit. The parameter α is therefore supposed to be positive: only when the expected price p^e_{t-1} is higher than the current price will positive inventories be carried forwards; in the opposite case, negative inventories should be carried forwards.

The market equilibrium condition reads now:

$$S_t - D_t = I_t - I_{t-1}$$

where the right-hand side represents the stock newly created during the period $(t-1, t)$. We shall not go into the details of Muth's derivation as it does not involve really new ideas; instead we shall summarize some of his major findings (1961, p.328-330). Under the assumption of white noise exogenous disturbances, speculation is found to reduce the variance of prices by spreading the effect of a disturbance over several time periods; the larger the speculative factor α, the smaller the standard deviation of prices $\sigma(p)$. The formulas for the two asymptotic cases are the following:

- $\alpha \ll \beta + \gamma \;:\; \sigma(p) \sim (\sigma/\beta)(1 - \alpha/\beta) \longrightarrow \sigma/\beta$ when: $\alpha \to 0$
- $\alpha \gg \beta + \gamma \;:\; \sigma(p) \sim \sigma/[\alpha^{1/4}(\alpha + \beta)^{3/4}] \longrightarrow 0$ when: $\alpha \to \infty$

Nonlinear models In the previous linear inventory model negative inventories cannot be avoided. Crops, however, cannot be consumed before they are grown and one has therefore to get rid of this unrealistic feature. To take into account this non-negativity constraint is one of the main motivation of more recent nonlinear models. As an example of such models, we shall mention a recent attempt at modelling commodity prices by A.Deaton and G.Laroque (1992). One of the purposes of their paper is to explain the existence of rare but violent explosions in prices coupled with a high degree of price autocorrelation in more normal times. In the course of their study, they are able to prove an existence and uniqueness theorem for the solution of an expectational functional equation. This is a remarkable property in so far as uniqueness is the exception rather than the rule for expectational equations. The next paragraph briefly discusses non-uniqueness in expectational equations.

2.4 More about expectional equations

The basic expectational equation in Muth's (1961) model (equation (2.3)) can be generalized to the following form:

$$p_t = \sum_{i=1}^{p} a_i E(p_t | I_{t-i}) + u_t$$

without loosing its main property, namely the uniqueness of its solution for given initial conditions. On the contrary, *future* expectational equations of the form:

$$p_t = aE(p_{t+1} | I_t) + u_t \tag{2.7}$$

usually have multiple solutions as we shall show presently. An equation of the form (2.7) is known as Cagan's equation; a more detailed discussion can be found in Broze and Szafarz (1992).

Let us try to solve (2.7) by the method of recursive substitution which we already used in the discussion of Muth's model. We introduce the notation: $E(.|I_t) = E_t(.)$. First, we make the substitution $t \to t+1$ in (2.7); then we apply the operator E_t to both sides:

$$E_t(p_{t+1}) = aE_t(E_{t+1}(p_{t+2})) + E_t(u_{t+1})$$

By the law of iterated expectations one has: $E_t(E_{t+k}(.)) = E_t(.)$. Substituting in (2.7) one obtains:

$$p_t = a^2 E_t(p_{t+2}) + aE_t(u_{t+1}) + u_t$$

By repeating this operation an infinite number of times, one obtains a solution of (2.7) in the form:

$$p_t = u_t + \sum_{i=1}^{\infty} a^i E_t(u_{t+i}) + \lim_{T \to \infty} a^T E_t(p_{t+T}) \tag{2.8}$$

A multiplicity of solutions can be obtained according to the behaviour of the last term. Often this term is set equal to zero by assuming the so-called transversality condition:

$$\lim_{T\to\infty} a^T E_t(p_{t+T}) = 0$$

In order to obtain an expression for the series in (2.8) one has to know the stochastic properties of the exogenous process u_t. If for instance, the u_t are independent white noises: $u_t = \epsilon_t$, then:

$$E_t(u_{t+i}) = 0 \qquad i = 1, 2, \ldots$$

and the solution reduces to: $p_t = u_t$.
Alternatively, let us assume that u_t satisfies a first-order autoregressive process of the form:

$$u_t = \gamma u_{t-1} + \epsilon_t \qquad |\gamma| < 1$$

where u_t represents white noise. The solution can be obtained from (2.8) in a way similar to the one used in the discussion of Muth's model (long memory case). However, one can also use the method of undetermined coefficients. In this method, one assumes a solution of the form:

$$p_t = \alpha u_t + \beta$$

The price expectation becomes:

$$E_t(p_{t+1}) = \alpha E_t(u_{t+1}) + \beta = \alpha E_t(\gamma u_t + \epsilon_{t+1}) + \beta = \alpha\gamma u_t + \beta$$

substituting in (2.7) one obtains:

$$\alpha u_t + \beta = a(\alpha\gamma u_t + \beta) + u_t$$

identifying the constant terms as well as the u_t terms, leads to:

$$\alpha = \frac{1}{1 - a\gamma}, \qquad \beta = 0$$

It follows that the process defined by:

$$p_t = \frac{u_t}{1 - a\gamma}$$

is a solution of the Cagan equation.

The method of undetermined coefficients has been generalized by Gouriéroux, Laffont and Montfort (1982) in a celebrated paper in which these authors also attracted attention to the fact that rational expectations equations are "compatible with an embarrassing infinity of solutions". It may be shown that, while an initial condition is unable to generate a unique solution, a terminal condition selects a unique solution. This asymmetry between past and future in rational expectations equations is of course not surprising: at any point in time, the past is known for sure but the future is only predicted.

3 Oligopoly theory and spatial competition

In this section we direct our attention to the producer's optimum. To begin with we examine the case of a single (monopolistic) producer. Then we discuss the case of several producers at different locations.

3.1 The monopoly optimum

3.1.1 The firm is able to sell all it wishes

We assume that:

- Only one product is being produced.
- The firm exercise no control over selling price because the established "normal" price has served the industry well and there is no desire to disturb a stable situation.
- Subject to the given price the firm attempts to maximize its profits.

Let $C(q)$ and $R(q)$ be the firm's cost and revenue functions for an output q. For its profits $\pi(q) = R(q) - C(q)$ to be maximized, the output $\hat{q}$ should be chosen such that:

$$\frac{dR}{dq}(\hat{q}) = \frac{dC}{dq}(\hat{q})$$

In other words, the optimum output is determined by the equality of marginal cost and of marginal revenue. When the revenue function can be approximated by the simple form: $R(q) = qp$ where p is the selling price, then at the optimum the price is given by the marginal cost.
We can note in passing that for an agricultural commodity, the marginal cost function is in general increasing with q.

3.1.2 The firm cannot sell all it wishes

The previous elementary marginal reasoning is of course open to various improvements; by way of illustration we shall mention two extensions allowing the limited character of demand to be taken into account.

Let $q = D(q)$ be the demand function; the profit reads now:

$$\pi = pD(p) - C(D(p)) \tag{3.1}$$

The optimum selling price is determined by the condition:

$$\frac{d\pi}{dp} = D(p) + p\frac{dD}{dp} - \frac{dC}{dq}\frac{dD}{dp} = 0$$

Introducing the elasticity of demand with respect to price: $\eta = -\frac{dD}{dp}/(D/p)$ we obtain (Tirole 1985, p.8):

$$\frac{1}{p}(p - \frac{dC}{dq}) = \frac{1}{\eta} \tag{3.2}$$

When $\eta = \infty$ (3.2) reduces to the previous case.

3.2 The duopoly equilibrium

The discussion of duopoly equilibrium goes back to Cournot's "Recherches sur les Principes mathématiques de la Théorie des Richesses" (Paris 1838). Renewed interest arose one century later with the work of Hotelling which opened up the way for the introduction of game theory into oligopoly theory. We shall present Cournot's argument mainly for the sake of its historical interest.

3.2.1 Cournot's model

Cournot considers the case of two proprietors of mineral springs which are supposed to produce mineral waters of identical quality. Let c be the production cost and $p = h(q)$ the global demand function, where p is the demand price. The profits of the firms are respectively:

$$\pi_1 = q_1(h(q_1 + q_2) - c)$$

$$\pi_2 = q_2(h(q_1 + q_2) - c)$$

The first firm adjusts its production q_1 so that its profit will be as great as possible; this leads to:

$$h(q_1 + q_2) + q_1 h'(q_1 + q_2) = c$$

In the same way the second proprietor adjusts its production so that:

$$h(q_1 + q_2) + q_2 h'(q_1 + q_2) = c$$

Because of the symmetry of the equations, there is at least one solution $q_1 = q_2$. It should however be remarked that depending on the form of the demand function, another solution $q_1 \neq q_2$ may exist too.

It has been argued that the solution $q_1 = q_2$ is in fact instable; indeed, either firm may by a slight reduction in price be able to take away all its opponent's business. This objection amounts to saying that instead of specifying a *global* demand function one should know from which firm consumers are going to buy. We indeed have unstability when the demand functions for each firm are defined in the following discontinuous way:

$$q_1 = D(p_1|p_2) = \begin{cases} D(p_1) & \text{if } p_1 < p_2 \\ \frac{1}{2}D(p_1) & \text{if } p_1 = p_2 \\ 0 & \text{if } p_1 > p_2 \end{cases} \tag{3.3}$$

with $D(p_1) = h^{-1}(q_1)$; and similarly for $q_2 = D(p_2|p_1)$.

Several solutions can be found to solve this apparent difficulty:

- It is possible to prove that the state $p_1 = p_2 = c$ actually is an equilibrium in the special sense introduced by Nash in game theory.
- Alternatively, one may observe that a discontinuous demand function such as (3.3) is not realistic. The smoothing of the demand function may be attributed to various practical constraints which have not yet been incorporated into the model; for instance limitations in production capacity or spatial dispersion of firms.

We shall now briefly examine each of these solutions.

3.2.2 Nash equilibrium

Definition We consider a two-person game. Let a_1 and a_2 be the strategies of each player and $\pi_1(a_1, a_2), \pi_2(a_1, a_2)$ their payoff functions. (a_1^*, a_2^*) is called a Nash equilibrium if:

$$\pi_i(a_1^*, a_2^*) \geq \pi_i(a_1, a_2^*) \quad i = 1, 2 \qquad \forall a_1$$

In words: given the strategy of the second player the first player cannot increase his pay-off by selecting another strategy.

It is possible to prove (see Tirole 1985) that in Cournot's model there is only one Nash equilibrium, namely:

$$p_1^* = p_2^* = c$$

3.2.3 Spatial competition: two marketplaces

We consider the case treated by Hotelling in his celebrated 1929 paper. The buyers of a commodity with zero production cost will be supposed to be uniformly distributed along a line of length L which may represent the Main Street in a town or a transcontinental railroad. Each consumer consumes exactly one unit of the commodity. At distances a and b respectively from the two ends of this line are located two firms A and B (Fig. 2.4a). Each buyer transports its purchases home at a cost t per unit length. No customer has any preference for

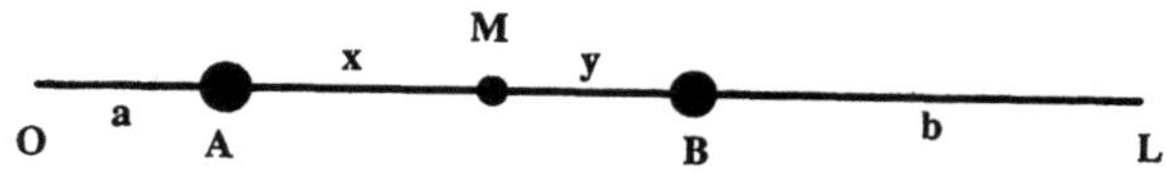

Fig.2.3 a Hotelling's duopoly model. The two firms are located at A and B. The customers buying from A (resp. B) are located in the interval AM (resp.BM).

either seller except on the ground of mill price plus transportation cost. Let p_1 and p_2 denote respectively the mill price of A and B. The point of division M between the regions served by the two firms is determined by the condition that at this place it is a matter of indifference whether one buys from A or from B. Let $AM = x$ and $BM = y$; x and y are defined by:

$$\begin{cases} p_1 + cx = p_2 + cy \\ a + x + y + b = L \end{cases}$$

Hence:

$$x = \frac{1}{2}(L - a - b - \frac{p_1 - p_2}{c}) \tag{3.4a}$$

$$y = \frac{1}{2}(L - a - b + \frac{p_1 - p_2}{c}) \tag{3.4b}$$

For these expressions to hold one has to assume that p_1 and p_2 are within a range such that $0 < x, y < L - a - b$; for the time being we shall make this assumption and we shall return to this point later on.
The quantities sold are: $q_1 = a + x$, $q_2 = b + y$ and the profits are:

$$\pi_1 = p_1 q_1 = p_1(a + x) \qquad \pi_2 = p_2 q_2 = p_2(b + y)$$

Substituting $(3.4a, b)$ into the profits π_1, π_2 and differentiating leads to the optimal prices:

$$p_1^* = t\ (L + \frac{a - b}{3}) \qquad p_2^* = t\ (L - \frac{a - b}{3}) \tag{3.5}$$

the price differential is:

$$p_1^* - p_2^* = \frac{2t}{3}(a - b) \tag{3.6}$$

We note that the price differential does not depend on the distance $L - a - b$ between A and B; moreover it vanishes when $a = b$.
The produced quantities are:

$$q_1 = 1/2(L + (a - b)/3) \quad q_2 = 1/2(L - (a - b)/3)$$

and the profits are given by:

$$\pi_1^* = \frac{t}{2}(L + \frac{a - b}{3})^2 \qquad \pi_2^* = \frac{t}{2}(L - \frac{a - b}{3})^2 \tag{3.7}$$

It can be proved that the validity of our result (3.5) extends beyond the somewhat restrictive assumptions under which it has been derived; it still holds for instance under the general assumption of a convex (and of course continuous and increasing) transportation cost function $c(x)$ (Gabszewicz and Thisse 1989, p.6). Finally let us mention that the duopoly model has been used to provide a qualitative description of the world wheat market in the period 1956-1965 (McCalla 1966).

Application As a matter of illustration we shall discuss how the equilibrium solutions (3.5) and (3.7) perform from the point of view of public welfare. Let us consider the total of transportation charges paid by the consumers. These charges for an interval of length l amount to

$$t \int_0^l u du = \frac{1}{2} t l^2$$

altogether the sum is:

$$S = \frac{1}{2} t \, (a^2 + b^2 + x^2 + y^2)$$

Given the constraint $a + b + x + y = L$, S will be minimum when:

$$a = b = x = y$$

By (3.4) this implies in particular that $p_1 = p_2$. In brief, public interest would require firms to be evenly distributed over the distance L and to charge the same price; this is not likely to be the case under competition and profit maximization.

3.2.4 Spatial competition: several marketplaces

We consider n sellers evenly distributed along a line (Tirole 1985) as shown on Fig.2.4b. In the above duopoly case, end effects at each side of the line of

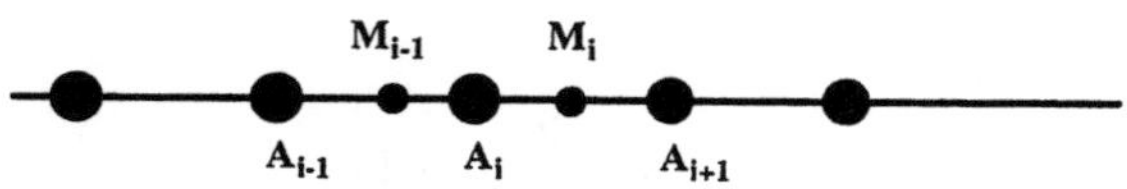

Fig.2.3 b Generalization of Hotelling 's model to n firms. Located at A_i the firms are evenly distributed on the line. The customers buying from A_{i-1} (resp. A_i) are located in the interval $A_{i-1}M_{i-1}$ (resp. A_iM_{i-1}). .

length L played an essential role. This will no longer be the case here at least for the markets that are not close to the boundaries. Let p_i denote the mill price of firm i. The reasoning of the previous section still applies. The firm i will, if it sells anything, sell to all buyers in the strip $M_{i-1}M_i$, where $A_iM_i = x_i$ is defined by:

$$p_i + t x_i = p_{i+1} + t(a - x_i)$$

thus: $x_i = (p_{i+1} - p_i + ta)/2t$.
Hence the profit of firm i is:

$$\pi_i = (p_i - c)(a - x_{i-1} + x_i) \quad c: \text{ production cost}$$

and profit maximization reads:

$$\partial_{p_i}\pi_i = a - x_{i-1} + x_i + (p_i - c)(-\partial_{p_i}x_{i-1} + \partial_{p_i}x_i) = 0$$

which leads to the condition

$$4p_i - p_{i-1} - p_{i+1} = 2(c + at)$$

A particular solution of this inhomogeneous second order difference equation is: $p_i = c + at$. With s_1, s_2 denoting its characteristic roots, the general solution is:

$$p_i = As_1^i + Bs_2^i + c + at$$

s_1 and s_2 are real and positive; for p_i to be bounded both at $i = -\infty$ and at $i = \infty$ we require that $A = B = 0$. Hence: $p_i^* = c + at$; in other words all firms will charge the same price, a result which is consistent with our previous model when $a = b$.

The models presented so far are rather formal; let us discuss to what extent they may apply to the grain markets of the nineteenth century on which we shall focus in following chapters. Let us assume that grains have already been stored in appropriate merchant's facilities located at the A_i. Our previous assumptions then are not completely unrealistic: grains are an homogeneous product; the transport is under the customers' control; in first approximation, customers may be thought of as being uniformly distributed if the intervals between the A_i include a large number of cities. Yet empirical evidence given in chapters 4 and 6 does not match the previous conclusion; in particular the price differentials show a marked tendency to increase along with distance between marketplaces. What is wrong?
It would of course be easy to mention many features of real markets which have not been taken into account in our model: no demand function has been introduced, the process of collecting grains from the producers has been discarded, several merchants are operating at each marketplace, and so on. This would not be a very constructive criticism however; after all a model is nothing more than an idealization of reality. Nonetheless, a *dynamic* description of the merchant's selling and arbitrage strategies as provided for instance by the inventory models in Sections 1 and 2, seems to be lacking in some essential way. Sequential game models (see for instance Maskin and Tirole 1988 or Gabszewicz and Thisse 1989) are an attempt in that direction. Such a direction also has been explored in a recent paper by Sheppard, Haining and Plummer (1992). The Enke-Samuelson trade model which we introduce in the next chapter is an attempt to take demand functions into account.

A Appendix A: Conditional expectation: a mathematical reminder

The probabilistic concept of conditional expectation plays a crucial role in the theory of rational expectations. In this Appendix we summarize its definition and its basic properties.

A.1 Conditional expectation: two random variables

A.1.1 Definitions

Definition 1 Let X and Y be two random variables with joint density functions $f(x, y)$. The conditional density function of Y, assuming $X = x$, is defined as:

$$f_Y(y \mid X = x) = \frac{f_{XY}(x, y)}{f_X(x)}$$

Definition 2 The conditional expectation of the function $g(Y)$, assuming $X = x$, is given by:

$$E\left(g(Y) \mid X = x\right) = \int_{-\infty}^{\infty} g(y) f_Y(y \mid X = x)\, dy$$

For any given x, this expectation is a number which we shall denote by $\mathcal{E}_{g(y)}(x)$:

$$\mathcal{E}_{g(y)}(x) \stackrel{def}{=} E\left(g(Y) \mid X = x\right)$$

The special case $g(y) \equiv y$ is particularly important:

$$\mathcal{E}(x) \stackrel{def}{=} E\left(Y \mid X = x\right) = \int_{-\infty}^{\infty} y \frac{f_{XY}(x, y)}{f_X(x)} dy \tag{1a}$$

Definition 3 The conditional expectation $E\left(Y \mid X\right)$ of the random variable Y, assuming X, is a random variable defined as:

$$E\left(Y \mid X\right) = \mathcal{E}(X) \tag{1b}$$

More generally the conditional expectation $E\left(g(Y) \mid X\right)$ is defined as:

$$E\left(g(Y) \mid X\right) = \mathcal{E}_{g(y)}(X)$$

A.1.2 Basic properties of conditional expectation

It is the following property which provides the main motivation for the introduction of the concept of conditional expectation (Papoulis 1965, p.217).

Proposition 1 We consider two dependent random variables X and Y and we want to approximate Y by a suitable function $h(X)$ in such a way that the mean square error $E\left[(Y-h(X))^2\right]$ is minimum. It is the conditional expectation of Y, assuming X, which provides the solution of this minimization problem:

$$h(X) = E(Y \mid X)$$

Proof In order to find the extremum of the following integral:

$$\mathcal{L}(h) = E\left[\left(Y - h(X)\right)^2\right] = \int_{-\infty}^{\infty} f(x)dx \int_{-\infty}^{\infty} \left(y - h(x)\right)^2 f(y \mid x)\, dy$$

we differentiate $\mathcal{L}$:

$$\delta\mathcal{L} = \mathcal{L}(h+\epsilon) - \mathcal{L}(h) = \int_{-\infty}^{\infty} f(x)\epsilon(x)dx \left[h(x) - \int_{-\infty}^{\infty} yf(y \mid x)\, dy\right]$$

Hence:

$$h(x) = \int_{-\infty}^{\infty} yf(y \mid x)\, dy = E(Y \mid X = x)$$

It is easy to check that the extremum is indeed a minimum.

The essential meaning of the previous result is that the conditional expectation $E(Y|X)$ is the best predictor among all (square integrable) functions of X. In other words, it "extracts" out of the realizations of X all the possible information about Y. Conditional expectations have two other properties which are extremely interesting from a statistical point of view, namely:

- $E(\ E(Y|X)\ ) = E(Y)$ (see below) which says that it is unbiased
- $\mathrm{Var}[E(Y|X)] \leq \mathrm{Var}(Y)$ which means that the variability of conditional expectation is not larger than the one of the variable to be approximated.

Proposition 2
a) If X and Y are independent, $E(Y \mid X)$ is an almost certain random variable, namely the expectation of Y:

$$E(Y \mid X) = E(Y)$$

b)

$$E(Y \mid Y) = Y$$

To prove these relations we have to get the corresponding $\mathcal{E}(x)$ functions.

a) By taking into account the independence of X and Y we obtain:

$$f_{XY}(x,y) = f_X(x) f_Y(y) \Longrightarrow \mathcal{E}(x) = \int_{-\infty}^{\infty} y f(y \mid x)\, dy = E(Y)$$

b)

$$f_{YY}(x,y) = \delta(x-y) f_Y(y) \Longrightarrow \mathcal{E}(x) = \int_{-\infty}^{\infty} y\delta(x-y) dy = x$$

Proposition 3 $\quad E\big[E\big(Y \mid X\big)\big] = E(Y)$

Proof The definition of conditional expectation leads to:

$$E\big[E\,(Y \mid X)\big] = \int_{-\infty}^{\infty} \left(\int_{-\infty}^{\infty} y \frac{f_{XY}(x,y)}{f_X(x)} \right) f_X(x) dx$$

hence:

$$E\big[E\,(Y \mid X)\big] = \int_{-\infty}^{\infty} y f_Y(y) dy = E(Y)$$

A.2 Conditional expectation: generalization to n random variables

The previous definition of conditional expectation can be easily generalized to the case of n random variables:

$$E\,(Y \mid X_1, \ldots, X_n) = \mathcal{E}(X_1, \ldots, X_n)$$

where:

$$\mathcal{E}(x_1, \ldots, x_n) = \int_{-\infty}^{\infty} y f_Y(y \mid x_1, \ldots, x_n) dy = \int_{-\infty}^{\infty} y \frac{f(y, x_1, \ldots, x_n)}{f(x_1, \ldots, x_n)} dy$$

The aforementioned properties may be generalized as well; for the sake of simplicity we restrict ourselves to the case of two variables.

Proposition 4
a) If Y is independent of both X_1 and X_2 the conditional expectation reduces to the ordinary expectation:

$$E\,(Y \mid X_1, X_2) = E(Y)$$

b)

$$E\,(Y \mid Y, X_1) = Y$$

c) If X' is independent of both X and Y:

$$E\,(Y \mid X, X') = E\,(Y \mid X)$$

To demonstrate the last property we note that from our assumption: $f(x, x', y) = f_{XY}(x, y) f_{X'}(x')$; integrating over y gives:

$$f_{XX'}(x, x') = f_X(x) f_{X'}(x')$$

Hence:

$$\mathcal{E}(x, x') = \int_{-\infty}^{\infty} y \frac{f_{XY}(x, y) f_{X'}(x')}{f_X(x) f_{X'}(x')} dy = E\big(Y \mid X = x\big)$$

Proposition 5 (Law of iterated conditional expectation): Let Ω_t be a sequence of decreasing subsets:

$$\Omega_t \supset \Omega_{t-1} \supset \Omega_{t-2} \supset \dots$$

Then for: $\Omega_k \supset \Omega_l$, one has:

$$E[\ E(Y|\Omega_k)\ |\Omega_l] = E(Y|\Omega_l)$$

A proof can be found in Billingsley (1979, theorem 34.3). The intuitive meaning of this result is the following in Billingsley's words: "Taking a conditional expected value can be thought of as an averaging or smoothing operation. This leads one to expect that averaging Y with respect to Ω_k and then averaging the result with respect to a coarser (smaller) field Ω_l should lead to the same result as would averaging with respect to Ω_l in the first place."

B Appendix B: Consumption, closing stocks and prices of cocoa, sugar and wheat.

COCOA

Year	**Consumption** 10^4 tons	**Closing Stocks** 10^4 tons	**Price** pounds/ton
1948	62.4	13.1	200
1949	68.6	22.0	139
1950	76.8	21.2	202
1951	76.5	25.2	281
1952	73.4	16.3	257
1953	78.7	17.9	242
1954	76.1	19.8	368
1955	73.5	27.0	327
1956	80.8	30.8	225
1957	89.8	31.2	203
1958	87.5	21.5	312
1959	87.0	25.9	288
1960	91.6	38.5	230
1961	100.	56.2	180
1962	109.	59.6	168
1963	114.	61.6	173
1964	118.	65.4	189
1965	129.	84.5	149
1966	137.	68.5	139
1967	138.	63.5	203
1968	140.	57.2	235
1969	136.	43.3	320
1970	135.	50.0	339
1971	140.	58.5	272
1972	153.	61.6	238
1973	158.	41.6	395
1974	151.	33.6	633
1975	145.	41.8	673
1976	152.	39.4	855
1977	143.	28.5	1757
1978	139.	39.1	1927
1979	145.	41.4	1781
1980	147.	55.2	1342
1981	157.	64.2	1034
1982	160.	75.7	1066
1983	164.	65.3	1171
1984	171.	46.1	1666
1985	184.	53.4	1901

Continued on next page

1986	186.	61.2	1670
1987	190.	68.0	1410
1988	200.	85.4	1140
1989	213.	116.	934
1990	220.	135.	776

Table 2.B.1 Consumption, stocks and prices of cocoa. The price column refers to unit value of imports in the U.K. (C.I.F.) Consumption in year n actually refers to consumption during the crop-year: Oct n-1, Sept n; similarly closing stocks represent the stocks at the end of the crop-year. *Sources: Gill and Duffus. Cocoa Market Report, 342 (1992) and 279 (1978)*

SUGAR

Year	Consumption 10^6 tons	Closing Stocks 10^6 tons	Price cents / lb
1964	54.2	11.1	6.90
1965	59.2	18.7	6.75
1966	61.9	19.0	6.99
1967	63.8	18.9	7.28
1968	65.6	18.8	7.52
1969	66.9	18.7	7.75
1970	70.5	21.1	8.07
1971	73.0	19.1	8.52
1972	74.0	17.2	9.09
1973	75.8	17.0	10.3
1974	78.7	16.3	29.4
1975	76.5	17.5	22.5
1976	78.2	20.4	13.3
1977	82.3	24.8	11.0
1978	85.8	30.2	13.9
1979	89.9	31.0	15.5
1980	90.8	25.1	30.0
1981	88.9	24.2	19.7
1982	92.2	32.6	19.9
1983	93.8	38.7	22.0
1984	94.2	39.8	21.7
1985	97.1	40.3	20.3
1986	98.8	25.9	20.9
1987	103.	23.4	21.8
1988	105.	20.4	22.1
1989	108.	19.4	22.8
1990	109.	19.4	23.2

Table 2.B.2 Consumption, stocks and prices of sugar. The price column refers to unit value of imports in the U.S. Consumption in year n actually refers to consumption during the crop-year: Sept n-1, Aug n; similarly closing stocks represent the stocks at the end of the crop-year. *Sources: Consumption and stocks: The McGrawHill Handbook of commodities trend futures. Pring Ed. (1985) and Chalmin (Ph): Cyclope, les marchés mondiaux. Economica (1990,1991). Prices: International Financial Statistics FMI Annuaire 1979, 1991.*

WHEAT

Year	**Consumption** 10^6 tons	**Closing Stocks** 10^6 tons	**Price** (index)
1947	144	7	75.0
1948	138	11	67.3
1949	153	15	56.0
1950	159	20	49.6
1951	165	20	57.4
1952	171	17	60.2
1953	183	34	54.6
1954	187	52	47.5
1955	190	53	45.8
1956	201	54	45.8
1957	220	55	44.5
1958	226	50	43.7
1959	239	61	45.3
1960	239	61	44.5
1961	235	63	45.1
1962	236	54	46.8
1963	248	55	47.4
1964	252	46	49.7
1965	262	46	46.6
1966	284	34	49.7
1967	286	35	49.2
1968	294	43	47.1
1969	308	60	45.6
1970	329	65	44.8
1971	342	51	45.3
1972	349	49	50.5
1973	366	28	104.0
1974	363	26	148.0
1975	368	30	128.0
1976	364	38	105.0
1977	380	56	82.0
1978	413	53	95.
1979	428	56	122.0
1980	440	49	135.0
1981	451	47	139.0
1982	446	54	118.0
1983	459	65	120.0
1984	483	65	117.0
1985	497	71	122.0
1986	503	85	113.0
1987	523	81	94.0

Table 2.B.3 Consumption, stocks and prices of wheat. The closing stocks figures refer to the stocks of the five major exporters: Argentina, Australia, Canada, EEC, USA. Consumption in year n actually refers to consumption during the crop-year: July n-1, June n; similarly closing stocks represent the stocks at the end of the crop-year. *Sources: World Wheat Statistics; International Wheat Council, 1987 and World Bank.*

I would like to express my gratitude to Dr John Tjaadstra of the IWC and to Dr Ron Duncan of the World Bank for their kind assistance.

Chapter 3
The stochastic Enke-Samuelson arbitrage model

In this chapter we introduce the stochastic Enke-Samuelson model whose purpose it is to describe the process of spatial arbitrage. In chapters 8 and 9 it will be generalized to non equilibrium situations. While the assumptions on which this model relies are similar to those of the spatial price equilibrium model its approach is different in many important respects. As has often been noted (see for instance Batten 1990, p.139) spatial price equilibrium models often generate quite unrealistic trade patterns in which all but a few trade flows vanish; moreover, being a deterministic model it is unable to describe local price fluctuations and their relationship to the volume of trade. The model we shall develop has none of these drawbacks. Furthermore, because it can be solved analytically in a number of simple but nevertheless pertinent cases, it is able to provide an intuitive insight into the mechanisms of spatial arbitrage. To convince the reader that the model can safely be extended to different realistic contexts it will be shown that the simplifying assumptions on which it relies can be relaxed without notably changing its main features.

In the first section, we briefly review the line of arguments on which the spatial price equilibrium model is based and we qualitatively describe the alternative approach provided by the stochastic Enke-Samuelson model along with its major predictions. In section two, we put the model to work in the case of two markets. In section three we study a one-dimensional chain of markets, a case which can be considered as being representative of more complex market configurations. Finally, in section three we consider the case of a two-dimensional network of markets. The predictions of the model are confronted with empirical evidence in the next chapter.

1 Defining the stochastic Enke-Samuelson model

1.1 The spatial price equilibrium model

1.1.1 General presentation

The process of spatial price arbitrage has been formalized in the fifties by Stephen Enke (1951, with an acknowledged contribution of H. Germond from the Rand Corporation) and particularly by Paul Samuelson (1952,1957). The main problem they intended to solve was the generalization to an arbitrary number of markets of the standard graphical construction of Figure 3.1. Enke's solution relied on a nonlinear electric network analogue. This was quite in tune with the current interest at that time in analogue computers (in this respect see also Morehouse et al 1950). By giving a variational formulation of the problem, P.Samuelson was able to reduce it to the so-called transportation problem in linear programming. The latter had provided one of the earliest illustration of the newly introduced methods of linear programming (Hitchcock 1941; Koopmans and Reiter 1951; Dorfman, Samuelson and Solow 1958). Samuelson's 1952 paper can be considered as having set up the framework of the so-called spatial price equilibrium model. In the following years this model has been used in connection with various commodity markets:

1) Lifestock-feed market (Fox 1953)
2) American market for eggs (Judge 1956)
3) International grain and beef markets (Bawden 1966)
4) World sugar market (Bates and Schmitz 1969)
5) Broiler market (Lee and Seaver 1972)

Very readable and helpful reviews on some of these topics are to be found in two books which have appeared at the beginning of the seventies, namely Bressler and King (1970) and Labys (1973). One may think the validity of a model that has been used so frequently to be established beyond all question. This is not true however, for many of the previous papers rely on simulations based on hypothetical or semi-hypothetical data. Let us for instance consider the paper by Fox (1953). Among the aforementioned papers it is one of the most interesting for the following reasons:

- In contrast to many later papers it is based on real not hypothetical data.
- It provides the first application of the theoretical papers by Enke and Samuelson (he also makes reference to a working report by Baumol 1952). This approach was quite novel at that time; indeed, as Fox points out in his introduction "although the basic facts about the geographic structure of feed prices and the directions of feed grain shipments were well known to agricultural economists, until the recent appearance of the spatial equilibrium model, no

none would have proposed to formulate these complex relationships in a specific, quantitative way."

- As a member of the US Department of Agriculture Fox continues a long tradition of research on spatial market equilibrium initiated about forty years before by Zapoleon (1918,1919).

Fox analyses the spatial pattern of the feed market in the United States on the basis of a ten-region subdivision. He relies as much as possible on actual empirical data[1]. Of course, a number of simplifying assumptions are required; for instance, the price of corn (which makes up about 60% of the total concentrate supply) is taken as representative of the price of the whole group of feed concentrates; moreover, the form of the regional demand functions for feed is supposed to be the same throughout the United States regardless of local livestock characteristics. The results of the paper mainly consist in price and trade patterns based on simulations (effect of a possible drought, increase in freight rates, etc). The only empirical test is the confrontation of predicted price differentials with actual ones, neither trade flows or local consumption figures are compared to actual data; the test shows that nearly half of the geographical variation in corn prices is due to factors not allowed in the model (the average determination coefficient is equal to 0.49). One can guess that the predictions of the model in terms of trade flows would be even poorer. In order to improve such a model two different strategies would be possible: either one may try to incorporate some of the missing factors into the model or treat them as exogeneous stochastic shocks. The first possibility implies a further disaggregation of the model and, as noted by Fox (1953,p.565), sooner or later it will be hampered by the unavailability of additional data. The second strategy is the one we shall use in developing a stochastic model. But first, let us briefly present the solution provided by the spatial price equilibrium model.

1.1.2 The spatial price equilibrium model for two markets

In the case of only two markets, the standard price equilibrium model can be solved by three different methods: graphical, algebraic and variational each of which has its own interest.

Graphical solution This is the most standard and straightforward approach. Its only drawback is that it cannot be extended to more than two markets. Let us denote the equilibrium demand and supply functions of both markets by:

$$D_i = D_i(p_i) \quad S_i = S_i(p_i) \quad i = 1, 2$$

[1]One weak point in the paper is that is does not give the sources from which the data have been drawn

That S_i is the *equilibrium* supply function is clear from the fact that it depends on the equilibrium price p_i rather than on the expected price p_i^e as was the rule in the dynamic models of Chapter 2. If goods are permitted to flow from one market to another we must determine the excess supply that is available in each region in prospect of exportation. These are:

$$s_i = s_i(p) = S_i(p) - D_i(p) \quad i = 1, 2$$

To summarize, the opening of trade between both regions has the effect of

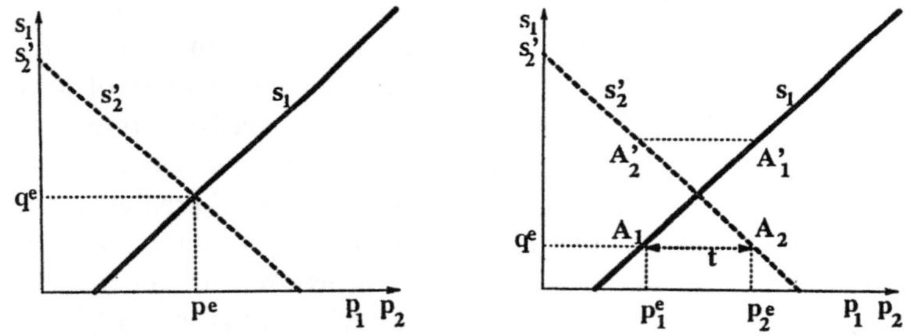

Fig.3.1 a,b Equilibrium of exports and imports between markets 1 and 2. In (a) transportation costs are assumed to be negligible; the equilibrium then is defined by the intersection of the excess-supply functions of both markets. In (b) one assumes a fixed transport cost t; market 1 then exports a quantity q^e (at a price p_1^e) to market 2; market 2 imports these goods at a price p_2^e such that p_2^e - $p_1^e = t$.

bringing the combined demand of the regions to bear on the combined supply so that they now have to be thought of as a new global (and isolated) market: $1 \cup 2$. Let us assume that the exporting market will be market 1. We now have to work out which amount market 1 is going to export. It is determined by the equilibrium condition for market $1 \cup 2$. Let us first assume that transportation costs are negligible; in this case equilibrium is defined by the intersection of the curves representing s_1 and s_2 in Fig.3.1a. In this Figure s_2 has been replaced by $s_2' = s_{12} = -s_2(p)$ because imported quantities are in fact negative supplies. The equilibrium price is then seen to be p_e and the exported amount q_e.

Suppose now that transportation costs between markets 1 and 2 are represented by t; the amount to be exported will be determined by the spatial arbitrage condition:

$$p_2 - p_1 = t$$

The resulting export and import prices p_1^e and p_2^e are shown in Fig. 3.1b. Assume for a moment that region 2 is exporting. Then we would look for two points A_1' and A_2' in Fig. 3.1b such that:

$$p_1 - p_2 = p(A_1') - p(A_2') = t$$

The point A_2', however, corresponds to a positive value of $s_2' = s_{12}$ which implies that region 1 is still exporting, a conclusion which is inconsistent with our assumption.
If the solution of each of the following equations:

$$p_1 - p_2 = t, \qquad p_2 - p_1 = t$$

leads to an inconsistency, this means that the transportation cost t represents too high a barrier for an exchange of goods to take place.

To anticipate subsequent developments figure 3.1b could be redrawn in a sightly different way. First, we exchange x and y axes so that prices become represented as ordinates; we are thus in a better position to draw the curve:

$$\Delta p = p_2(-s) - p_1(s) \qquad s = s_{12}$$

Now the amount exported q^ewill be given by the intersection of this curve with the discontinuous arbitrage curve:

$$\Delta p = t\phi(s), \quad \phi(s) = Y(-s) + Y(s)$$

where:

$$Y(s) = \begin{cases} 0 & \text{if } s \leq 0 \\ 1 & \text{if } s > 0 \end{cases}$$

This gives the standard "back-to-back diagram" representation. In Fig 3.2a,b,c we have summarized three situations:

- Fig.3.2a : region 1 exports
- Fig.3.2b: the price differential is too small and trade remains equal to zero. In fact the solution $s = 0$ cannot be obtained graphically: because of the jump in the function $Y(s)$ there is no intersection between the two curves in this case.
- Fig.3.2c: region 2 exports.

1.1.3 Algebraic solution

The main advantage of the former graphical solution is the fact that it applies to linear as well as to nonlinear excess-supply functions. In the linear case it may of course be easily written down algebraically as follows. Let:

$$D_i(p_i) = -\beta_i p_i + b_i \quad S_i(p_i) = \gamma p_i - c_i$$

$$s_i = s_i(p_i) = a_i(p_i - \overline{p}_i) \quad a_i = \gamma_i + \beta_i \quad \overline{p}_i = (c_i + b_i)/(\gamma_i + \beta_i) > 0 \quad i = 1, 2$$

be the two excess-supply functions; $\overline{p}_1$ and $\overline{p}_2$ denote the equilibrium prices when each market is isolated. We shall assume that the a_i and the $\overline{p}_i$ are such

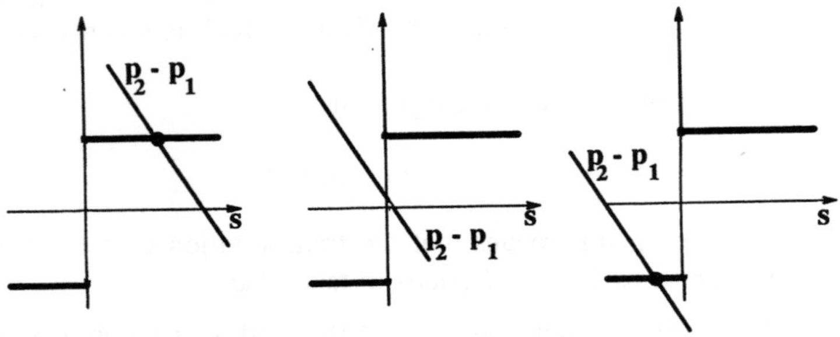

Fig.3.2 a,b,c Types of equilibrium situations for markets 1 and 2. In (a), $p_2 > p_1$ which means that market 1 exports; it is the opposite in (c); in (b) the price differential is too small to surmount transport costs, so trade is zero; in this case the two curves have no intersection.

that the exporting region is region 1. This assumption is precisely the tricky point however and we shall return to it later. Then the function Δp reads:

$$\Delta p = p_2(-s) - p_1(s) = -s(1/a_1 + 1/a_2) + \overline{p}_2 - \overline{p}_1 \tag{1.1}$$

and the relation $\Delta p = tY(s)$ becomes:

$$-s(1/a_1 + 1/a_2) + \overline{p}_2 - \overline{p}_1 = tY(s) \tag{1.2}$$

that is, when $s > 0$:

$$s = \frac{\overline{p}_2 - \overline{p}_1 - t}{1/a_1 + 1/a_2} \tag{1.3}$$

1.1.4 Variational solution

Any algebraic equation can of course be cast in the form of a minimization problem. For instance, solving the equation $f(x) = 0$ is equivalent to the minimization of any of the following pay-off functions:

$$\mid f(x) \mid, \quad f^2(x), \quad \int_0^x f^2(u)du$$

Samuelson (1952) selected as pay-off function:

$$h(s) = \int_0^s (\Delta p(u) - t\phi(u))du$$

It is easy to check that the minimization condition $dh/ds = 0, s > 0$ indeed leads to our previous solution (1.3). We shall postpone the discussion of the special advantages of this variational method until the next paragraph; let us just remark that an economic interpretation of Samuelson's pay-off function has been given in Smith (1963).

1.2 Possible generalizations to more than two markets

As we have already mentioned the graphical solution cannot be extended to more than two markets; thus when discussing possible generalizations we need only consider the algebraic and the variational method.

1.2.1 The algebraic solution

The main difficulty which we meet when we try to extend the algebraic solution to more than two markets is to decide between which market pairs trade is to take place. Once this is done one has to solve the system of equations defining the inter-market flows. Thus the following steps have to be taken:

1) Try every possible combination of trade versus non trade assumptions.

2) Solve the system of equations: $p_i - p_j = t_{ij}$ where t_{ij} denotes the transportation cost between markets i and j.

3) Check the consistency of each solution and reject those which do not fit.

In principle, one should end up with the *single* solution giving the flows between each market pair. For a market network of some complexity, these steps represent a formidable task however. Suppose we have n markets; there will be $P = n(n-1)/2$ inter-market links and $C = 2^P$ different combinations of trade/non trade assumptions. For instance:

$$n = 5 \rightarrow C = 2^{10} = 1024, \qquad n = 10 \rightarrow C \sim 10^{13}, \qquad n = 20 \rightarrow C \sim 10^{57}$$

For $n \geq 20$, the task is out of reach even for fast computers.

1.2.2 The variational solution

Fortunately the variational solution is not subjected to the same defect: the pay-off function may be written out without any specific trade versus non trade assumption having to be made. This is a definite advantage. Furthermore, because of the integration which occurs in its definition the pay-off function will be smooth (although not differentiable). In the case of a network containing 20 markets, we are then required to find the solution of a minimization problem involving 190 unknowns either by the method of linear programming or by some of its improved version (Takayama and Judge 1964, Takayama 1964). Whatever method one employs, this represents a notable amount of computation; above all, it does not provide the clear insight one could expect from an analytical solution.

1.3 The stochastic Enke-Samuelson model

The model we shall develop will be referred to as the stochastic Enke-Samuelson model in order both to emphasize that it constitutes an extension of the approach originally set up by S.Enke and P.Samuelson an to draw attention to the fact that it is quite distinct from the spatial price equilibrium model. Our line of arguments includes the following steps:

1) In order to match observed price differentials, the spatial price equilibrium model requires specific statistical data about local excess-supply functions and transportation costs; such data are rarely available however. This motivates the move to a random framework in which information about *averaged* quantities will be sufficient.

2) The spatial price equilibrium model basically is a nonlinear model. However, we shall show that because of compensations occurring in the averaging of the random model, its linearized form leads to results which are close approximations to the exact model. This opens up the possibility of obtaining *analytical* solutions which may provide a clearer view of the salient features of the model. Let us now develop these different points.

1.3.1 The rationale of a stochastic model

In discussing Fox' paper we have already seen that when using a deterministic model one is hindered by the availability of adequate data. This not only concerns the specification of excess-supply functions; even freight rates usually are unknown on specific routes as is made clear by the following quotation from the US Department of Agriculture (Economic Research Service, personal communication 1992):

> "Most of the wheat shipped long distance by rail within the United States moves under rates prescribed by contracts between the shipper and the railroad. These rates are deemed to be proprietary information of both parties and are not made public."

The fact that freight rates are shrouded in secrecy is by no means special to our time. The question of confidential differential rates has been a permanent theme in the railway debate during the second half of the nineteenth century, either in the US, in the UK or in France (see for instance Hadley 1885). Such uncertainties as to freight rates makes it almost impossible to check a given model on a specific route. While micro-statistics are unavailable, regional freight data are regularly published for instance by the US Interstate Commerce Commission. Thus, to be testable a model should describe the market at a *global* level.

1.3.2 Smoothing and linearization of the model

Mathematically, the main difficulty stems from the discontinuous form of the arbitrage function $\Delta p = t\phi(s)$ which defines the price differential Δp as a function of the trade flow s (see Fig.3.2). As we pointed out in paragraph 1.2.2 one of the main reason for converting the initial problem into a maximum problem is precisely to get rid of this discontinuity; thereby one has to rely on linear programming techniques however. In fact, this discontinuity is rather artificial for in Hotelling's (1929) words "discontinuity like vacuum is abhorred by nature". In other words replacing the discontinuous function $\phi(s)$ by a continuous approximation will both be more realistic and simpler from a mathematical point of view. Such an approximation has been considered by P.Samuelson in a subsequent paper (1957) in a slightly different context. One possible continuous approximation is displayed in Fig.3.3; it corresponds to the

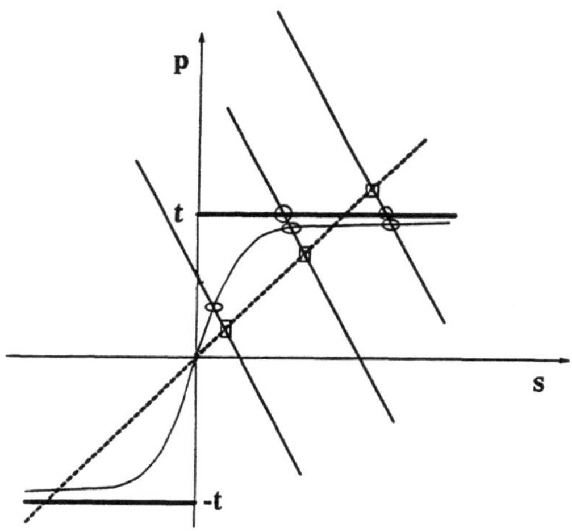

Fig.3.3 Different types of arbitrage functions. The figure compares the discontinuous model, the continuous nonlinear model and the linear model. As s becomes larger than t, the solution of the linear model becomes more and more different from those of the two other models.

family of functions:

$$\varphi_c(s) = \tanh(cs), \qquad \tanh x = \frac{e^x - e^{-x}}{e^x + e^{-x}} \tag{1.1}$$

Subsequently such an approximation will be used in the nonlinear Enke-Samuelson model. The smoothing of the arbitrage function can be carried a step further by assuming ϕ to be not only continuous but also linear, that is by replacing $\varphi_c(s)$ by its development to first order around $s = 0$. Such an approximation is displayed in Fig.3.3; as can be seen it is a reasonable approximation except for large values of s. Mathematically such an approximation transforms a problem which had to be solved numerically into one that may be solved analytically. From an economic point of view, two arguments can be given in favour of such a linearization.

1) The assumption is not unreasonable from an empirical point of view. For instance, the linear coefficient of correlation between the wheat exports from Prussia to Britain (in the period 1828-1859) and the corresponding price differentials turns out to be equal to -0.62 (Engel 1861, p.288-289 and chapter 4, Appendix B).

2) By comparing the solutions of the linear and of the nonlinear model it can be seen that the first one provides a fairly close approximation to the second one. This should not be too surprising if one keeps in mind that a set of 30 markets comprises as many as 435 market pairs; thus even if the linear approximation works rather poorly for some pairs, the error for the market as a whole may be reduced by possible compensations.

To sum up, the idea which is behind our line of argument is that the trade problem may be considered in two different ways. In the first perspective, one is interested in a small number n of regions ($n \leq 5$) for which sufficient local data are available to allow all excess-supply functions to be realistically estimated; these estimations will most certainly turn out to have some nonlinear form; then the only possible approach will be to resort to numerical solution; in this case it would be pointless to linearize the arbitrage function. In the second perspective, one considers a large number of regions ($n \geq 20$) for which local excess-supply functions are anyway not available. Our hope then is that due to the large number of exchanges that are likely to take place the linear model may provide sensible results.

1.3.3 Consistency tests of the model

To determine the range of validity of our subsequent results two tests are of crucial importance.

- First, one has to examine under which conditions the linearized model is indeed an acceptable approximation.
- Secondly, one has to prove that the predictions of the model are to a large extent independent of the specific pattern of inter-market links. Only then can the model be accepted as a generic description of spatial arbitrage in commodity markets.

These tests, however vital they are, should not divert our attention from the results themselves; for that reason we devote the following paragraph to listing the main predictions of the model.

1.3.4 Predictions of the model

The model provides predictions about four related questions.

1) The evolution of price dispersion on one market with respect to transport cost: Fig.3.4a

2) The evolution of price differentials (or of price correlations) with respect to transport cost: Fig.3.4b.

3) The evolution of trade with respect to transport cost: Fig.3.4c.

4) The variation of price differentials (for given transport cost) with respect to intermarket distance: Fig.3.4d.

It is the second of these phenomena which is usually considered as characterizing the process of market integration. The third one, the increase of trade along with diminishing transport costs, could at first be seen as quite obvious. World trade in wheat for instance has expanded very rapidly between 1850 and 1913 (Harley 1980, p.229). What we actually mean is variation in trade under the assumption of constant production. With this qualification, it is no longer obvious that trade should necessarily increase in the long run when transportation costs decrease. The fourth phenomenon is of special interest for it provides detailed information about the spatial structure of prices. At the same time it provides a solution to the following paradox: according to the spatial price equilibrium model, for prices on two distant markets to be arbitrage regulated, their differential should be larger than (or equal to) transport costs; yet statistical observation rather supports the opposite view that markets remain interconnected even when posted prices become smaller than the transportation margin. From Fig.3.4.d it can be seen that, while price differentials first increase along with distance, for larger distances a saturation effect sets in.
All the results shown in Figures 3.4a-d have been obtained for a two-dimensional network of markets (with trade links between each market and its nearest neighbours). It may be of interest to mention that these results are not much modified when we consider instead a one-dimensional chain of markets.

2 The stochastic Enke-Samuelson model for two markets

To get an idea of how the model works, we apply it here to the simple case of two interacting markets (Fig.3.5). One should of course keep in mind that the main motivation for developing the model is to provide an easy treatment for networks with an *arbitrary number* of markets.

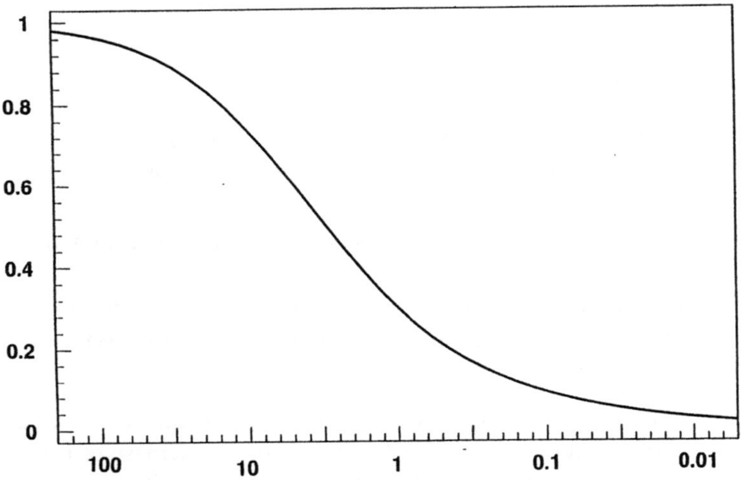

Fig.3.4 a Standard deviation of prices in each single market. The horizontal scale represents the dimensionless parameter $\theta = at$, where t is the transport cost and a denotes the slope of the excess-supply functions. The axis is labelled from right to left in analogy with the direction of historic evolution. The decrease of the standard deviation shows the stabilizing effect of improved market integration. Here, as well as in the following three figures, the standard deviation of local shocks is taken equal to one.

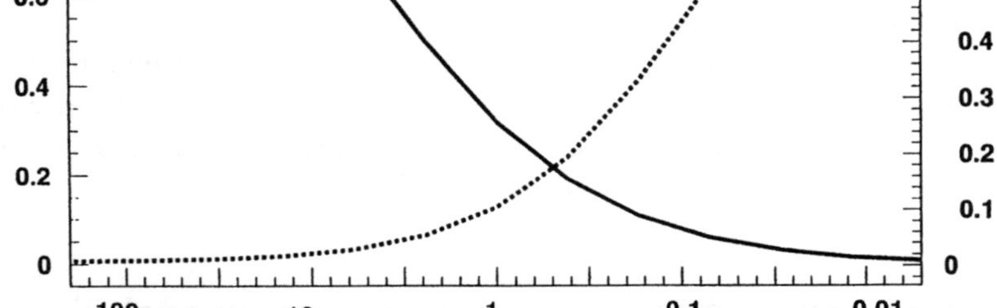

Fig.3.4 b Price differential and price correlation (per unit of distance) between geographically separated markets. The horizontal scale represents the dimensionless parameter $\theta = at$, where t is the transport cost and a denotes the slope of the excess-supply functions. The axis is labelled from right to left in analogy with the direction of historic evolution. In the sample, each (integral) distance is represented by one market pair; the largest intermarket distance considered is equal to 10, the unit of distance being the interval between two neighbouring markets. Solid line: average price differential; broken line: average price correlation.

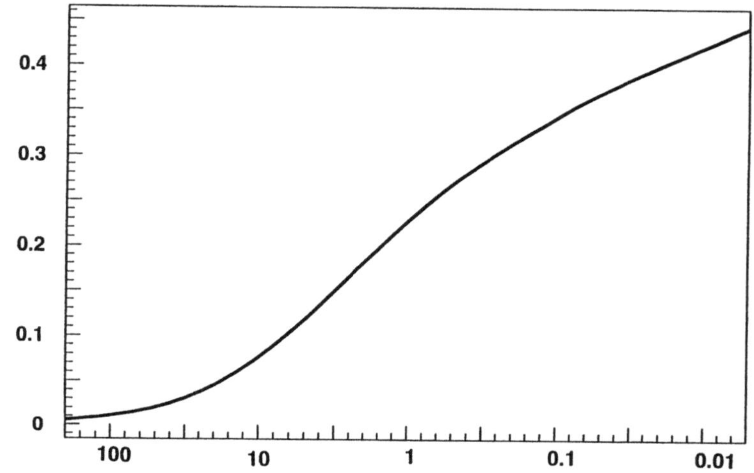

Fig.3.4 c Average trade within a network of markets. The horizontal scale represents the dimensionless parameter $\theta = at$, where t is the transport cost and a denotes the slope of the excess-supply functions. The axis is labelled from right to left in analogy with the direction of historic evolution. The chart shows that in spite of the fall in price differentials brought about by improved market integration, the net result of a fall in transport cost is an expansion of trade.

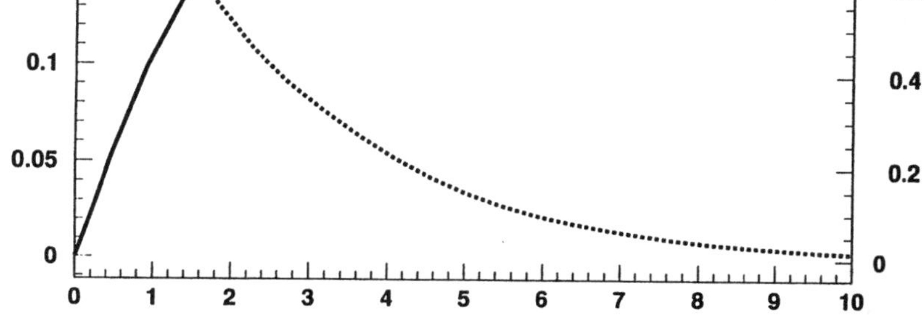

Fig.3.4 d Price differential and price correlation as a function of intermarket distances. Transport cost is fixed and equal to 0.5, $a = 1$.

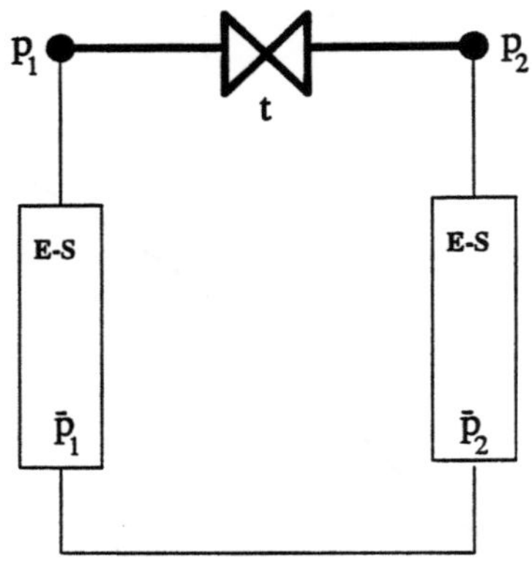

Fig.3.5 Schematic representation of the equilibrium equations between markets 1 and 2. The blocks labelled E-S correspond to the excess-supply functions of each market; the fact that trade takes place only when the price difference exceeds the transportation cost t is represented by a threshold gate.

2.1 Basic equations

Let:

$$D_i(p_i) = -\beta_i p_i + b_i, \qquad S_i(p_i) = \gamma_i p_i - c_i \tag{2.1}$$

be the two demand and supply functions. Then, the excess-supply functions become:

$$s_i = S_i - D_i = (\gamma_i + \beta_i)p_i - (c_i + b_i)$$

Introducing the notations:

$$a_i = \gamma_i + \beta_i \qquad \overline{p}_i = (c_i + b_i)/(\gamma_i + \beta_i)$$

where the $\overline{p}_i$ denote the equilibrium prices when each market is isolated, one obtains:

$$s_i = s_i(p_i) = a_i(p_i - \overline{p}_i) \qquad i = 1,2 \qquad \overline{p}_i > 0$$

The arbitrage condition reads:

$$\Delta p = p_2(-s) - p_1(s) = t\varphi_c(s) \tag{2.2}$$

where t denotes the transportation cost. The linear model requires the linearization of the right-hand side of (2.2), that is to say the replacement of $t\varphi_c(s)$ by ts; one thus obtains:

$$s = \frac{\overline{p}_2 - \overline{p}_1}{1/a_1 + 1/a_2 + t}$$

where s is taken positive when the flow is from market 1 to market 2. This result is of course different from the result (1.3) of the nonlinear model, although its form is somewhat similar.
In the following, we shall assume that the excess-supply functions of both markets have the same slope $a_1 = a_2 = a$, we obtain therefore:

$$s = \frac{\overline{p}_2 - \overline{p}_1}{2/a + t}$$

Furthermore, from the definition of the excess-supply functions one obtains:

$$p_1 = \overline{p}_1 + s/a = \frac{(1+\theta)\overline{p}_1 + \overline{p}_2}{2+\theta} \tag{2.3a}$$

$$p_2 = \overline{p}_2 - s/a = \frac{\overline{p}_1 + (1+\theta)\overline{p}_2}{2+\theta} \tag{2.3b}$$

where: $\theta = at$ is a dimensionless parameter. Equations (2.3a) and (2.3b) are the basic defining equations of the linear two-market model. But before proceeding let us first establish a formula which proves essential in studying spatial price differentials.

Expectation of spatial price differentials

A possible characterization of the spatial price differential between two markets 1 and 2 is by means of the following expectation:

$$\Delta_{12} = E\left(|p_1 - p_2|\right)$$

We shall now give an explicit expression of this expectation under the assumption that p_1, p_2 have a jointly normal distribution. First of all we observe that since:

$$E\left(|p_1 - p_2|\right) = E\left(\ |(p_1 - m) - (p_2 - m)|\ \right)$$

we need only consider random variables with zero means. The joint normal distribution of two variables X and Y with zero mean reads :

$$f_{XY}(x,y) = \frac{1}{2\pi\ \sigma^2\sqrt{1-r^2}} \exp\left[-\frac{x^2 - 2rxy + y^2}{2(1-r^2)\ \sigma^2}\right]$$

Let: $Z = X - Y$. The density function of Z is given by:

$$f_Z(z) = \int_{-\infty}^{\infty} f(z+y, y)dy$$

By writing the exponent as a sum of squares, the integral becomes after a change of variables:

$$f_Z(z) = \frac{\exp\left[\frac{-z^2}{4(1-r)\ \sigma^2}\right]}{2\pi\sigma^2\sqrt{1-r^2}} \int_{-\infty}^{\infty} \exp\left(-\frac{u^2}{\sigma^2(1+r)}\right) du$$

Hence:

$$f_Z(z) = \frac{\exp\left[\frac{-z^2}{4(1-r)\ \sigma^2}\right]}{2\sigma\sqrt{\pi(1-r)}}$$

Furthermore:

$$f_{|Z|} = 2 f_Z(z) Y(z)$$

$$Y(z) = \begin{cases} 0 & \text{if } z \leq 0 \\ 1 & \text{if } z > 0 \end{cases}$$

We obtain therefore:

$$f_{|Z|}(z) = \frac{\exp\left[\frac{-z^2}{4(1-r)\ \sigma^2}\right]}{\sigma\sqrt{\pi(1-r)}}\ Y(z) \tag{2.4}$$

Here we shall only need the expectation $E(\ |Z|\ )$; we have worked out the expression of $f_{|Z|}$ because it will prove useful subsequently. From (2.4) one obtains:

$$E(\ |X-Y|\ ) = \frac{2\sigma}{\sqrt{\pi}}\sqrt{1-r} \tag{2.5}$$

2.2 Solutions of the linear model

We shall now review different cases corresponding to various assumptions as to the distribution of the random variables $\overline{p}_1$ and $\overline{p}_2$.

2.2.1 Uncorrelated local shocks (identical means)

We assume $\overline{p}_1$ and $\overline{p}_2$ to be identically and independently distributed with a normal $N(m,\sigma)$ distribution; from $(2.3a,b)$ we shall derive the expressions of the relevant variables in the model: correlation between prices, price dispersion, price differential and trade. For the correlation $r_{p_1p_2}$ between prices one has:

$$r_{p_1p_2} = \frac{E\left((p_1-m_1)(p_2-m_2)\right)}{\sigma_{p_1}\sigma_{p_2}} = \frac{E(p'_1p'_2)}{\sigma_{p'_1}\sigma_{p'_2}}$$

where p'_1 and p'_2 denote the centered variables:

$$p'_1 = a\overline{p}'_1 + b\overline{p}'_2 \quad p'_2 = b\overline{p}'_1 + a\overline{p}'_2 \tag{2.6}$$

where: $a = (1+\theta)/(2+\theta)$, $\quad b = 1/(2+\theta)$; thus:

$$\sigma^2_{p'_1} = \sigma^2_{p'_2} = \sigma^2(a^2+b^2) \quad E(p'_1p'_2) = 2ab\sigma^2$$

and:

$$r_{p_1p_2} = 2\frac{1+\theta}{2+2\theta+\theta^2} \tag{2.7}$$

The price dispersion is given by:

$$\sigma_p^2 = \sigma^2 \frac{2 + 2\theta + \theta^2}{(2+\theta)^2}$$

From (2.5) it follows that the expected price differential is given by:

$$E\left(|p_1 - p_2|\right) = \frac{\theta}{2+\theta} E\left(\ |\overline{p}_1 - \overline{p}_2| \ \right) = \frac{\sigma}{\sqrt{\pi}} \frac{\theta}{1+\theta/2} \tag{2.8}$$

The expectation of the absolute trade flow becomes:

$$T = \frac{1}{2} E\left(\ |s| \ \right) = \frac{\sigma}{\sqrt{\pi}} \frac{a}{\theta + 2} \tag{2.9}$$

where we have used the fact that: $s = a(\overline{p}_2 - \overline{p}_1)/(2+\theta)$; the factor $1/2$ has been introduced as a normalizing coefficient with respect to the total number of marketplaces.

It is interesting to investigate the limits for vanishing and large transportation costs. For the price correlation one has:

$$r_{p_1 p_2} \sim \begin{cases} 1 - \theta^2/2 & \text{if } \theta \to 0 \\ \frac{2}{\theta} & \text{if } \theta \to \infty \end{cases} \tag{2.10}$$

For the price differential one obtains:

$$E\left(\ |p_1 - p_2| \ \right) \sim \begin{cases} \frac{\sigma}{\sqrt{\pi}} \theta & \text{if } \theta \to 0 \\ \frac{2\sigma}{\sqrt{\pi}} (1 - \frac{2}{\theta}) & \text{if } \theta \to \infty \end{cases} \tag{2.11}$$

As could be expected the price differential goes to zero at the limit of vanishing transportation costs.
For the trade expectation we obtain:

$$T \sim \begin{cases} \frac{\sigma a}{2\sqrt{\pi}} & \text{if } \theta \to 0 \\ \frac{\sigma}{t\sqrt{\pi}} & \text{if } \theta \to \infty \end{cases} \tag{2.12}$$

In the limit of perfect market integration, the trade-flow converges to a finite limit: it is precisely this trade-flow which makes prices become nearly equal in spite of the differences in local production and demand conditions. If local conditions become more and more identical (i.e. $\sigma \to 0$), then, of course, the trade between both markets vanishes.

2.2.2 Correlated local shocks (identical means)

In the previous case there is already a built-in structural similarity in local demand and supply conditions in so far as we assumed the slopes of the excess-supply functions to be identical in each market. This similarity can be extended by assuming a correlation r between the prices $\overline{p}_1$ and $\overline{p}_2$. The previous derivation can be easily generalized to this case; one obtains:

$$\sigma_{p_1}^2 = \sigma_{p_2}^2 = \sigma^2(a^2 + 2abr + b^2)$$

thus the price dispersion is given by:

$$\sigma_p^2 = \frac{\sigma^2[2(1+r)(1+\theta) + \theta^2]}{(2+\theta)^2}$$

Furthermore:

$$E(p_1' p_2') = \sigma^2 \left(2ab + (a^2 + b^2)r\right)$$

Thus the equations (2.7), (2.8) and (2.9) become:

$$r_{p_1 p_2} = \frac{r + \lambda(\theta)}{1 + r\lambda(\theta)} \qquad \lambda(\theta) = 2\frac{1+\theta}{2 + 2\theta + \theta^2} \tag{2.13}$$

$$E(\,|p_1 - p_2|\,) = \frac{1}{\sqrt{\pi}} \frac{\theta}{1 + \theta/2}\, \sigma\sqrt{1-r} \tag{2.14}$$

$$T = \frac{a}{\sqrt{\pi}(\theta + 2)}\, \sigma\sqrt{1-r} \tag{2.15}$$

As far as price differential and trade expectation are concerned, it is therefore equivalent to consider correlated $N(m, \sigma; r)$ prices or to consider uncorrelated $N(m, \sigma\sqrt{1-r}; 0)$ prices. Accordingly, the uniformization of local market conditions which usually goes along with increased market integration can be described by a decrease in σ. It should also be noted that in contrast to the price differential, the price correlation does *not* depend on the dispersion σ of local shocks, a result which shows the correlation to be a "better" measure for the level of market integration; this can be of special interest in economic history.

2.2.3 Correlated local shocks (different means)

We now assume for the local shocks a joint distribution $N(m_1, m_2; \sigma; r)$ with two different means: m_1 and m_2; this corresponds for instance to different comparative advantages. First, it should be noted that the expression of the price correlation remains the same under this more general assumption. This again shows the correlation to be a " cleaner" measure for market integration than is the price differential; the latter will be seen to depend, not only on transportation costs, but also on the levels of m_1, m_2, a rather unwanted feature.

A second important remark is that the expected trade factorizes in the following way:

$$T = F(\theta)A(d,r,\sigma) \qquad d = m_2 - m_1$$

where:

$$F(\theta) = \frac{a/2}{\theta+2}$$

$$A(d,r,\sigma) = \frac{2\sigma}{\sqrt{\pi}}\sqrt{1-r}$$

$$\exp\left(\frac{-d^2}{4\sigma^2(1-r)}\right) + \frac{d}{2}\left[\text{Erfc}\left(\frac{-d}{2\sigma\sqrt{1-r}}\right) - \text{Erfc}\left(\frac{d}{2\sigma\sqrt{1-r}}\right)\right]$$

In deriving the above result, we have used the following lemma (see chapter 8, lemma 2):

If X is a normal $N(m,\sigma)$ random variable, one has:

$$E(|X|) = \sigma\sqrt{\frac{2}{\pi}}\,\exp(-m^2/2\sigma^2) + \frac{m}{2}\left[\text{Erfc}(-m/\sigma\sqrt{2}) - \text{Erfc}(m/\sigma\sqrt{2})\right]$$

where the complementary error function is defined by:

$$\text{Erfc}(x) = \frac{2}{\sqrt{\pi}}\int_x^\infty e^{-u^2}du$$

Thus, the functional dependence of trade with respect to transport cost is the same as in the case of identical means but for a global multiplying factor A.

there is a similar expression for the price differential:

$$E(|p_1 - p_2|) = G(\theta)A(d,r,\sigma) \tag{2.16a}$$

$$G(\theta) = \frac{\theta}{\theta+2} \tag{2.16b}$$

Remark The previous expression can be simplified if $\sigma \ll d$ for in this case the price difference keeps a constant sign.

As can be seen from the above formulas, the assumption $m_1 \neq m_2$ introduces formal (in the sense of being non essential) complications in the various expressions of trade, price correlations or price differentials. It is mainly for this reason that we shall subsequently restrict ourselves to the case of local shocks with identical means. From an economic point of view this is justified by the fact that as far as wheat production is concerned comparative advantages are largely of non climatic character; indeed due to the introduction of differentiated varieties, wheat can be grown almost everywhere and with comparable yields. As an illustration let us mention the fact that in recent years Saudi Arabia has become a major wheat exporter: it is ranked 6th just before Hungary which traditionally is a substantial wheat exporter (Charvet 1990,p.81). In fact, during the last years favourable exchange rates have been the main source of comparative advantages. The results obtained in this section are summarized in Table 3.1-3 respectively for large and small transport costs.

2.2.4 Linear versus nonlinear model

Fig.3.6a shows three different representations of the price differential between two markets. They correspond respectively to:

1) The solution of the linear model as given by the expectations in the previous paragraph.

2) The solution of the linear model obtained by random simulation.

3) The solution of the nonlinear model obtained by random simulation.

They show that the solutions of the linear and of the nonlinear model are rather close; in fact, the random fluctuations of the simulated linear solution are larger than the differences between the linear and the nonlinear solutions (the two simulations have been arranged to go through the same sequence of random values). Fig.3.6b shows the same three representations for the trade between the two markets.

We do not expect the linear approximation to hold when large price differences (and hence large trade flows) develop. This conclusion results also from the expression of the price differential; indeed as $\sigma \longrightarrow \infty$, the price differential becomes very large (see for instance (2.14)), whereas in the nonlinear model it is of course bounded by the transport cost. In other words, for the linear approximation to lead to sensible results the dispersion in local conditions σ should remain small. From Fig.3.6c which compares the standard deviations of the linear and of the nonlinear model as a function of σ the permitted range may be seen to be:

$$\sigma < t$$

3 Chain of markets

There are four main motivations for analysing a chain of markets.

1) From producer to consumer there is usually a chain of intermediaries: from Topeka (Kansas) to Radom next to Warshaw a bushel of wheat goes through a number of different hands.

	Segmented market	Unified market
Transport cost	$\theta = at \to \infty$	$\theta = at \to 0$
Uncorrel. shocks	$\frac{2}{\theta} \to 0$	$1 - \frac{\theta^2}{2} \to 1$
Correl. shocks		
$m_1 = m_2$	$r + \frac{2(1-r)}{\theta} \to r$	$1 - \frac{\theta^2}{2(1+r)} \to 1$
$m_1 \neq m_2$	$r + \frac{2(1-r)}{\theta} \to r$	$1 - \frac{\theta^2}{2(1+r)} \to 1$

Table 3.1 Asymptotic expressions of the correlation of prices on two distant markets under different assumptions regarding the joint distribution of local shocks. a is the slope of the excess-supply functions and t is the transport cost between both markets; r is the correlation of local shocks.

	Segmented market	Unified market
Transport cost	$\theta = at \to \infty$	$\theta = at \to 0$
Uncorrel. shocks	$\frac{2\sigma}{\sqrt{\pi}}$	$\frac{\sigma\theta}{\sqrt{\pi}} \to 0$
Correl. shocks		
$m_1 = m_2$	$\frac{2\sigma\sqrt{1-r}}{\sqrt{\pi}}$	$\frac{\sigma\sqrt{1-r}\theta}{\sqrt{\pi}} \to 0$
$m_1 \neq m_2$	$A(d, r, \sigma)$	$A(d, r, \sigma)(\theta/2) \to 0$

Table 3.2 Asymptotic expressions of the price differential for two distant markets under different assumptions regarding the joint distribution of local shocks. a is the slope of the excess-supply functions and t is the transport cost between both markets; r is the correlation of local shocks; $d = m_1 - m_2$; the expression of $A(d, r, \sigma)$ is given in the text.

	Segmented market	Unified market
Transport cost	$\theta = at \to \infty$	$\theta = at \to 0$
Uncorrel. shocks	$\frac{\sigma}{t\sqrt{\pi}} \to 0$	$\frac{a\sigma}{2\sqrt{\pi}}$
Correl. shocks		
$m_1 = m_2$	$\frac{\sigma\sqrt{1-r}}{t\sqrt{\pi}} \to 0$	$\frac{a\sigma\sqrt{1-r}}{2\sqrt{\pi}}$
$m_1 \neq m_2$	$\frac{1}{t}(A/2) \to 0$	$\frac{a}{2}(A/2)$

Table 3.3 Asymptotic expressions of the trade between two distant markets under different assumptions regarding the joint distribution of local shocks. a is the slope of the excess-supply functions and t is the transport cost between both markets; r is the correlation of local shocks; the expression of A is given in the text.

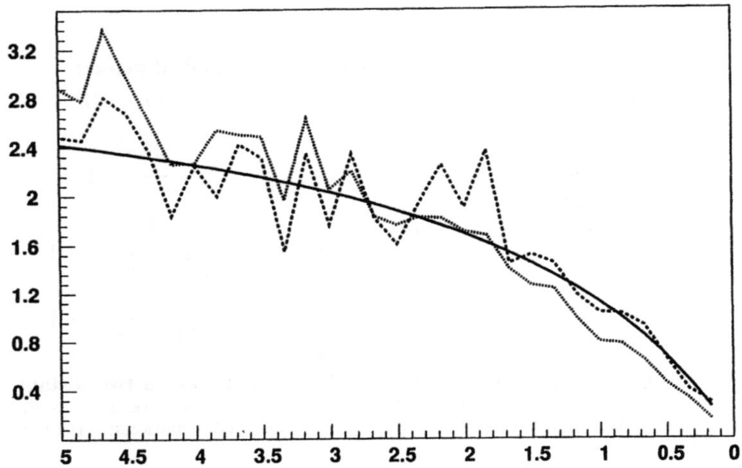

Fig.3.6 a Expected price differential between two markets. The figure compares the probabilistic linear model (solid curve), a simulation of the linear model (dashed curve) and a simulation of the nonlinear model (dotted curve). The horizontal axis has been labelled in decreasing transportation costs to compare to the course of historic evolution. The standard deviation of local shocks is equal to 3, $a = 1$; 30 iterations.

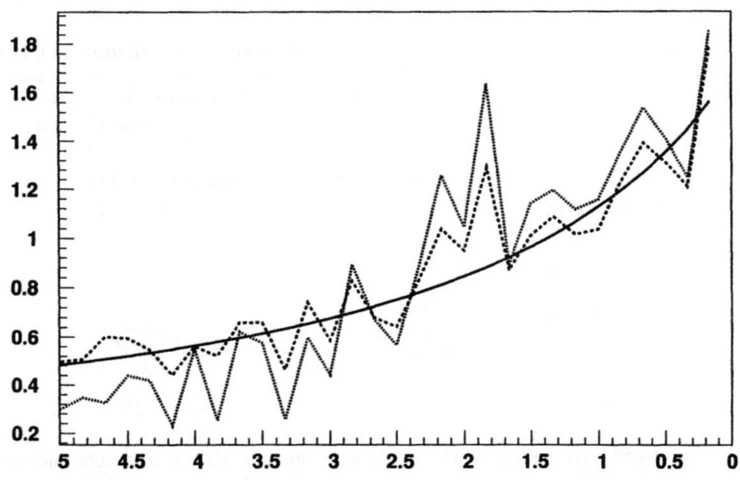

Fig.3.6 b Expected trade between two markets. The figure compares the probabilistic linear model (solid curve), a simulation of the linear model (dashed curve) and a simulation of the nonlinear model (dotted curve). The horizontal axis has been labelled in decreasing transportation costs to compare to the course of historic evolution. The standard deviation of local condition is equal to 3, a=1; 30 iterations.

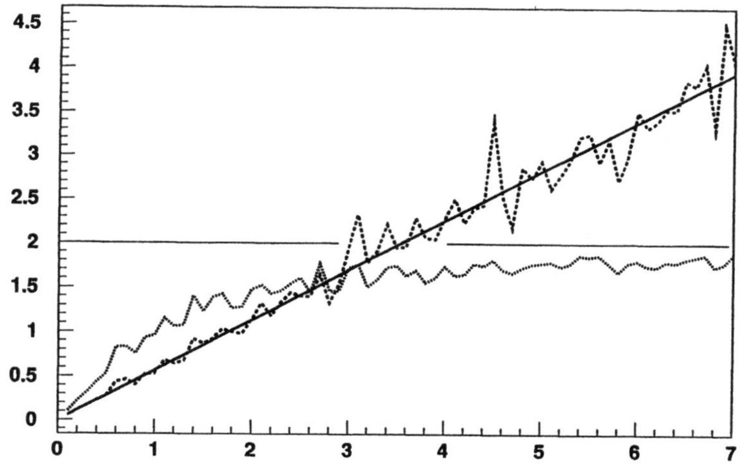

Fig3.6 c Expected price differential between two markets as a function of the standard deviation of local shocks. The figure compares the probabilistic linear model (solid curve), a simulation of the linear model (dashed curve) and a simulation of the nonlinear model (dotted curve). The transportation costs is equal to 2 (horizontal line); as the standard deviation of local conditions becomes larger than 2, the behavior of the linear and of the nonlinear models become more and more different. 60 iterations.

2) In Harold Hotelling's terms (1929), the market chain corresponds to "Main street in a town or to a transcontinental railroad". The last mention is particularly appropriate when one remembers that the United States as well as Russia are stripe-shaped countries: USA: 4500km x 1600km; Russia: 6000km x 2200km. Even in a rather square-shaped country such as France, the communication channels from North to South are concentrated in two rather narrow strips, one West of the Massif Central and the other in its East (Rhône valley).

3) The market chain provides the simplest example of a network with an *arbitrary* number of markets, a condition which is essential in order to study the spatial pattern of price differentials.

4) The market chain provides the opportunity of comparing the linear and the nonlinear model in a case which remains tractable.

3.1 Chain of markets: direct trade relations restricted to closest neighbours

First we consider the case where each market has (direct) trade relations only with its closest neighbours (Fig.3.7); subsequently, this case will for short be referred to as the market chain with two neighbours. Apart from price differentials our analysis focuses on the evolution of the standard deviation of prices

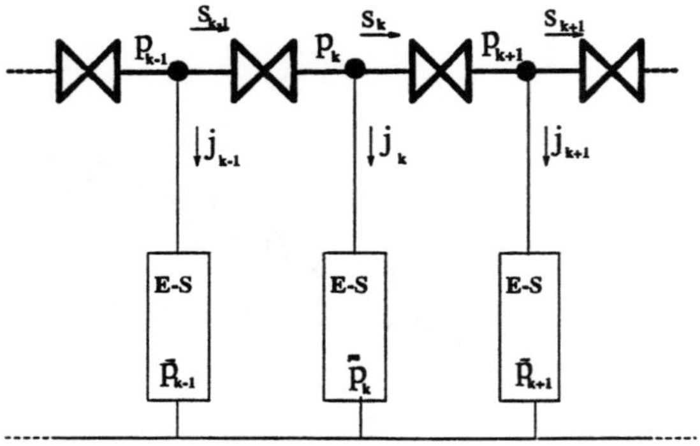

Fig.3.7 Schematic representation of the equilibrium equations of a chain of markets. The E-S blocks contain the excess-supply information on each market. The direction of the arrows are conventional. s_{k-1} (s_{k+1}) represents the amount that is exported from market k to market $k-1$ ($k+1$); j_k represents the excess-supply for market k.

and of the overall trade with respect to transport cost.

3.1.1 Solving the linear model

Equations of the model and results The equations of the model are established in the same way as in the case of two markets; the (linearized) arbitrage assumption reads:

$$p_k - p_{k-1} = ts_{k-1} \qquad k = \ldots -1, 0, 1, \ldots \tag{3.1a}$$

The excess-supply of market k is:

$$j_k = (\overline{p}_k - p_k)a \qquad k = \ldots -1, 0, 1, \ldots \tag{3.1b}$$

At market k the conservation of trade flows reads:

$$s_{k-1} - s_k = j_k \qquad k = \ldots -1, 0, 1, \ldots$$

Substituting the above expressions, we obtain:

$$(2 + at)p_k - p_{k-1} - p_{k+1} = (at)\overline{p}_k \qquad k = \ldots -1, 0, 1, \ldots \tag{3.2}$$

In this equation $\overline{p}_k$ are independent, identically distributed random variables; therefore (3.2) is a spatial second-order autoregressive process (see chapter 7). Our first concern with equation (3.2) is to examine whether stationarity is ensured. The boundary conditions are of the form:

$$p_{-\infty} < \infty \qquad p_{\infty} < \infty$$

Once stationarity is guaranteed we know that the actual values of $p_{-\infty}$ and p_{∞} become unimportant. The roots of the characteristic equation are reciprocal since their product is equal to one. Explicitly we have:

$$x_1 = \frac{\gamma}{2}(1 + \sqrt{1 - 4/\gamma^2}) \quad x_2 = \frac{\gamma}{2}(1 - \sqrt{1 - 4/\gamma^2}) \qquad \gamma = 2 + at$$

This means that the solution of the homogeneous equation must be discarded and that the stationary solution is provided by a particular solution of the non homogeneous equation. From second order stationarity, we infer that the expectation $E(p_k)$ is independent of k.

One has the following result:

Theorem 1 Chain of markets with two neighbours For a chain of N markets each of which maintains trade relations with two neighbouring markets the standard deviation of prices and the trade within the chain of markets have the following expressions:

$$\sigma_p = \frac{\sigma}{2} \frac{\theta^{1/4}(1 + \theta/2)^{1/2}}{(1 + \theta/4)^{3/4}} \qquad \theta = at$$

$$T = \frac{1}{2\sqrt{2\pi}} \frac{a\sigma}{\theta^{1/4}(1 + \theta/4)^{3/4}} \tag{3.3}$$

where t is the transportation cost, a the slope of the excess-supply function and σ the standard deviation of local demand and supply conditions. For small, respectively large transportation costs, one has the following developments:

$$\sigma_p^2 \sim \begin{cases} \frac{\sigma^2}{4}\theta^{1/2} & \theta \to 0 \\ \sigma^2(1 - \frac{2}{\theta}) & \theta \to \infty \end{cases}$$

$$T \sim \begin{cases} \frac{1}{2\sqrt{2\pi}} \frac{a\sigma}{\theta^{1/4}} & \theta \to 0 \\ \frac{1}{\sqrt{\pi}} \frac{\sigma}{t} & \theta \to \infty \end{cases}$$

3.1.2 Proof

Mathematically, it is the covariance function

$$c_p(h) = E[(p_{k+h} - m)(p_k - m)]$$

which is the crucial variable. Once we get its expression, the results for the standard deviation and the trade may be easily derived. From Fourier analysis, $c_p(h)$ is given by (see chapter 7):

$$c_p(h) = \frac{(at)^2}{\pi} \int_0^{\pi} \frac{\cos(\omega h)}{(2+\theta-2\cos\omega)^2}\, d\omega$$

This integral can be evaluated by the theorem of residues; alternatively it can be derived from a result given in Gradshteyn (1965; p.366 3.613 (1)). One obtains:

$$c_p(h) = \frac{x_2^{|h|}}{(x_2-x_1)^3}[|h|(x_1-x_2)+x_1+x_2](at)^2\,\sigma^2 \qquad (3.4)$$

Subsequently we shall confine ourselves to positive values of h; therefore the absolute value notation becomes useless. By replacing x_1, x_2 by their expressions, one obtains:

$$c_p(h) = \frac{(\sqrt{1+\alpha^2}-\alpha)^h(\sqrt{1+\alpha^2}+h\alpha)}{4\alpha^3}\,\theta^2\,\sigma^2, \quad \theta = at, \quad \alpha = \sqrt{\theta+\frac{\theta^2}{4}}$$

Taking $h = 0$ in $c_p(h)$ we obtain the expression of σ_p. The developments of σ_p for small and large θ may be easily derived; they have been stated explicitly with the idea of comparing them to the two-market case. We note that $\sigma_p^2 \to \sigma^2$ when $t \to \infty$ as expected since the markets become disconnected when transportation costs become large. The chart of the variance with respect to transport cost is shown in Fig.3.8a

Next we define the total trade T as being half the sum of all exports and imports; in order to allow comparisons between chains of markets regardless of their size, we normalize by the total number of markets.

$$T = \frac{1}{2(N+1)} \sum_{k=1}^{N} E(\,|s_k|\,)$$

Because of spatial stationarity (and discarding the markets located near the boundaries which do not satisfy the stationarity requirement) $E(\,|s_k|\,)$ is independent of k. From (3.1a) we have (for large N):

$$T = \frac{1}{2t}E(|p_{k+1}-p_k|)$$

Using (2.5) for the expectation leads to:

$$T = \frac{\sigma_p}{t\sqrt{\pi}}[1-c_p(1)/c_p(0)]^{1/2}$$

From the expression of $c_p(h)$ we finally obtain the expression of T stated above. The variations of trade with respect to transport cost are shown in Fig.3.8b.

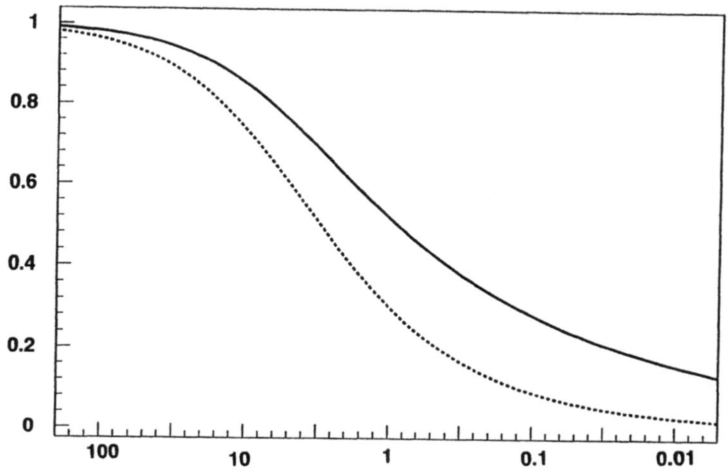

Fig.3.8 a Standard deviation of prices in a market chain (solid line) and in a market network (dashed line). Transportation costs are represented on the horizontal axis (logarithmic scale). The standard deviation of local conditions is equal to 1; $a = 1$.

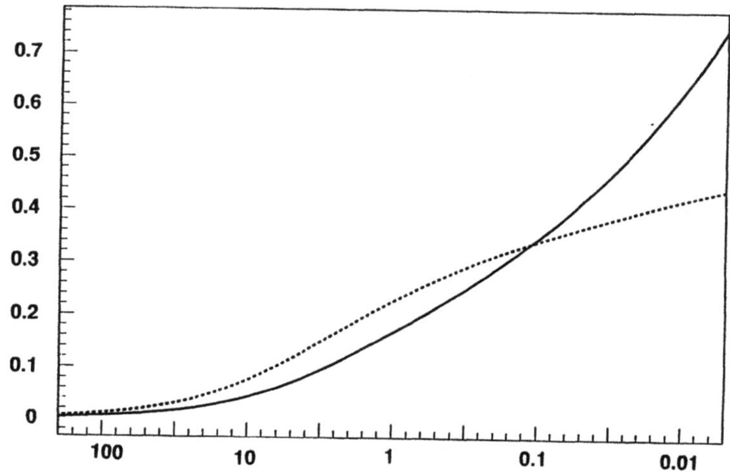

Fig.3.8 b Comparison of trade expectation in a market chain (solid line) and in a market network (dashed line). Transportation costs are represented on the horizontal axis (logarithmic scale). The standard deviation of local conditions is equal to 1; $a = 1$.

3.1.3 Price differentials as a function of distance

In the introduction we emphasized that our knowledge of transport costs is beset with great uncertainties. Therefore, a reliable estimating procedure should rely on a relationship in which transport costs do *not* occur. Analysing price differentials as a function of distance precisely provides such a relationship. From (2.5) we derive the price differential between markets k and l:

$$\Delta(h) = E\left(|p_k - p_l|\right) = \frac{2\sigma_p}{\sqrt{\pi}}\sqrt{1 - c_p(h)/\sigma^2}, \qquad h = |k - l| \tag{3.5}$$

3.1.4 Linear versus nonlinear model

In contrast to the linear model, the nonlinear one has to be solved numerically; but this is not the only difference, nor is it the most important. In fact, in the nonlinear case, with $t\varphi_c(s_k)$ substituted for ts_k, we can no longer solve equations (2.1a) for the s_k. As a result, one first has to solve a problem in which the variables j_k and s_k (instead of the p_k) are the unknowns. This makes a great difference for the number of inter-market links usually is much larger than the number of markets. More specifically, the number of links depends on how many neighbours each market has. In the case of a chain, links and markets are in equal number and the previous difficulty does not manifest itself. On the contrary it becomes serious in the case of a two dimensional network where each market has about four neighbours.

Fig.3.9 shows the variations of the price differential as a function of distance both in the linear and in the nonlinear model. As expected it can be seen that there is an overall agreement provided that t does not become smaller than σ.

3.2 Chain of markets with an arbitrary exchange pattern

The market chain we have considered until now could seem rather peculiar in so far as direct long range trade connections are missing. In this section we shall investigate more complex market chains where each market is in direct business relation with an arbitrary number of other markets: p markets on its left and p markets on its right (Fig.3.10). Subsequently such a market chain will for short be called a market chain with $2p$ neighbours. We shall be able to carry out this investigation only in the limit of a well integrated market, i.e; when transport costs go to zero; in this case most of our previous results will be seen to hold true at least qualitatively. As can be guessed from a general argument which we develop below in paragraph 3.2.6 a similar conclusion certainly applies for non vanishing transport costs as well.

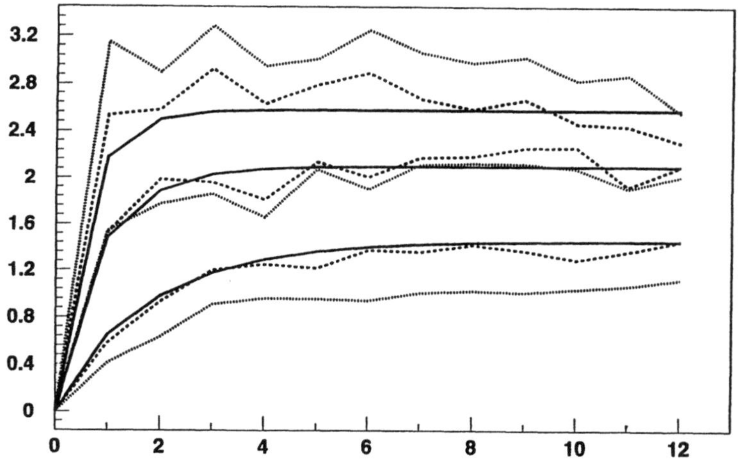

Fig.3.9 Price differentials in a market chain with respect to distance. The Figure compares the probabilistic linear model (solid curve), a simulation of the linear model (dashed curve) and a simulation of the nonlinear model (dotted curve). From highest to lowest the curves correspond to transportation costs equal to 5, 2 and 0.5. In the latter case the standard deviation of local conditions is larger than the transportation cost; there is then, as expected, a pronounced difference between the linear and the nonlinear model. The standard deviation of local condition is equal to 3; $a = 1$; 60 iterations, 61 markets.

3.2.1 Equations and results

We consider a market chain where each market is connected to $2p$ neighbours. The equilibrium equation for the prices p_k may be written down in the same way as in the previous section. Thus we obtain:

$$(2\rho + \theta)p_k - \sum_{l=1}^{p} \frac{p_{k-l} + p_{k+l}}{l} = \theta \overline{p}_k, \quad \rho = 1 + \frac{1}{2} + \ldots + \frac{1}{p} \qquad \theta = at \quad (3.6)$$

With the $\overline{p}_k$ still being a set of independent identically distributed normal variables, (3.6) is a spatial autoregressive process of order $2p$. Once the prices p_k are known, the direct trade flow between market k and market l will be given by:

$$s_k^{(l)} = \frac{p_{k+l} - p_k}{lt}$$

We shall investigate the behaviour of this system in the limit of a perfectly integrated market and state the following theorem.

Theorem 2 Chain of markets with $2p$ neighbours We consider a chain of markets with $2p$ neighbours; in the limit of small transportation

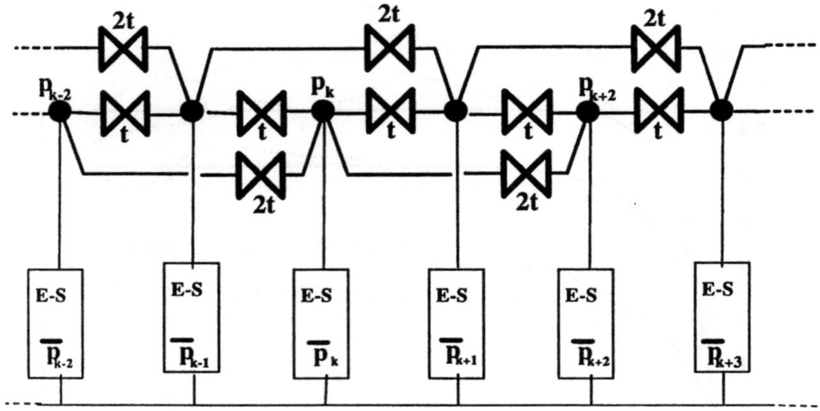

Fig.3.10 Schematic representation of the equilibrium equations of a chain of markets with $2p$ neighbours. In this figure $p = 2$: each market has direct links with 2 neighbours on each side. The E-S blocks represent the excess-supply functions for each market.

costs, the spatial variance of prices and the overall trade are given by:

$$\sigma_p^2 \underset{\theta\to 0}{\sim} \frac{\sigma^2}{2\sqrt{2}\, p^{9/2}\sqrt{p+1}}\sqrt{\theta} \tag{3.7}$$

$$T \underset{\theta\to 0}{\sim} \frac{a\sigma}{\sqrt{2\pi}\sqrt{p^5(p+1)}}\left(\sum_{l=1}^{p}\frac{\sqrt{p-l}}{l}\right)\sqrt{\frac{1}{\theta}} \tag{3.8}$$

where $\theta = at$, a is the slope of the excess-supply function and t is the transport cost

By comparison of these results with the corresponding expressions in the previous section, we observe that the dependence with respect to θ is basically the same as here. Indeed, the $\theta^{-1/4}$ dependence of T in theorem 1 (instead of $\theta^{-1/2}$ here) is an unessential feature as will become clear later on.

3.2.2 Roots of reciprocal equation

We first prove the following lemma.

Lemma The reciprocal equation:

$$f(x,\theta) = \sum_{l=1}^{p}\frac{1}{l}(z^l + z^{-l}) - (2\rho + \theta) = 0 \tag{3.9}$$

has one, and only one, pair of roots of the form:

$$z_1, z_1' \underset{\theta \to 0}{\sim} 1 \pm \alpha\sqrt{\theta}, \qquad \alpha = \sqrt{\frac{2}{p(p+1)}} \tag{3.10}$$

Proof The roots of equation (3.9) occur in the form of reciprocal pairs $(z, 1/z)$. We shall first obtain the form (3.10) of the pair of roots; uniqueness will be examined subsequently.
With $\sqrt{\theta} = \epsilon$, we set: $z = 1 + \alpha\epsilon$ where α is yet unknown; then developing to second order:

$$z^l + z^{-l} = 2 + l^2\alpha^2\epsilon^2 + O(\epsilon^3)$$

Substituting in equation (3.9) we obtain:

$$2\rho + \alpha^2\epsilon^2 \sum_{l=1}^{p} l = 2\rho + \epsilon^2 + O(\epsilon^3)$$

This leads to:

$$\alpha^2 = 1/\sum_{l=1}^{p} l = \frac{2}{p(p+1)}$$

Would we have another pair of roots in the vicinity of 1, then 1 would be, for $\epsilon = 0$, a root of order at least equal to 4; thus, we should have: $f''(1,0) = 0$. This is not true however since:

$$f''(1,0) = p(p+1)$$

3.2.3 Covariance function

With $c_p(l)$ denoting the covariance of the p_k, we have (see chapter 7):

$$c_p(l) = \sum_{D(0,1)} Res\left[\, |h(z)|^2 z^{l-1}\right] \tag{3.11a}$$

where:

$$h(z) = \frac{\theta}{2\rho + \theta - \sum_{k=1}^{p} \frac{1}{k}(z^k + z^{-k})} \tag{3.11b}$$

Res denotes the residue of the function inside the bracket at one of its poles and $\sum_{D(0,1)}$ indicates summation over all poles inside the unit disk centered at the origin. By factorizing its denominator, we may write $h^2(z)$ in the form:

$$h^2(z) = \frac{\theta^2}{p^2} \frac{z^{2p+l-1}}{\prod_{k=1}^{p} (z - z_k)^2 (z - z_k')^2}$$

Since the roots occur in reciprocal pairs (z_k, z'_k) there are p second-order poles $z_k, \quad k = 1, \ldots, p$ inside the unit disk. Replacing the residue by its expression leads to:

$$c_p(l) = \frac{\theta^2}{p^2} \sum_{k=1}^{p} \frac{d}{dz} \left[\frac{z^{2p+l-1}}{(z - z'_k)^2 \, u_k^2(z)} \right]_{z=z_k} \tag{3.12}$$

with:

$$u_k(z) = \prod_{j \neq k} (z - z_j)(z - z'_j)$$

Since there is only one pair of roots whose difference is of order ϵ, it can be seen from (3.12) that these roots provide the dominant contribution to $c(l)$. We shall now work out this argument in detail for $\sigma_p^2 = c(0)$ and for the trade T.

3.2.4 Variance

Let us introduce the notations:

$$u_1 = u_1(z_1), \qquad u'_1 = u'_1(z_1)$$

The residue at $z = z_1$ becomes:

$$Res(z_1) = \frac{z_1^{2p-2+l}}{(z_1 - z'_1)^3 u_1^3} \; \{ \, (2p + l - 1)(z_1 - z'_1)u_1 - z\,[2u_1 + (z_1 - z'_1)u'_1] \, \} \tag{3.13}$$

With $z_1 - z'_1 \sim -2\alpha\epsilon$, the dominant term in the bracket of the right-hand side is: $-2u_1$. Collecting all factors, we obtain for $l = 0$:

$$c_p(0) = \sigma_p^2 \underset{\theta \to 0}{\sim} \frac{\sigma^2}{4p^2\alpha^3 u_1^2} \sqrt{\theta} \tag{3.14}$$

We now calculate u_1 to zero-order, along with u'_1 which will be required later on. Let us denote the denominator of $h(z)$ in (3.11b) by $P(z)$:

$$P(z) = (2\rho + \theta)z^p - \sum_{k=1}^{p} \frac{1}{k}(z^{k+p} + z^{-k+p}) \tag{3.15}$$

Between $P(z)$ and $u_1(z)$ we have the following relation:

$$P(z) = (-\frac{1}{p})(z - z_1)(z - z'_1)u_1(z) \tag{3.16}$$

By successive derivations, we obtain:

$$u_1 = \left(-\frac{p}{2}\right) P''(1) \qquad u'_1 = \left(-\frac{p}{6}\right) P'''(1) \tag{3.17}$$

We now differentiate $P(z)$ three times and set $t = 0$ i.e. $z = 1$; collecting all terms, we obtain:

$$P''(1) = -p(p+1), \qquad P'''(1) = (-3p)(p^2-1) \quad p \geq 2$$

and:

$$u_1 = \frac{p^2(p+1)}{2}, \qquad u_1' = \frac{p^2}{2}\,(p^2-1) \tag{3.18}$$

Substituting the first expression in (3.14) gives the final result for σ_p^2.

3.2.5 Trade

We now come to the evaluation of the global trade:

$$T = \frac{1}{2N} \sum_{l,k=1}^{p} E\left(\left|s_k^{(l)}\right| \right)$$

Substituting $s_k^{(l)} = (p_{k+l} - p_k)/lt$, and using (2.5), T becomes:

$$T = \frac{\sigma_p}{\sqrt{\pi}t} \sum_{l=1}^{p} \frac{1}{l} \sqrt{1 - \frac{c_p(l)}{c_p(0)}} \tag{3.19}$$

For the evaluation of $c(l)/c(0)$ we again make use of (3.13):

$$\frac{c_p(l)}{c_p(0)} = z_1^l \left. \frac{(2p-1+l)(z_1 - z_1')u_1 - z_1[2u_1 + (z_1 - z_1')u_1']}{(2p-1)(z_1 - z_1')u_1 - z_1[2u_1 + (z_1 - z_1')u_1']} \right|_{z_1 = 1+\alpha\epsilon}$$

Collecting dominant terms we obtain:

$$\frac{c(l)}{c(0)} = 1 + \epsilon[l - (2p-1) + \frac{u_1'}{u_1}] + O(\epsilon^2) \tag{3.20}$$

At this point, let us pause for a moment to examine the special case $p = 1$. Then one has: $u_1 = 1, \quad u_1' = 0$ and of course $l = 1$. Thus the coefficient of ϵ vanishes, so to say by accident, and one has to carry out the development in ϵ to second order.
Replacing u_1'/u_1 by its expression (3.18) in (3.20) we obtain the global trade in the form stated in the theorem.

3.2.6 Discussion

First we note that the similarity between the results for the $2p$-neighbour chain and the 2-neighbour chain could have been expected. Indeed in the later case the average price differential between two markets is as a rule smaller than (or equal to) the transportation cost between them. This is obvious in the nonlinear model; we have seen it to be true for the linear model too as long as $\sigma < t$. This makes the higher order links between k and $k+2, k+3, \ldots$ almost useless on average. A second comment is in order. In defining the $2p$-neighbour model we have explicitly assumed that transportation costs are proportional to distance. Thus we have ignored the loading and unloading costs; this is admissible whenever long range transportation is considered. Changing transportation costs from lt into $b + lt$ would produce but minor modifications in the previous derivation.

4 Market networks

In this section we consider the market network represented in Fig.3.11. It is

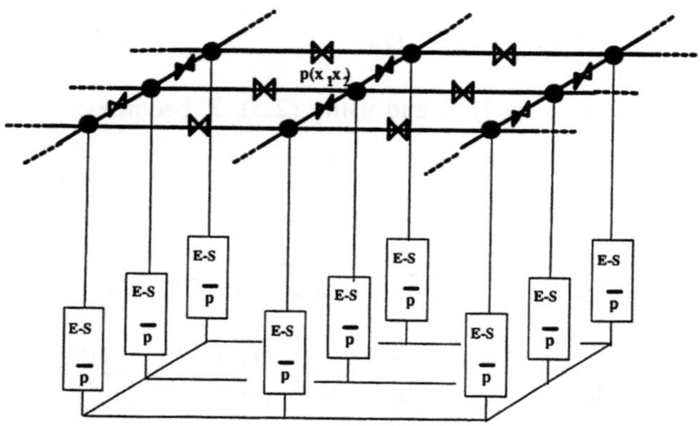

Fig.3.11 Schematic representation of the equilibrium equations of a network of markets. The E-S blocks represent the excess-supply functions on each market.

one of the simplest two-dimensional arrangements of markets. Yet our previous experience with market chains makes us believe that its properties may be representative of the broader class of two-dimensional networks.

4.1 Solving the linear Enke-Samuelson model

4.1.1 Equations of the model

The model's equations may be derived from Fig.3.11 in the same way as in the former sections. We thus obtain:

$$(4+\theta)p(x_1, x_2) - [p(x_1, x_2 - 1) + p(x_1, x_2 + 1) + p(x_1 - 1, x_2) + p(x_1 + 1, x_2)]$$

$$= \theta\overline{p}(x_1, x_2) \tag{4.1a}$$

With the standard notation:

$$\Delta u = u(x+1,y) + u(x-1,y) + u(x,y-1) + u(x,y+1) - 4u(x,y)$$

the equation may be written in the form:

$$\theta p(x_1, x_2) - \Delta p(x_1, x_2) = \theta\overline{p}(x_1, x_2) \tag{4.1b}$$

With $\overline{p}(x_1, x_2)$ still being a set of independent and identically distributed normal variables, (4.1) defines a bivariate autoregressive process.

4.1.2 Solution by Fourier transformation

Although we shall return to this method of solution in chapter 7 let us for the sake of completeness briefly sketch the main steps. We introduce the generating function $\widetilde{G}(\theta_1, \theta_2)$:

$$\widetilde{G}(\theta_1, \theta_2) = \sum_{x_1=-\infty}^{\infty} \sum_{x_2=-\infty}^{\infty} G(x_1, x_2) \exp(-ix_1\theta_1 - ix_2\theta_2) \tag{4.2a}$$

In other words $\widetilde{G}(\theta_1, \theta_2)$ is the Fourier series transform of $G(x_1, x_2)$. The inverse transformation reads:

$$G(x_1, x_2) = \frac{1}{(2\pi)^2} \int_{-\pi}^{\pi} \int_{-\pi}^{\pi} d\theta_1 d\theta_2 \widetilde{G}(\theta_1, \theta_2) \exp(ix_1\theta_1 + ix_2\theta_2) \tag{4.2b}$$

Let us now represent by the same notation $G(x_1, x_2)$ the solution of equation (4.1) when the right-hand side is replaced by $\delta(x_1, x_2)$:

$$\delta(x_1, x_2) = \begin{cases} 1 & x_1 = x_2 = 0 \\ 0 & x_1^2 + x_2^2 \neq 0 \end{cases}$$

Then the Fourier series transform of the covariance function will be given by:

$$\widetilde{C}(\theta_1, \theta_2) = \left|\widetilde{G}(\theta_1, \theta_2)\right|^2 \tag{4.3}$$

4.1.3 Integral representation of the covariance function

We now prove the following lemma:

> **Lemma 2** The covariance function of the bivariate autoregressive process:
>
> $$(a - 4 - \Delta u)G(x_1, x_2) = \delta(x_1, x_2), \qquad a > 4 \tag{4.4}$$

has the following integral representation:

$$\gamma(x_1, x_2) = \frac{1}{4} \int_0^\infty dq \exp(-qa/2) q I_{x_1}(q) I_{x_2}(q) \tag{4.5}$$

where I_x is the modified Bessel function.

Proof

By replacing (4.2a) into (4.4) we obtain:

$$\tilde{G}(\theta_1, \theta_2) = \frac{1}{a - \left(e^{-i\theta_1} + e^{i\theta_1} + e^{-i\theta_2} + e^{i\theta_2}\right)}$$

Substituting into (4.2b) gives:

$$G(x_1, x_2) = \frac{1}{(2\pi)^2} \int_{-\pi}^{\pi} \int_{-\pi}^{\pi} d\theta_1 d\theta_2 \frac{\exp(ix_1\theta_1 + ix_2\theta_2)}{a - 2\cos\theta_1 - 2\cos\theta_2} \tag{4.6}$$

From (4.3) we deduce that the covariance function will be given by:

$$\gamma(x_1, x_2) = -\frac{\partial G}{\partial a} \tag{4.7}$$

Since the integral is over a finite domain without singularities, we may indeed carry the derivation inside the integral. We now make the following changes in (4.6); first in the product $e^{ix_1\theta_1} e^{ix_2\theta_2}$ we get rid (because of their odd parity) of all terms containing a sinus; then we replace the denominator by the following obvious integral representation:

$$\frac{1}{a/2 - \cos\theta_1 - \cos\theta_2} = \int_0^\infty dq \exp[\, q(\cos\theta_1 + \cos\theta_2 - a/2)\,], \qquad a > 4$$

This gives:

$$G(x_1, x_2) = \frac{1}{2} \int_0^\infty dq e^{-qa/2} A(q, x_1) A(q, x_2)$$

where:

$$A(q, x) = \frac{1}{\pi} \int_0^\pi d\theta e^{q\cos\theta} \cos(x\theta)$$

The second and the third integral may be identified as integral representations of the modified Bessel function $I_{x_1}(q)$ and $I_{x_2}(q)$ (Magnus 1966, p79); this leads to:

$$G(x_1, x_2) = \frac{1}{2} \int_0^\infty dq e^{-qa/2} I_{x_1}(q) I_{x_2}(q)$$

For $a > 4$, the integral is absolutely convergent and it may be differentiated with respect to a; thus from (4.7) we get (4.5).

4.1.4 Asymptotic expressions of the price covariance function

In Appendix A we prove the following:

Theorem 3 Market network with 4 neighbours. We consider a network of N markets each of which maintains trade relations with four neighbouring markets. For small, respectively large, transportation costs the price covariance function admits the following developments:
1) $\theta \to 0$:

$$c_p(x_1, x_2) \underset{\theta\to 0}{\sim} \frac{\sigma^2}{4\pi}\left[\theta - \frac{x_1^2 + x_2^2 - 1/2}{4}\,\theta^2 \ln(1/\theta)\right] \qquad (4.7a)$$

2) $\theta \to \infty$:

$$c_p(x_1, x_2) = \left(\frac{\sigma}{1+\frac{4}{\theta}}\right)^2 \frac{1}{(\theta+4)^{x_1+x_2}} \sum_{m=0}^{\infty} \frac{L_m(x_1, x_2)}{(\theta+4)^{2m}} \qquad (4.7b)$$

where:

$$L_m(x_1, x_2) = (2m + x_1 + x_2 + 1)\frac{[\,(2m + x_1 + x_2)!\,]^2}{m!(m + x_1)!(m + x_2)!(m + x_1 + x_2)!}$$

In particular one has to first order:

$$c_p(x_1, x_2) \underset{\theta\to\infty}{\sim} \frac{L_0(x_1, x_2)}{\theta^{x_1+x_2}}\,\sigma^2, \qquad L_0(x_1, x_2) = \binom{x_1+x_2}{x_1}(x_1 + x_2 + 1)$$

4.1.5 Approximation formula

In Appendix A we obtain as a side product the following approximate expression of the covariance function:

$$c_p(x_1, x_2) \simeq \hat{c}_p(x_1, x_2)$$

where:
$\hat{c}_p(x_1, x_2) =$

$$\frac{\sigma^2}{(\theta+4)^{x_1+x_2}}\left[L_0(x_1, x_2)\left(\frac{\theta}{\theta+4}\right)^2 + 2\frac{4^{x_1+x_2+2}}{\pi}\frac{\theta}{(\theta+8)(\theta+4)^2}\right] \qquad (4.8)$$

As an accuracy check of this approximation formula, let us compare the results that it provides for $\theta \to 0$ and for $\theta \to \infty$ with the exact results.

1) $\theta \to 0$ The first term in the bracket is of order θ^2 while the second one is of order θ; thus:

$$\hat{c}_p(x_1, x_2) \underset{\theta \to 0}{\sim} \frac{\sigma^2}{4\pi}\theta$$

which equals the exact result to lowest order.

2) $\theta \to \infty$ The first term in the bracket is of order θ^0, while the second one is of order θ^{-2}; thus:

$$\hat{c}_p(x_1, x_2) \underset{\theta \to \infty}{\sim} \frac{\sigma^2}{\theta^{x_1+x_2}} L_0(x_1, x_2)$$

which again matches the exact result to lowest order; in particular: $\hat{c}_p(0,0) \underset{\theta \to \infty}{\sim} \sigma^2$

4.2 Process of market integration

Proposition For small, respectively large, transportation costs the variance σ_p^2 of the prices and the global trade T have the following developments:

$$\sigma_p^2 \sim \begin{cases} \frac{\sigma^2}{4\pi}\theta & \theta \to 0 \\ \sigma^2[1 - \frac{8}{\theta}] & \theta \to \infty \end{cases}$$

$$T \sim \begin{cases} \frac{a\sigma}{4\pi}\sqrt{\ln(1/\theta)} & \theta \to 0 \\ \frac{2a\sigma}{\pi\theta}(1 - \frac{1}{\theta}) & \theta \to \infty \end{cases}$$

For σ_p^2 the result is an obvious consequence of $(4.7a, b)$; for T it is straightforward too. Indeed with

$$a_{x_1,x_2} = (1/t)[p(x_1+1, x_2) - p(x_1, x_2)] \quad b_{x_1,x_2} = (1/t)[p(x_1, x_2+1) - p(x_1, x_2)]$$

denoting the trade flows in horizontal and vertical links:

$$T = \frac{1}{2N^2} \sum_{x_1,x_2}^{N} [E(\,|a_{x_1,x_2}|\,) + E(\,|b_{x_1,x_2}|\,)] = \frac{1}{2}\sqrt{\frac{2}{\pi}}\,(\sigma_a + \sigma_b)$$

where:

$$\sigma_a^2 = \frac{2}{t^2}[c_p(0,0) - c_p(0,1)], \quad \sigma_b^2 = \frac{2}{t^2}[c_p(0,0) - c_p(1,0)]$$

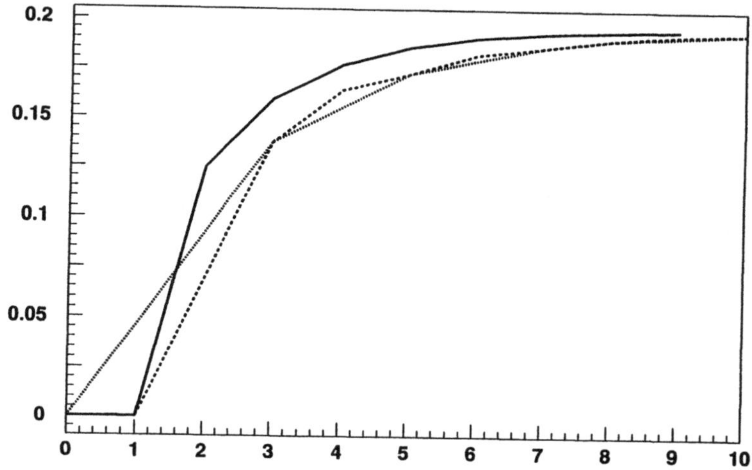

Fig.3.12 Evolution with distance of the expectation of price differentials in a network of markets. The solid line, the dashed line and the dotted line respectively correspond to directions making angles of 0°, 30° and 60° with a given bearing. At distances beyond 7, the model becomes almost isotropic. The standard deviation of local conditions is equal to 1; the transport cost is equal to 0.5; $a = 1$.

Since $c_p(0,1) = c_p(1,0)$ we have $\sigma_a = \sigma_b$ and:

$$T = \frac{2}{t\sqrt{\pi}}[c_p(0,0) - c_p(1,0)]^{1/2}$$

Replacing c_p by its developments leads to the result above.

The former results may be compared with those given in theorem 1 for the simple market chain and with those for the p-neighbours market chain in theorem 2. The behaviour of the global trade in the limit $\theta \to 0$ is of particular interest. We may remember that in the case of a market chain, trade diverged as $1/\theta^{1/4}$ or $1/\theta^{1/2}$ according to whether is was a simple or a $2p$-neighbour chain. Here we formally still have a divergence, but compared to a power-like divergence the divergence of the logarithm is so slow that it may be almost unnoticed. Of course, the stage of a perfectly integrated market can never be reached; nonetheless it is satisfactory that the trade function does not have a true singularity in the vicinity of this point. The evolution of σ_p^2 and of T for decreasing transportation cost is shown by the dashed curves in Fig.3.8a,b. When drawn on the same graphic the results given by the approximation formula (4.8) would be almost indiscernible from the exact curves.

4.3 Price differentials as a function of inter-market distance

The price differential will be derived from the covariance function in the usual way:

$$\Delta(x_1, x_2) = \frac{2\sigma_p}{\sqrt{\pi}}\sqrt{1 - \frac{\mathcal{C}_p(x_1, x_2)}{\mathcal{C}_p(0, 0)}} \tag{4.9}$$

Its variations with respect to distance between markets is shown in Fig.3.12. Because we are dealing here with a discrete network we have used the Manhattan distance $|x_1| + |x_2|$ rather than the Euclidian distance $(x_1^2 + x_2^2)^{1/2}$. Fig.3.12 allows a comparison of the increase of price differentials in three different directions. As could be expected the behavior of the model becomes more and more isotropic as distance from the origin increases.

A Appendix A: Covariance function of a network of markets

A.1 Development for vanishing transportation costs

We rewrite the covariance function (4.5) of lemma 2 as:

$$\gamma(x_1, x_2) = \frac{1}{4} K(\epsilon; x_1, x_2)$$

where:

$$K(\epsilon; x_1, x_2) = \int_0^\infty q e^{\epsilon q} e^{-2q} I_{x_1}(q) I_{x_2}(q) dq \qquad \epsilon = \theta/2 \qquad (A1)$$

We are interested in the development of $K(\epsilon; x_1, x_2)$ in the vicinity of the singular point $\epsilon = 0$. Guided by the asymptotic expansion of the modified Bessel function (Bateman 1953, p.86) we write $K(\epsilon; x_1, x_2)$ in the form:

$$K(\epsilon; x_1, x_2) = \int_0^\infty q e^{-(2+\epsilon)q} B(q, x_1) B(q, x_2)$$

where:

$$B(q, x) = I_x(q) - \frac{e^q}{\sqrt{2\pi q}} + \frac{e^q}{\sqrt{2\pi q}}$$

Developing we obtain:

$$K(\epsilon; x_1, x_2) = \frac{1}{2\pi\epsilon} + \frac{1}{\sqrt{2\pi}} f(\epsilon; x_1, x_2) + g(\epsilon; x_1, x_2) \qquad (A2)$$

$$f(\epsilon; x_1, x_2) = \int_0^\infty \sqrt{q} e^{-\epsilon q} e^{-q} f(q) dq \qquad (A3a)$$

$$f(q) = I_{x_1}(q) + I_{x_2}(q) - 2\frac{e^q}{\sqrt{2\pi q}} \qquad (A3b)$$

$$g(\epsilon; x_1, x_2) = \int_0^\infty q e^{-(2+\epsilon)} \left(I_{x_1}(q) - \frac{e^q}{\sqrt{2\pi q}} \right) \left(I_{x_2}(q) - \frac{e^q}{\sqrt{2\pi q}} \right) dq \qquad (A4)$$

$g(0; x_1, x_2)$ is finite since the integrand is $O(1/q^2)$; on the contrary, $f(\epsilon; x_1, x_2)$ is still singular at $\epsilon = 0$ since its integrand is $O(1/q)$. First we split the integration interval into two parts:

$$f(\epsilon; x_1, x_2) = f_0(\epsilon; x_1, x_2) + f_1(\epsilon; x_1, x_2)$$

$$f_0(\epsilon; x_1, x_2) = \int_0^1 \sqrt{q} e^{-(1+\epsilon)q} f(q) dq$$

$$f_1(\epsilon; x_1, x_2) = \int_1^\infty \sqrt{q} e^{-(1+\epsilon)q} f(q) dq$$

The first integral is finite and in fact analytic in ϵ. Still guided by the asymptotic development of the modified Bessel function we rewrite f_1 as:
$f_1(\epsilon; x_1, x_2) =$

$$\int_1^\infty \sqrt{q}e^{-(1+\epsilon)}\left[f(q) + \frac{e^q}{\sqrt{2\pi q}}\frac{x_1^2+x_2^2-1/4}{2q} - \frac{e^q}{\sqrt{2\pi q}}\frac{x_1^2+x_2^2-1/4}{2q}\right]dq$$

$$f_1(\epsilon; x_1, x_2) = -\frac{x_1^2+x_2^2-1/4}{2\sqrt{2\pi}}\,a(\epsilon) + b(\epsilon; x_1, x_2) \qquad (A5)$$

$$a(\epsilon) = \int_1^\infty \frac{e^{-\epsilon q}}{q}dq$$

$$b(\epsilon; x_1, x_2) = \int_1^\infty \sqrt{q}e^{-(1+\epsilon)}\left[f(q) + \frac{e^q}{\sqrt{2\pi q}}\frac{x_1^2+x_2^2-1/4}{2q}\right]dq$$

$b(0; x_1, x_2)$ is finite since the integrand is $O(1/q^2)$; $a(\epsilon; x_1, x_2)$ reads, with $u = \epsilon q$:

$$a(\epsilon) = \int_\epsilon^\infty \frac{e^{-u}}{u}du = -Ei(-\epsilon)$$

where Ei denotes the exponential-integral function (Gradshteyn 1965, p.925). Now, the exponential-integral has the following series expansion (Gradshteyn 1965, p.927):

$$Ei(x) = C + \ln(-x) + \sum_{k=1}^{\infty}\frac{x^k}{k\ k!} \qquad x < 0$$

where C denotes Euler's constant. Hence:

$$a(\epsilon) = -\ln\epsilon - C + O(\epsilon) \qquad (A6)$$

Collecting all terms, we obtain:
$K(\epsilon; x_1, x_2) =$

$$\frac{1}{2\pi\epsilon} + \frac{x_1^2+x_2^2-1/4}{4\pi}\ln\epsilon + g(\epsilon; x_1, x_2) + b(\epsilon; x_1, x_2) + \sum_{k=0}^{\infty} a_k\epsilon^k \qquad (A7)$$

The terms $g(\epsilon; x_1, x_2)$ and $b(\epsilon; x_1, x_2)$ are finite at $\epsilon = 0$ but neither of them is analytic; their expression is of the form:

$$g(\epsilon; x_1, x_2), b(\epsilon; x_1, x_2) = \sum_{k=0}^{\infty} c_k[(\ln\epsilon + 1)\epsilon\ln\epsilon]^n$$

Remark The first term in our result ($A5$) could have been obtained more directly by invoking a theorem giving the behavior of the Laplace transform in the vicinity of singular points (Doetsch 1950, p.498, 501). It states that:

$$f(q) \underset{q\to\infty}{\sim} c(-1)^{p+1}p!\,\frac{e^{\lambda_0 q}}{q^{p+1}} \Rightarrow [\mathcal{L}f](\lambda) \underset{\lambda\to\lambda_0}{\sim} c(\lambda-\lambda_0)^p \ln(\lambda-\lambda_0)$$

When applied to the Laplace transform $(A3a)$ with $p = 0, \lambda_0 = 0$, this result gives back the first term in $(A5)$

A.2 Asymptotic expression for large transportation costs

Starting again from the expression (4.5) of the covariance function, we make use of the following series expansion (Bateman 1953, p.11):

$$I_{x_1}(q)I_{x_2}(q) = \sum_{m=0}^{\infty}\left(\frac{q}{2}\right)^{2m+x_1+x_2} C_m$$

where:

$$C_m = \frac{\Gamma(2m+x_1+x_2+1)}{\Gamma(m+1)\Gamma(m+x_1+1)\Gamma(m+x_2+1)\Gamma(m+x_1+x_2+1)}$$

$\Gamma()$ denotes the gamma function. Integrating this series term by term, with the help of:

$$\int_0^{\infty} x^n e^{-ax}dx = \Gamma(n+1)/a^{n+1}$$

we obtain:

$$\gamma(x_1,x_2) = \sum_0^{\infty} C_m \frac{\Gamma(2m+x_1+x_2+2)}{a^{2m+x_1+x_2+2}} \tag{A8}$$

Let us check that this series converges; we use the duplication formula (Magnus 1966, p.3):

$$\Gamma(2z) = \frac{2^{2z-1}}{\sqrt{\pi}}\Gamma(z)\Gamma(z+1/2)$$

together with Stirling's asymptotic formula (Magnus 1966, p.12):

$$\frac{\Gamma(n+a)}{\Gamma(n+b)} \underset{n\to\infty}{\sim} n^{a-b} \tag{A9}$$

Thus we obtain:

$$C_m \frac{\Gamma(2m+x_1+x_2+2)}{a^{2m+x_1+x_2+2}} \underset{m\to\infty}{\sim} \left(\frac{4}{a}\right)^{2m+x_1+x_2} \tag{A10}$$

Since $a > 4$, the series converges geometrically.

Series $(A8)$ constitutes an asymptotic expansion of the covariance function for $\theta \to \infty$. Noting that $\Gamma(x+1) = x!$ we rewrite it in the form:

$$c_p(x_1, x_2) = \frac{\sigma^2}{(1+4/\theta^2)^2(\theta+4)^{x_1+x_2}} \sum_{m=0}^{\infty} \frac{L_m(x_1, x_2)}{(\theta+4)^{2m}} \qquad (A11a)$$

$$L_m(x_1, x_2) =$$

$$(2m + x_1 + x_2 + 1)\frac{[\,(2m + x_1 + x_2)!\,]^2}{m!(m + x_1)!(m + x_2)!(m + x_1 + x_2)!} \qquad (A11b)$$

To lowest order, $c_p(x_1, x_2)$ is given by the first term in this development:

$$c_p(x_1, x_2) \underset{\theta\to\infty}{\sim} \frac{\sigma^2}{\theta^{x_1+x_2}} L_0(x_1, x_2) \qquad L_0(x_1, x_2) = (x_1 + x_2 + 1)\binom{x_1+x_2}{x_1}$$

in particular: $\sigma_p^2 = c_p(0,0) \underset{\theta\to\infty}{\sim} \sigma^2$ as should indeed be the case for disconnected markets.

A.3 Approximation formula

It turns out that Stirling's asymptotic formula is pretty good even at small n: for 1!, 2!, 3! it provides (at first order) the following approximation: 0.92, 1.92, 5.83. Therefore it is tempting to make use of $(A10)$ for any $m > 0$ in order to obtain an approximate expression of the covariance function. Substituting $(A10)$ in series $(A8)$ with the first term singled out, we obtain:

$$\gamma(x_1, x_2) \simeq \hat{\gamma}(x_1, x_2)$$

with:

$$\hat{\gamma}(x_1, x_2) = \frac{L_0(x_1, x_2)}{a^{x_1+x_2+2}} + \frac{2}{\pi a^2}\left(\frac{4}{a}\right)^{x_1+x_2} \sum_{m=1}^{\infty} \left(\frac{4}{a}\right)^{2m}$$

Summing up the geometrical series, we obtain:

$$\hat{\gamma}(x_1, x_2) = \frac{L_0(x_1, x_2)}{a^{x_1+x_2+2}} + \frac{2}{\pi}\left(\frac{4}{a}\right)^{x_1+x_2+2} \frac{1}{a^2 - 4}$$

and $\hat{c}_p(x_1, x_2) = \sigma^2\theta^2\hat{\gamma}(x_1, x_2)$ becomes:

$$\hat{c}_p(x_1, x_2) = \sigma^2\theta^2 \left[\frac{L_0(x_1, x_2)}{(4+\theta)^{x_1+x_2+2}} + \frac{2}{\pi}\left(\frac{4}{(4+\theta)}\right)^{x_1+x_2+2} \frac{1}{\theta(\theta+8)}\right] \qquad (A12)$$

How accurate is $(A12)$?
One would expect its accuracy to improve as the relative weight of the first terms in series $(A8)$ decreases. This weight is greatest when the series has a fast convergence which happens when a is large. Therefore one expects the accuracy of $(A12)$ to become poorer when θ becomes large; to first order it remains satisfactory even when $\theta \to \infty$ as shown in the discussion that follows Theorem 3. Furthermore using Stirling's formula introduces an error whose magnitude is by $(A9)$ largely independent of x_1, x_2; in relative terms, this error becomes therefore larger when $c_p(x_1, x_2)$ becomes smaller i.e. for large x_1, x_2 values. Having thus pointed out the limitations of the approximation formula, we must emphasize that in fact it constitutes the only way to calculate $c_p(x_1, x_2)$ for x_1, x_2 larger than 10 say, for numerical integration then becomes very difficult:

- in the expression (4.5) the numbers $I_{x_1}(q)$ and $I_{x_2}(q)$ become very large
- in the Fourier expression (4.6) the integration of the rapidly oscillating function becomes rather tricky.

Chapter 4
Empirical evidence about transport costs, price differentials and trade development

The stochastic Enke-Samuelson model that has been developed in the previous chapter brought about a number of specific predictions regarding for instance:

- The variations in price differentials between spatially separated markets with respect to inter-market distances.
- The evolution of price dispersion with respect to transport costs.
- The development of trade as markets become increasingly integrated.

In this chapter our purpose is to describe the crucial features of the transportation business and to confront the predictions of the model with empirical evidence. The examination of price correlations will be postponed until chapter 6 for two reasons. Although price correlations have many advantages over price differentials for measuring market integration (see section 2 of chapter 3) they are of marginal interest to the trader whose profits rather depend upon price differentials. Secondly, the statistical measure of correlation hinges upon the time series characteristics of prices and accordingly it is appropriate to discuss it in Part III devoted to time dependent models.

Trade has to be examined at different levels for it is clearly quite a different business to ship a cargo of wheat from Chicago to Rouen (8000 km) than to haul it from Rouen to Bernay (50 km); between these extremes there is a wide range of intermediate cases. In spite of the diversity in transportation conditions, two facts distinctly emerge: the introduction of railroads and the shift from sail- to steam navigation. Each of these technical mutations brought about an economic revolution by reducing transport costs by a factor of two or three. The railroad revolution was especially important; previously, transportation by road was so expensive and slow that its economic role remained very limited. Although we shall in this chapter mainly focus our attention on wheat (for reasons which have been explained in chapter 1) there are other goods which would deserve attention; pork prices for instance display both interesting cyclical fluctuations and non trivial spatial patterns; the main obstacle in such investigations is the difficulty of finding reliable price and freight series. In section one we examine the evolution of transport costs. In section two, we consider the patterns of spatial price differentials. In section three we examine the implications of the reduction in price differentials; first for the volatility of prices, secondly for the development of trade. In section four we estimate the parameters of the stochastic Enke-Samuelson model.

1 Transportation costs

The difficulty in estimating transportation rates has already been pointed out in chapter 3. It is almost impossible to know the exact cost of shipping (at a given moment) one ton of wheat from Kansas-City to Portland (Oregon). The figures given below should be considered rather as average estimates. We successively examine nineteenth century and twentieth century markets; finally, we sketch the long range evolution of transportation rates.

1.1 European nineteenth century wheat markets

It is in a sense easier to find data about transportation costs in the nineteenth century than it is for present time. The following references proved very helpful in that respect: Engel (1861), Foville (1881), Toutain (1967), Price (1983).

1.1.1 Inter-regional trade

First we discuss the relative importance of waterways, of roads and of railroads in nineteenth century France. Table (4.1) provides an overall picture for the years 1867 and 1896; it highlights the preponderance of railroads for inter-regional trade. Next let us try to estimate transportation rates. One could at first think that railroads may provide the most reliable estimates: since in France there is only one railroad company in each region, is it not sufficient to look at their tariff-books? Unfortunately, there are many different rates. Of course the rates depend on the types of the freight (coal, grains, cattle, etc), and on the speed of transportation, but even for a given product hauled at a given speed, there are different rates: special rates, differential rates, export rates, maximum rates (Foville 1880, p.66). Table 4.2a gives a sample of such rates.
It is plausible that the lowest rates named special rates, which could legally move within large bounds, fluctuated according to demand. Thus, with scarcity turning up in some regions and requiring additional shipping, transportation prices were expected to increase. The elasticity of transportation prices with respect to demand was even greater in the case of transportation by road. Foville (1880, p.63) mentions that during the subsistence crisis of 1847 and 1855, transportation prices by road have been multiplied by a factor ranging from 3 to 5. Even "normal" rates are more difficult to estimate for road than they are for railroads. Table 4.2b gives some indicative figures. As far as waterways are concerned,

	Trade in 1867 billion tonxkm			Trade in 1896 billion tonxkm	
Navigation	4			6.2	
Coastal navigation		2.0			2.0
Waterways		2.0			4.2
Canals			1.2		
Rivers			0.8		
Roads	8				
National roads		1.7			
Regional roads		1.1			
Local roads (including cities)		5.2			
Railroads	8			13.2	
Total	20				

Table 4.1 Relative importance of various means of transportation in France. In spite of the fact that the railroad network had not achieved its full development in 1867, it already played a major role in long and medium range transportations: 8 billion tonxkm as compared to 2.8 for roads and 4.0 for navigation. *Sources: Foville (1880) p.222, 295; Statistique de la Navigation Intérieure 1896, Vol I, Ministère des Travaux Publics. Paris. p.81; Mitchell (1978) p.328.*

the average price is about 2 to 4 centimes/(tonxkm) in the second half of the nineteenth-century (Foville 1880, p.137). This is notably lower than by rail and explains the sustained development of waterways traffic shown in Table 4.1. For cereals however, the average price was rather about 5 centimes/(tonxkm) (Foville 1880, p.138).

To summarize, we shall retain the following orders of magnitude for transportation costs of cereals in the period around 1870.

- transportation by road: 20 centimes/(tonxkm)
- transportation by rail: 7 centimes/(tonxkm)
- transportation by waterway: 5 centimes/(tonxkm)

1.1.2 International trade

Two preliminary observations are in order regarding international sea-trade. The first one again concerns the great variability of freight rates in the course of time (Foville 1880, p.159). Secondly, transportation costs by sea are no longer proportional to distance: in 1879 the freight from Marseilles to Aden is 2.8 centimes/(tonxkm), whereas it is only about 1.1 centimes/(tonxkm) from Marseilles to Yokohama. Such a variability is quite understandable at a time when wind conditions still played a major role. Sometimes the freight rates fell as

	Transportation rate centimes/ tonxkm
Maximum rate for grains, low speed,1875	14
applicable to all companies	
Legal margin for minimum rates, grain, 1867	
Eastern network	2.7 - 8
Northern network	3.4 - 6
Western network	3.3 - 9
Orleans network	2.4 - 8
Southern network	3.0 - 8

Table 4.2a Legal rates for grain transportation. *Source: Foville 1980, p.65, 239.*

	Roads centime/ tonxkm	Rail centime/ tonxkm	Waterw. centime/ tonxkm	Roads centime/ hecx100km	Rail centime/ hecx100km	Waterw. centime/ hecx100km
1800-1824	30			225		
1825-1844	25		3.3	187		24
1845-1854	20	10	3.0	150	75	22
1855-1864	20	8.7	2.6	150	65	19
1865-1874	20	7.5	2.6	150	56	19
1875-1884	17	6.8	2.1	127	51	16
1885-1894	17	6.0	1.5	127	45	11
1895-1904	17	5.4	1.4	127	40	10
1905-1914	15	4.8	1.4	112	36	10
1921-1924	10	5.8	1.0	75	43	7
1925-1934	7	5.0	0.7	52	37	5
1935-1938	8	5.8	0.8	60	43	6

Table 4.2b Average transportation rates. The rates are given in centimes of 1900; the correction for inflation becomes significant after 1900 only. The three columns on the right have been established to facilitate subsequent comparisons with wheat-price differentials; it has been computed on the basis of 1 hectolitre wheat = 0.075 ton. Let us mention that loading and discharching costs b are not included; thus the total transportation cost c over a distance d should be: $c = ad + b$. *Sources: Foville 1980, p.70, 63; Toutain 1967, p.279; Price 1983, p.234, 270.*

low as 0.4 centimes/(tonxkm) for instance between New York and Liverpool; this helps to explain how American wheat could become competitive even on European markets. In Engel (1861) we find an estimate of the transportation cost from Prussia to England which is of special interest for it includes all subsidiary costs occurring from producer to consumer (Table 4.3). Before clos-

	Cost shilling/quarter
Collecting and stocking wheat in Prussia	12
Discharching	1
Insurance	3
Freight	5
Stocking and distributing wheat in England	5
Total	**26**

Table 4.3 Total transportation cost for wheat from Prussia to England about 1860. The total price of 26 shillings represents 12 centimes/tonxkm (on the basis of 1 quarter wheat =0.22 ton, 1sh = 124 French centimes; Seuffert 1857, p. 351). Freight alone represents 2.3 centimes /tonxkm which is consistent with the estimates given in Foville. *Source: Engel (1861), p.289.*

ing this section an additional remark is in order. In Mémoires (1765-1798) an anonymous author observes that after having been kept for a long time in the hold of sea vessels up to Rouen and then in barges from Rouen to Paris, grains usually are in such a bad condition that they have to be given away to the poor people. This raises the question of the transportation time which was of crucial importance not only from the point of view of preserving the quality of goods but also because it conditioned the commercial risks taken by the merchant.

1.2 Twentieth century commodity markets

1.2.1 Inter-regional trade in the United States

As has already been mentioned most transportation contracts are not made public and we can offer but an incomplete picture. The data are summarized in Tables 4.4a,b and in Table 4.5. We may notice that transportation down the Mississippi River is about two or three times cheaper than transportation by rail. Regarding rail rates, a comparison between the lowest rates in Table 4.4a and the rates in Table 4.4b shows that their decrease during the twentieth century has been rather modest.

	Chicago to Baltimore		Chicago to Portland (Maine)	
	1916 cent/ tonx100km	1985 $/ tonx100km	1916 cent/ tonx100km	1985 $/ tonx100km
Local rate				
for domestic use	43	3.0	39	2.7
for exports	38	2.6	29	2.0
Reshipping rate				
for domestic use	31	2.2	31	2.1
for exports	26	1.8	26	1.5

Table 4.4a All-rail freight rates for wheat (carload lots) in the US 1913-1916. The rates are degressive with distance. Chicago-Baltimore: 1000km; Chicago-Portland: 1400km. The conversion has been carried out on the basis of: 1 cent 1916 = 114.4/16.4 cent 1985 (Liesner 1989, p.90). *Source: Zapoleon 1918a, p.18.*

	To Pacific NW ports $/tonx100km	To Texas Gulf ports $/tonx100km
1986	1.63	0.82
1987	1.54	0.78
1988	1.67	0.97
1989	1.66	1.06
Average	**1.62**	**0.90**

Table 4.4b Average rates for rail shipments either to the Pacific coast or to Texas Gulf. The average rate to Pacific ports is $1.62 as compared with $0.90 for shipments to Texas ports. There are several factors which may contribute to this substantial rate difference: 1) Different levels of competition: the Texas Gulf market is served by at least 4 major rail carriers while the Pacific Northwest market is served directly by only 2 carriers. 2) The average train size is much larger in the Texas Gulf market; this provides greater economies of scale and improved rail asset structure. 3) Unlike the Texas Gulf and the southern plains, the upper plains and the Pacific Northwest are separated by a large expanse of mountainous terrain; this can contribute to higher operating costs for carriers. *Source: Interstate Commerce Commission, Carload Waybill Sample.*

I am indebted to Dr. J.D. Norton of the US Department of Agriculture for bringing these figures and their interpretation to my attention.

	Freight rates			Freight rates
	current$/ (tonx100km)	$ of 1980/ (tonx100km)		$ of 1980/ (tonx100km)
1877	0.46	3.34	**1984**	0.42
1878	0.39	3.30	**1985**	0.41
1879	0.40	3.41	**1986**	0.47
1880	0.42	3.23	**1987**	0.58
1881	0.44	3.28	**1988**	0.53
1882	0.44	3.14	**1989**	0.53
1883	0.39	3.00	**1990**	0.46
1884	0.31	2.38	**1991**	0.57

Table 4.5 Navigation rates on the Mississippi River. Grain shipments from St Louis (Missouri) to New Orleans (Louisiana). Navigation rates are about two to three times cheaper than rates for rail shipments. *Source: Transportation Situation. Illinois Dept of Agriculture.*

I am grateful to Dr. J.R. Gonzales of the US Department of Agriculture for pointing these figures to my attention.

1.2.2 International trade

One of the major markets for freight operations is the "Freight Market" at the "Baltic Mercantile and Shipping Exchange" in London. Offers and demands are introduced by the "charterers agents" and the "owner brokers". The resulting rates show dramatic fluctuations (Figure 4.1) with rates being multiplied by a factor of 4 within a couple of years.
Figures for sea-transportation of wheat have already been given in Chapter 1 (Table 1.3). When translated in the units used in Table 4.4a,b, these rates are seen to be of the order of $0.5/(tonx100km). One should keep in mind that such rather low rates are free on board prices and do not therefore include loading and discharging costs. Zapoleon (1918) provides the following figure for ocean freights from New York to Liverpool in 1913: $ 2.12/ton which represents 3.5 cents of 1913/(tonx100km) that is to say: 21 cents of 1976/(tonx100km).

1.3 Long term evolution of transportation costs

A systematic analysis of the long term evolution of transportation costs would be desirable. To our best knowledge it still has to be undertaken. Therefore, in order to link up the twentieth century data with those for the nineteenth century, we have to resort to fragmentary information.

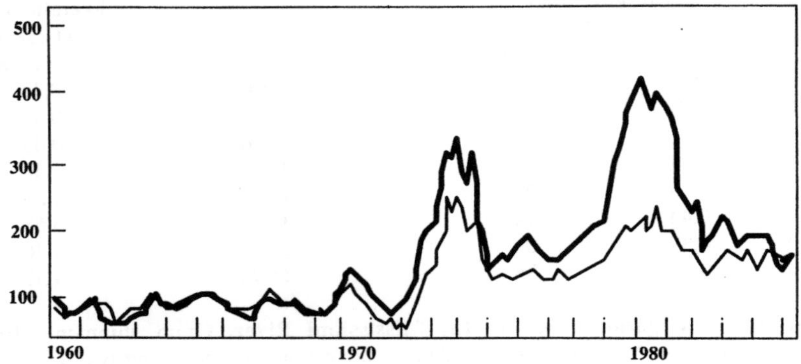

Fig.4.1 Index of ocean-freight rates: 1960-1984. Thick line: time-charter; thin-line: trip-charter. Between 1971 and 1973, the index has been multiplied by a factor of 4: for time-charter it rose from a level of 80 to about 330; the respective figures for trip-charter are 40 and 250. *Source: Norwegian Shipping News, cited in Bauchet (1991).*

1.3.1 Rail and waterways freight rates

For wheat transportation in 1930, Etling (1937, p.79) gives:

4 centimes /(kgx100km)

After adjustment for inflation, we obtain (Liesner 1989, p.184): 45 centimes of 1900/(hectox100km). This is consistent with the figure provided by Toutain (Table 4.2b). Thus, between 1875 and 1930 there has been no price decrease comparable to the rapid decline that occurred from 1845 to 1875.

In the same way let us see how the figures in Table 4.4a (USA 20th century) compare with those in Table 4.2b (France 19th century). This time we have not only to adjust for inflation but also for exchange rates. Fortunately during the nineteenth century exchange rates were fairly stable.

- 1$ of 1885 = 5.1 Fr of 1885 (The Bank of Japan 1966, p.318)
- 1$ of 1986 = 11.2/114 $ of 1885 (Liesner 1989, p.90)

Hence: 1$ of 1986/(tonx100km)= 0.37 Fr of 1885 /(hectox100km). Needless to say such monetary conversions which cover a whole century may be fraught with some uncertainties. For instance the exchange rate is determined by other factors than just the cost of living; the volume and structure of trade must be taken into consideration. Nonetheless, it appears that the decrease in transportation costs has been slower after 1913 than between 1850 and 1913.

Fig.4.2 is an attempt to provide an overall view of the evolution of rail freight rates. It relies on two series: one for Germany and another for the United States.

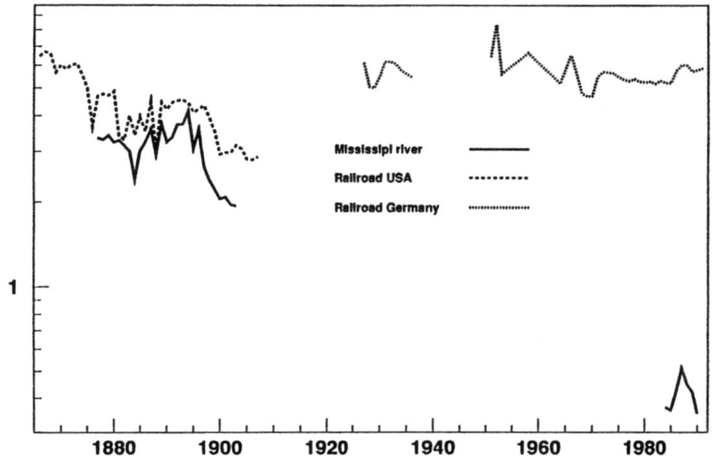

Fig.4.2 a Railroad freights and waterways freights. The vertical scale is logarithmic and is expressed in dollars of 1980 per (tonx100 km). *Sources: Mississippi river: Statistical Abstract of the US; Transportation situation, Illinois Dept of Agriculture. Railroad USA: Statistical Abstract of the US; Interstate Commerce Commission. Carload Waybill Sample. Railroad Germany: Statistisches Jahrbuch für das deutsche Reich; Statistisches Jahrbuch für die Bundesrepublik Deutschland.*

The German series shows almost constant freight rates from 1927 to 1990; in the United States, on the contrary there has been a substantial fall. Although the specifications of the series are somewhat different (in terms of weight and distance of shipment), their difference is large enough to be of significance. Figure 4.2 and Table 4.5 give a hint as to the evolution of freight rates for wheat on the Mississippi river. Because of the outstanding importance of this route for US agricultural exports, the sharp decrease that has occurred between World War I and present is of great economic moment.

1.3.2 Ocean freight rates

Let us set side by side three figures (converted in US cents) on diminishing ocean freight:

- 1879 (Foville 1880, see above) 240 cents of 1976/(tonx100km)
- 1913 (Zapoleon 1918, p.17) 21 cents of 1976/(tonx100km)
- 1976 (World Wheat Statistics 1987) 15 cents of 1976/(tonx100km)

In 1879 sail navigation still predominated over steam navigation: when expressed in tonnage the ratio was 3 to 1. The dramatic decline in freight which occurred between 1879 and 1913 resulted from the shift to steam navigation; after 1913 the decrease slowed down. One should of course keep in mind that ocean freights fluctuate greatly; fortunately, 1879, 1913 and 1979 were rather "normal" years. Freight series for the period before World War I have been published by Isserlis (1938) and by North (1958); a rather complete review of standard freight series up to 1913 is given in Harley (1990). Fig.1.5a,b (chapter 1) displays the long range evolution of ocean freight rates. As both series are drawn from completely independent sources, their comparison provides a useful overall check.

1.3.3 Tariffs

In this book we are only occasionally concerned with international trade. This is why we usually give but limited attention to the evolution of tariff levels. Here is a short account of this important question. Schematically five different periods can be distinguished. The 17th and 18th centuries saw the growth of mercantilist policies which were based on the concept that one nation can increase its trade only at the expense of other nations. A typical illustration of the mercantilist spirit is the famous English Navigation act of 1651; it prohibited the import of goods of non-European origin unless transported in ships flying the English flag; the Navigation Act lingered on until 1849. By the end of the 18th century Adam Smith and the French economists known as Physiocrats demanded liberty of trade. The Anglo-French trade agreement of 1786 was a first step in that direction. Between 1860 and 1885 the duties[1]on French wheat imports were about 5%. The Anglo-trade agreement of 1860 marked the triumph for liberal ideas but is was soon followed by a period of restrictive policies. In the United States the McKinley Tariff Act (1890) was ultra-protectionist. Germany too progressively adopted a protectionist policy: it increased its rates for wheat from about 5% in 1879, to 13% in 1885 and 30% in 1887. But on average the protectionism of the last quarter of the 19th century was mild by comparison with the mercantilist policies that have been common in the 17th and 18th century and were to be revived between the two world wars. From 1933 onward, the recommendations of all the postwar conferences based on the fundamental postulates of economic liberalism were ignored; mercantilist policies dominated the world scene until after World War II. The General Agreement on Tariffs and Trade (GATT) was signed on October 30, 1947 by 23 countries. Under GATT a series of conferences have been organized for the purpose of lowering trade barriers. In the United States the Trade Expansion Act of 1962 authorized tariff reductions of up to 50 percent, subject to reciprocal concessions from the European partners. This marked a fundamental shift away from the traditional protectionist posture of the United States and led to the co-called Kennedy

[1]For an hectolitre of wheat imported in April 1887 from New York to Le Havre the decomposition of the price is the following: purchase price in New York: 13.52F, freight rate: 2.20F (16%), duty: 5%, insurance: 1.8% (Grande Encyclopédie 1887).

Round negotiations in the GATT.

2 The spatial patterns of price differentials

Keeping the former figures in mind we can now turn to the analysis of spatial price differentials. One important issue will be the following. If trade can be thought of as operating through a chain structure as in the models of chapter 3, the spatial price differential between two markets A and B should be smaller than the transportation cost $C(A, B)$ from A to B:

$$|p_A - p_B| < C(A, B)$$

If, on the contrary, p_A and p_B are fixed in a single arbitrage operation, then the price differential should be approximately equal to the transportation cost:

$$|p_A - p_B| \simeq C(A, B)$$

2.1 European nineteenth-century wheat markets

2.1.1 Comparison between the evolution of price differentials and of transportation costs

According to the spatial price equilibrium model there should be a clear-cut deterministic relation between price differentials and transport cost. Such a relationship cannot be observed however. The fact that a stochastic model has to be used is shown by Table 4.6 and by Figure 4.3a,b. These figures are illustrative of a much larger sample. The markets in Fig.4.3a,b have been chosen with a view to discussing the impact of the railroad revolution on price differences: Bordeaux and Angoulême were connected to the railroad network as early as 1854, while the construction of the line between Avignon and Digne was delayed until the end of the nineteenth century. Yet there is no clear evidence that the Bordeaux-Angoulême price gap narrowed significantly after 1854. Furthermore the Avignon-Digne price-difference seems to be higher (probably because the area is mountainous) regardless of whether we consider the pre-or post-railroad period. Such observations again point out that the impact of the railroad revolution, whereas well marked at a global level, is somewhat obscured at the level of individual markets. Would the markets be perfectly efficient, then any price difference larger than the transportation cost should at once be levelled off. The Bordeaux-Angoulême market pair shows so many "exceptional" years that it seems difficult to attribute them to temporary under-estimation of transportation costs.

	Distance from Lille	January 1847 Price	Differ.	July 1847 Price	Differ.	January 1900 Price	Differ.
	km	cent.	cent.	cent.	cent.	cent.	cent.
Lille	0	30 80	0	39 30	0	15 00	0
Arras	50	29 03	1 77	35 19	4 11	13 81	1 19
Nantes	500	31 05	35	30 57	8 73	13 75	1 25
Lyon	550	31 00	20	23 29	16 01	13 94	1 06
Bordeaux	700	30 20	60	27 75	11 55	14 25	75

Table 4.6 Prices and price differentials between Lille and four other wheat markets at three different dates. These dates have been selected so as to provide examples of high as well as of low prices. In January 1847 and in January 1900 the price gap between Lille and Arras (50 km apart) is larger than the differential between Lille and Bordeaux (700 km). Likewise the differential between Lyon and Bordeaux (450 km) is smaller or of the same order than the differential between Lille and Arras. *Source: Drame et al (1991).*

2.1.2 Methodology for the observation of price differentials

In the previous paragraph we have seen that for a regular pattern to emerge local conditions must be averaged out. In studying the variations of price differentials with respect to intermarket distances we shall make use of a grouping technique which is standard in nonlinear regression analysis: the pairs of markets will be sorted according to their spacings and arranged in successive batches. For the curve of the price differential with respect to distance to be defined with adequate precision, it should be specified by about 20 or 30 points. Furthermore, it appears that about 30 to 40 market-pairs should be used in each batch in order to smooth out the statistical fluctuations of local conditions. Thus we should work with a total of about 800 market pairs; this corresponds to a sample of 40 markets. In general annual prices lead to neater results than do monthly or fortnight prices. This should be no surprise; in fact, it could hardly be expected that arbitrage between two distant markets could be set into effect within such short delays. Among the samples to be analysed subsequently only three truly meet the above specifications. They concern the French nineteenth-century wheat market and the twentieth-century wheat and potato markets in the United States. We shall also occasionally use some other less optimal data sets.

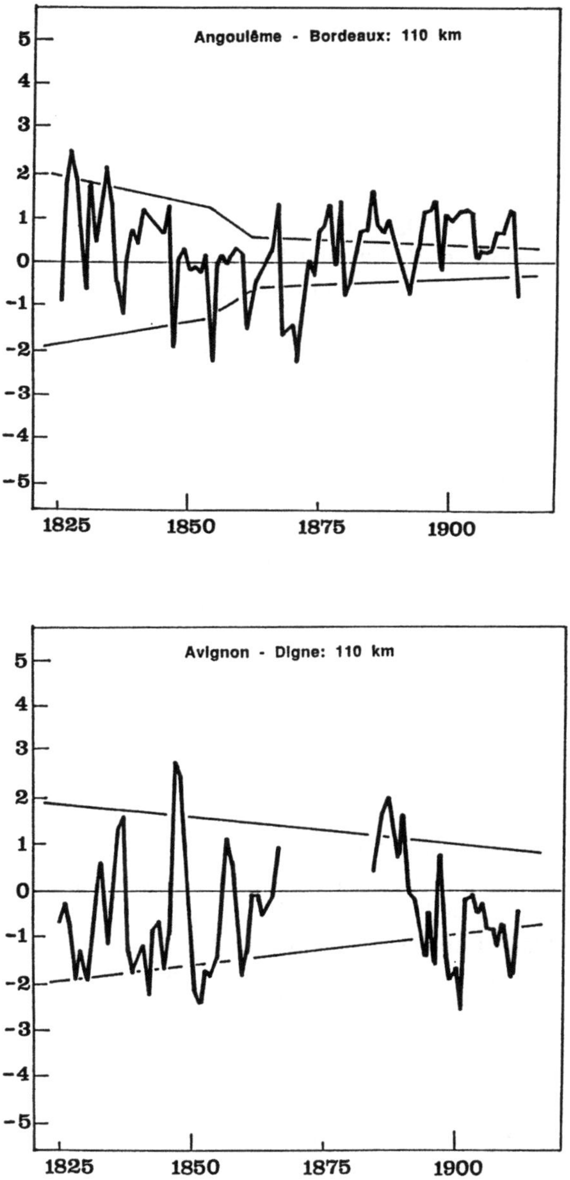

Fig.4.3. a,b Annual price differentials at the regional level in nineteenth-century France. The decrease in the differential after the connection of Angoulême and Bordeaux to the railroad network in 1855 came about very gradually. *Source: Drame et al (1991).*

2.1.3 Price differentials at the regional level

The analysis of price differentials between markets which are relatively close to each other is interesting for two reasons. Firstly , it will give us some estimates about loading and discharging costs. Secondly, it will throw some light on the transition between transportation by road and transportation by rail: the former is the rule over distances smaller than 50 km, whereas transportation by rail predominates for distances over 150 or 200 km (see Section 1.1). Two ranges of distances have been investigated:

• Distances between 10 km and 80 km: see Fig.4.4a,b. Because the samples of markets are rather small price differentials have been displayed for every market pair. In such a small area weather conditions are likely to be fairly similar; accordingly the price differentials in Fig.4.4a,b are largely to be attributed to non climatic factors. Furthermore, at a time when regional traditions were important the dispersion in cultivated wheat varieties could be considered as being negligible in such a limited region. By the way let us emphasize that even for larger areas the component of price differentials to be attributed to differences in wheat varieties probably remains small; indeed the price records (Archives nationales $F^{11*}1779-2678$) do not differentiate between wheat varieties; the only distinction concerns "old" grains (i.e.from last year crop) versus "new" grains (i.e. current year crop). Estimation of the regression lines yields the following results:

1) Nord 1855 — 7.2 ± 1.5 Fr/(hecto x100km)
2) Côtes d'Armor 1855 — 3.2 ± 1.0 Fr/(hecto x100km)

These figures turn out to be rather high in comparison with transport costs. The reason is probably related to the fact that we used "instantaneous" (fortnight) prices while subsequent results refer to prices averaged over longer time spans.

• Distances between 30 km and 300 km; two samples have been analysed: one for Brittany (Fig.4.5), the other for Bavaria. Both samples do not really meet the requirements listed above: The Brittany prices are fortnight (January 1-15) prices, (instead of annual averages); the Bavaria prices are annual prices but the sample contains only 10 markets. Their comparison nevertheless is informative. In the limit of small inter-market distances the price-gap in either case ranges between 0.40 and 0.80 French Francs. If this figure is taken as an estimate of fixed costs (loading, discharging, storing, etc) we see that it represents a substantial amount of the total transportation cost over short distances. Furthermore estimating the slopes of the regression lines leads to the following results:

1) Bavaria 1815 — 1.11 Fr/(hecto x100km)
2) Bavaria 1841 — 0.74 Fr/(hecto x100km)
3) Brittany 1855 — 0.81 Fr/(hecto x100km)
4) Bavaria 1875 — 0.46 Fr/(hecto x100km)

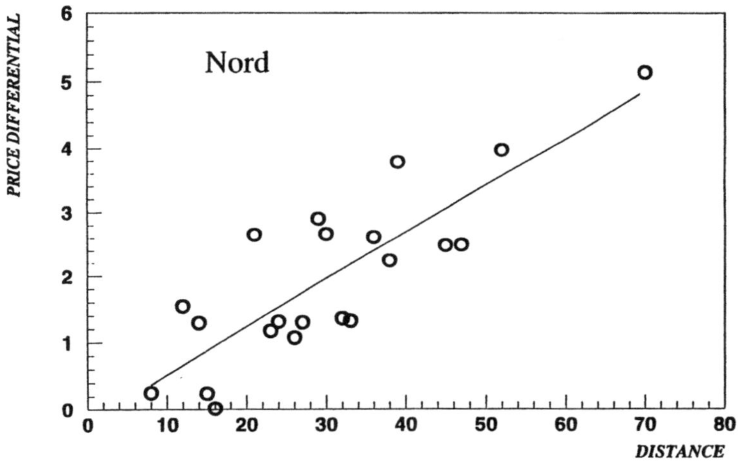

Fig.4.4a Price differentials within the district "Nord"(France). Horizontal scale: distance in kilometres; vertical scale: price differential in French francs. The prices refer to the first fortnight of January 1855. The coefficient of correlation is equal to 0.83. *Source: Archives Nationales, Paris, F^{11*}* 1779 – 2678.

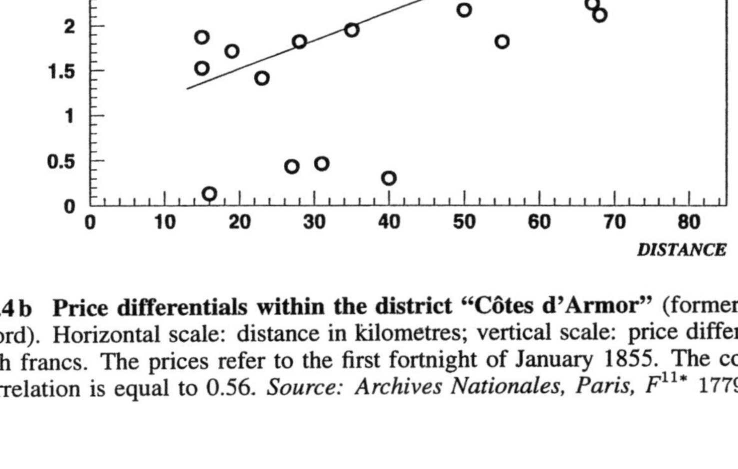

Fig.4.4b Price differentials within the district "Côtes d'Armor" (formerly Côtes du Nord). Horizontal scale: distance in kilometres; vertical scale: price differential in French francs. The prices refer to the first fortnight of January 1855. The coefficient of correlation is equal to 0.56. *Source: Archives Nationales, Paris, F^{11*}* 1779 – 2678.

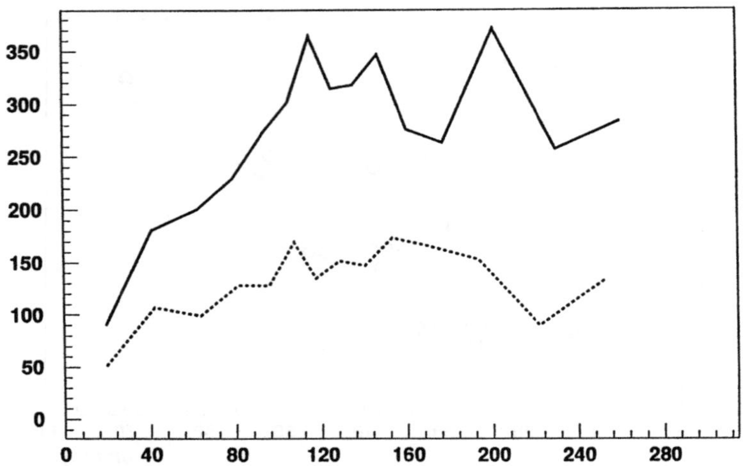

Fig.4.5 Wheat-price differentials as a function of distance in nineteenth-century Brittany. Solid line: 1855, dashed line: 1875. Horizontal scale: kilometre. Vertical scale: centime/hectolitre The sample includes 31 markets; prices are fortnight prices (January 1-15; differentials are averaged over 30 market-pairs. *Source: Archives Nationales, Paris,* F^{11*} 1779 – 2678.

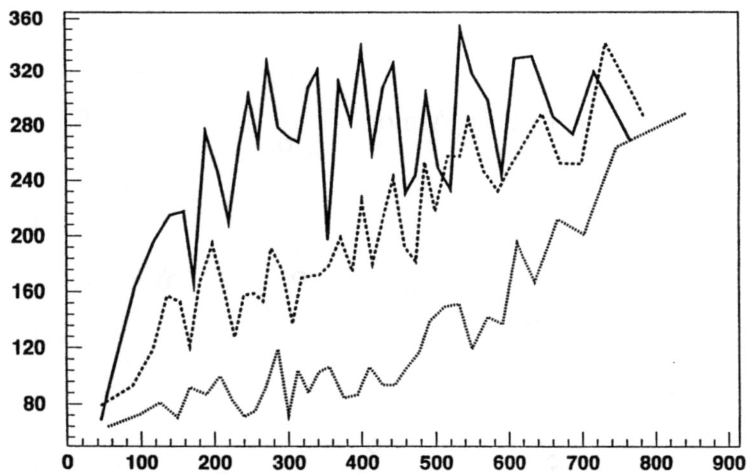

Fig.4.6 Wheat price differentials as a function of distance in nineteenth-century France. Solid line: 1825, dashed line: 1858, dotted line: 1908. Horizontal scale: kilometre. Vertical scale: centime/hectolitre The sample includes 51 markets; differentials are averaged over 30 market-pairs. The decrease in transportation costs may account for the global decline in the value of the differentials; yet it does not explain the dramatic change in the concavity of the curve. *Source: Drame et al (1991).*

In Bavaria the railroad was introduced in the years 1850-1855 (Seuffert 1857, p.414) and about twenty years later in Brittany (Price 1983, p.217). The first three figures are somewhat smaller than the rate of transportation by road while the third is smaller than an average between road and rail rates.

2.1.4 Price differentials at the national level

The theoretical price differential curves (Fig.3.4d, 3.9, 3.12) are asymptotically increasing towards a limit. One point at issue in this paragraph is to examine whether the larger range of inter-market distances which we consider here will permit this limiting value to be determined. The data set we shall consider is ideally suited to our needs. It has been published in Drame et al (1991). The number of markets ($\sim$ 50) is adequate and the data cover a span of time which encompasses the railroad revolution. The main results are summarized in Fig.4.6. The most conspicuous feature is the decrease in the course of time of the price differentials for each distance interval. In spite of the random fluctuations, the asymptotic trend is clearly visible on the 1825 curve. It is somewhat less marked for the 1858 curve; but it is the 1908 curve which is the most surprising: its concavity turns out to be oriented in the wrong direction. The year 1908 is in no ways an "exceptional" year: the same phenomenon can be observed in almost any year between 1900 and 1913 and year after year it becomes more apparent.
How may we explain this curious feature? One may remember that there are three parameters in the model: the cost of transportation t, a parameter a related to the elasticities of offer and demand, and the spacing between successive markets. An increase in the average inter-market distance has the effect of pushing up the asymptotic limit. This idea is supported by the fact that between 1825 and 1913 the number of active markets diminished regularly. Between 1825 and 1895 for instance it decreased from 871 to 540 (Drame et al 1991, p.62) and after 1900 this decrease became even more pronounced. This effect may account for the high asymptotic limit of the price differentials but their unexpected concavity still remains a mystery.

The second example we shall present in this paragraph is rather a counter-example in the sense mathematicians give to this word: we shall see that if the prices are not real (free) market prices then price differentials do not display the expected pattern. This example concerns the distribution of rye prices in Sweden. Series of rye prices have been thoroughly edited by Lennart Jörberg along with the price-series of many other products in his "History of prices in Sweden: 1732-1914" (1972). These prices are "price scales" rather than market prices. What is meant by this expression is best explained by L.Jörberg himself (p.8,11). Taxes were originally payable by means of commodities. Gradually the need to fix cash values of these commodities became increasingly urgent and

price scales became accepted as the method by which these cash values were determined. The procedure of assessment of price scales underwent several changes in the course of time. In 1815 it was decided that at the parish meeting one or two members of the parish should be chosen in order that, in cooperation with the High Bailiff, they could establish the price which could be used for price assessment in the jurisdictional district. This price should be the average of the current price for each parish issued by the parish representatives. There were however departures from a strict average calculation at the level of the deputies who, with a knowledge of "general economic conditions" were able to adjust the prices sot that they reflected "actual prices". What the real impact of these adjustments was is of course a critical issue.
We have analysed the spatial distribution of rye prices for the three years 1805, 1855 and 1905. They have a similar increasing trend; their regression slopes is summarized in Table 4.7. The increase rate of price differentials with distance

	Increase rate of price differential kronor/ (hectox100km)	**Increase rate of price differential** centimes/ (hectox100km)
1805	3.3	4.7
1855	7.0	9.8
1905	7.7	10.8

Table 4.7 Increase rates of the differentials of rye prices in Sweden. The reason why these increase rates are about 3 to 10 times smaller than in France or in Bavaria may be found in the fact that the prices are not true market prices. The conversion to French centimes has been made on the basis of 1 kronor = 1.39 French Franc (Földes 1905 , p.490). *Source: Jörberg (1972).*

happens to be three to ten times smaller than in France or in Bavaria. For instance in 1858 we have in France a figure of 32 centimes/(hectox100km). A hint about how to resolve this apparently paradoxical situation can be got by imagining that the adjustment of prices carried out by the deputies have had the effect of smoothing out spatial price differences.

2.1.5 Price differentials at the international level

What makes international trade interesting in our perspective is the possibility opened by foreign commerce statistics to confront price differentials with the resulting trade flows. Unfortunately the data at our disposal at the international level are rather scanty. One such set of data is given in Appendix B. It may be remembered that in the linear Enke-Samuelson model we assumed a linear relationship to hold between price differentials and resulting trade. For wheat exchanges between Prussia and England, the linear correlation coefficient turns out to be $r = -0.62$; this gives some plausibility to the linear assumption.

The second piece of evidence we would like to present concerns nine European markets, namely: Arnheim (Netherlands), Berlin, Hamburg, Köln, Königsberg (Kaliningrad), Leipzig, Mannheim, München, Odessa (Ukraine). Although many of these markets are inside the nineteenth-century borders of Germany, they fairly well cover most of Central Europe. The resulting distribution of price differentials is shown in Fig.4.7 for the period 1861-1896. In spite of the

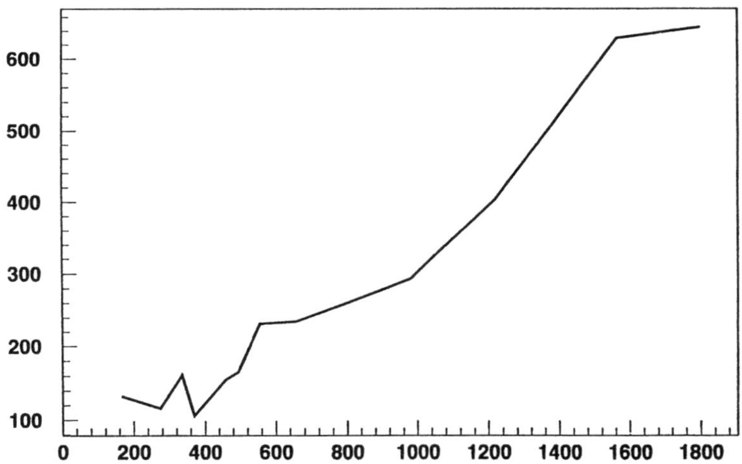

Fig.4.7 Rye-price differentials as a function of distance in Central Europa, 1861-1900. Horizontal scale: kilometre. Vertical scale: 0.1 Mark/ton. The sample includes 9 markets: six within the 1992 border of Germany + Arnheim(Netherlands) + Kaliningrad(Poland) + Odessa (Ukraine). Differentials are averaged over 3 market-pairs. The curve represents an average over the period 1861-1900 which saw an increase in tariffs due to overall over-production. *Source: Jacobs and Richter (1935).*

large range of distances covered, there is no asymptotic limit to be observed. This however, is scarcely surprising because the tariffs on wheat and rye imports increased after 1865, not only between Germany and foreign countries but even between Prussia and other parts of Germany (Jacobs and Richter 1935, p.281).

2.2 Twentieth-century commodity markets

2.2.1 Wheat market in the United States

In Europe the consumption centers are disseminated among production areas. Such a pattern strongly contrasts with that in the US where the production areas are separated from the large consumption centers of the East and West coasts. One could then expect a simpler price pattern to hold, with low prices occurring in the productive regions and higher prices prevailing in urban areas. Table 4.8a lists the States where the lowest, respectively highest, prices occurred. While

Year	Lowest price	cents/ bushel	Highest price	cents/ bushel
1871-1875	Nebraska	66	South Carolina	174
1882-1886	Nebraska	57	Maine	130
1891-1895	North Dakota	49	South Carolina	95
1901-1905	Nebraska	62	South Carolina	108
1911-1915	Idaho	72	Alabama	120
1951	Montana	196	Michigan	221
1961	Pennsylvania	171	North Dakota	226
1971	Wyoming	114	West Virginia	157
1981	New York	321	Washington	392

Table 4.8a Locations of lowest (respectively highest) wheat prices in the United States. With the notable exceptions of 1961 and 1981, the lowest price in general occurs in States belonging to the wheat belt. The location of the maximum is more fluctuating. *Sources: 1871 - 1915: Zapoleon (1918a); 1951 - 1981: Langley (1989).*

the minimum is most often located in the wheat belt, the position of the maxima is rather changing. We next turn to the spatial analysis of price differentials. Are the data provided by the US Department of Agriculture adequate for that purpose? They give the average price paid to producers for every State except the smallest North Eastern States. The uncertainties come from the very definition of the inter-market distances for the prices are averaged over extended areas some of which, such as Texas for instance, may be even larger than France. Fig.4.8a shows the curve of price differentials with respect to distance. In the (100 km, 2000 km) range, it increases almost linearly with a slope of about 21 cents/(tonx100km), a figure which, as expected, is somewhat lower than the average freight rate. Between 2000 km and 3500 km, the growth rate decreases.

2.2.2 Potato market in the United States

While of modest value in total agricultural output (and even of less importance in international trade), potatoes are a crop of great interest for the analysis of spatial

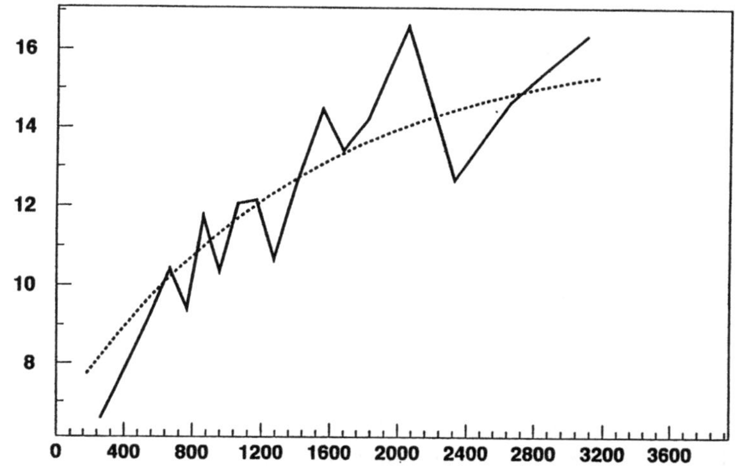

Fig.4.8 a Wheat price differentials as a function of distance in the United States, 1951-1981. Solid line: observations; dashed line: Enke-Samuelson model. Horizontal scale: kilometre. Vertical scale: cent/bushel The sample includes 34 States. Differentials are averaged over 30 market-pairs. The solid curve is an average over the years 1951,1961,1971,1981. The theoretical curve corresponds to the following parameters: ratio of transportation cost to excess-supply slope = 0.030, standard deviation of local shocks = 41 cents/bushel, average inter-market distance = 177 km. *Source: Langley (1989).*

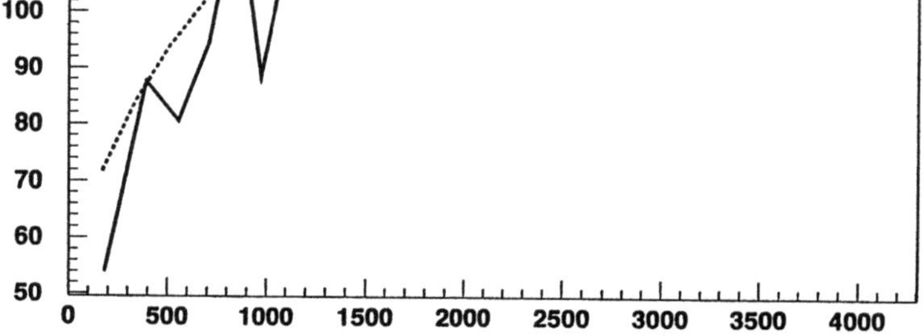

Fig.4.8 b Potato price differentials as a function of distance in the United States, 1951-1981. Solid line: observations; dashed line: Enke-Samuelson chain model. Horizontal scale: kilometre. Vertical scale: cent/centweight The sample includes 35 States. Differentials are averaged over 30 market-pairs. The solid curve is an average over the years 1951,1961,1971,1981. The theoretical curve corresponds to the following parameters: ratio of transportation cost to excess-supply slope = 0.12, standard deviation of local shocks = 216 cents/centweight, average inter-market distance = 170 km. *Source: Lucier et al (1991)*

interactions; indeed, by comparison with wheat, potatoes have a comparatively low value per ton. In 1961 the average US price of wheat was (Langley 1989, p.5):

$$\$ \ 1.8/\text{bushel} \simeq \$ \ 67/\text{ton}$$

whereas the average price of potatoes was (Lucier 1991):

$$\$ \ 1.36/\text{hundredweight} = \$ \ 26/\text{ton}$$

In 1981, the corresponding figures are:

wheat: $\$ 3.7/\text{bushel} \simeq \$ 135/\text{ton}$ potatoes: $\$ 5.4/\text{cwt} = \$ 106/\text{ton}$

Thus, the value of potatoes per unit of weight ranges between 38% and 78% of the value of wheat. There are other differences between the two products.

- Whereas the US are one of the major wheat exporting countries, they neither exports nor imports potatoes. In 1981 the exports amounted to 0.17 million ton and the imports to 0.11 million ton; these figures are negligible when compared to a total production of 17 millions tons (Lucier 1991, p.11,105).
- Because there may be four different potato crops (spring, summer, fall and winter), potatoes are grown in almost every region (even in Alaska!). As a result the production is more evenly distributed throughout the country than the production of wheat. Table 4.8b parallels Table 4.8a by listing the occurrences

Year	**Lowest price**	cents/ cwt	**Highest price**	cents/ cwt
1951	New-Jersey	178	Connecticut	368
1961	Wahington	98	Illinois 295	
1971	North Dakota	123	Tennessee	415
1981	South Dakota	365	Louisiana	1170

Table 4.8b Locations of lowest (respectively highest) potato prices in the United States. A comparison with Table 4.8 shows at once that in relative terms the spatial dispersion of prices is more than two times larger. *Source: Lucier et al (1991).*

of lowest and highest prices.

To summarize, one would expect the incentive to trade potatoes to be significantly smaller than in the case of wheat. This is indeed confirmed by the price differential curve shown in Fig.4.8b. Its increase is almost linear for distances up to 1400 km, with a slope of about 95 cents/(tonx100km), instead of 23 cents/(tonx100km) for wheat. For distances above 1400 km, the price differentials converge to a limiting value of about 130 cents/cwt = $ 25/ton as compared to $ 16/ton in the case of wheat. The same kind of conclusion can be drawn from the comparison of wheat and potato markets in Germany during the nineteenth century (Roehner 1989a).

2.3 Is the spatial distribution of prices Gaussian?

Time distributions of stock-prices are known to be approximately lognormal (Fama 1965). So are time distributions of wheat prices (Roehner 1990b). What about the *spatial* distribution of prices? As a first guess one could expect it to be less leptokurtic than the time distribution. Indeed the skewness of the latter is mainly a consequence of the existence of huge price peaks; while possibly triggered by adverse climatic conditions, these peaks build up as a result of speculative storage. Whereas speculative storage just requires a definite selling- and buying-strategy spatial arbitrage requires a real*transfer* of goods[2], an operation which is much more demanding. Before analysing specific price series, we shall review statistical tests for departure from normality.

2.3.1 χ^2 test versus cumulant tests

A number of goodness-of-fit tests have been designed specifically for the normal distribution. Because the question of testing the normal distribution is of central importance in price theory, we shall devote this paragraph to a comparison of two kinds of tests:

- Pearson's standard χ^2 test
- A cumulant test (D'Agostino 1986, p. 377, 388) based on the coefficients of skewness and kurtosis:

$$b_1 = m_3/m_2^{3/2}; \qquad b_2 = m_4/m_2^2$$

In the various cumulant tests statistical variables are devised which, in the null hypothesis (H_0) that the distribution is normal, have a known distribution or converge towards a known distribution. For instance in the Z_1, Z_2 tests which we shall use subsequently the Z_1, Z_2 variables are respectively associated with b_1 and b_2; under the null hypothesis they may be approximated by a normal $N(0,1)$ variable. The Z_1 test is claimed to be appropriate for samples larger than 8; for the Z_2 test the size of the sample should not be less than 20.

For the purpose of comparing the powers of both tests, one would have to analyse their operating characteristics which implies a large number of iterations. We shall be somewhat less ambitious and restrict our comparison to a given confidence level. Table 4.9 establishes a comparison between the performances of the χ^2 test and those of the Z_1, Z_2 tests for a confidence level of 0.95. The Z_1, Z_2 tests can be said to be more selective since they achieve better results at the level of errors of the second kind. From a computational point of view they have the advantage of not requiring any subdivision of the sample into classes

[2]We discard future markets; they appeared only in the late 19th century and for the period we are investigating here their influence is probably negligible

	Error of the first kind Rejecting a distribution which is normal	Error of the second kind Accepting as normal a distribution which is not		
		Lognormal	**χ^2(l=4)**	**Johnson(0,2)**
χ^2 Test	5%	0%	0%	35%
Z_1 Test	5%	0%	0%	50%
Z_2 Test	15%	0%	0%	30%
Z_1 Test + Z_2 Test	20%	0%	0%	20%

Table 4.9 Comparison of statistical tests of the normal distribution. The Johnson (0,2) distribution has a shape which is rather similar to the normal distribution: unlike the lognormal and the χ^2 distributions, it is symmetric; this explains that the asymmetry test Z_1 performs rather poorly. The size of the sample is 150; the number of iterations is equal to 20; the confidence level is 0.95 (the Z_2 test is somewhat out of bounds due to statistical fluctuations).

as does the χ^2 test. In the next paragraph we use the Z_1, Z_2 tests to analyse the spatial distribution of prices.

2.3.2 The spatial distribution of prices

Once a statistical test of reasonable efficiency has been selected the next step is to pick up a sample of adequate size. The larger the sample the most conclusive the test. Figure 4.9 shows the histograms of two samples of 250 prices for the years 1855 and 1875. They immediately appear as being very dissimilar; in fact he normal hypothesis is accepted in 1855 ($Z_1 = 0.15; Z_2 = 0.056$) while it is sharply rejected in 1875 ($Z_1 = 5.6; Z_2 = 2.1$). When testing the lognormal distribution instead, we still get acceptance in 1855; for the year 1875 the skewness is reduced ($Z_1 = 4.42$ instead of $Z_1 = 5.6$) but the H_0 hypothesis is rejected.

We now turn to the examination of a larger number of smaller samples. Table 4.10 summarizes the results. Unfortunately one has the same inconclusiveness as before. Nonetheless, the assumption of a normal spatial distribution of prices does not appear altogether unreasonable.

3 The reduction in spatial price differentials and its implications

The spatial equalization of commodity prices is of major economic importance in many respects. Its implications for factor price equalization are well known. Let us briefly recall the standard argument. Let falling transport costs and declining tariff barriers tend to equalize prices of traded commodities. Countries

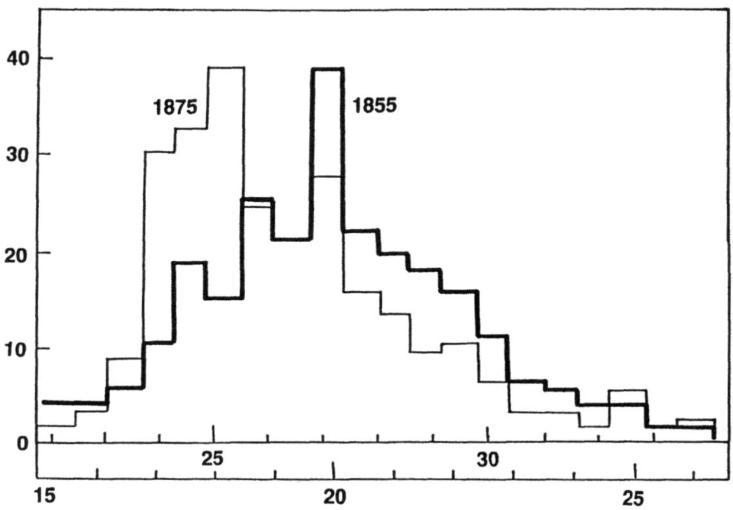

Fig.4.9 Histograms of wheat prices on 250 markets in nineteenth-century France. Thick line: 1855, thin line: 1875. Horizontal scales: franc/hectolitre, upper scale: 1855, lower scale: 1875. Vertical scale: frequency. The 1855 histogram is consistent with a normal distribution, while the 1875 histogram is not. *Source: Archives Nationales, Paris,* F^{11*}1779 – 2678.

will now export more of the goods which exploit their favourable factor endowment. An illustration is provided by the "New World invasion of grains" (O'Rourke and Williamson 1992): by 1870 Europe had plenty of labor and little land while America had the opposite. Accordingly America had low land rents (and high real wages) while Europe had the opposite. Responding to the growing, export-driven demand for grains, land rents tended to rise in America and to decrease in Europe[3]. For short, commodity price equalization tends to produce factor price equalization. This is in substance the content of Samuelson's price equalization theorem (Samuelson 1948, 1954) although the theory is ambiguous about how fast the process takes place and how far it proceeds. In this section we shall rather be interested in microeconomic implications namely its impact on the volatility of prices and its significance for the development of trade.

[3]In the late 20th century a similar evolution is to be observed in Europe: due to the lowering of agricultural tariffs, there is an extension of land left fallow land which implies a reduction in land rent.

	Normality				Lognormality			
	Yes	No	Z1	Z2	Yes	No	Z1	Z2
France, wheat 250 markets, 1855	1	0	1.5	0.56	1	0	0.02	0.15
France, wheat 250 markets, 1875	0	1	5.6	2.1	0	1	4.42	1.41
France, wheat 51 markets, 89 years	45	44	1.60	2.41	58	31	1.19	1.93
USA, wheat 34 States, 4 years	2	2	2.33	1.65	1	3	2.37	1.79
USA, potato 34 States, 4 years	2	2	1.71	0.89	3	1	0.86	1.78

Table 4.10 Testing normality versus lognormality of the spatial distribution of prices. The tests are performed with a 95% level of significance for every single year. Z_1 and Z_2 are N(0,1) random variables respectively corresponding to skewness and to kurtosis; the table shows their average values over time; the critical value for rejection is 1.96.

3.1 Evidence of long term price convergence

The process of market integration has two facets: the decrease in the spatial price dispersion and the related trade increase. Theoretical predictions have been given for both evolutions in the framework of the Enke-Samuelson model. In this section, we investigate the most obvious of both phenomena, namely the dispersion decrease.

3.1.1 How to measure spatial price dispersion?

The most standard measure of dispersion is of course the standard deviation σ. In the case of market prices p_k, their differences have such a strong intuitive appeal that one may be tempted to use alternative measures of dispersion which are rather based on variates differences, as for instance (Kendall et al 1987):

1) **The mean difference**

$$\Delta = \frac{2}{n(n-1)} \sum_{k<l} |p_k - p_l|$$

2) **The range (largest price difference)**

$$R = \max |p_k - p_l|$$

The relations between σ, Δ and R are examined in Appendix A. One has for instance the following inequality:

$$\Delta \leq (2/\sqrt{3})\sigma$$

As a rule σ and Δ lead to rather similar results while R is obviously very sensitive to the possible occurrence of a few outliers. The range has been used for the purpose of analysing market integration in Drame (1991, p.97,98). In this section, we shall use the standard deviation.

3.1.2 Spatial price convergence

To make contact with the predictions of the Enke-Samuelson model, we should analyse the spatial standard deviation of prices as a function of transportation costs. This is scarcely feasible however because transportation costs fluctuate a great deal and our information about them is anyway too scanty. Thus we shall take time as the independent variable; in so doing we should keep in mind that the decrease in transportation costs is not a linear function of time. The evidence accumulated in Section 1 shows that it rather goes through a succession of periods of acceleration or of slowdown .
Spatial price convergence in the period 1820-1914 has been documented by many authors. Let us mention for instance: Dupriez et al (1966), Drame et al (1991), Williamson (1992), Ljungberg (1993); Fig.4.10 provides still an other

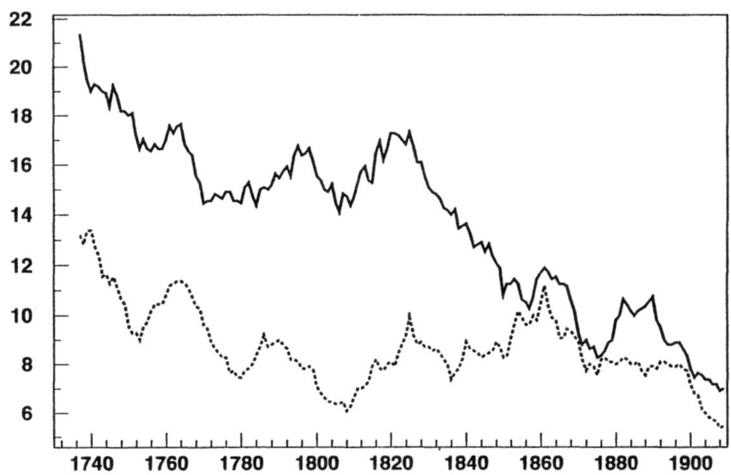

Fig.4.10 Spatial price convergence in Sweden. Solid line: rye; dashed line: wheat. Vertical scale: spatial coefficient of variation. The interesting point in this chart is the fact that, in contrast to rye, wheat does not exhibit any clear spatial price convergence. Why? The question remains open. The figures for rye are based on a number of regions which varies between 19 and 30; the figures for wheat are based on a number of regions which varies between 11 and 23. *Source: Jörberg (1972, p.632-636).*

example for this period[4]. However, to our best knowledge, the extension of this study to present time has rarely been considered. Figure 4.11 is an attempt

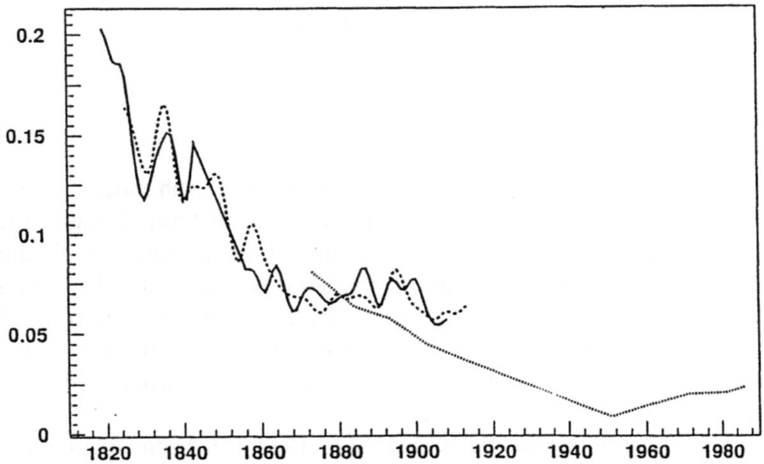

Fig.4.11 Decrease trend in the spatial dispersion of the logarithms of wheat prices. Solid line: Germany, 1790-1913; dashed line: France, 1825-1913; dotted line: USA, 1873-1986. Vertical scale: differences of logarithms of prices. The sample includes 5 markets for Germany, 51 markets for France and 31 States for the US. In order to make the curves comparable the dispersions have been normalized to a same intermarket distance of 1000km. Using logarithms has the advantage of making the curves insensitive to multiplication of the prices by any conversion factor; on the other hand it has the drawback that arbitrage takes into consideration prices rather than logarithms of prices. *Sources: Jacobs and Richter (1935); Drame et al (1991); Zapoleon(1918); Langley(1989).*

in that direction at national level. It represents the standard deviation of the *logarithms* of prices. Taking logarithms makes the curves insensitive to multiplication by any conversion factor. From Fig.4.11 it is clear that after World War II progress in the process of market integration has been much slower than before World War I. A similar conclusion emerged from Fig.1.7a,b (Chapter 1) at the international level.

3.2 The relationship between price convergence and decrease in price volatility

The Enke-Samuelson model predicts that, as market integration improves, price volatility in each single market should decrease. But for this conclusion to hold

[4]At the European level an interesting source should be mentioned namely, Archives Nationales (Paris) F[11] 2985 – 3046: Prix des grains sur les marchés étrangers 1828-1860.

the correlation r of exogenous shocks in different markets should be different from one; indeed from the expression of σ_p in section 2.2.2 of chapter 3 one obtains:

$$\frac{d\sigma_p^2}{d\theta} = \frac{2\sigma^2(1-r)}{(2+\theta)^3}$$

Thus for $r = 1$ there is no decrease in price volatility, a conclusion which is consistent with intuitive reasoning.
For grain prices, a decrease in volatility has indeed been reported: Persson (1993) has investigated a large sample of long-range grain series. Some of its results are summarized in Table 4.11a along with our own findings. Evidence of a long term decrease is also documented in Roehner (1990b). While Table 4.11a provides an illustration of the relationship of spatial price convergence and decrease in price volatility Table 4.11b gives what could be called "a contrario" evidence. Indeed metal prices do *not* show any significant decrease in volatility. As shown by the series of lead prices, even the effect of the nineteenth century transport revolution resulted but in a slight decrease. The evolution after 1913 may be related to the evolution of ocean-freight rates, although other explanations could of course be proposed for instance a change in the dynamics of price fixation. The previous results should be considered as rather preliminary; in particular, we did not at this stage try to assess the statistical significance of dispersion changes from one period to another.

3.3 The relationship between price convergence and trade development

Historically this consequence of diminishing transportation costs has been somewhat masked by the extraordinary development of production which accompanied the process of market integration. In order to get rid of the effect of a changing production (P) on the trade (T), we shall analyse the ratio T/P; more general forms T/P^α could be used, but since we have no definite evidence about the adequate value of α, we shall take $\alpha = 1$.

3.3.1 Trade development at the level of single commodities

There can be little doubt about the short-term effect of a fall in transport costs; assuming every other factors to remain constant, it should result in an increase in the volume of trade. In the *long-run* however, smaller transport costs lead to more integrated markets and lowered price differentials make trade less attractive [5]In this section, we shall examine whether or not this second effect

[5]Obviously the fall in price differentials lags behind the decrease in transport costs, but the static theory of chapter 3 is unable to provide an order of magnitude for this lag. Its determination requires a dynamic model. This lag is of crucial importance for the transportation

	1790-1820	1825-1913	1920-1938	1950-1983
1) Persson (1993)				
WHEAT				
1) Toulouse, France	0.083	0.048		
2) Vienna, Austria	0.092	0.061		
RYE				
Vienna, Austria	0.105	0.067		
2)				
WHEAT				
Toulouse, France	0.205	0.140		
RYE				
Breda, Netherlands	0.283	0.178	0.259	0.156

Table 4.11a Changes over time in standard deviation of grain prices. Persson's results for Toulouse are corroborated by our own. Although he used a different method of computation (by first substracting a noise component, hence the smaller orders of magnitude of dispersions) the changes from period 1790-1820 to period 1825-1813 are similar: 42% in one case, 32% in the other. Incidentally, the above results also provide confirmation of the well known rule that rye prices have a larger dispersion than wheat prices. *Sources: Persson (1993); Toulouse: Drame et al (1991); Breda: Tijms (1970).*

	1819-1850	1851-1913	1920-1938	1950-1990
COPPER, London		0.134	0.190	0.181
LEAD,London	0.132	0.115	0.229	0.206
		1869-1913	**1920-1938**	**1950-1990**
TIN,London		0.161	0.239	0.218
		1875-1913	**1920-1938**	**1950-1990**
ZINC,London		0.150	0.200	0.255

Table 4.11b Change over time in standard deviation of non-ferrous metal prices. The effect of the nineteenth century transport revolution can be observed in the case of lead prices; its result is but a slight fall in the standard deviation. After, World War I, there is no decrease for any of the metals; this can be attributed to the fact that metal prices are more tighly connected to business cycles than are grain prices; the fact that there has been no further increase in market integration can be also be part of the explanation. *Sources: Up to 1878: Schmitz (1979); 1979-1990: Metall Statistik (1991).*

eventually could offset the short term increase. From the freight series that we have established above, we are in a good position to discover the periods of fast changing rates; these will be particularly appropriate for the testing of the model.

The evolution of trade may be studied either at a *bilateral* or at a *multilateral* level. As an example of the first approach one could for instance consider the wheat exports between the United States and the United Kingdom. Table 4.12a shows that imports from the US represented a share of total British wheat imports that ranges between 75% (1880) and 23% (1891); most of the time, however, it is of the order of 40% to 50%. Such a bilateral approach has two notable advantages: tariffs on British imports were almost negligible and freight rates on North Atlantic routes are relatively well known. There is a snag, however, in so far as other suppliers could hardly be ignored. In some years (1888,1889) Russia even had a larger market share than the United States. Modelling US-UK wheat trade by a bilateral trade model is not tenable therefore. The second option is to model wheat trade at world level. This time the difficulties rather are of a statistical nature since we have to estimate tariffs and freight rates (not only ocean rates, but also rates on waterways and railroads) on a world wide basis. Even if the required data were available, it would be difficult to construct such an index without making some arbitrary choices. Thus, we have selected the Chicago-Liverpool transport costs (by rail and steamer) as representative of the revolution in freight rates which occurred in the late nineteenth century. Duties have been considered as extra transport costs and have been schematically represented by error bars. This leads to the chart in Fig.4.12. Additional evidence is provided by Table 4.12b which shows the evolution of the ratio T/P for wheat and for cocoa. In the first case there is a stumbling increase trend; in the second case the starting values of the ratio are already so high that a further increase is scarcely possible. To get a better idea of the general trend, we would need series covering larger periods and particularly series going back to the nineteenth century.

Remark To avoid the bias introduced by tariffs, one could be tempted to use national trade statistics. True, in many countries wheat trade data are available for railroads. There is a problem however: the decrease in freight rates and the construction of the network have taken place almost simultaneously. Theoretically it is difficult to model a network whose structure is changing over time.

---

business; indeed, being a highly capital-intensive business, it requires guarantees as to the length of asset life (or amortization period). In other words if the decrease in transport costs is to be shortly followed by a comparable decrease in price differentials there will be no incentive for further investments in the transportation business.

	Total imports in percentage of consumption %	**Imports from the US** in percentage of total imports %	**Imports from RUSSIA** in percentage of total imports %
1878	44	57	18
1879	62	50	13
1880	51	**74**	**5**
1881	51	75	7
1882	50	53	15
1883	63	52	21
1884	38	49	11
1885	56	47	19
1886	43	44	8
1887	48	51	10
1888	48	37	**37**
1889	49	28	36
1890	49	33	32
1891	47	**23**	22
1892	49	54	7
1893	52	57	15
1894	49	38	24
1895	67	34	28
1896	55	32	25
1897	49	46	24

Table 4.12a British wheat imports according to source of supply. *Source: Das Getreide im Weltverkehr (1900)*

	Wheat Trade / Production %	**Cocoa** Trade / Consumption %	**Total world trade** Trade / World GDP %
1933-1939	9		
1946-1951	16		
1951-1955	13	91	
1956-1960	15	89	
1961-1965	20	94	10
1966-1970	16	78	11
1971-1975	17		17
1976-1980	18		22
1980-1987	20		19

Table 4.12b Evolution of trade at fixed levels of production for wheat, cocoa and for total world trade. For cocoa the starting values of the trade / consumption ratio are already so close to 100% that subsequent increases are scarcely possible. *Sources: World Wheat Statistics, 1987 p.15; Cocoa Statistics. FAO. Rome 1958 - 1974; FMI Annuaire 1990; National Account Statistics UNO 1965 - 1989.*

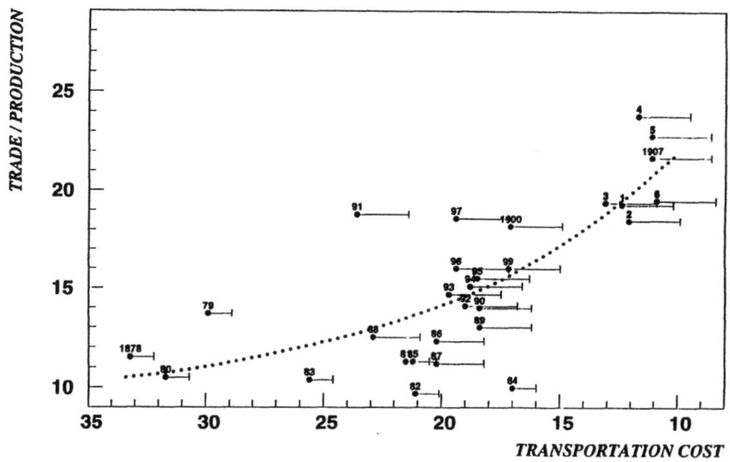

Fig.4.12 Variation of trade (reduced to constant production) with respect to transport cost (in cents/bushel) in the period 1878-1907. This period has been selected because it was marked by a substantial decrease in freight rates. The errors bars give estimates of the extra transport cost represented by custom duties. The dotted curve shows a best fit to the data. *Sources: Trade: Harley (1980); FAO Monograph. Le blé (1950). Production: Das Getreide im Weltverkehr (1900); FAO Monograph. Le blé (1950). Transport cost: Statistical Abstract of the US.*

3.3.2 Trade development at the macroeconomic level

The third column in Table 4.12b gives the ratio of world exports to the world Gross Domestic Product. Should the observed increase trend to be attributed to the decrease in transport costs? One may argue that it is rather related to structural macroeconomic changes in national economies. In fact, all industrialized nations experienced an increase in the ratio of foreign commerce to GDP; in the case of Netherlands for instance it rose from 9% in 1900 to 38% in 1980; in the case of the United States it increased from 3% to about 20% in the same period (Roehner 1984). We could however also take the argument the other way round. In an economy where transportation costs are low, any comparative advantage, however small, may give rise to a new trade "niche" (we take the word in its ecological sense). This argument is nothing but an other form of Samuelson's reasoning leading to the factor price equalization theorem. Of course, the one-product models of Chapter 3 do not provide a description of the complementarity and substitution effects which should play a major role in any model of international trade.

4 Estimation of the Enke-Samuelson trade model

4.1 Methodology

The Enke-Samuelson models are spatial auto-regressive models. The maximum-likelihood estimators of such models are well known, at least formally (Cliff and Ord 1981, Upton and Fingleton 1985, p.361); they are discussed in chapter 7. Apart from the coefficients of the autoregressive equations, there is here an additional parameter, namely the average spacing between markets. Accordingly the standard estimators cannot be used. The average spacing between markets provides the link between the theoretical sampling set $\{n\Delta x, n = 1, 2, \ldots\}$ and the inter-market distances $\{d_1, d_2, \ldots\}$. At this point, we prefer not to embark on an attempt to propose maximum likelihood estimators; instead we shall use the method of moments which constitutes a rather conservative estimating approach, even if it may not be the most efficient. Our model estimation should anyway be considered as a *preliminary* attempt. Indeed, to reduce the number of free parameters and thereby improving the accuracy of the hypothesis test, one would need additional statistical data regarding the slope of the excess-supply curve.

4.2 Results

We shall estimate the parameters of the model in three instances:

1) Wheat market in France (1825); sample of 50 markets; data from Drame et al (1991).

2) Wheat market in the United States (1951-1981); sample of 34 states; data from Langley (1989).

3) Potato market in the United States (1951-1981); sample of 35 states; data from Lucier (1991).

We did not try to estimate the model for the wheat market in France in the late nineteenth century or in the early twentieth century for, as shown in Fig.4.6, prices then have a rather different spatial pattern; the source of which has to be understood qualitatively before an estimation could reasonably be attempted. In principle one should use the network model; we shall rather use the chain model. It constitutes a reasonable and simple approximation. Furthermore price differentials have a similar behaviour with respect to distance in both models. In Figures 4.8a and 4.8b the statistical curve and the theoretical fitted curve are displayed side by side in the second and in the third case. Table 4.13 summarizes the values of the parameters. A reasonable guess regarding the slope of the excess-supply functions would be to assume that their changes have been slower than the changes in transportation costs. Accordingly the parameter θ may be considered as a crude measure of transportation costs;

	θ Transport cost / slope of exc.-sup.	σ Standard dev. of local shocks	Δ Average intermar. distance	η^2 Index of curvilin. correlation	**k** Number of interv.	χ^2
France, Wheat 1825	0.10	743	43	0.55	40	41
USA, Wheat 1951-1981	0.03	41	177	0.82	18	7.6
USA, Potato 1951-1981	0.126	216	170	0.74	19	10.8

Table 4.13 Estimation of the Enke-Samuelson model

with this interpretation in mind we see that the estimates in Table 4.13 seem plausible.

The Table provides two measures of goodness of fit:

- The index of curvilinear correlation:

$$\eta^2 = 1 - \sum_1^k (y_i - Y_i)^2 / \sum_1^k (y_i - \overline{y})^2$$

where y_i denotes the observations and Y_i the theoretical predictions.

- The usual χ^2 test:

$$\chi^2 = \sum_1^k (y_i - Y_i)^2 / \sigma_i^2$$

where σ_i denotes the standard deviation of the y_i

The values of χ^2 listed in Table 4.13 are rather small; this, however, does not necessarily indicate excellence in the adjustments; it is more likely to be connected with rather large values of σ_i due to limited sample size; let us observe that the magnitudes of the σ_i fortunately turn out to be comparable in every distance interval.

To conclude one may say that to put these estimations on a sound basis what seems most required are additional data about local excess-supply functions.

A Appendix A: Dispersion measures for spatial distributions

When studying the distribution of the weights w_i in a sample of adult males, it makes little sense to consider the differences $|w_i - w_j|$. On the contrary, when analysing the distribution of prices p_i in a sample of wheat markets, the price differences $|p_i - p_j|$ have a definite economic meaning. For this very reason it is tempting to characterize the dispersion of a spatial distribution of prices by measures based on price differences, such as for instance:

- The mean difference:

$$\Delta = \frac{1}{n(n-1)} \sum_{j \neq k} |x_j - x_k|$$

- The range of the sample:

$$R = x(n) - x(1)$$

where $x(n)$ denotes the largest value in the sample and $x(1)$ the smallest. In this Appendix we shall summarize some of the statistical properties of the mean difference and of the range; our review is chiefly based on Kendall et al (1987).

A.1 The mean difference

A.1.1 Existence

The probabilistic definition of the mean difference for a continuous distribution reads:

$$\Delta = \int_{-\infty}^{\infty} \int_{-\infty}^{\infty} |x - y| f(x) f(y) dx dy \qquad (A1)$$

It is essentially a linear rather than a quadratic measure of dispersion and its defining integral can be shown to converge whenever the mean exists. Thus the mean difference may provide a measure of dispersion for long-tailed distributions such as the Pareto distribution for which the standard deviation does not exist.

Remark The appearance of an absolute value in the definition (A1) leads to difficulties in the theory of sampling. It might be thought that this inconvenience may be overcome by an alternative definition:

$$E^2 = \int_{-\infty}^{\infty} \int_{-\infty}^{\infty} (x - y)^2 f(x) f(y) dx dy \qquad (A1)$$

E^2 however is nothing but twice the variance: $E^2 = 2\sigma^2$ and it has of course none of the convergence advantages of the mean difference.

A.1.2 Relation with Gini's coefficient

Gini's coefficient of concentration G is a measure of dispersion which has the property of being independent of the variate scale; it is a pure number and moreover it lies between 0 and 1. Gini's coefficient is closely related to the mean difference:

$$G = \Delta/2m$$

where m is the mean.

A.1.3 Sampling properties

In samples of size n drawn from a normal $N(m, \sigma)$ population the standard error of the sample mean difference $\hat{\Delta}$ is:

$$\sigma_{\hat{\Delta}} = 0.806 \frac{\sigma}{\sqrt{n}}$$

Hence its convergence properties in the limit of large samples are similar to those of the standard deviation. In the case of the range to which we turn now, the situation will be completely different.

A.2 The range of the sample

The range constitutes a particular case of the rth order-statistics, by which we mean the rth-largest variate value in the sample. The order-statistics are not symmetric functions of the observations and require specific methods of analysis.

A.2.1 The limiting distributions

Let us denote by $F_n(x)$ the asymptotic distribution function (for large samples) of the largest value $x(n)$ in the sample. For a normal population, one has (Kendall et al 1987, p.456):

$$F_n(x) \underset{n \to \infty}{\sim} \exp\left[-e^{-\sqrt{\ln n}\,(x - \sqrt{2 \ln n})}\right]$$

Thus $F_n(x)$ does not converge toward the normal distribution; moreover it converges very slowly (because of the $\ln n$ terms) toward its limiting distribution. A similar result holds for the smallest value $x(1)$ in the sample and since $x(1)$ and $x(n)$ are asymptotically independent the range has an asymptotic distribution of the same kind.

A.2.2 Sampling properties

In the case of a normal $N(0,\sigma)$ population, one has (Kendall et al 1987, p. 461):

$$\sigma_{\hat{R}} \underset{n\to\infty}{\sim} \frac{0.906}{\sqrt{\ln n}}$$

Thus R converges rather slowly toward its expectation:

$$E(\hat{R}) = \frac{0.408}{\sqrt{\ln n}}\,\sigma$$

The main advantage of the range as a measure of dispersion is of course the fact that it may be obtained without computation. However, the above properties show that it should be used with caution even in large samples.

B Appendix B: Trade and wheat differentials between England and Prussia 1828-1859

	Price in England Silvergros.	**Price in Prussia** Silvergros.	**Price**(England) – **Price**(Prussia) Silvergros.	**Exports** Prussia -->England thousand quarters
1828	110	57	53	253
29	127	66	61	348
1830	122	63	59	520
31	126	78	48	298
32	112	65	47	119
33	100	46	54	93
34	88	43	45	41
35	75	45	30	13
36	88	43	45	122
37	106	47	59	350
38	121	63	58	586
39	133	75	58	767
1840	125	70	55	807
41	121	65	56	890
42	108	73	35	738
43	94	62	32	659
44	96	57	39	551
45	95	65	30	424
46	103	86	17	360
47	131	110	21	493
48	95	63	32	528
49	83	61	22	618
1850	76	58	18	835
51	72	62	10	696
52	76	72	4	452
53	98	86	12	1145
54	136	108	28	675
55	141	119	22	540
56	130	113	17	223
57	106	85	21	870
58	83	76	7	626
59	101	75	26	772

Table 4.B Wheat price differentials and trade between England and Prussia 1828-59. England's major sources of supply in this period were Prussia, Russia and the United States. The elimination of the Corn Laws in 1846 under Robert Peel does not seem to have had a great impact on the level of British imports. The cost of transportation between Prussia and England was about 22 Silvergroschen. The price differentials show a clear decreasing trend. The coefficient of linear correlation between price differentials and exports is -0.62. *Source: Engel 1861, p.288, 289.*

C Appendix C: Conversion tables for volumes, weights and currencies

Country	Volumes and weights	Reference
	1 hectolitre wheat ≅ 0.075 ton	Statist. Agricole de la France (1890)
Bavaria	1 schäffel = 2.22 hectolitre	Seuffert 1857 p.351
USA	1 bushel = 0.35 hectolitre	Paquette et al 1991, p.156
England	1 imperial quarter = 2.91 hectolitre	Paquette et al 1991, p.155
	1 centweight or hundredweight = 50.8 kg	Paquette et al 1991, p.156
Country	**Exchange rates**	**Reference**
Bavaria	1 Gulden 1850 = 2.12 French Francs (Fr)	Seuffert 1857, p351
England	1 Shilling 1875 = 1.25 Fr 1875	Bank of Japan 1966, p.318
Germany	1 Mark 1875 = 1.24 Fr 1875	Földes 1905, p.498
Sweden	1 Kronor 1875 = 1.39 Fr 1875	Földes 1905, p.490
USA	1 Dollar 1875 = 5.1 Fr 1875	Bank of Japan 1966, p.318
Country	**Inflation rates**	**Reference**
USA	Consumer price index, all items 1800-1970	Historical Statistics of the US, 1975
USA	Producer price index, all items 1885-1987	Liesner 1989, p.90
USA	Consumer price index, all items 1885-1987	Liesner 1989, p.90

Table 4.C Conversion tables for volumes, weights and currencies.

Chapter 5

Grain markets and demographic phenomena

In this chapter we examine two demographic phenomena which are closely related to the economic themes of this book. The first one, the distribution of city-sizes and its evolution in the course of time, is directly related to the level of transport costs. In fact, the distribution of city-sizes is shaped by two antagonistic forces: on one side concentrating population and services in large cities allows obvious economies of scale (especially in the perspective of a rapidly growing population), on the other side provisioning large cities represents a major technical and economic challenge in terms of transportation costs and infrastructure; the penetrating study by S.Kaplan (1984) regarding Paris in the 18th century is quite revealing in this respect. In the first section of this chapter we formalize the transportation constraint for a network of cities and we discuss its implications for urban growth. In the second section we consider the consequences on vital rates of the fluctuations in the (real) cost of living (and especially in grain prices). We shall observe that even in the 19th century grain prices had a significant influence on birth rates and on marriage rates.

1 The green-belt model for city-size distributions

A simple way to characterize the pattern of urban networks is to analyse the statistical distribution of their city-sizes. If X denotes the population of a city, the cumulative distribution function $G(x)$ of a system of cities is defined as:

$$G(x) = N(X > x)$$

where $N(X > x)$ is the cumulative number of cities with a population above a specified population x. Going back to Auerbach (1913) and to Zipf's work in the 1940s, conclusive evidence has shown the distribution of city-sizes to be of Pareto form. Accordingly, the distribution of city-sizes can be described by:

$$G(x) = N(X > x) = \frac{C}{x^{\alpha}} \qquad x_1 \leq x \tag{1.1}$$

x_1 is the urbanization threshold and α is the Pareto index of the distribution; C is a normalization constant.
It can be noted that when $x_1 = 1$, (1.1) gives $C = N(X > 1)$; thus C has the interpretation of being the total number of cities when the urbanized threshold is equal to one; admittedly, this is a rather unrealistic threshold; nevertheless, it will be considered as a limiting case in section 1.2.1.
The description of equation (1.1) is equivalent to the so-called rank-size rule (or Zipf's law):

$$r_i P_i^\alpha = C \qquad \text{or} \qquad r_i^a P_i = K \quad a = 1/\alpha, \ K = C^{1/\alpha} \tag{1.2}$$

where r_i is the rank (in decreasing order of size) of city i having population P_i. The slope of the line representing the distribution of city-sizes in a $(\ln r_i, \ln P_i)$ plot is $-a$. In the following we shall use the Pareto index α rather than the slope a because α has an easy interpretation in statistical terms as the slope of the log-log plot of the cumulative distribution (1.1) of city-sizes. Empirical values of α turn out to be in the range between 0.8 and 1.5. One of the questions which we shall address is whether it is possible to predict the value of α in a specific country, as well as its evolution in the course of time, from underlying socio-economic phenomena.

Our analysis involves two steps. First the notion of Pareto distribution has to be extended to include *truncated* Pareto distributions; indeed, insofar as standard Pareto distributions extend to arbitrarily large city sizes the very notion of a maximum city size is ill defined; thus our first task is to discuss the basic statistical properties of truncated (or finite) Pareto distributions. In this framework an urban system is defined by three parameters: the total number of cities, the index of the Pareto law and the population of the largest city. While these parameters can be considered as being independent from a mathematical point of view, we shall see that given the total urbanized population they become subject to specific constraints. These constraints provide clearer insight into the process of urbanization which has made dramatic progress during past decades in a number of countries such as for instance Mexico, Brazil or Egypt.
Then, in a second step we shall be able to formalize the production and transportation constraints. Conveying to the heart of cities indispensable goods such as water, foodstuff, energy, building materials, etc has a cost; this cost turns out to increase along with city's population x as $x^{3/2}$, that is to say significantly faster than the population itself. In investigating how the urban system finds its way around these constraints it is enlightening to look at its trajectories in the Pareto-plane. This plane has the Pareto index as the horizontal scale and on the vertical scale there is the ratio x_1/x_2 of the smallest (actually the city-threshold) to the largest city. In such a plane, the origin represents the ultimate stage of urban systems with the whole urban population gathered in a single capital-city. Before we develop this programme, let us have a look at Fig.5.1; it shows

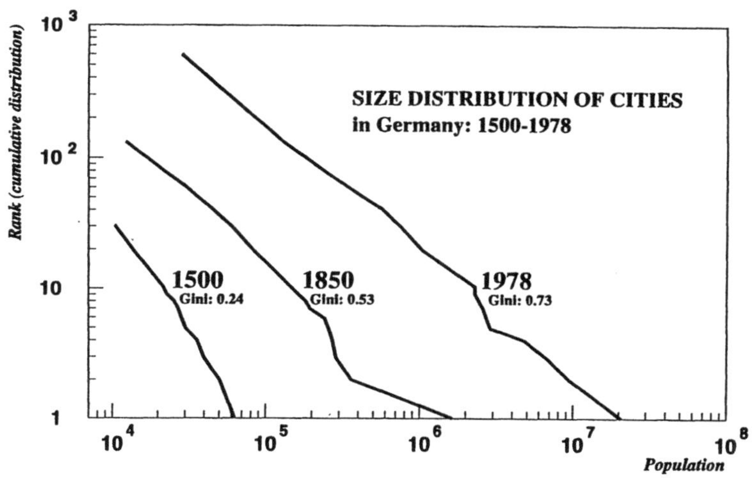

Fig.5.1 Evolution of the size distribution of cities in Germany 1500-1978. The evolution is marked by an overall growth in city-sizes and by a steady decrease of the Pareto index. As a result urban networks have become more concentrated as shown by the increase of Gini's coefficient. *Source: De Vries (1984).*

the evolution of the size distribution of cities in Germany; there is a similar evolution in France and in Britain (see Table 5.1b). Our objective is to explain this evolution. Admittedly, the increase in city sizes may be seen as an almost trivial consequence of overall population growth. But why should there be a simultaneous decrease in the value of the Pareto index?

Let us briefly place our study in the wider literature on city-size distributions. Crudely speaking the proposed models fall into two broad classes. The probabilistic (and usually static) models (Simon 1955, Steindl 1965, Hill 1974) exhibit global mechanisms through which Pareto distributions can be generated. The second class consists in dynamic models (Parr 1985) which are either deterministic (Malecki 1975) or stochastic (Vining 1976,1977) or provide comparisons between deterministic and stochastic versions (Roehner and Wiese 1982). In the latter paper as well as in Vining (1977), it is in particular pointed out that deterministic models are usually adequate except when the average rate of urban growth becomes small, in which case fluctuations turn out to play a crucial role. Basically, all these approaches rely on assumptions regarding growth rates of individual cities; accordingly they meet with some difficulties due to the great dispersion in empirical growth rates (Guérin-Pace and Pumain 1990). In this chapter, we try to combine the advantages (in terms of smoothness) of the holistic approach (which considers cities in a given region as a global entity) and the benefit of an explanation in terms of underlying economic determinants.

1.1 The finite Pareto distribution

The infinite Pareto distribution (1.1) has no standard deviation as soon as $\alpha \leq 2$; it has no mean either as soon as $\alpha \leq 1$. This has obvious probabilistic and statistical implications: the central-limit theorem fails to hold true and the statistical estimators of any parameter related to the Pareto distribution have poor convergence properties. There are two ways out of this difficulty.

- The first solution is to accept the infinite range of the Pareto distribution; one then has to tackle the ensuing mathematical problems of the so-called stable distributions. This is the approach that has been tried by B.Mandelbrot(1960).
- The second alternative is to consider a truncated Pareto distribution. For such a distribution all convergence problems are solved ipso facto. The passage from an infinite distribution $f(x)$ to a finite distribution $\tilde{f}(x)$ implies that the random variable X is only to be observed within a bounded interval (x_1, x_2). The relationship between the density functions $f(x)$ and $\tilde{f}(x)$ only requires an obvious renormalization:

$$\tilde{f}(x) = \frac{f(x)}{\int_{x_1}^{x_2} f(x)dx} = \frac{f(x)}{F(x_2) - F(x_1)}$$

In spite of its simplicity, this solution will be seen to have a number of interesting implications.

1.1.1 Cumulated distribution of the finite Pareto distribution

The infinite Pareto distribution (or equivalently the rank-size rule) has a straight-line representation on a log-log plot. Yet many observed distributions bend away from the linear fit in the region of large city-sizes. Let us note in passing that it is for this very reason that one is often tempted to use a lognormal distribution instead. The finite Pareto distribution is another possible candidate as is made clear by Fig.5.2. It is of course not surprising that the finite Pareto distribution has more flexibility than the infinite one since it involves an additional parameter. Its density function $\tilde{f}(x)$ and its cumulated distribution function $\tilde{G}(x)$ read:

$$\tilde{f}(x) = C\frac{Y[(x - x_1)(x_2 - x)]}{x^{\alpha+1}} \qquad C = \frac{\alpha}{1/x_1^\alpha - 1/x_2^\alpha} \tag{1.2a}$$

where:

$$Y(x) = \begin{cases} 0 & x \leq 0 \\ 1 & x > 1 \end{cases}$$

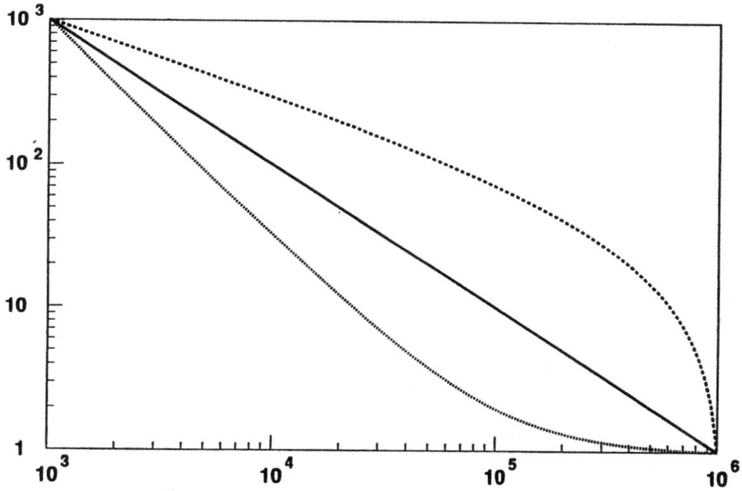

Fig.5.2 Cumulated distribution functions for a finite Pareto distribution. Solid line: $\alpha = 1$; dashed line: $\alpha = 0.5$; dotted line: $\alpha = 1.5$. Plotted on (log, log) scales the curve is no longer a straight line as in the case of an infinite Pareto distribution. Here we have a sample of $N = 1000$ cities; the urbanization threshold x_1 is 1000 and the size of the largest city x_2 is one million. The fact that it is the $\alpha = 1$ curve which is almost a straight line depends on the relation between N and x_2/x_1.

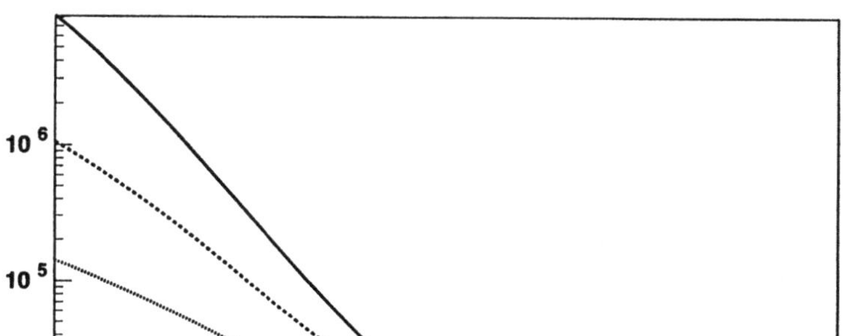

Fig.5.3 Average number of inhabitants per city as a function of the Pareto index α The different curves correspond to following values for the size of the largest city x_2; from bottom to top: $x_2 = 10^5,\ 10^6,\ 10^7,\ 10^8$; $x_1 = 1000$.

and:

$$\widetilde{G}(x) = \begin{cases} 1 & x \leq x_1 \\ \dfrac{(x_1/x)^\alpha - (x_1/x_2)^\alpha}{1-(x_1/x_2)^\alpha} & x_1 \leq x \leq x_2 \\ 0 & x \geq x_2 \end{cases} \tag{1.2b}$$

1.1.2 Expectation of the finite Pareto distribution

Let us denote by P_u the total urban population and by N the number of cities above the threshold x_1; the expectation of the finite Pareto distribution (i.e. the average city size) is given by (see Appendix B):

$$P_u/N = \frac{\alpha x_1}{\alpha - 1}\frac{1-\epsilon^{\alpha-1}}{1-\epsilon^\alpha} \qquad \epsilon = x_1/x_2 \tag{1.3}$$

When $x_2 = \infty$, we recover the standard result for the infinite Pareto distribution. Fig.5.3 shows the curve of the function P_u/N for different values of the ratio ϵ.

Let us examine whether this Figure might shed some light on how an urban system adapts to growing urban population. There are basically three possible responses to an increase in P_u:

a) An increase in the number N of cities

b) An increase in the size of the largest city x_2

c) A decrease of the Pareto index α

Statistical evidence shows that N increases at a much slower rate than P_u. The only exception to this rule seems to be the settlement periods, such as for instance in the United States between 1800 and 1900 (see in this connection Roehner and Wiese 1982, p.1457). The first possibility should therefore be ruled out. As a first approximation we may even assume that N remains almost constant. Regarding the second possibility, Fig.5.3 shows that it is almost useless to increase x_2 unless α is smaller than 1. When starting from an initial distribution of cities characterized by a value of α of the order of 1.2, which is a standard figure in developing countries, we therefore know for sure that α is bound to decrease in order to make the urban system able to absorb large additional urban populations.

Remark We can note in passing that this argument also have interesting implications for the distribution of income. It has been pointed out by the Pareto school that the value of α tends to decrease in "good times" and to fall in "bad times" (Davis 1941, p.17-53). Now, we may argue that, from a mathematical point of view, there is a formal equivalence between urban distributions and income distributions when both of them are considered as the result of an underlying birth and death process (Simon 1955, Steindl 1965, Roehner and Wiese 1982). Thus, one may draw the following parallel between distributions of income and distributions of city-sizes.

Total income	$\longleftrightarrow$	Total population
Number of people	$\longleftrightarrow$	Number of cities
Subsistence level of income	$\longleftrightarrow$	Urbanization threshold

From the previous argument we see that in the case of a strong increase in total income (and provided the size of the population remains almost constant, a condition that is clearly fulfilled in a short term perspective), there will be an almost "mechanical" decrease of α in order for the system to absorb the additional revenue. The argument applies even better to incomes, where α is of the order of $3/2$, than to cities where α is somewhat lower.

1.1.3 Concentration of a finite Pareto distribution

How should the degree of concentration of an urban network be defined? Concentration is but another term for dispersion. Pearson's coefficient of variation σ/m (where σ denotes the standard deviation and m the expectation) is a relative measure of dispersion; the entropy $S = -\sum_i p_i \ln p_i$ is another one. However, neither of them has an upper bound; accordingly these measures cannot be used to define an unambiguous scale of concentration. As is well known, Gini's coefficient of concentration, g, provides a measure of concentration that remains bounded between 0 and 1 (Kendall et al 1987,p.60):

$$g = \frac{1}{2m}\int_{-\infty}^{\infty}\int_{-\infty}^{\infty} |x-y| f(x)f(y)dxdy$$

Gini's coefficient may also be derived from the Lorenz curve (Atkinson 1975, p.45). In appendix A we derive an alternative expression of g which turns out to be convenient for analytical calculations:

$$g = 1 - \frac{\int_0^\infty G^2(x)dx}{\int_0^\infty G(x)dx} \tag{1.4}$$

Let us examine whether Gini's coefficient has indeed the properties that one would expect intuitively. To this end we consider two extreme situations:

1) A sample of N cities all of which have same population $\overline{x}$

2) A sample which consists of one large city of size x_2 surrounded by $N-1$ small cities of size x_1.

In the fist case, $G(x) = Y(x-\overline{x})$ and (1.4) gives at once $g = 0$, i.e. the concentration is at its bottom level.

In the second case, the expression of g depends on x_1, x_2 and N but g increases toward 1 when:

$$x_2 \longrightarrow \infty, N \longrightarrow \infty$$

The expression of Gini's coefficient for a finite Pareto distribution is derived in Appendix A; one obtains:

$$g = \frac{1-(2\alpha-1)\epsilon^{\alpha-1}(1-2\epsilon)-2\alpha\epsilon^{2\alpha-1}}{(2\alpha-1)(1-\epsilon^{\alpha-1})} \qquad \alpha \neq 1, 1/2 \tag{1.5a}$$

where $\epsilon = x_1/x_2$. When $\alpha = 1$, one has:

$$g = \frac{\ln 1/\epsilon - 2 + \epsilon \ln 1/\epsilon + 2\epsilon}{(1-\epsilon)\ln 1/\epsilon} \tag{1.5b}$$

As $x_2 \longrightarrow \infty$, $g \longrightarrow 1$ i.e. the concentration becomes maximal.
Fig.5.4 shows graphically how the concentration increases from 0 to 1 as x_2

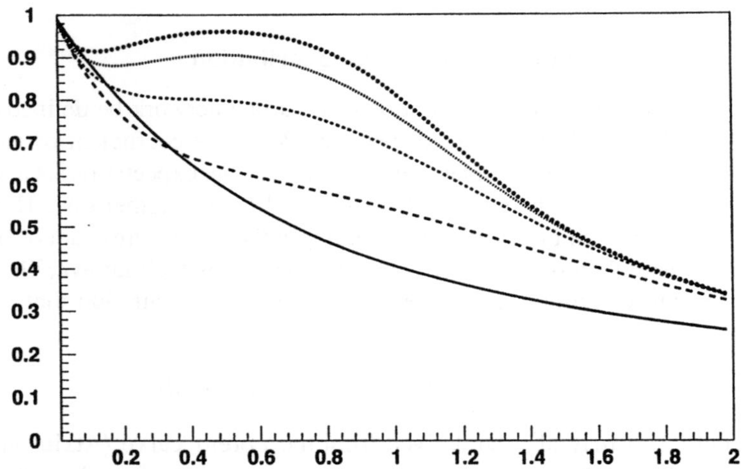

Fig.5.4 Gini's coefficient of concentration for a finite Pareto distribution as a function of the Pareto index. The different curves correspond to the following values of the size of the largest city x_2; from bottom to top: $x_2 = 10^4,\ 10^5,\ 10^6,\ 10^7,\ 10^8$; $x_1 = 2000$.

increases and/or α decreases. The value $\alpha = 1$ seems to play a special role in so far as the curves show a plateau between $\alpha = 1$ and $\alpha = 0.5$, at least for $x_2/x_1 > 10^6$

1.2 Evolution of urban systems in the Pareto plane

In almost every business or public service, whether one considers hospitals, libraries, retail stores, etc, economies of scale would give an incentive to ran ever larger units. Apart from a number of operating problems inherent to gigantic installations that we choose to ignore here, the main obstacle to such an evolution is the very existence of transportation costs. Accordingly, the thesis we shall formalize subsequently is that the pattern of city-sizes is controlled by two competing forces:

• a trend toward increased concentration under the combined pressure of an inflated population and of the quest for economies of scale.

• a resistance to further concentration on account of increased transportation charges. The green-belt model that we introduce in the next paragraph formalizes this effect.

The first of these points, the problem of scale economies due to agglomeration, has been investigated in Abdel-Rahman and Fujita (1990). In the present paper we shall in a sense take up the problem at the point where these authors have brought it, that is to say we take for granted that city distributions follow finite Pareto distributions and we investigate the *parameters* of these distributions. Regarding the second point, let us emphasize that the interactions between cities and the surrounding agricultural neighbourhood have been studied from an historic and economic point of view by Chartres (1991) as part of a large scale investigation which covered the adjacent questions of market organization and trade fluctuations (Chartres 1990), as well as the evolution of means of transportation (Chartres 1977). For the late Middle Age estimates for the population of major European cities have been published by Russel (1972).

1.2.1 The transportation constraint in the green-belt model

In the light of the finite Pareto distribution, we re-examine and extend the green-belt model that has been introduced in Roehner (1991); in particular we carry out a number of numerical applications with the purpose of assessing the magnitude of the transportation constraint.

Assumptions and definitions We consider a specific product, labelled k, which is consumed in a city. We assume that it may be gained from the area surrounding the city and we introduce the following variables:

• c, the annual consumption per inhabitant

• q, the yield per square-kilometre; it is related to the area h required to produce the quantity c: $h = c/q$

• $\tilde{t}$, the work (in man-year) required to transport one unit of k over a distance of one kilometre; it is related to the work t required to transport c over a distance of one kilometre: $t = c\tilde{t}$.

• $\tilde{p}$, the work (in man-year) required to produce one unit of k; it is related to the work p required to produce c: $p = c\tilde{p}$.

One city with a single inhabitant The radius $R(1)$ of the area required for the production of the quantity c is such that:

$$q\pi R^2(1) = c \Longrightarrow R(1) = \sqrt{c/q\pi}$$

The production in the circular crown $(r, r+dr)$ (Fig.5.5) amounts to $2\pi r dr\ q$. The work required to transport this quantity to the city is given by: $(2\pi r dr\ q) r\tilde{t}$; the transportation work required to transport the production of the whole disk is:

$$W_{Tr}(1) = 2\pi q\tilde{t}\int_0^{R(1)} r^2 dr = \frac{2\pi}{3} qR^3(1)\tilde{t} = (\pi R^2(1)q)(\frac{2R(1)}{3})\tilde{t} = c(\frac{2R(1)}{3})\tilde{t}$$

In words, the transportation work amounts to transferring the whole quantity c from a distance $2R(1)/3$ to the city.

Numerical example The product we consider is wheat for available data are probably more detailed for wheat than for any other product. We take our figures from the "Album de Statistique Agricole. Résultats Généraux de l'Enquête Décennale de 1882". Another source of empirical data should be mentioned in this respect, namely the studies by Slicher van Bath (reedition 1967,1977).

- $c = 2.5$ hectolitre (hl); moreover, the average production per inhabitant is equal to 3.43 hl/(man-year)
- The average yield for wheat is: $q_0 = 18$ hl/ha; taking into account that the acreage grown in wheat represents only 13% of total land surface, we obtain: $q = 0.13 q_0 = 234\,\text{hl}\,/\,\text{km}^2$; thus $h \simeq 1$ ha[1].
- To estimate $\tilde{t}$ we argue as follows. When evaluated in money, we have (Foville 1880): $\tilde{t} = 3$ centimes/(hl.km); now the salary earned in one year by a transportation hand approximately amounts to its annual consumption of wheat, that is to say, assuming an average price of wheat of 15 Fr/hl, to 37 Fr; hence: $\tilde{t} \simeq 10^{-3}$ man-year/(hl.km)

From the above expression of $W_{Tr}(1)$ we obtain: $W_{Tr}(1) = 10^{-4}$ man-year. As a matter of comparison let us evaluate the work p required to produce this quantity of wheat:
$\tilde{p} =$ Total number of man-years available/Total production $=$ 1/average production per capita. Thus, $\tilde{p} = (1/3.4)$(man-year/hl) and $p = c\tilde{p} = 0.73$ man-year. To summarize, in the hypothetical case of a city with one inhabitant, the work required for transportation is completely negligible when compared to the work required for production. We next consider a single city of about two millions inhabitants such as Paris at the end of the nineteenth-century; the result then will be very different.

[1]As a matter of comparison, in the 20th century the land requirement for American type food consumption for one person is estimated by Clark (1968,p.153) to be of the order of 0.22 ha

One city with x inhabitants The radius $R(x)$ of the area required for the production of the quantity cx is such that:

$$q\pi R^2(x) = cx \Longrightarrow R(x) = \sqrt{cx/q\pi} = R(1)\sqrt{x} \tag{1.6}$$

Accordingly, the work $W_{Tr}(x)$ required for transportation becomes:

$$W_{Tr}(x) = (cx)\left(\frac{2R(x)}{3}\right)\widetilde{t} = W_{Tr}(1)x^{3/2} \qquad W_{Tr}(x)/x = W_{Tr}(1)\sqrt{x} \tag{1.7}$$

We observe that $W_{Tr}(x)$ increases with x as $x^{3/2}$, that is to say substantially faster than the size of the city itself. The numerical implication of this observation is made clear by the following example.

Numerical examples
a) 1870 With $x = 2.10^6$ we obtain: $R(x) = 82\,\text{km}$ and $W_{Tr}(x)/x = 0.14$ man-year.
The annual fraction of work to be devoted to wheat transportation is no longer negligible.

b) 1750 Before 1800 the data are less precise. Nonetheless, as a matter of illustration, let us estimate the radius $R(x)$ around 1750 for a large city such as Paris, which already had about half a million inhabitants. Regarding the consumption, production and transportation of wheat, we shall use the following figures (Braudel 1967,p.90; Foville 1880):

$$c = 4 \text{ hl} \qquad q_0 = 6 \text{ hl/ha} \qquad q = 78\,\text{hl}\,/\,\text{km}^2$$

$$\widetilde{t} = 6 \text{ centimes/(hl.km)} = 2.10^{-3} \text{ man-year/(hl.km)}$$

With these values we obtain:

$$R(1) = 0.128 \text{ km} \qquad R(0.5.10^6) = 90 \text{ km}$$

$$W_{Tr}(1) = 6.8\ 10^{-4} \text{ man-year} \Longrightarrow W_{Tr}(x)/x = 0.48 \text{ man-year}$$

The last figure could seem somewhat too large especially if one remembers that it does not include work required for production. On the other hand, one should keep in mind that the area within a radius of about 100 km around Paris was populated, Paris excepted, by about 1.5 million people living in rural districts and for whom transportation costs were therefore almost negligible. When reduced to that total population x', the previous figure becomes more reasonable:

$$W_{Tr}(x')/x' \simeq W_{Tr}(x)/x' = (x/x')\left(W_{Tr}(x)/x\right) = 0.12 \text{ man-year}$$

Pareto distribution of city-sizes We now make the more realistic assumption that the distribution of city-sizes is of the Pareto-type (Fig.5.5); the total work

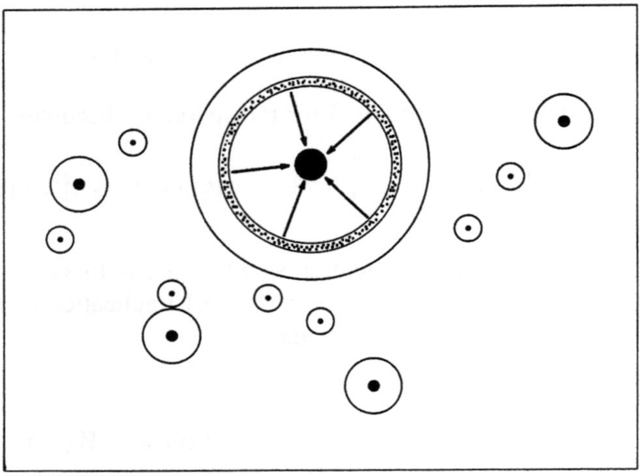

Fig.5.5 Supplying areas of cities. Solid black disks represent cities; the circles represent the supplying zones of each city. For the largest city, a crown $(r, r+dr)$ is depicted.

required for transportation then becomes:

$$W_{Tr} = \int_{x_1}^{x_2} W_{Tr}(x) f(x) dx$$

where $f(x)$ is the density function of the Pareto distribution:

$$f(x) = C/x^{\alpha+1} \qquad x_1 < x < x_2$$

with C being the normalization constant.
Substituting, we obtain:

$$W_{Tr} = W_{Tr}(1)\ C \int_{x_1}^{x_2} \frac{x^{3/2}}{x^{\alpha+1}} dx = W_{Tr}(1) C \frac{x_2^{3/2-\alpha} - x_1^{3/2-\alpha}}{3/2-\alpha}$$

From the expression of $W_{Tr}(1)$ we observe that the following variables introduces themselves in a natural way:

$$h = c/q \qquad t = c\tilde{t}$$

h: area required to produce c
t: labor required to transport c over one kilometre

Introducing these notations, the expression of W_{Tr} becomes:

$$W_{Tr} = C\frac{2t}{3}\sqrt{\frac{h}{\pi}}x_2^{3/2-\alpha}\frac{1-\epsilon^{3/2-\alpha}}{3/2-\alpha} \qquad \epsilon = x_1/x_2 \tag{1.8}$$

Numerical example
The expression of C is (see Appendix B):

$$C = N\frac{\alpha x_1^\alpha}{1-(x_1/x_2)^\alpha}$$

With: $\alpha = 1 \quad x_1 = 1000 \quad x_2 = 2.10^6$, we obtain:

$$W_{Tr} = 2.10^6$$

The urban population above the threshold $x_1 = 1000$ was in 1911 (Annuaire Rétrospectif INSEE 1966,p.24): $P_u = 28$ millions. Thus: $W_{Tr}/P_u = 0.07$ man-year. For periods prior to the nineteenth century, it is clear that we would get a larger figure.

The production-transportation constraint We denote by $W_{Pr}(k)$ and $W_{Tr}(k)$ the work required for production and transportation of product k; with P being the total population, the production-transportation constraint reads:

$$P \geq \sum_k [W_{Pr}(k) + W_{Tr}(k)] \tag{1.9a}$$

The work required for production is:

$$W_{Pr} = P\sum_k q_k$$

Thus inequality (1.9a) becomes:

$$P\left(1-\sum_k q_k\right) \geq \sum_k W_{Tr}(k) \tag{1.9b}$$

We shall now state this condition explicitely. Denoting by P_u the urban population and by u the urbanization rate, one has (see Appendix B):

$$P = \frac{P_u}{u} = C\frac{x_2^{1-\alpha}}{u}\frac{1-\epsilon^{1-\alpha}}{1-\alpha} \tag{1.10}$$

Replacing (1.8) and (1.10) in inequality (1.9b) we see that the factor C (which involves the total number of cities) drops from each member and disappears from the model. Thus, we are left with:

$$\frac{x_2^{1-\alpha}}{u}\frac{1-\epsilon^{1-\alpha}}{1-\alpha}\left(1-\sum_k p_k\right) \geq \frac{2x_2^{3/2-\alpha}}{3\sqrt{\pi}}\frac{1-\epsilon^{3/2-\alpha}}{3/2-\alpha}\sum_k t_k\sqrt{h_k}$$

We introduce global values $\overline{p}$, $\overline{t}, \overline{h}$ such that:

$$\overline{p} = \sum_k p_k \qquad \overline{t}\sqrt{\overline{h}} = \sum_k t_k \sqrt{h_k}$$

We may divide both members by $(1 - \epsilon^{1-\alpha})/(1 - \alpha)$ for this ratio is always positive (when $\epsilon < 1$); thus we obtain finally:

$$u\sqrt{x_2}\frac{1-\alpha}{3/2-\alpha}\frac{1-\epsilon^{3/2-\alpha}}{1-\epsilon^{1-\alpha}} \leq \left(\frac{3\sqrt{\pi}}{2}\right)\frac{1-\overline{p}}{\overline{t}\,\overline{h}} = A(\overline{p}, \overline{t}, \overline{h}) \qquad (1.11)$$

Inequality (1.11) is the basic relation expressing the production-transportation constraint.

- In the left member we have the three variables defining the distribution of city-sizes, namely $x_2, \epsilon = x_1/x_2$ and α, along with the rate of urbanization u.
- The right-hand side, on the contrary, contains productivity rates which are conditioned by the technological level of the society.

1.2.2 Graphical representation in the Pareto plane: possible trajectories

Presently, we shall interpret relation (1.11) which expresses the production-transportation constraint, in terms of the evolution of urban systems in the Pareto plane (α, ϵ). A graphical display is given in Fig.5.6. On this chart we have represented three elements:

1) Relation (1.11) is of the form:

$$g(\alpha, \epsilon, u) \leq A(\bar{p}, \bar{t}, \bar{h}) \qquad (1.11a)$$

If the global productivity factors $\bar{p}, \bar{t}, \bar{h}$ are assumed fixed as well as the urbanization ratio u and the urbanization threshold x_1, then $(1.11a)$ defines a curve in the (α, ϵ) plane. These curves are represented by solid lines for three different values of A. What remains to be settled is which part of the plane is allowed by inequality $(1.11a)$ and which part is forbidden. When x_2 goes to infinity (i.e. $\epsilon \to 0$) and α goes to zero, the left-hand side of (1.11) becomes equivalent to $(2/3)u\sqrt{x_2}$ which goes to zero; accordingly, the inequality is not satisfied in the part of the plane which includes the origin $(\alpha = 0, \epsilon = 0)$. This is represented symbolically by the hatched side of the curves. This constraint is especially of significance for countries that experience a rapid growth in their urbanized population. In contrast, it is clear that given their technological level countries such as Denmark or Sweden could "afford" an urban system with a much larger capital city; in 1990, Copenhagen had 1.3 million inhabitants (total population of Denmark: 5.5 millions), while Stockholm had only 0.67 million (total population of Sweden: 8.4 million).

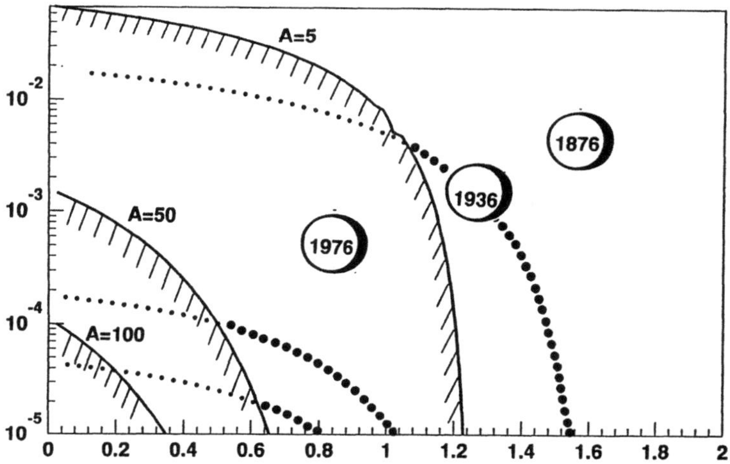

Fig.5.6 Possible trajectories of urban systems in the Pareto plane. Horizontal axis: Pareto index; vertical axis: ratio of urbanization threshold to largest city. The hatched side of the solid lines corresponds to regions which, for given productivity values, are forbidden by the production-transportation constraint. For a given value of the ration P_u/N the large dots correspond to possible positions of the urban system. From top to bottom $P_u/N = 5000,\ 10^4,\ 10^6$. The years inside the circles refer to the urban networks of French regions as given in table 1a. A is a parameter defined in inequality (1.11) in terms of productivity of production and of transportation.

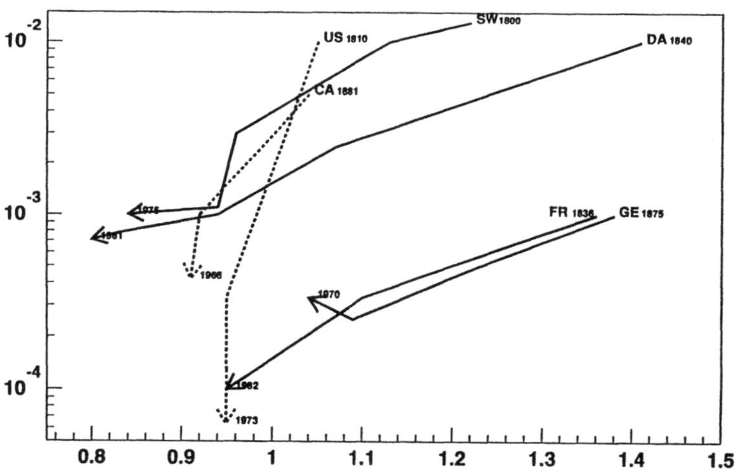

Fig.5.7 Actual trajectories of urban systems in the Pareto plane. Horizontal axis: Pareto index; vertical axis: ratio of urbanization threshold to largest city. The trajectories correspond to the data in Table 5.1b. All trajectories tend towards the origin which represents the ultimate state of urban systems. There is an obvious difference between the trajectories of "old" European countries and "new" countries such as Canada and the United States.

2) Assuming the urbanization threshold to be fixed, relation (1.3) is of the form:

$$f(\alpha, \epsilon) = \frac{P_u}{N}$$

P_u/N represents the average size of a city. An urban system for which this average size would remain constant in the course of time can, in some sense, be said to experience a "balanced" urban growth. The dotted curves show such balanced trajectories for different values of the ratio P_u/N. Only the parts of these trajectories which are outside the forbidden region are of course possible. Insofar as the ratio P_u/N in general shows a marked increase trend, *real* urban growth is not balanced. To what extent real trajectories are unbalanced is shown by the divergence between balanced growth trajectories and real ones. Thus, from the comparison of Fig. 5.6 and 5.7 it can be seen that almost all trajectories are strongly unbalanced except those of Denmark, Sweden and Germany in the last twenty years.

3) The positions of the three disks show the collective evolution of French (regional) urban systems as given by the data in Table 5.1a.

1.3 Confronting the implications of the model with empirical evidence

We shall carry out two sorts of empirical tests. Firstly, we analyse the trajectories of urban systems in the Pareto-plane; secondly, we test our assumptions about transportation charges by comparing commodity prices respectively in large and in small cities. The fact that these tests remain somewhat qualitative is mainly due to the lack of adequate data which would permit a more accurate estimation of the term A in the left-hand side of inequality (1.11).

1.3.1 Sources

We mainly used two sources:

1) The special issues of the United Nations Demographic Yearbooks which contain a section devoted to urban demography. They are published every three or four years and give the number of cities in each of about 7 or 8 size classes.

2) In order to specify the distribution in the range of large cities we have made use of lists of major cities in each country provided by the Europa World Yearbook; cities are recorded by decreasing size and their number varies depending on the country (from about 80 in the case of Japan for instance, to about 7 for Ghana).

Let us first point out that these urban statistics are not always free of ambiguities or gaps. It is of course well known that the very definitions of cities are not

Region	Year	Number of cities	Total popul.	Average city-size	Pareto index	Largest city	Gini's coeff.
		N	P	P/N	α	x_2	
			thousands	thousands		millions	
Loire	1876	144	590	4.1	1.45	0.12	0.47
	1911	124	640	5.1	1.25	0.15	0.54
	1936	96	650	6.8	1.09	0.20	0.60
	1954	92	654	7.1	1.01	0.20	0.63
	1975	93	722	7.8	0.92	0.20	0.66
Loire - Atlantique	1876	191	613	3.2	2.00	0.12	0.33
	1911	186	670	3.6	1.77	0.17	0.38
	1936	165	659	4.0	1.68	0.20	0.41
	1954	164	733	4.5	1.54	0.22	0.45
	1975	161	861	5.3	1.08	0.40	0.64
Rhône	1876	122	705	5.8	1.57	0.30	0.45
	1911	103	915	8.9	1.38	0.50	0.52
	1936	93	1028	11.0	1.11	0.70	0.64
	1954	91	966	10.6	0.98	0.70	0.71
	1975	124	1325	10.7	0.76	1.00	0.80
South - East	1876	280	1499	5.3	1.27	0.30	0.56
(Alpes-Marit.	1911	264	1971	7.4	1.10	0.50	0.64
+Bouches Rh.	1936	252	2637	10.4	1.07	0.80	0.67
+Hérault +Var)	1954	265	2447	9.2	0.98	0.70	0.70
	1975	322	3338	10.4	0.86	1.00	0.77

Table 5.1a Evolution of regional urban systems in France 1876-1975. What makes the analysis of regional urban systems attractive is that their characteristics are more contrasted than those of urban systems at national level (see for instance the steep distribution of Loire-Atlantique in 1876). x_2 denotes the size of the largest city. It is apparent that increases in P/N trigger both a decrease in α and an increase in x_2. The urbanization threshold is x_1=1000; P is the total population; given the low urbanization threshold, P is not very different from the urban population. *Sources: Dénombrements INSEE. Paris, various years.*

identical in all countries, but the ambiguities we are referring to seem to go beyond that. Let us just give two examples:

- In the 1969 issue of the Europa World Book, Osaka (Japan) is reported to have a population of 5.9 millions; in the 1989 issue, the population of the same city has fallen to 2.5 millions.

- In the 1979 issue of the UN Demographic Yearbook, only two cities in 1971-India are reported to be larger than 500 000 (this is probably a misprint); ten years later, in the issue of 1989, one has 218 cities above the same threshold of 500 000: a tremendous increase!

1.3.2 Empirical trajectories in the Pareto plane

The trajectories shown in Fig.5.7 correspond to the data in Table 5.1b in which the Pareto index is obtained by standard least squares. The most conspicuous feature is that all trajectories tend toward the origin which represents the ultimate state of urban systems (a state which can of course only be approached asymptotically). The overall directions of evolution are, at least qualitatively, consistent with the production-transportation constraint. Yet, there are marked differences in the way different countries are converging towards the origin. Three groups are to be distinguished:

- France and Germany have almost parallel trajectories except for a pronounced divergence that has set in during the last thirty years.
- Denmark and Sweden which remain at relatively high ϵ levels
- The "new" countries such as Canada and the United States which are characterized by frontier systems whose Pareto indexes remain almost constant in the course of time.

Table 5.1c parallels Table 5.1b for developing countries; unfortunately for many of them reliable statistics are rather sparse.

1.3.3 Prices of commodities in small versus large cities

In nineteenth-century Europe wheat markets were hold two or three times a week in almost all cities of some importance. By virtue of the strong centralization of the French administration, the corresponding price records have been compiled and conserved at the "Archives Nationales" in Paris. The sample of data we shall use is drawn from these archives.
According to the assumptions on which the green-belt model is based, wheat prices should be higher in large cities; let us examine whether this is confirmed by the data. In order for the test to be significant, the price comparisons have to be carried out "ceteris paribus", i.e. in situations that are identical with regard to all other conditions. For instance wheat used to be cheaper in Brittany than in the South-East; it would therefore be meaningless to compare prices in Montfort (Ille et Vilaine, population: 1700) and in Avignon (Vaucluse, population: 32 000). For the same kind of reasons we have excluded from our sample all major ports such as Bordeaux, Brest, Marseille, Nantes or Rouen; the communication patterns of these cities clearly do not fit the green-belt model. Furthermore to make the test effective, one has to select pairs of cities exhibiting large population gaps. Finally, we came up with the 38 market pairs which are listed in Table 5.2. Wheat prices are indeed higher in large cities in 66% of the cases; this proportion could be expected to become even higher if the previous fortnight prices were replaced by annual averages with the effect of smoothing out short run fluctuations. Moreover, one should keep in mind that even in the nineteenth century wheat prices in large cities were a matter of concern for the

Country	Year	Pareto index	Largest city millions	Gini's coeff.	Source
Canada	1881	1.04	0.2	0.62	Z(p.417)
	1931	0.92	1.0	0.75	Z(p.417)
	1966	0.91	2.4	0.79	UN(1971)
Denmark	1801	1.64	0.1	0.41	Stewart
	1840	1.41	0.1	0.47	Stewart
	1890	1.07	0.4	0.65	Stewart
	1945	0.94	1.0	0.74	UN(1955)
	1970	0.83	1.3	0.79	UN(1973)
	1981	0.80	1.4	0.80	UN(1981),EY
England & Wales	1801	1.26	0.9	0.59	Robson
	1851	1.14	3.0	0.68	Robson
	1911	1.16	4.0	0.67	Robson
	1921	1.06	8.0	0.74	Z(p.439)
	1961	not Pareto	11.0		UN(1962)
France	1500	1.56	0.09	0.43	De Vries
	1600	1.48	0.15	0.46	De Vries
	1836	1.36	1.0	0.54	P(p.97)
	1906	1.10	3.0	0.70	P(p.97)
	1982	0.95	10.0	0.81	GP
Germany	1500	2.52	0.04	0.24	De Vries
	1600	2.10	0.06	0.31	De Vries
	1800	1.41	0.15	0.48	De Vries
	1875	1.38	1.0	0.53	Z(p.427)
	1900	1.23	2.0	0.62	Z(p.427)
	1939	1.09	4.0	0.71	Z(p.427)
	1970	1.04	3.0	0.73	UN(1973),EY
Sweden	1800	1.22	0.08	0.52	Stewart
	1850	1.13	0.1	0.55	Stewart
	1913	0.96	0.3	0.67	Stewart
	1945	0.94	0.9	0.73	UN(1955)
	1975	0.84	1.0	0.77	UN(1983),EY
USA	1810	1.05	0.1	0.58	Z(p.420)
	1900	0.95	3.0	0.77	Z(p.420)
	1930	0.95	8.0	0.80	Z(p.420)
	1973	0.95	16.0	0.82	AU

Table 5.1b Urban evolutions in industrialized countries. The 1970 figures for Germany refer to East and West Germany together. *Sources: References to sources are as follows: AU: Atlas Universalis; De Vries: 1984; EY: Europa World Yearbook; GP: Guérin-Pace (1990); P: Pumain (1982); Robson: 1972; Stewart: 1958; Z: Zipf (1972); UN: United Nations Demographic Yearbook.*

Country	Year	Pareto index	Largest city millions	Gini's coeff.	Source
Ghana	1960	1.42	0.6	0.51	UN(1962) AU
	1970	1.27	0.8	0.58	UN(1973) AU
Mexico	1960	1.18	5.0	0.66	UN(1962)
	1970	1.11	9.0	0.71	UN(1973)
Tunisia	1946	1.14	0.4	0.62	UN(1956)
	1984	1.03	0.8	0.70	UN(1988)

Table 5.1c Urban evolution in developing countries. *Sources: Same as in Table 5.1b.*

government because large price increases could result in civil disturbances (such disturbances for instance took place on a rather large scale as a result of the price increase of 1847); although the years we have selected are rather "normal" years, the few regulations (as compared to previous centuries) that remained in effect in the nineteenth century might have had the effect of lessening the price gap between large and small cities.

1.4 Conclusion

An urban revolution is clearly in progress in many developing countries. In this study we have modelled the direction of this evolution with the help of a few basic parameters: the growth rates of the urban population and of the number of cities, the productivity in production and in transportation (this last expression being taken in a wide sense so as to include transmission of electricity, water, gas, etc). Given the current rates of (urban) population increase, the huge metropolitan areas are bound to become even larger. Whether this should bring about difficulties in the supplying process mainly depends on future productivity gains in transportation (in this connection see Deakin 1969). What we have tried to do in this study is to provide a quantitative assessment by analysing the trajectories of urban systems in the Pareto plane. In order to sharpen the investigation one would need additional statistical data about the routing of various products to cities.

From the point of view of system theory, we may say that urban organisations can be approached in two alternative ways: by analysing the various services that operate *within* cities or by focusing on inputs and outputs of cities considered as "black boxes". In this study, we have used the second approach. The former has been tried in Roehner (1985,1991) with a similar emphasis on the evolution of the Pareto index. There too, the analysis was somewhat hampered by the lack of accurate data (in that case concerning the various occupation

Region	City	Population 1836 thousands	Price dif. 1855	Price dif. 1875	Price dif. 1880
AIN	Bourg	9.5		-123	108
	Gex	2.9			
AISNE	Saint-Quentin	20.5	-42		
	Vervins	2.5			
AUBE	Troyes	25.5	126; 52	20	
	Bar/Aube	3.9			
	Arcis	2.7			
CANTAL	Aurillac	10.9	-15	425	275
	Murat	2.5			
CHARENTE	Angoulême	16.9	248	-123	318
	Cognac	3.8			
CHER	Bourges	25.3	64	77	145
	Saint-Amand	7.3			
DOUBS	Besançon	29.7		73	43
	Beaume	2.5			
Hte-	Toulouse	77.3	-119; -31	25; 45	32; -12
GARONNE	*Villefranche*	2.7			
	Muret	3.9			
LOIRET	Orléans	40.2	-17	-210	-6
	Pithiviers	4.0			
MAINE-et-	Angers	35.9	88	109	
LOIRE	*Baugé*	3.4			
MEURTHE	Nancy	31.4	-294		
	Sarrebourg	2.3			
NIEVRE	Nevers	16.9		-16	125
	Cosne	6.2			
NORD	Lille	72.0	397	85	171
	Cambrai	17.8			
PAS-de-	Arras	23.4	26	115	46
CALAIS	*Béthune*	6.8			
PUY-de-	Clermont	32.4	144	168	45
DOME	*Riom*	11.4			
VAUCLUSE	Avignon	31.7	404		
	Apt	5.9			

Table 5.2 Market prices of wheat in large versus small cities. In each of the mentioned "departement" two (in some cases three) marketplaces have been selected: one with a large population, the other(s) (italics) with a small population. Price differences (in centimes) are given between large cities and small ones; the prices refer to the first fortnight of January. Prices are indeed higher in larger cities in 66% of the above cases. *Sources: Statistique de la France (1837) p.267-279; Archives Nationales (Paris) F11* 1779-2678.*

groups within cities).

2 The impact of price fluctuations on vital rates

The impact of *severe* recessions on the level of birth rates is unquestionable. Let us give two examples.

- After the reunification of Germany in 1988, former East Germany faced a major social and economic crisis: unemployment rose from zero to about 20% between 1988 and 1991. As a result the birth rate fell from 12.9 per thousand to 6.6 in 1991.
- At the time when the Great Depression hit the United States the birth rate dropped from 22.2 per thousand in 1928 to 18.4 in 1933 while, at the same time, unemployment rose from 4.2 % to 24.9 %.

Yet the influence of economic fluctuations of smaller magnitude is not so obvious. Its statistical estimation is one of the objective of this study. The nineteenth century is of special interest in this respect for it provides the opportunity to analyse demographic comportment during the transition from an agricultural economy to an industrial economy.

A number of papers have already been devoted to the connection between the economic situation and the short-term fluctuations in births, deaths and marriages: Richards (1983), Grenier (1984), Galloway (1985,1986,1992), Weir (1989), Roehner (1990), Blum et al (1992). Galloway's 1992 paper is of special interest for it analyses different European countries over long time spans. This is precisely the point of view we shall adopt in this section. Since our sources are distinct from those used by Galloway it is of interest to note that in many respects our findings confirm his results.

Did fluctuations in grain prices have a significant impact on the number of births, deaths and marriages in the nineteenth century? If so, were the patterns of influence similar in different European countries? One would expect the connection between prices and vital rates to become weaker at the beginning of the twentieth century; is such a trend actually to be observed? These are some of the questions we shall address in this study. But first of all we have to delineate the methodological framework.

2.1 The methodology

We are interested in measuring correlations between wheat prices on one hand and marriage, birth and death rates on the other. Let us, for the sake of shortness, refer to these correlations as: p-m, p-b and p-d correlations.

2.1.1 Selecting the data

Availability of data Fortunately, for the 19th century vital rate statistics exist for almost all industrialized countries. The United States are a notable exception. Massachusetts has the longest annual series of vital rates but it starts only in 1860 (Historical Statistics of the US, 1975). Estimated birth rates are given from 1855 forward for the entire US in Coale and Zelnick (1963)[2]. 1855 is too late a date, however, for one of our purposes is to carry out comparisons between the first and the second half of the nineteenth century. Another important country which will be omitted in this study is Japan; Mitchell(1982) gives vital rates from 1875 onward; this again is somewhat too late. Accordingly, our analysis will be restricted to European countries.

Calendar year versus cereal-year Let us refer to the 12 months from July to June as the cereal-year. Averages over cereal-years have been claimed (see for instance Meuvret 1971) to be more appropriate than calendar-year averages for the purpose of measuring the connection between cereal prices and vital rates. This question has been discussed in some detail in Roehner (1990a,p.306-310). The conclusion is that the p-b and p-m correlations are almost unaffected by the substitution of the calendar year for the cereal-year; only the p-d correlations might be adversely affected. As we are primarily interested in the p-b and p-m correlations (p-d correlations are not very significant anyway) using calendar-year data will cause no problem.

Wheat versus rye prices In each country those grain prices will be used which play the major role: wheat in France and England, rye in Sweden and Finland. In Germany, wheat and rye are of comparable importance: in 1885 the production figures were respectively: 3.5 and 6.9 million tons; therefore, we have used a weighted average of both prices.

2.1.2 Alternative options for estimating the correlation

To begin with, let us point out that we are not interested in the whole sequence of intercovariance coefficients between prices and vital rates:

$$c(l) = E\left[(X_t - m_X)(Y_{t+l} - m_Y)\right]$$

Lags larger than two years correspond to rather indirect effects of prices on vital rates. For instance a jump in the rate of marriages is likely to be followed one year later by a jump (of a somewhat smaller amplitude) in the number of births. The latter may in turn result in an increase in the number of marriages some

[2] I am grateful to P. Galloway for bringing this reference to my attention

twenty years later and so on. The same kind of reasoning can be applied to deaths. In this study, we investigate *direct* effects of price fluctuations; therefore we shall be interested in the zero- and one-year lags. The significance of one-year lags have already been discussed in some detail in Roehner (1990), so we shall actually focus on zero-lag correlations.
In order to get rid of possible trends in each of the series different methods may be used. "Pre-withening" the series by taking its first differences is one of them; subtracting a moving average background is another possibility. A number of different options have been compared in Roehner (1990, p.312). It turns out that one of the best compromise is to take correlations between deviations of the series with respect to a moving average performed over the same period that is used to estimate the correlation. This way, possible trends are almost eliminated and, at the same time, the impact of possible statistical errors is kept under control.

2.2 Results

2.2.1 Nineteenth century

England, France and Germany Our results for England & Wales, France and Germany are best illustrated by referring to Fig.5.8a,b,c. The upwards trends in the p-m and p-b correlations are a clear indication of the transition from an agricultural economy to an industrial economy. Indeed, in the society of the end of the eighteenth century high prices are associated with periods of contraction and dearth, while in modern economies periods of recession are on the contrary characterized by deflation. In the process of this transition England is in the lead: this appears most distinctly on the p-b curves; the lag tends to vanish by the end of the century especially between England and Germany. In fact, the curves for Germany and France are very close until 1870-1885; after this date Germany catches up with England while France lags behind. The same features more or less appear on the p-d curves; however because correlations are lower on average, statistical fluctuations are more important. Nevertheless, the deep through which occurs around 1870 in the curve for England seems to be too pronounced to be nothing but a statistical fluctuation. Its interpretation remains an open question.

Baden To clarify the relations between the evolutions in France and in Germany somewhat further we next consider the case of the Land of Baden (presently Baden-Wurtemberg). Baden is a frontier zone facing Alsace across the Rhine. Is its evolution to resemble that of France or that of Germany? The answer is provided by Fig.5.9a,b. Demographic comportment turns out to be much closer to the German average than to the French, especially after 1870.

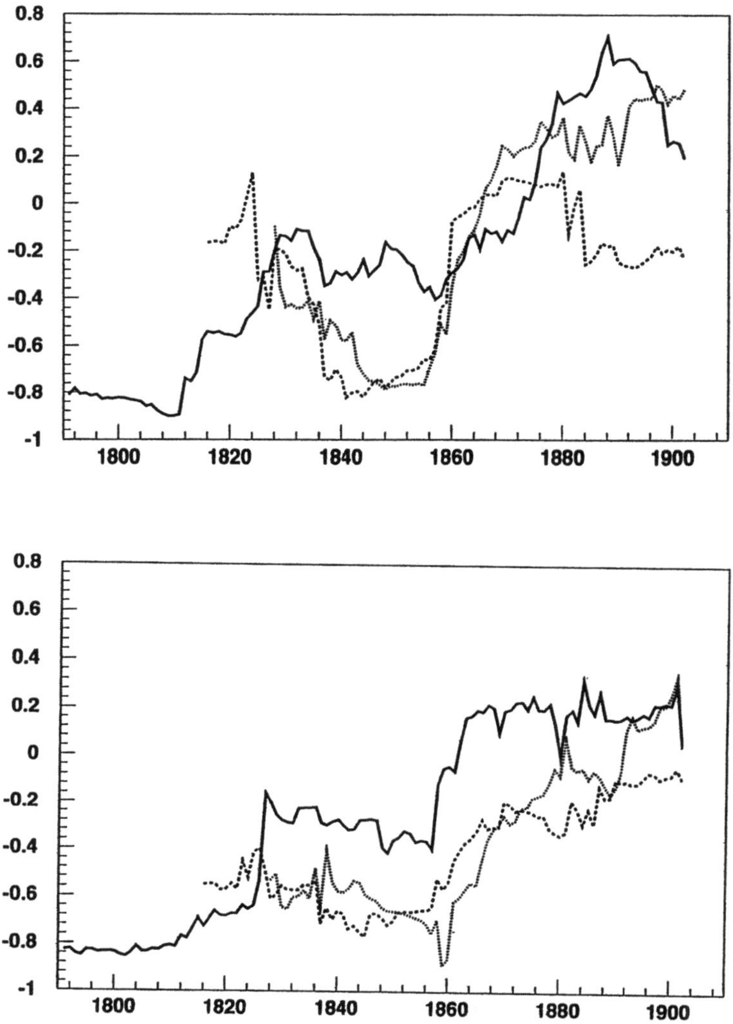

Fig.5.8 a,b Evolution of (marriage rates / cereal prices) correlation (a) and of (birth rates / cereal prices) correlation (b) in England (solid line), France (dashed line) and Germany (dotted line). The transition from an agricultural economy (where high prices are associated with periods of dearth) to an industrialized economy (where price increases are associated with periods of prosperity) is especially clear for England and Germany. As in all figures thereafter the width of the moving window is 21 years. *Sources: Wheat prices in England: Mitchell (1971); wheat prices in France: Labrousse et al (1970); grain prices in Germany: Jacobs and Richter (1935); vital rates: Mitchell (1978).*

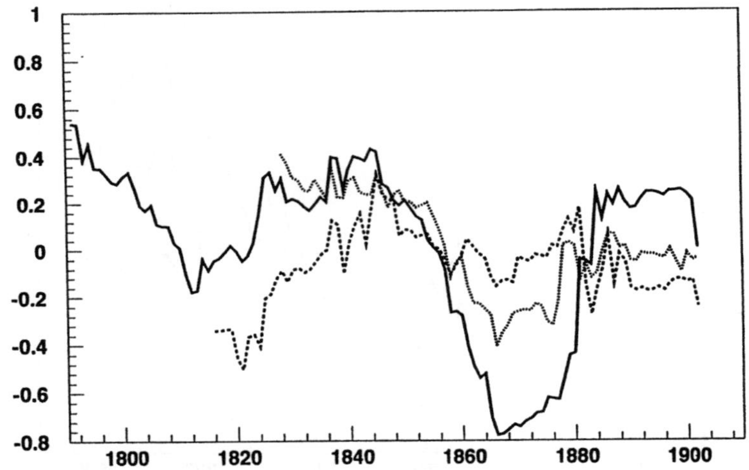

Fig.5.8c Evolution of the correlation between cereal prices and death rates in England (solid line), France (dashed line) and Germany (dotted line). *Sources: Same as in Fig.5.8a,b.*

The data for Baden come from completely different sources than the data for Germany: grain prices are prices of rye in Mannheim and the demographic data are from the "Statistisches Jahrbuch des Großherzogtum Baden"(1915). Consequently, the results for Baden constitute a confirmation of the results for Germany.

Cereal versus bread prices Since a series of bread prices was available for Stuttgart, the capital-city of Baden (Hirschberg 1893), it was possible to compare its correlations to those corresponding to rye prices. Results are shown in Fig.5.9c,d for marriages and births. The most conspicuous fact is that both curves are rather parallel. This again provides a useful check. At closer inspection, the correlations with bread prices can be seen to be somewhat more pronounced, i.e. they are lower as long as correlation is significantly negative, and after the turning point, they become higher. Unfortunately the bread price series is much shorter than the series for rye prices in Mannheim.

Sweden and Finland Analysing the cases of Sweden and Finland provides some confirmations but it also raises a number of questions. The correlations for Sweden in Fig.5.10a,b follow the same pattern as the correlations in Fig.5.8a,b

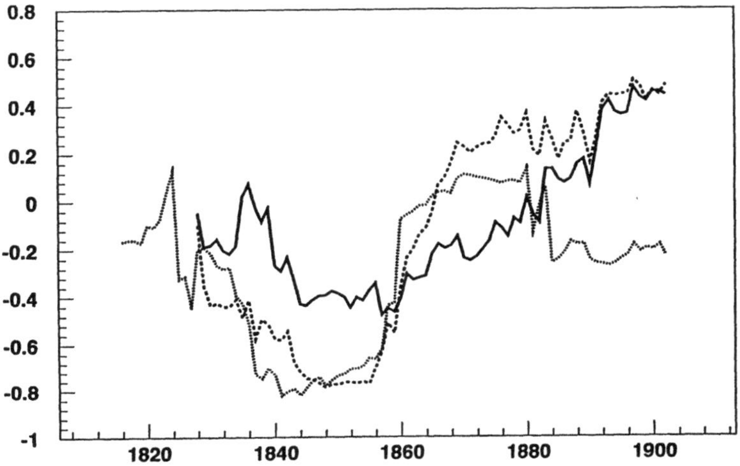

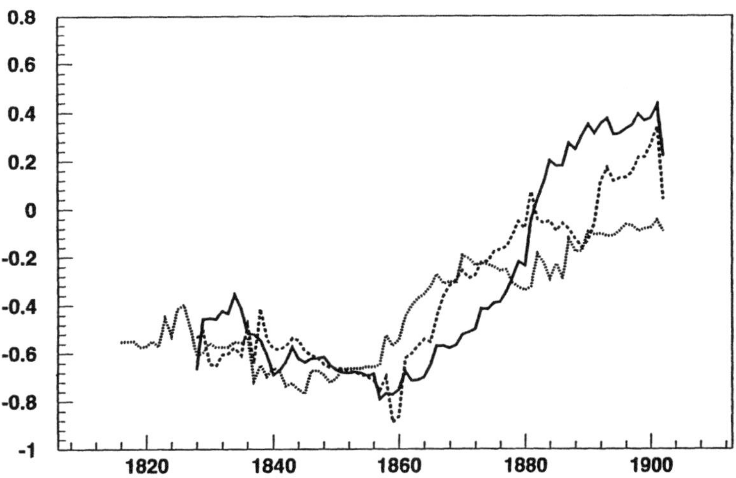

Fig.5.9 a,b Comparison between (marriage rates / cereal prices) correlations (a) and (birth rates / cereal prices) correlations (b) in Baden (solid line), France (dotted line) and Germany (dashed line). In the course of time the correlation for Baden moves closer to the average correlation level in Germany, especially after 1870. *Sources: Rye prices in Mannheim (Baden): Jacobs and Richter (1935); vital rates in Baden: Statistisches Jahrbuch für Baden (1915). France and Germany: same as in Fig.5.8.*

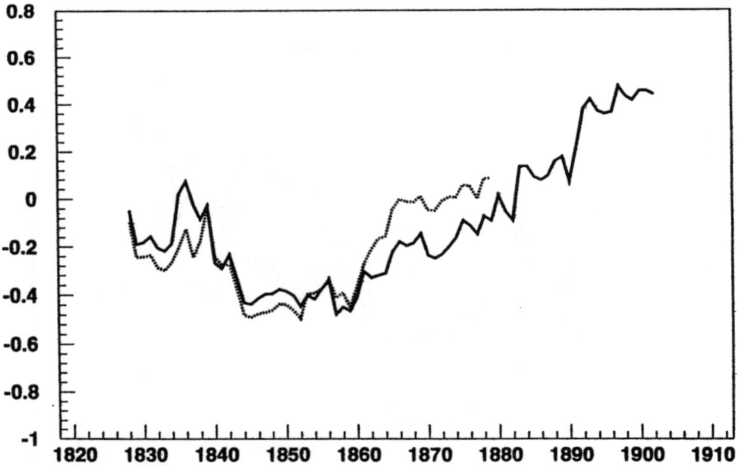

Fig.5.9 c Comparison between (marriage rates / rye prices) correlations (solid curve) and (marriage rates / bread prices) correlations (dotted curve) in Baden. *Sources: Bread prices: Hirschberg (1893); vital rates: same as in Fig.5.9a,b.*

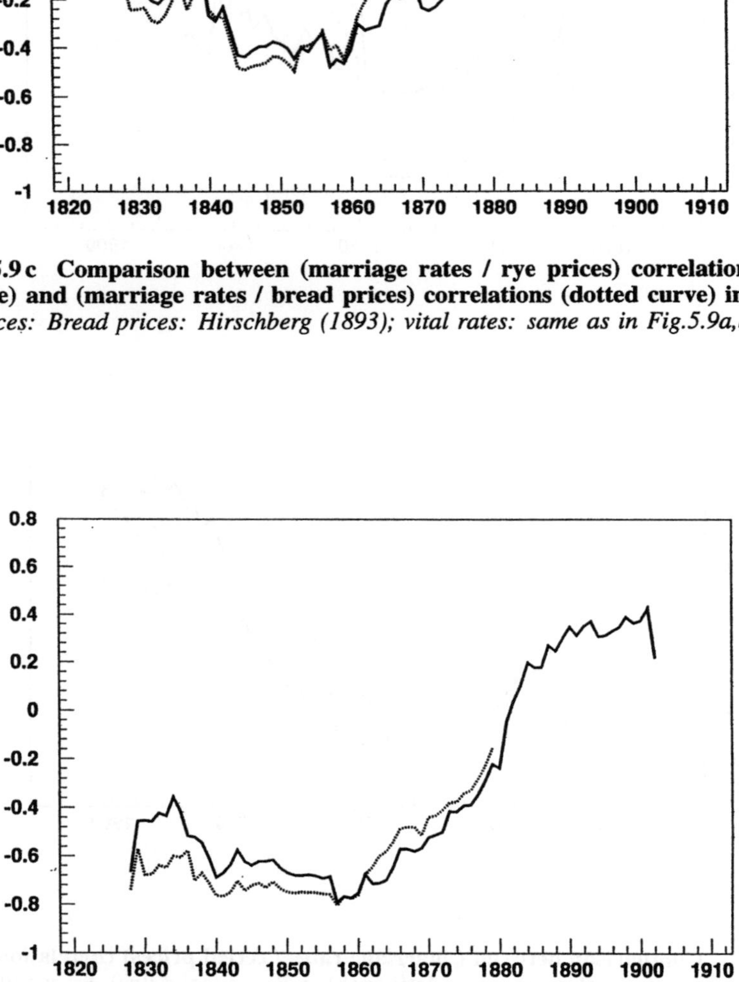

Fig.5.9 d Comparison between (birth rates / rye prices) correlations (solid curve) and (birth rates / bread prices) correlations (dotted curve) in Baden. *Sources: Same as in Fig.5.9c*

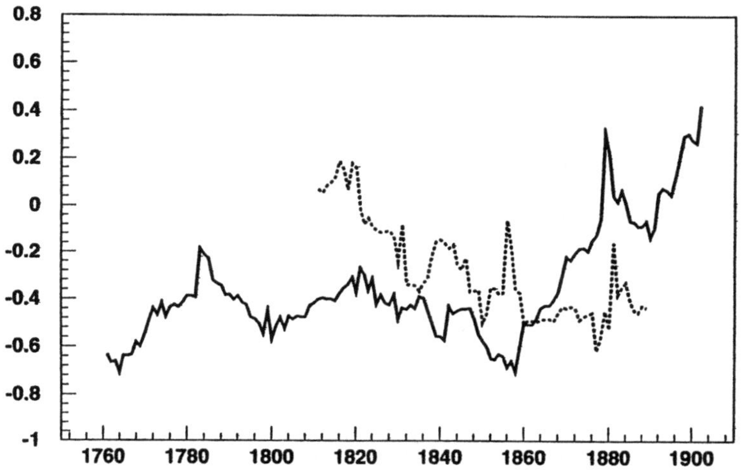

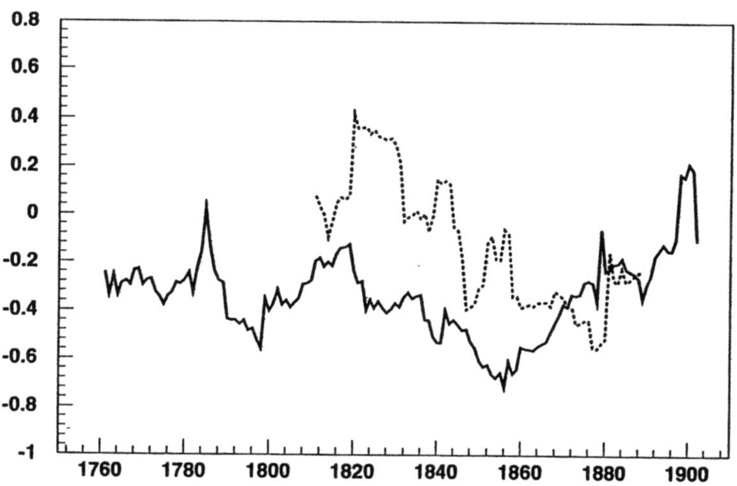

Fig.5.10 a,b Evolution of (marriage rates / rye prices) correlation (a) and of (birth rates / cereal prices) correlation (b) in Sweden (solid line) and in Finland (dashed line). The pre-1860 level of the price/birth correlation in Sweden is notably less negative than in Germany. The curves for Finland are somewhat more puzzling. *Sources: Rye price in Finland: Földes (1905,p.492); rye prices in Sweden: Jörberg (1972,p.633); vital rates: Mitchell (1978).*

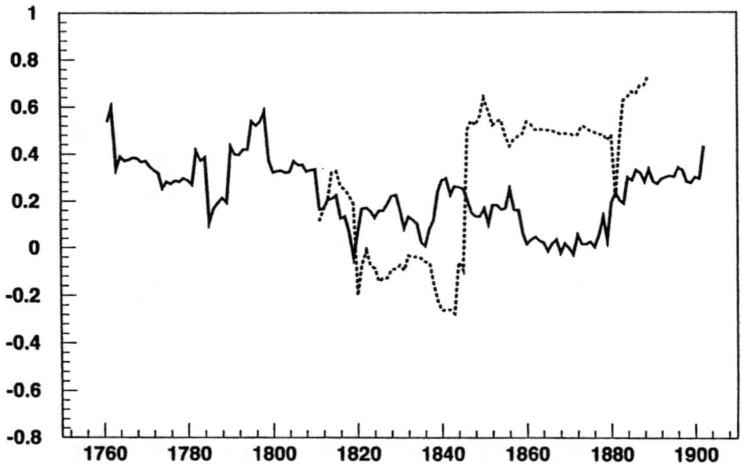

Fig.5.10 c Evolution of the correlation between rye prices and death rates in Finland (dashed line) and in Sweden (solid line). *Sources: Rye price in Finland: Földes (1905,p.492); rye prices in Sweden: Jörberg (1972,p.633); vital rates: Mitchell (1978).*

with an increase trend for birth and marriage correlations; this trend sets in around 1860 likewise to the evolutions in France and in Germany. The decrease trend of deaths rates is less marked than in Germany.

The case of Finland is more puzzling. The trends, if any, go almost the opposite way. Whether this should be attributed to some peculiar rationality in demographic comportment or simply to flaws in the data remains an open question.

2.2.2 Discussion of the period after World War I

Obviously, grain prices are no longer a pertinent economic indicator after World War I. Instead one could think of using GNP/capita figures or unemployment rates. Unfortunately, the occurrence of World War II had a disturbing effect on vital rates. For instance, in the United States the marriage rate jumped from 10.9 per thousand in 1944 to 16.4 in 1946; likewise, the birth rate increased from 20.4 in 1945 to 26.6 in 1947. These large increases were not accompanied by a comparable rise in GNP (on the contrary GNP decreased) or by a decrease in unemployment (on the contrary unemployment rose from 2% to 4%). We shall here restrict our attention to a special but important point: the effect of the Great Depression on birth rates. Table 5.3 summarizes the relevant data for France and for the United States from 1921 to 1940. During the whole decade

	1921	22	23	24	25	26	27	28	29	30
USA	132	123	122	123	118	114	110	104	100	100
France	115	107	106	104	106	104	101	102	98	100
	1931	**32**	**33**	**34**	**35**	**36**	**37**	**38**	**39**	**40**
USA	95	92	86	89	88	86	88	90	88	91
France	97	96	90	90	85	83	82	81	81	76
	1951	**52**	**53**	**54**	**55**	**56**	**57**	**58**	**59**	**60**
USA	117	118	117	119	117	118	119	115	113	111
France	108	107	104	104	103	102	102	101	101	99

	Average (1921-1930)	Average (1931-1940)	Average (1951-1960)
USA	115	89	116
France	104	86	103

Table 5.3 Comparison of birth rates in the decades 1921-1930, 1931-1940, 1951-1960. To facilitate comparisons the rates have been normalized to 100 in 1930; actual rates for 1930 are: USA: 21.3 per thousand, France: 18.0 per thousand. The number of births remains below the 1921-1930 average during the whole 1931-1940 slump that followed the Great Depression. In a sense the so-called baby-boom that occurred after World War II can be seen as a continuation of the situation that prevailed before the onset of the Great Depression; in terms of ten-years averages there is an almost exact correspondance between the periods 1921-1930 and 1951-1960 both in the US and in France. *Source: Mitchell (1978).*

1931-1940 marked by the Great Depression the level of birth rates is notably lower than during the previous decade. After the Great Depression decade, birth levels resumed their 1921-30 levels both in the US and in France. In the light of this observation the post war "baby-boom" may be seen rather as a return to a "normal" state.

A Appendix A: Measure of concentration for a finite Pareto distribution

As the following expression of Gini's coefficient:

$$g = 1 - \frac{\int_0^\infty G^2(x)dx}{\int_0^\infty G(x)dx} \tag{A.1}$$

was not to be found in standard textbooks (for instance Kendall et al 1987) we shall devote a few lines to its derivation. At the same time we shall obtain the conditions under which formula $(A.1)$ holds true.

A.1 Expression of Gini's coefficient

Gini's coefficient may be defined geometrically in terms of the Lorenz curve by the following expression:

$$g = 1 - 2B$$

where B denotes the area under the Lorenz curve. As the standard application of Lorenz curves refers to income distribution we shall in this derivation adopt this terminology. A parametric representation of the Lorenz curve in the plane (p, r) is given by:

$$\begin{cases} p = F(u) \\ r = \frac{1}{R}\int_0^x uF'(u)du \end{cases}$$

p denotes the percentage of income units smaller than x and r denotes the percentage share of the total income R which is received by these p per cent. $F(.)$ is the probability distribution function. The area B under the Lorenz curve is:

$$B = \int_0^1 rdp = \int_0^\infty r(u)p'(u)du = \frac{1}{R}\int_0^\infty F'(u)du \int_0^u vF'(v)dv \tag{A.2}$$

where:

$$R = \int_0^\infty uF'(u)du \tag{A.3}$$

We now integrate integral $(A.3)$ by parts; but before this can be done, we have to shift from $F(u)$ to $G(u) = 1 - F(u)$ for, unlike F, $G(u)$ goes to zero as u tends to infinity. Thereby, we obtain:

$$R = \int_0^\infty G(u)du \tag{A.4}$$

In the process of integration by parts, we had to assume that: $\lim_{u \to \infty} uG(u) = 0$.

We now come to the evaluation of the numerator in $(A.2)$; expressed in terms of G it reads:

$$I = \int_0^\infty J(u)G'(u)du \qquad J(u) = \int_0^u vG'(v)dv$$

$J(u)$ can be integrated by parts in the same way as we did for R, but this time the integrated term is no longer equal to zero:

$$J(u) = uG(u) - \int_0^u G(v)dv$$

Replacing $J(u)$ in the integral I, one obtains:

$$I = I_1 - I_2 \qquad I_1 = \int_0^\infty uG(u)G'(u)du \qquad I_2 = \int_0^\infty \left(\int_0^u G(v)dv\right) G'(u)du$$

Integrating both I_1 and I_2 by parts, we obtain:

$$I_1 = -\frac{1}{2}\int_0^\infty G^2(u)du \qquad I_2 = -\int_0^\infty G^2(u)du$$

where the following assumptions had to be made:

$$\lim_{u\to\infty} uG^2(u) = 0 \qquad \lim_{u\to\infty} G(u)\int_0^u G(v)dv = 0$$

Collecting all terms, leads to the result $(A.1)$.

A.2 Application to finite Pareto distributions

We now consider the cumulative distribution function of a finite Pareto distribution:

$$G(x) = \begin{cases} 1 & x \le x_1 \\ \dfrac{(x_1/x)^\alpha - (x_1/x_2)^\alpha}{1-(x_1/x_2)^\alpha} & x_1 \le x \le x_2 \\ 0 & x \ge x_2 \end{cases}$$

Tedious but straightforward integrations lead to:

$$g = \frac{1-(2\alpha-1)\epsilon^{\alpha-1}(1-2\epsilon) - 2\alpha\epsilon^{2\alpha-1}}{(2\alpha-1)(1-\epsilon^{\alpha-1})} \qquad \alpha \ne 1, 1/2 \qquad (A.5)$$

The correctness of this result may be checked in two ways:

1) For the infinite Pareto distribution corresponding to $\epsilon = 0$, $(A.5)$ should reduce to the well-known expression:

$$g = \frac{1}{2\alpha - 1} \qquad \alpha > 1$$

From this expression it can be seen that the distribution becomes more concentrated ($g \rightarrow 1$) as α decreases toward 1.

2) For $\alpha = 1$, g must be of indeterminate form $0/0$
Both requirements can be seen to be satisfied.

The particular case $\alpha = 1$ is of some importance too for most empirical distributions of city-sizes are bordering on this value. The integrations then lead to the appearance of logarithmic terms:

$$g = \frac{\ln 1/\epsilon - 2 + \epsilon \ln 1/\epsilon + 2\epsilon}{(1-\epsilon)\ln 1/\epsilon}$$

B Appendix B: First moments of a finite Pareto distribution

In this appendix, we shall establish a few results which are used in the text, in particular in equation (1.3) and (1.10). We consider a distribution of cities characterized by the probability density function:

$$f_p(x) = C_p \frac{Y(x - x_1)(x_2 - x)}{x^{\alpha+1}} \qquad (B.1)$$

where α is the urbanization threshold, x_2 the size of the largest city and α the Pareto index. The constant C_p is defined by the normalization condition:

$$\int_{x_1}^{x_2} f_p(x) = 1$$

which leads to:

$$C_p = \frac{\alpha x_1^\alpha}{1 - \epsilon^\alpha} \qquad \epsilon = x_1/x_2 \qquad (B.2)$$

First order moment Denoting the total urban population by P_u and the total number of cities by N, the average size of a city will be given on one hand by P_u/N, and on the other by the expectation of the distribution $(B.1)$; thus:

$$\frac{P_u}{N} = \int_{x_1}^{x_2} x f_p(x) dx$$

Taking into account $(B.1)$ this leads to:

$$\frac{P_u}{N} = \frac{C_p}{\alpha - 1} \frac{1 - \epsilon^{\alpha-1}}{x_1^{\alpha-1}} = C_p \frac{x_2^{1-\alpha}}{1 - \alpha}(1 - \epsilon^{1-\alpha})$$

When replacing the normalization constant C_p by its expression one obtains:

$$\frac{P_u}{N} = x_1 \frac{\alpha}{\alpha - 1} \frac{1 - \epsilon^{\alpha-1}}{1 - \epsilon^\alpha}$$

which is equation (1.3).

In the text, we reasoned on the statistical density function $f_s(x)$ rather than on the probabilistic density function, the only difference between them being their normalization:

$$f_s(x) = C \frac{Y(x - x_1)(x_2 - x)}{x^{\alpha+1}}, \qquad \int_{x_1}^{x_2} f_s(x) dx = N \quad \Rightarrow \quad C = NC_p$$

Thus:

$$C = N\alpha \frac{x_1 \alpha}{1 - \epsilon^\alpha} \quad \text{and} \quad P_u = C \frac{x_2^{1-\alpha}}{1 - \alpha}(1 - \epsilon^{1-\alpha})$$

which is (1.10).

Second order moment The expression of the standard deviation of the truncated Pareto distribution is given in Roehner (1991, p.1740).

Chapter 6
Interdependence between markets and autoregressive modelling

In February 1990, on the day following the elections in the Lower House of the Japanese Diet, the Nikkei index at the Tokyo Stock Exchange lost 3%. At this time, Tokyo was the world largest Stock Market in terms of capitalization. In the following months, there was a steady decline of the Nikkei index; a key issue then was whether or not this drop would be transmitted to European and American markets, in which case a downward spiralling of stock prices could result. This did not happen, however, and the relative disconnection between Tokyo and other major stock markets came as a surprise to most analysts. This example concerning stock markets could be rephrased for commodity markets as well. It highlights the importance of being able to assess the strength of interactions between markets. Price differentials which have been discussed in chapters 3 and 4 do in fact provide a measure of market interdependence, but this measure has but a limited range of applicability since it is only appropriate for transactions in one commodity and in the same currency; it is for instance useless when it comes to analysing the coupling between the fluctuations of the Nikkei and the Dow-Jones indexes. A number of general methods have been developed by statisticians and econometricians in order to analyse the inter-relationship between two time-series:

- Correlation analysis
- Cross-spectral analysis
- Autoregressive modelling and causality tests
- Cointegration tests

First we discuss some of these methods, then we apply correlation analysis and autoregressive modelling to the analysis of market interdependence. It will be shown that by using autoregressive modelling it is possible to extract detailed information from price series not only about the strength of the interaction but also about its direction. In this chapter our analysis is completely phenomenological in the sense that it does not directly rely on specific assumptions about arbitrage processes or about profit maximization. Later on in chapter 8 we shall see that the parameters of our autoregressive models can be given an economic interpretation in terms of transportation costs and of supply-elasticities. Section one is devoted to preliminary methodological tests. In section two we estimate the *strength* of the interdependence between markets and its evolution in the course of time. In section three, by using multivariate autoregressive models we are able to assess the *direction* of the interdependence; this technique is firstly tested on pairs of markets of unequal importance; then it is applied to major grain markets.

1 Analysing market interdependence

1.1 From price differentials to correlation analysis

We have already pointed out that a measure of market interdependence should be independent of the absolute level of prices or indexes; let us first elaborate on this point. Arbitrage is the most obvious characteristic of an integrated market; as a result price differentials can be considered as a measure of market integration. The main disadvantage of this approach is that it relies upon the magnitude of prices; this could lead to misleading results. Let us for instance consider retail markets in nowadays France. Although it should be considered as a well integrated market, there are still irreducible price differentials due to extra transportation costs for instance between Marseilles and Ajaccio in the island of Corsica. In order to avoid this difficulty, it may be in order to consider the *correlation* of prices in Marseilles and Ajaccio rather than their differences. Then, if the market is well integrated, prices in Marseilles and Ajaccio will undergo parallel changes regardless of their respective levels and as a result their correlation will be close to one.
Correlation analysis has further practical advantages:

- As already mentioned it applies to indexes such as for instance Stock Exchange indexes.
- It applies to commodity prices regardless of specific grades. This turns out to be of special importance in modern markets where grades are specified with great precision; in the case of wheat for instance, one distinguishes between: Hard Red Winter (ordinary protein), Hard Red Winter (13% protein), Hard Winter, Soft Red Winter, etc.
- It applies to commodity prices regardless of the currency or of the unit of weight (or volume) in which prices are expressed. This is especially important when comparing historical price records for establishing conversion tables is not always easy for the periods before 1800.

Under the assumption of a normal price distribution, there is of course a direct correspondence between expectation of differences on one hand and correlations on the other hand. While the normality assumption was not found to be unrealistic for *spatial* price distributions of prices (see chapter 4), it is no longer valid for distributions of prices in the course of time; in this case, log-normality definitely constitutes a more realistic assumption. In the following we shall mainly be concerned with correlations between logarithms of prices for, in contrast to arbitragers, consumers are more concerned about percentage price increases than by the increases themselves.

1.2 General methods for measuring market interdependence

1.2.1 Model-independent measures of market integration

Correlation analysis Correlation analysis has been widely used to study market integration in an historical perspective. Let us mention the works of Achilles (1959), Jörberg (1972), Latham and Neal (1983), Ravallion (1986,1987), Roehner (1989a,1991a,b). Correlation analysis is a measure of interdependence which is both simple and robust; however, it has the following shortcomings. First, being a symmetrical measure of interaction, it is unable to provide any information about the direction of the interaction; to this end we shall resort to autoregressive models. The second drawback is more subtle. A time series can be regarded as the superposition of different periodical components. For instance, components with a period of several years are usually ascribed to the overall business cycle or, in the case of pre-industrial markets, to long-range fluctuations in climatic conditions; components with a period of a few months on the other hand are usually related to local price fluctuations. In the process of computing intercorrelations all these components combine and mix up. A great deal of the difficulties that we shall experience in interpreting the results of correlation analysis in remote periods can be traced to this problem. Cross-spectral analysis provides a way to obviate this difficulty.

Cross-spectral analysis The coherence square gives an estimate of the degree of correlation between separate frequency components in both series. The main reason why we shall refrain from using this method is the fact that estimating the spectrum involves rather large confidence intervals even for time-series of substantial length (Priestley 1981,p.510). Cross-spectral analysis has been used by Beveridge (1922), and by Bengtsson and Jörberg (1975) for a (static) description of market integration in Sweden.

1.2.2 Model-dependent measures of market integration

The previous measures can be considered to be largely model-independent in the sense that they do not require prior knowledge of the following elements.

- The number of markets that are actually influencing each other

• The statistical properties of exogenous shocks, in particular their auto- and intercorrelation

• The adequate sampling-time.

The main difficulty with model-dependent measures is that they may give misleading results whenever the model is incorrectly specified.

Autoregressive models Broadly speaking all the models we shall consider are of the autoregressive type. This should be no surprise since autoregressive equations are just the discrete analog of (stochastic) differential equations and therefore have a very large scope of applicability. Autoregressive processes may be classified into four categories (Table 6.1):

	Local integration market pairs	**Global integration**	**Considered in this chapter**
1) MODEL-INDEPENDENT MEASURES			
Dispersion	yes	yes	no
Correlation	yes	yes (correlation length)	yes
Cross spectral analysis	yes	no	no
2) MODEL-DEPENDENT MEASURES			
Transfer function models	yes	no	no
VAR models (Vector autoregressive)	yes	no	yes
MVARIMA models (Multivariate autoregressive integrated moving average)	yes	no	no
Bidimensional processes (STAR i.e. space-time autoregressive models)	no	yes	see chapters 7 and 8

Table 6.1. Measuring market integration

1) Univariate models which describe single markets

2) Transfer function models; these models relate two time series one of which is considered as an input and the other as an output (Box and Jenkins 1976)

3) Multivariate models; these models constitute a generalization of transfer function models and describe the connections within a set of N different markets (Priestley 1981, p.685)

4) Bidimensional models; these provide a description both in time and in space (Whittle 1954, Priestley 1981,p.718).

In addition, causality tests have been developed within the framework of autoregressive models (Granger 1969b).

Let us examine the relevance of the aforementioned models for the investigation of interdependence between markets. Of course, univariate models are not appropriate for that purpose. Neither are transfer function models: in fact these models are reasonable candidates only when the input and the output can be clearly identified as for instance for a chemical reactor or an electronic device. In the case of markets, one could think of "large" markets as inputs while "small" markets would be considered as outputs; it is not obvious, however, that the direction of causality should go this way; it is precisely the purpose of section 3 to test this assumption. Bidimensional models are the main subject of chapters 7 and 8 and we shall leave them aside in this chapter.
Since their introduction in the 1960s autoregressive models have been used extensively by economic historians in particular in connection with commodity or stock price fluctuations. Let us for instance mention the works of: Lévy-Leboyer and Bourguignon (1985); Heffer (1986); Aftalion (1988); Neal (1990), Roehner (1991d), Chevet and Saint Amour (1991).

Cointegration tests Analysis of cointegrated time series has become a rather popular subject in econometric research in the 1980s. The cointegration framework was proposed by Granger (1981); it has been related to error-correction models in the bivariate case by Engle and Granger (1987); the generalization to the multivariate case was carried out by Engle and Yoo (1987) and by Johansen (1988). Let us briefly present some of the ideas on which cointegration tests are based.
A time series $X(t)$ is called integrated of order one if the series of first differences $\Delta X(t)$ has a *stationary* autoregressive moving average (ARMA) representation. As a result $\Delta X(t)$ is mean stationary; if a denotes this mean: $a = E[\Delta X(t)]$, $X(t)$ will on average grow as the (discrete) integral of a; in other words, it will exhibit a trend of slope a: $E[X(t)] = at + x(0)$. $X(t)$ is said to follow an ARIMA process. We now assume that the series $X(t)$ and $Y(t)$ are both integrated of order one. They are called cointegrated if there is a number α such that:

$$Z(t) = X(t) - \alpha Y(t)$$

has a stationary ARMA representation. In other words the non-stationarities of $X(t)$ and $Y(t)$ are combined in such a way as to make $Z(t)$ stationary. Then (if one assumes that $E(X) = 0$) $X(t)$ is expected to fluctuate around $\alpha Y(t)$ without drifting apart in the long run.

Let us now point out by an example the economic significance of cointegration tests (Hagen 1989). The Prebisch-Singer hypothesis conjectures a secular decline in the price of primary commodities relative to the price of manufactured goods. The reasoning behind this assertion rests on the assumptions that the productivity of the manufacturing sector grows faster than the productivity of the primary sector and that the income elasticity of the demand for agricultural products is less than unity. How do cointegration tests step in? Let $X(t)$ and $Y(t)$ be the logarithms of a primary-goods and a manufactured-goods price index respectively. If the two prices are cointegrated (with $Z(t)$ denoting their ARMA representation), the difference between both prices may be expressed in the following way in terms of $Y(t)$ and $Z(t)$:

$$X(t) = Z(t) + \alpha Y(t) \Longrightarrow D(t) = X(t) - Y(t) = (\alpha - 1)Y(t) + Z(t)$$

Since $Z(t)$ is stationary, the trend of $D(t)$ is the trend of the first term. If $Y(t)$ is assumed to be increasing in the long run the Prebisch-Singer assumption can be expressed in the framework of cointegration by the condition $\alpha > 1$; thus estimation and testing of the critical parameter α may settle the issue. From empirical evidence given in Hagen (1989) it turns out that the test does *not* support the Prebisch-Singer hypothesis.

To summarize, cointegration primarily appears as a way to deal with non stationary time series. Cereal prices could be considered as being stationary in the mean during the whole nineteenth century; accordingly, as far as market integration is concerned, the relevance of cointegration is not evident.

1.3 Simulations of autoregressive modelling

Technicalities of autoregressive modelling are dealt with in Appendix B. In this paragraph we shall carry out some simulated experiments in autoregressive modelling in order to gain a better understanding of the possibilities and of the limitations of autoregresive models.

1.3.1 Adjusting ARMA processes to a simulated multivariate process

We generate two time series through the following vector autoregressive process:

$$\begin{cases} X_1(t) = a_{11}X_1(t-1) + a_{12}X_2(t-1) + N_1(t) \\ X_2(t) = a_{22}X_2(t-1) + a_{21}X_1(t-1) + N_2(t) \end{cases} \quad (1.1)$$

$N_1(t), N_2(t)$ are two white noises having the correlation r_{12} at equal times . The process (1.1) has been selected because it provides one of the simplest realistic model for the interaction between two markets. The autoregressive terms a_{11}, a_{22} take into account the fact that prices usually have a rather high autocorrelation. The interaction terms a_{12}, a_{21} respectively describe the influence of market 2 on market 1 and that of market 1 on market 2. The disturbances $N_1(t), N_2(t)$ describe local perturbations in supply and demand on each market. On the side of supply it includes in particular meteorological factors; since weather conditions are to some degree spatially autocorrelated (see Section 2.3.2) it is natural to assume $N_1(t)$ and $N_2(t)$ to be correlated.

The tables 6.2a,b summarize the results obtained for the estimation of different autoregressive and moving average processes. The two columns on the left give the estimated parameters; the third column gives the residual sum of squares; the fourth gives a Durbin-Watson estimate for the autocorrelation of residuals; the fifth column gives the value of Akaike's criterion (Akaike 1969). Criteria of this kind have been proposed because of the failure of maximum likelihood to provide consistent estimates of the autoregressive and moving average orders, p and q, of a model. Their general form is:

$$A = \ln \widehat{\sigma}^2_{pq} + (p+q)\frac{C(T)}{T} \qquad \frac{C(T)}{T} \longrightarrow 0 \tag{1.2}$$

$\widehat{\sigma}^2_{pq}$ is the estimated residual sum of squares. The intuitive interpretation of (1.2) is clear: increasing the order of the model has in general the effect of decreasing the residual sum of squares; beyond a given point, however, further complication of the model becomes inefficient; the "penalty" term $(p+q)C(T)/T$ provides a measure of the complexity of the model. One particular function $C(T)$ deserves special attention, namely: $C(T) = \ln T$ (Hannan and Rissanen 1982,1983); this is the choice that have been made in Table 6.2.

From the results in Table 6.2a, it is clear that the first order processes AR(1) and MA(1) are not acceptable. This is in fact not surprising . What is more unexpected is that the second order autoregressive process AR(2) turns out to be "better" than the more general mixed process both in terms of residual sum of squares and in term of Akaike's criterion. When one turns to estimating the true model, correct values of the parameters are indeed obtained; in terms of residual sum of squares the fit is not outstanding however. For short, had the type of the model been unknown, it would have been very difficult indeed, due to statistical fluctuations, to guess it correctly on the basis of the results in Table 6.1a. The same remarks more or less apply to Table 6.2b.

1.3.2 Estimation of a multivariate autoregressive process

The previous example has shed some light on the way the accuracy of the fit increases along with model's complexity. A clear intuitive interpretation of the estimated parameters was lacking however. The second example displayed in Table 6.3 is meant to provide such an interpretation. The simulated process we consider now is generated by a set of equations which differs from (1.1) by one additional term, namely $b_{21}X_1(t)$:

$$\begin{cases} X_1(t) = a_{11}X_1(t-1) + a_{12}X_2(t-1) + N_1(t) \\ X_2(t) = a_{22}X_2(t-1) + b_{21}X_1(t) + a_{21}X_1(t-1) + N_2(t) \end{cases} \tag{1.3}$$

Process	Estimated parameters	Variance of disturbances	Residual sum of squares	Auto-correlation of residuals	Akaike's criterion
AR(1)	0.53	1.48	371	1.67	0.42
MA(1)	0.62	1.50	374	1.70	0.42
ARMA(1,1)	0.38 0.38	1.39	349	1.94	0.38
AR(2)	0.69 -0.31	1.34	335	1.99	0.31
ARMA(2,1)	0.82 -0.39	1.37	342	2.01	0.38
	-0.11				
VAR(2,1)	0.64 -0.52	1.00	367	2.06	
	0.32 0.56	1.06		1.90	
	r_{12}=0.01				

Table 6.2a

Process	Estimated parameters	Variance of disturbances	Residual sum of squares	Auto-correlation of residuals	Akaike's criterion
AR(1)	0.34	1.67	418	1.75	0.542
MA(1)	0.50	1.54	385	2.05	0.453
ARMA(1,1)	-0.07 0.54	1.54	384	2.01	0.471
AR(2)	0.46 -0.37	1.42	355	2.10	0.390
ARMA(2,1)	0.90 -0.52	1.38	344	1.96	0.386
	-0.54				
VAR(2,1)	0.65 -0.62	1.04	345	1.97	
	0.29 0.54	1.06		1.86	
	r_{12}=0.81				

Table 6.2a,b Simulation of the modelling of two series of market prices by various ARMA processes. The time series are generated through the following multivariate VAR(2,1) autoregressive process:

$$X_1(t) = 0.6X_1(t-1) - 0.5X_2(t-1) + N_1(t)$$
$$X_2(t) = 0.4X_2(t-1) - 0.5X_1(t-1) + N_2(t)$$

$N_1(t)$, $N_2(t)$ are Gaussian white noises with intercorrelation r_{12}; in Table 6.2a r_{12}=0, in Table 6.2b, r_{12}=0.8. The parameters of the univariate processes are estimated on a maximum likelihood basis: the variance of the noise is estimated by the residual sum of squares. The parameters, variances and intercorrelation of disturbances for the bivariate VAR(2,1) process are Yule-Walker estimates. Akaike's criterion in the last column is given by:

$$A = \ln\sigma^2_{p,q} + (p+q) \ln N / N$$

where p,q are respectively the autoregressive and moving average orders of the process. $\sigma^2_{p,q}$ is the residual sum of squares. N is the length of the time series: N=250. In Table 6.2a, due to statistical fluctuations, the AR(2) process provides a better fit in terms of residual sum of squares than the more general ARMA(2,1) process or even than the correct VAR(2,1) process. The results in Table 6.2b are more in line with intuition: the best results in terms of residual sum of squares are indeed obtained with the ARMA(2,1) and the VAR(2,1) process.

	Exact parameters	b_{21}=0	b_{21}=0.5	b_{21}=1	b_{21}=-1
a_{11}	0.40	0.49	0.42	0.53	0.35
a_{22}	0.40	0.31	0.33	0.37	0.13
a_{12}	0.10	0.01	0.03	0.06	0.00
a_{21}	0.60	0.69	0.87	1.42	0.10
s_1	1.00	0.97	1.01	1.04	0.89
s_2	1.00	1.06	1.41	1.77	1.01
r_{12}	0.50	0.49	0.91	1.15	-0.49

Table 6.3 Estimating the parameters in the model defined by equations (1.1) when the time series are generated by the process (1.3) containing the extra term: $b_{21}X_1(t)$. The estimated parameters try to compensate for the term which is lacking. When b_{21}=1 which implies a strong positive dependence between $X_1(t)$ and $X_2(t)$, a_{21} and r_{21} both become large (r_{12} even becomes larger than one!). The opposite happens when b_{21}=-1. The estimates are Yule-Walker estimates. The length of the series is N=100.

The term $b_{21}X_1(t)$ represents an influence of market 1 on market 2 that is to take place almost without delay. Given these time series, we have tried to estimate a model of the form (1.1). From the results in Table (6.3) it can be seen that estimated parameters tend to counterbalance the effect of the missing term; for instance, when b_{21} increases from 0 to 1 (which implies a growing correlation between $X_1(t)$ and $X_2(t)$) both a_{21} and r_{12} become large. The opposite happens when b_{21} becomes negative.

1.3.3 Inadequate sampling time

Most often the sampling time of time series does not coincide with the "natural" unit of time of the process that has generated these time series. For instance, wheat markets were held two or even three times a week in nineteenth century France, whereas the series at our disposal are monthly or at best fortnight series. How does this gap distort parameter estimation? To answer this question we performed the following simulation. Two series are generated through process (1.1); the series then are sampled using sampling times of increasing length and the parameters in equations (1.1) are successively estimated for each of the sampled series. The results of this procedure are summarized in Table 6.4. Apart from the expected decrease in the autocorrelation parameters a_{ii}, one observes a steady increase in the estimated correlation between the disturbances $N_1(t)$

	Exact values	Sampling times					
		1	2	3	4	5	6
$(\hat{a}_{11}+\hat{a}_{22})/2$	0.55	0.54	0.45	0.28	0.21	0.15	0.10
$(\hat{a}_{12}+\hat{a}_{21})/2$	0.27	0.27	0.29	0.23	0.20	0.22	0.28
$(s_1+s_2)/2$	1.00	0.98	1.20	1.32	1.32	1.38	1.40
r_{12}	0.20	0.21	0.40	0.53	0.53	0.57	0.63

Table 6.4 Estimating a vectorial autoregressive process using sampling times of increasing length. Two time series (of length 2000) have been generated through the process:

$$X_1(t) = 0.54X_1(t-1) + 0.27X_2(t-1) + N_1(t)$$
$$X_2(t) = 0.54X_2(t-1) + 0.27X1(t-1) + N_2(t)$$

The series then have been sampled with sampling times of increasing length (the sampling time equal to 1 represents the initial series). It is of course not surprising that the coefficients a_{ii} measuring autocorrelation tend to zero; what is more unexpected is the increase in the correlation r_{12} between the disturbances $N1(t)$ and $N_2(t)$.

and $N_2(t)$. Thus inadequate sampling times may be a possible source of bias.

2 Correlation analysis

2.1 Methodology

2.1.1 The influence of foreign trade

It would be somewhat meaningless to analyse market interdependence in a country (such as Great Britain for instance) where prices are predominantly influenced by the world market. This, however, is not the case in nineteenth century France. Throughout most of the century, France was the world's largest wheat producer; even by the end of the century, when the United States emerged as a major producer both countries achieved comparable levels of production; in 1885 the figures are as follows: France: 8.5 millions tons, United States: 10.4 millions tons. As shown in Table 6.5, French imports represented on average about 6% of domestic production. Except in 1890 and 1891-1892, shipments from the United States never accounted for a high proportion of wheat consumption.

2.1.2 Structural versus temporary interdependence

> "The influence of the metropolitan trade ruled in times of dearth; the influence of local stability was predominant in years of plenty."
>
> Usher (1913)

	Total	From the United States	From Russia and Black Sea
1880	17.0	16.0	4.3
81	16.9	8.4	2.5
82	13.8	4.6	2.8
83	12.8	3.4	3.1
84	11.9	1.7	2.2
85	7.5	1.7	2.2
86	8.6	3.0	3.1
87	10.3	4.8	2.3
88	15.2	2.3	5.4
89	13.7	2.5	4.5
1890	11.8	2.0	3.3
91	33.5	13.9	5.8
92	22.3	11.9	2.7
93	13.3	3.8	4.5
94	13.4	3.5	5.3
95	4.9	0.2	2.2
96	1.7	0	0.5
97	7.9	2.8	2.8
98	19.7	9.5	4.9
99	1.3	0	0.5
1900	1.5	0	0
01	1.9	0	0
02	2.7	0.1	0.3
03	4.8	0.5	1.8
04	2.5	0	0.7
05	2.0	0	0.7
06	3.4	0.2	1.2
07	3.4	0	0.7
08	0.9	0	0
09	1.5	0	0
1910	9.2	0.4	1.7
11	24.5	1.4	4.3
12	7.8	0.6	0.6
1913	17.8	1.5	1.2
Average (1811-1913)	**6.6**		

Table 6.5 French wheat imports in per cent of domestic production. Except for a few anomalous years (1890,1891,1898,1911) imports remained at levels that denote a rather weak connection with foreign grain markets; as a matter of comparison, the ratio of imports to GNP in 1970 France was of the order of 18%. Furthermore, the Table shows that imports came from a number of different countries, the relative importance of which changed a great deal in the course of time. *Sources: Statistique Agricole Annuelle de la France, various years; Das Getreide im Weltverkehr (1900).*

Market integration presupposes two conditions. First, crop yields must improve enough to allow the export of a marketable surplus. Second, the transportation network must be sufficient to ship the surplus. These, however, are only *necessary* conditions: depending on the economic situation transportation facilities may be used more or less intensively. During periods of dearth there was great pressure to achieve provisioning of cities at all costs. Many occasional traders (the so-called "blatiers" in France) entered the business and, as a result exchanges and prices were pushed up. For detailed descriptions of this process we refer to Biollay (1885), Afanassiev (1894), Usher(1913), Meuvret(1956), Kaplan(1984). It should therefore be no surprise that market interdependence was above average levels during these periods. On the contrary during times of plenty prices were depressed and since little could be gained in the business trade withered.

Remark The organization of the domestic rice market in present day Bangladesh as described in Ravallion (1986, p.130) bears some similarities with the previous description; in particular, the economic role of small local merchants (the so-called Aratdars) is crucial in times of dearth.

One of the issue we shall address in this chapter is how to distinguish between "structural" interdependence and short-lived interconnections. In its principle the solution is simple enough. Since, at least during the nineteenth century, periods of dearth were exceptional, they will materialize as temporary peaks on correlation curves. An example is provided by the peak in Fig.6.8a that corresponds to the dearth of 1817-18. However, there are two circumstances under which actual implementation of this method may become difficult:

1) If periods of dearth and famine are too frequent, correlation peaks are to follow each other so closely that it might be difficult to identify the background corresponding to a normal state of trade. As an illustration, this happened in France during the period 1650-1750 when as many as 9 subsistence crisis occurred in a row, namely (Dupâquier et al,1968):

1649-1650	1658-1665	1677-1680	1691-1695	1696-1702
1708-1715	1722-1727	1737-1742	1746-1755	

2) When the interdependence between markets is a rather weak one statistical fluctuations in the correlation become important (see Appendix A) so that it becomes difficult to distinguish between true correlation peaks (due to subsistence crisis) and spurious fluctuations. We shall meet both of these difficulties in our subsequent analysis of periods before the nineteenth century.

The main conclusion we draw from this discussion is that it is essential to use a moving window technique. It makes no sense to get precise statistical estimates for the period 1825-1850 say, if one is unable to ascertain that these results will not be altered when observation moves to adjacent periods such as 1835-1860 or 1845-1870.

2.1.3 The data

In the case of nineteenth century France there is an extensive body of price series. We shall take a few words to explain how these prices were recorded. The government required the mayor of every market town to fill out printed questionnaires twice a month and send them to the departmental prefect. That information then worked its way up through the various levels of the French government. First, one of the prefect assistant recopied the prices on a printed table for the entire department, which was relayed to the "Bureau des Subsistances", a division of the Ministry of the Interior (after the 1830s, those tables were sent instead to the Ministry of Commerce and Agriculture). At the Ministry the department tables were arranged alphabetically and bound in a large volume, month by month. These volumes, numbering more than a thousand, were eventually transferred to the Archives Nationales in two shipments. The first was deposited in 1909 and the second in 1934. The respective call numbers in the Archives Nationales are $F^{*11}1779 - 2678$ and $F^{*11}2877 - 2984$.

The number of markets for which wheat prices were recorded fell from almost 900 in 1825 to approximately 500 by the beginning of the twentieth century. That decrease can be explained by the changing nature of the trade: increasingly, grains bypassed the local marketplaces because farmers and merchants arranged their transactions individually, generally by the means of samples. From this huge number of markets, we selected a sample of 53 markets covering every part of France (Fig.6.1a). The northern part of France is more heavily covered than the south because wheat production was more intensive in the north than in the south. Prices were recorded every two weeks from 1825 to August 1903 and every month from September 1903 to December 1913. Within that sample, the maximum price, 49F70, occurred in the second fortnight of March 1847 at Blois (Loir-et-Cher) and the minimum price, 9F69, was recorded during the first fortnight of February 1850 in Bourges (Cher). Prices have thus been divided by five in less than three years and in the same area. There are some gaps in a number of series; therefore we shall rather use about 35 series. In this chapter we shall use monthly averages which are detailed enough for our present purpose.

For the nineteenth century, in addition to the French data set, we make use of annual grain prices in Germany (Jacobs and Richter 1935) and of monthly wheat prices in Bavaria (Fig.6.1b, Seuffert 1857). Regarding the twentieth century, we shall use annual wheat and potato prices in the United States (Langley et al 1989, Lucier et al 1991).

2.2 Local interdependence

As in chapter 4, we shall carry out the analysis at three different levels: regional, national and international.

Fig.6.1 a Selected wheat markets in nineteenth century France. During most of the nineteenth century, grain markets were held two or three times a week in every town of some importance. Records are potentially available for about 600 markets among which we have selected the 53 markets displayed in the Figure.

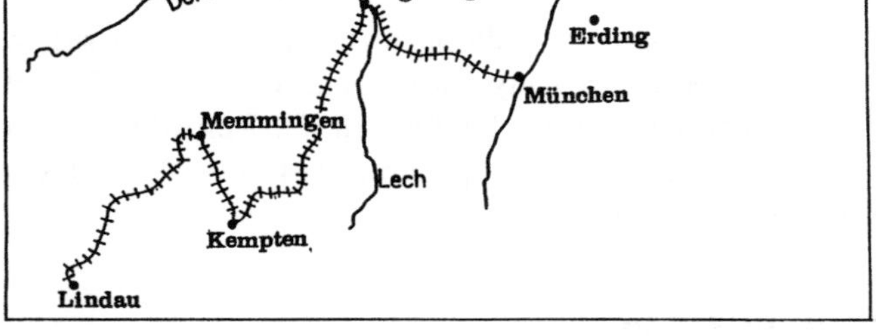

Fig.6.1 b Major grain markets in Bavaria: 1815- 1855. The figure also displays three important rivers and the railroad line that has come into operation in the years 1850-58.

2.2.1 Regional level

Before the railroad revolution, trade by land was confined to regional, small-distance exchanges. In support of this view which has been held by many historians (see for instance Braudel 1967,p.93) we shall provide the two following arguments. The first one concerns the correlation between wheat prices in Paris and in Toulouse. These markets are 600 km apart; the price series in Toulouse (1486-1849, Frêche 1967) and Paris (1521-1698, Baulant and Meuvret 1960) are among the longest monthly price series ever published. Now, between 1486 and 1698 the correlation between both series does not show any significant increase trend. The lesson we draw from this observation is that trade development during this stretch of two centuries must have been slow; as indicated above (Section 2.1.2) a modest increase trend would be difficult to detect because of the occurrence of many short run peaks due to subsistence crisis.

Unfortunately, no similar price series seem to be available for the same period at the regional level. The longest series at our disposal concerns Montauban and Toulouse (115 km apart). The evolution of their correlation is summarized in Fig.6.2. It is not quite clear whether there the increase between 1700 and

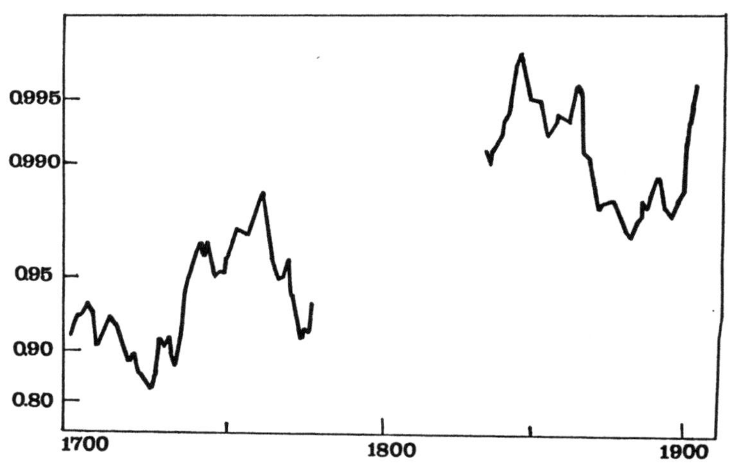

Fig.6.2 Correlation of annual wheat prices in Montauban and Toulouse (115 km apart). After 1850 there is no further increase in the correlation. The vertical scale is graduated in argth of correlation. The width of the moving window is 21 years. *Sources: Frêche et al (1967), Drame et al (1991).*

1780 and significant; yet the subsequent increase between 1750 and 1835 is unquestionable. Moreover, there is no further increase between 1825 and 1900, an observation which is consistent with the idea that the railroad revolution did not bring about much changes for small distance transportation for which loading costs played a major role. This evolution of correlation between 1825 and 1900 is confirmed by other pairs of neighbouring markets such as Arras and Douai (25 km), Louviers and Rouen (30 km) or Laval and Vitré (32 km).

2.2.2 National level

It is at this level that the impact of the railroad revolution is the most obvious. This is shown by two curves (Fig.6.3a,b); one for France: Arras-Toulouse (750 km), the other for Germany: Berlin-Munich (550 km). Although the trend is similar in both cases, market integration did not progress at the same pace in France and in Germany. This should be no surprise since Germany, in contrast to France, had to achieve political as well as economic unification. The process of market integration in Germany has been discussed in greater detail in Roehner (1989a).

2.2.3 International level

Nineteenth century The progression of market integration at the international level is somewhat similar to the evolution in Germany for in both cases trade barriers had to be surmounted . This is illustrated in Figure 6.4. by the correlation between the French market on one hand and those in a number of West European countries and in the United States on the other.

Long run evolution of correlation

• **1500-1900** Three series of wheat prices are available that extend from the fifteenth century up to the beginning of the twentieth century:

1) Monthly prices in Toulouse, a series that has already been mentioned above.

2) October prices in Douai (Mestayer 1963); unfortunately there is a gap from 1794 to 1825.

3) June prices in Maastricht (Netherlands, Tijms 1983)

The evolution of the correlation between Douai and Toulouse (765 km apart) on the one hand and between Maastricht and Toulouse (870 km) on the other hand is shown in Figure 6.5a. Between 1500 and 1800 there are large and apparently erratic fluctuations; this again comes in support of our argument in paragraph 2.2.1. After 1820, there is a strong increase in the interdependence. During the whole nineteenth century the correlation between Douai and Toulouse remained higher than the correlation between Maastricht and Toulouse, an observation

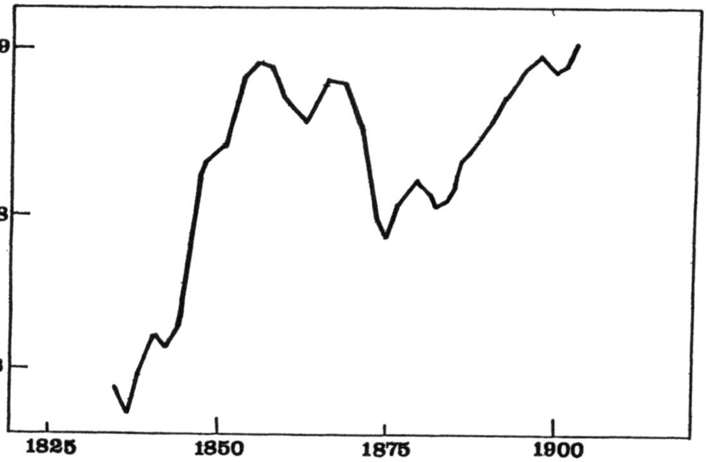

Fig.6.3 a Correlation of monthly wheat prices in Arras and Toulouse (750 km apart). The vertical scale is graduated in argth of correlation. The width of the moving window is equal to 201 months. *Source: Drame et al (1991).*

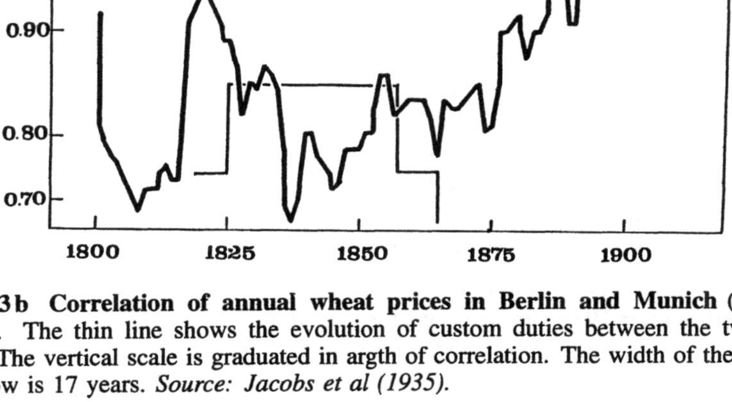

Fig.6.3 b Correlation of annual wheat prices in Berlin and Munich (515 km apart). The thin line shows the evolution of custom duties between the two markets. The vertical scale is graduated in argth of correlation. The width of the moving window is 17 years. *Source: Jacobs et al (1935).*

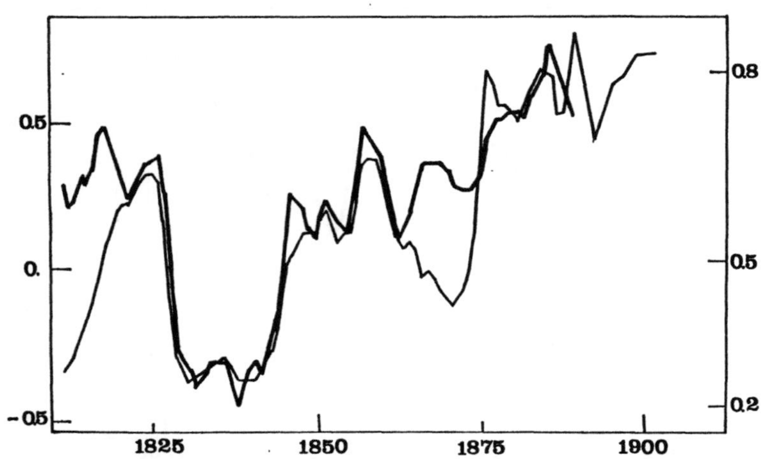

Fig.6.4 Correlation of annual international wheat prices. The thick line shows the evolution of correlation between wheat prices in Finland and France. The thin line represents the average correlation between prices in five countries: Finland, France, Germany, Great Britain, United States. The vertical scale is graduated in argth of correlation. The width of the moving window is equal to 21 years. *Sources: See appendix C.*

that should be related to the fact that the last two markets are separated by two borders.

It is somewhat frustrating that the first part of the curve between 1500 and 1800 could not be further exploited. At this point it may be worthwhile to fit an autoregressive model to the data. The process that has been used is defined by equations (1.1). The dotted curve in Fig.6.5a shows the variance of random shocks. Since we are dealing here with annual prices, these shocks mainly consist in meteorological factors; autoregressive analysis therefore reveals a secular decrease trend in the incidence of meteorological factors on prices.

- **1840-1980** Only few price series can be safely extended from the 19th century to present time. Because of their homogeneity and reliability price series of non ferrous metals can be considered as possible candidates. The correlation between annual prices in London and in New York is shown in Fig.6.5b for copper, lead, tin and zinc. Tin excepted, these series once they are deflated do not display any substantial trend. With regard to their correlations the first global observation to be made is the absence of any substantial increase in correlation after 1918 (tin again is an exception). This comes in confirmation of the conclusions reached in chapter 1 about the evolution of price differentials and of freight rates. Let us next consider each individual curve. If we make

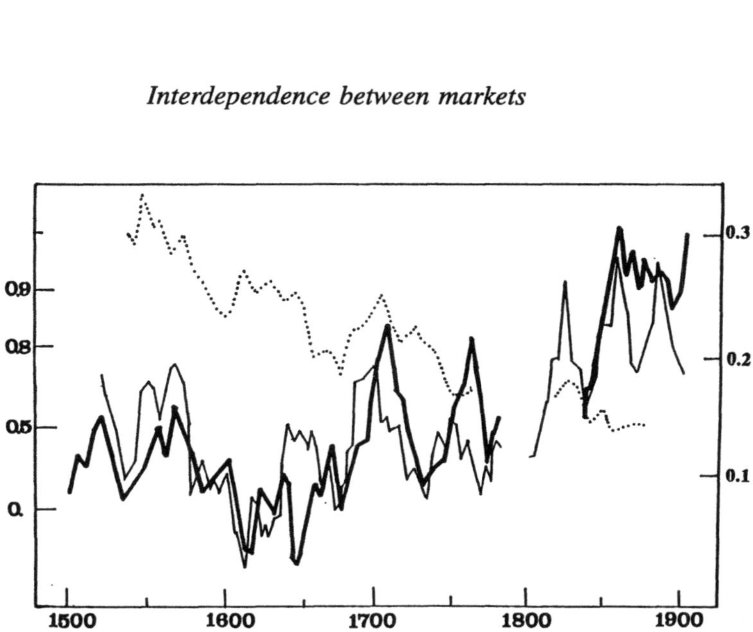

Fig.6.5 a Long range evolution of price correlation: 1500-1900. Thick line: correlation of annual wheat prices in Douai and Toulouse (765 km apart). The vertical scale is graduated in argth of correlation. The width of the moving window is 21 years. Thin line : correlation of annual wheat prices in Maastricht and Toulouse (870 km apart). Dotted line: variance of the disturbances affecting the market at Toulouse in the framework of a bivariate autoregressive model (right-hand vertical scale). *Sources: Frêche et al (1967), Mestayer (1963), Tijms (1983).*

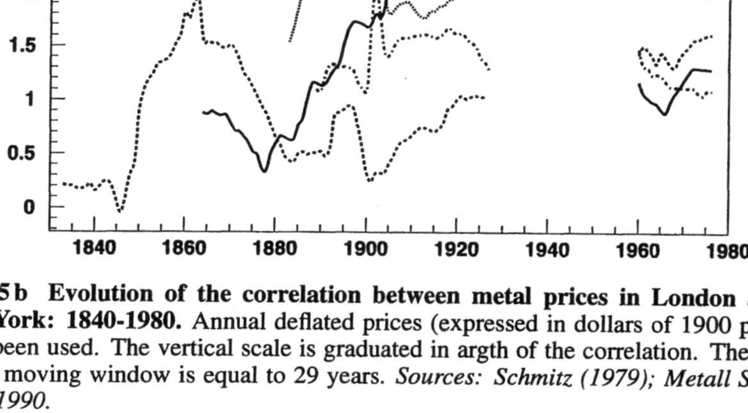

Fig.6.5 b Evolution of the correlation between metal prices in London and in New York: 1840-1980. Annual deflated prices (expressed in dollars of 1900 per ton) have been used. The vertical scale is graduated in argth of the correlation. The length of the moving window is equal to 29 years. *Sources: Schmitz (1979); Metall Statistik 1980-1990.*

abstraction of the huge peak around 1860 which may be due to the American Civil War lead correlations show a slow but steady increase trend. Copper shows a dramatic increase until 1918 and an even more dramatic decrease after World War II. The correlation of zinc prices almost remains at the same level either before or after World War II. One could be tempted to search for specific explanations of these different evolutions. This however would be of anecdotal interest since it only concerns one pair of market places. Of much more interest would be additional evidence about a number of other market places.

2.3 Global measure of interdependence: the correlation length

In this paragraph, we shall parallel the investigations of chapter 4 about spatial patterns of price differentials but this time in the framework of correlation analysis. While sets of about 30 to 40 markets have been used in chapter 4, sets of about 10 markets turn out to be sufficient here because correlations provide a measure of interdependence that is in a sense already time averaged.

2.3.1 The correlation length

Decrease of correlation with distance Because of the increase of transportation costs with distance the correlation between two markets separated by a distance d is expected to fall off as d increases. According to the non linear arbitrage model of chapter 3, the correlation should abruptly drop to zero as soon as the price differential becomes smaller than the expected transportation cost. Not surprisingly the transition rather turns out to be smooth, as shown in Fig. 6.7a,b,c,d. The way these figures have been set up is summarized in Figure 6.6a,b: given N markets, the correlations for each of the $N(N-1)/2$ possible market pairs have been computed and displayed as a function of distance.

Correlation length The decreasing exponential e^{-ad} is a function that is equal to 1 for $d = 0$ and tends to zero as $d \longrightarrow \infty$. It is therefore natural, at least as a first approximation, to describe the decrease of the correlation $c(d)$ with distance as:

$$c(d) = e^{-ad} \tag{2.1}$$

In chapter 8 we shall see that $c(d)$ may take a number of different analytical forms depending on the specific model; as a rule, however, the asymptotic expressions of these functions for $d \longrightarrow \infty$ are of the exponential form. The applicability of (2.1) therefore is larger than it could seem at first.
We shall now rewrite (2.1) in a slightly different form by substituting for a a parameter $L = 1/a$ which plays the role of a characteristic distance:

$$c(d) = e^{-d/L}$$

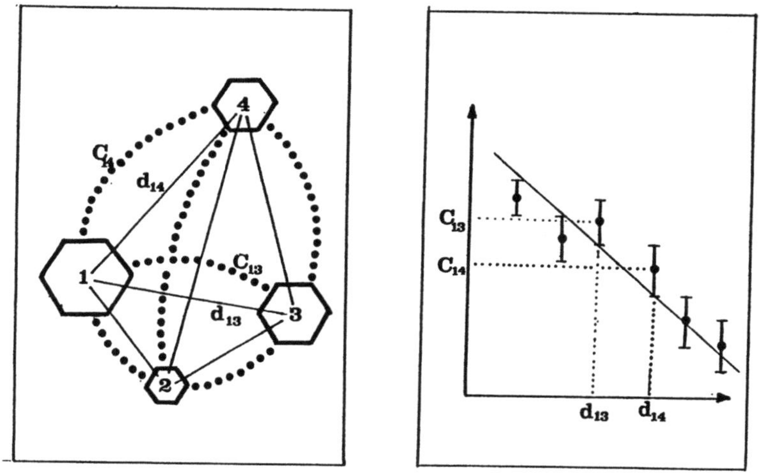

Fig.6.6 a,b Estimating the correlation length within a set of markets. The correlations between all market pairs are regressed against inter-market distances.

In fact, L happens to be too large a distance; for the set of markets in Fig.6.7a,b it would be equal to 5500 km; accordingly it is more convenient to introduce a submultiple of L: $L = 100l$. Thus we shall propose the following definition:

Definition The decrease of the correlation, $c(d)$, of prices on different markets with distance, d, is consistent with the exponential form:

$$c(d) = \exp(-d/100l)$$

l will be referred to as the correlation length; it has the following interpretation: when the distance between markets increases by l, the correlation $c(d)$ decreases by 0.01.

Estimates of correlation length Table 6.6 summarizes the estimates of correlation length for the following market sets.

Wheat

1) **Bavaria**, monthly prices, 9 markets:
Augsburg, Erding, Kempten, Landshut, Lindau, Memmingen, Munich, Nördlingen, Regensburg.

2) **France**, monthly prices

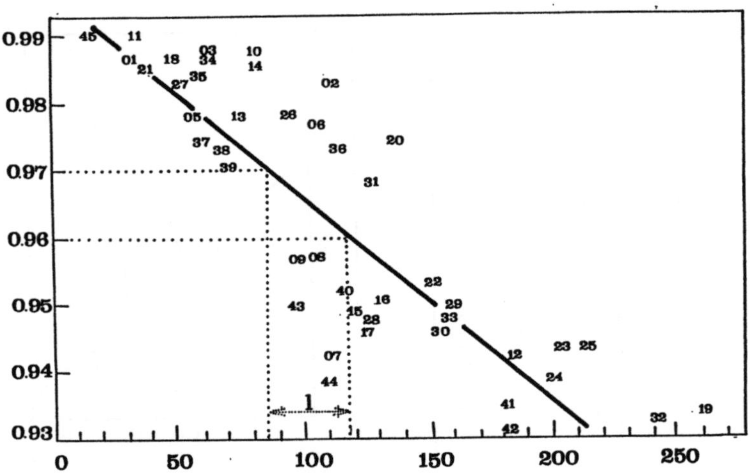

Fig.6.7 a Bavaria: decrease of wheat price correlations with distance. The sample contains 9 markets; the plotted numbers refer to the 45 possible market pairs. The correlation, R, of these points is equal to -0.85. The series are monthly prices 1825 - 1833. In Fig.6.7a-d the vertical scale is logarithmic and the horizontal scale is graduated in kilometres. *Source: Seuffert (1857).*

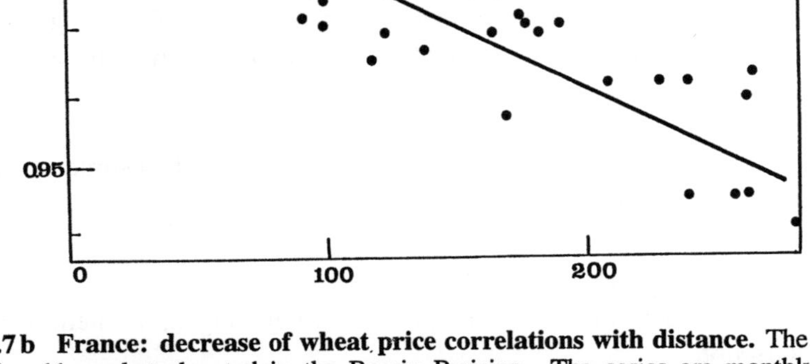

Fig.6.7 b France: decrease of wheat price correlations with distance. The sample contains 11 markets located in the Bassin Parisien. The series are monthly prices 1841-1858. $R = -0.91$. *Source: Drame et al (1991).*

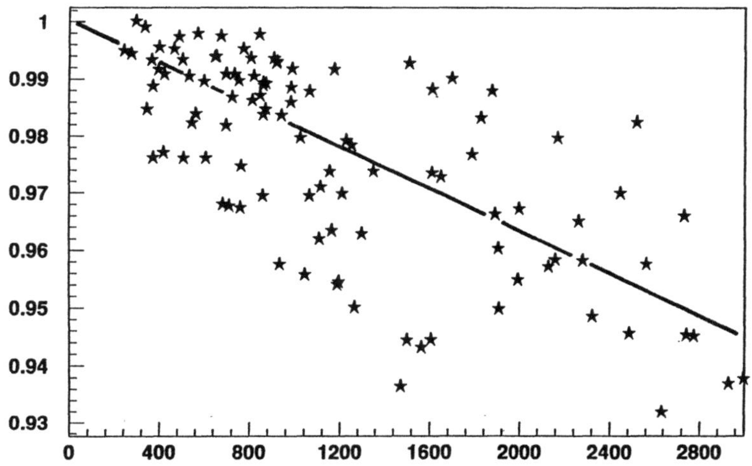

Fig.6.7 c United States: decrease of wheat price correlations with distance. The sample contains 15 States. The series are annual prices 1954-1986. $R = -0.70$. *Source: Langley et al (1989).*

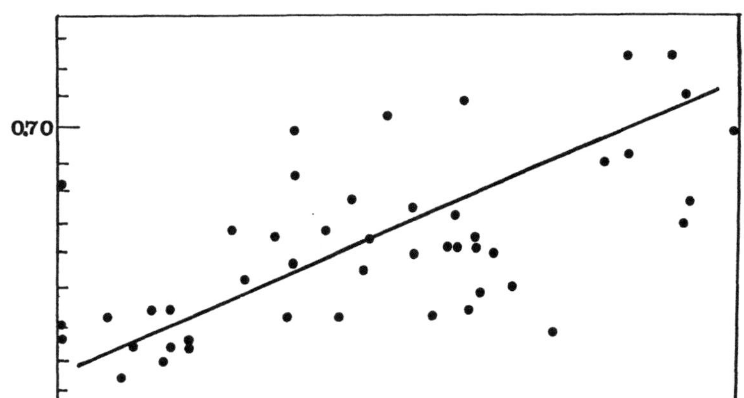

Fig.6.7 d France: increase of wheat price correlation (lag of 8 months) with distance. This figure is identical to Fig.6.7a except for the 8-months lag. The purpose of this figure is to show that for lagged correlations intuition no longer is an adequate guide, an econometric model is required; as will be seen in chapter 9 (sections 3.2 and 4.2.2) this chart is typical of an oscillatory second order pricing model. Needless to say the intercorrelation vanishes for large intermarket distances; in other words the chart shows only the first portion of the whole intercorrelation curve. The linear correlation is equal to 0.55. *Source: Drame et al (1991).*

	Correlation length	Goodness of fit
A - TIME AVERAGES		
Wheat, Bavaria (1815-1855)	60 km	0.85
Wheat, France (1825-1914)		
Bassin Parisien	55 km	0.85
Ports	231 km	0.60
France	64 km	0.45
B - EVOLUTION		
1) Wheat		
Bavaria (1829)	31 ± 5 km	0.85
France (1873)		
Bassin Parisien	55 ± 18 km	0.87
Ports	211 ± 41 km	0.58
France	71 ± 24 km	0.70
USA (1970)	560 ± 108 km	0.70
2) Potato		
Prussia (1837)	12 ± 4 km	0.63
USA (1970)	96 ± 27 km	0.50

Table 6.6 Correlation length for regions in France, Germany and in the United States. Three comments can be made. 1) Not surprisingly, the correlation length is smaller for potatoes than for wheat, the latter being traded more intensively. 2) It is larger for ports than for inland markets. 3) It increases in the course of economic development. *Sources: Bavaria: Seuffert(1857); France: Drame et al(1991); Prussia: Engel (1861); USA wheat: Langley et al(1989); USA potato: Lucier et al (1991).*

- **Bassin Parisien and Normandy**, 11 markets: Auxerre, Beaugency, Bernay, Blois, Bourges, Chartres, Châteauroux, Evreux, Louviers, Rouen.
- **Ports and cities on the Atlantic coast**, 10 markets: Bayeux, Bordeaux, Cherbourg, Dieppe, Marans, Nantes, Pont-L'Abbé, Rouen, Saint-Brieuc, Vannes.
- **A set of 12 French markets selected at random**: Bernay, Blois, Châteauroux, Le Puy, Marans, Mende, Montbrison, Pau, Peyrehorade, Saint-Brieuc, Toulouse, Vannes.

3) **United States**, annual prices, 15 States
Alabama, Arkansas, Colorado, Georgia, Idaho, Illinois, Indiana, Iowa, Kansas, Kentucky, Michigan, Minnesota, Mississippi, Missouri, Montana.

Potato

1) **Prussia**, annual prices, 7 markets
Berlin, Breslau(Wroclaw), Danzig(Gdansk), Königsberg(Kaliningrad), Magdeburg, Posen(Poznan), Stettin(Szczecin).

2) **United States**, annual prices, 13 States
Connecticut, Delaware, Illinois, Indiana, Maine, Maryland, Massachusetts, Mi-

chigan, New Jersey, New York, Ohio, Pennsylvania, Rhodes Island.
We may remark that (because of its smallness) the estimation of correlation lengths for potatoes requires samples of markets in which small intermarket distances are largely represented.

The intercorrelation function The intercovariance function is defined as:

$$c_l = E\,(X(t)X(t+l))$$

We have focused on zero-lag correlations for the same reasons that we already mentioned in chapter 5 in a different context; indeed, intercorrelations corresponding to a time lag of several months do not have an intuitive interpretation in terms of market interdependence. The full intercorrelation function only takes its significance in the frame of reference of stochastic models, the introduction of which we shall postpone to chapters 7 and 8. Just to show how non intuitive an 8 months lagged correlation can be, we refer to Fig. 6.7d: in this case the intercorrelation *increases* with distance at least in the range of small intermarket distances.

2.3.2 The correlation length of precipitation

An important component of the spatial interdependence between grain prices is constituted by the spatial autocorrelation embodied in meteorological fluctuations. What is the order of magnitude of this component? This is the question we shall try to answer in this paragraph. To this end we compute the correlation length of precipitation and compare its magnitude to that of cereal prices.
But why did we select precipitation among the many climatic factors that affect the growth of cereals? The relation between weather and grain yields has been studied by several authors, for instance: Hooker(1907), Beveridge(1921), Machali(1931), Timoshenko(1944) and more recently by Pfister(1986). Hooker points out that, at least in Western Europe, rain is the most important climatic factor: the correlation between rainfall (summed over the whole cereal year) and yields is about -0.65. Furthermore, rainfall is, along with temperature, the only meteorological variable for which nineteenth century records are available (Clayton 1944).
We selected the following series for the period 1850-1920: Berlin, Königsberg (Kaliningrad), Trier, Vienna, Breslau, Frankfurt, Gütersloh, Utrecht, Zürich.

The correlation, R, between rainfall correlations and distances turns out to be equal to 0.75 on average; this makes the results for the correlation length quite reliable: its order of magnitude is about 10 km which is comparable to the correlation length for grain prices at the very beginning of the nineteenth century; by the middle of the nineteenth century it is already four times larger.

One may say, therefore, that for most of the nineteenth century the contribution of meteorological factors to the spatial autocorrelation of wheat prices is nearly negligible by the end of the century.

2.3.3 Evolution of the correlation length during the nineteenth century

A distinctive advantage of the present approach over the investigation of correlation between pairs of markets is that it is much more systematic in the sense that one no longer needs to worry about local anomalies (for some reason, Saint Brieuc in Brittany for instance shows atypical correlations with most of other markets). The main results are summarized in Fig.6.8a,b. The huge peak around 1820 in Figure 6.8a is of special interest. It has its origin in the severe subsistence crisis of 1817-1818. This was the last period of famine in Western Europe if one excepts the potato crisis of 1846-1848 in Ireland.

3 Autoregressive modelling: dominant markets and satellite markets

Transposed to present time the questions we shall address in this section may be formulated in following ways. Both London and Paris are important markets for white sugar, but which one plays the leading role? Which between London, New York and Paris is in the lead for coffee futures?
Because our sample of nineteenth century prices includes markets of various sizes we shall be in a good position to *test* our methodology before applying it to economically significant markets.

3.1 Multivariate autoregressive models: identification and estimation

In the following, our purpose is to analyse trade interactions between two or three markets. One preliminary question is whether our model should be restricted to these markets or whether it should rather contain neighbouring markets as well. The latter choice in principle has definite advantages. Indeed by increasing the size of the sample, the weight of those interactions which are dealt with in the model is made predominant over the weight of external influences (due to markets outside the sample) which are not taken into account. Unfortunately, increasing the number of markets also raises a number of technical difficulties.

1) A multivariate autoregressive model of first order for a sample of 10 markets requires the determination of about 200 parameters. Estimating them with reasonable confidence intervals would require very long time series.

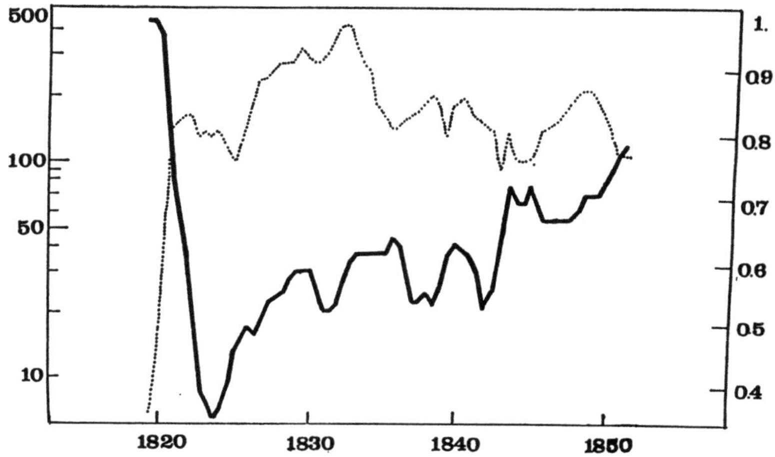

Fig.6.8 a Evolution of the correlation length in Bavaria (log scale). The peak is caused by the bad weather during the spring and summer of 1816 (the "year without a summer") which produced a very severe shortage of cereals. The dotted line shows the goodness of fit (right-hand scale). The sample contains 9 markets. The series are monthly prices with a moving window of 8 years. *Source: Seuffert (1857).*

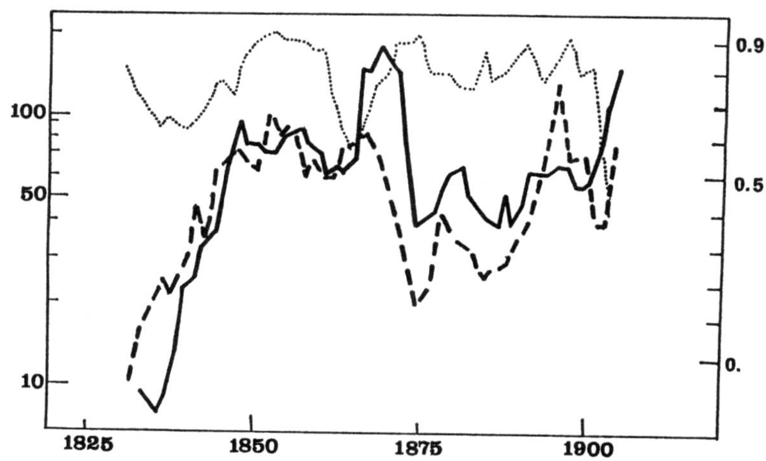

Fig.6.8 b Evolution of the correlation length in France (log scale). Solid line: the sample contains 12 markets selected at random; broken line: the sample contains the same 11 markets as in Fig.6.7b; dotted line: goodness of fit for the sample of 11 markets (right hand scale). *Source: Drame et al (1991).*

2) Due to stationarity requirements, estimated parameters show a marked tendency to become ever smaller as their number increases. Given standard confidence intervals, this adds some uncertainty to their determination.

In fact, the dilemma we are facing is well known in vector autoregressive modelling. In a very lucid review article, Arnold Zellner (1988) summarizes it by the assertion that "models are either too narrow or too broad".

Regarding identification, since it is not possible for the purpose of comparisons to use different models in different time intervals, we are compelled to select once and for all a model of a specific form.

3.2 Application of multivariate autoregressive models

3.2.1 Direction of interaction

As is clear from the discussion in the previous paragraph, the methodology of vector autoregressive modelling involves some thorny steps; therefore, it is pretty useful to perform some control tests.

Direction of interaction between markets on unequal importance Let us for instance consider the neighbouring markets at Bordeaux and Angoulême. Bordeaux is about ten times larger than Angoulême both in terms of population and in terms of grain sales (Table 6.7). Bordeaux can therefore be expected to be the dominant market. This is indeed confirmed by the results in Table 6.7. The same kind of test can be carried out for other market pairs similarly consisting of a large and of a small market; the examples given in Table 6.7 concern: Bordeaux-Marans, Bordeaux-Peyrehorade, Bordeaux-Marmande; Lyons-Montbrison, Lyons-Annecy, Lyons-Albertville; Marseilles-Digne; Munich-Erding; Lindau-Kempten

The results in Table 6.7 show that the directions of interaction revealed by bivariate autoregressive modelling do indeed coincide with those suggested by intuitive economic reasoning. Table 6.7 only gives time averages over the whole period, but a more detailed analysis shows that these results hold true for any time interval. Such a stability is rather comforting for it confirms that direction of interaction indeed is a *structural* feature of market interdependence.

Markets of comparable importance From a historical point of view it is of course of greater significance to investigate market interactions between major cities, such as for instance: Bordeaux, Lyons, Marseilles, Nantes; apart from Paris these are among the largest cities in nineteenth century France. One interesting issue is the following: is it global demand or rather global supply which gives a market its importance? The first factor may be roughly measured

Market A	Market B	A --> B	B --> A
A) Markets of unequal importance			
BORDEAUX (99,50)	ANGOULEME (15,4)	0.37	0.08
BORDEAUX	MARANS (3,20)	0.47	0.08
BORDEAUX	MARMANDE (7,3)	0.35	0.27
BORDEAUX	PEYREHORADE (2,3)	0.25	0.19
LYONS(133,--)	MONTBRISON (51,20)	0.42	0.07
LYONS	ANNECY (40,--)	0.52	-0.0
LYONS	ALBERTVILLE (15,--)	0.42	-0.20
MARSEILLES (145,50)	DIGNE (4,0.8)	0.27	0.03
TOULOUSE (133,12)	MONTAUBAN (25,1.5)	0.44	0.20
MUNICH (77,150)	ERDING (--,30)	0.39	0.16
LINDAU (-- ,100)	KEMPTEN (-- ,30)	0.58	-0.11
B) Markets of comparable importance			
Market A	**Market B**	**A --> B**	**B --> A**
BORDEAUX (99,50)	NANTES (77,15)	0.52	0.13
BORDEAUX	LYONS (133,--)	0.19	0.32
BORDEAUX	MARSEILLES (145,50)	0.14	0.20
LYONS (133,--)	MARSEILLES (145,50)	0.22	0.19

Table 6.7 Direction of interaction between different market pairs. The table gives average values of cross-regressive coefficients for a bivariate model with intercorrelated disturbations. The two figures in brackets respectively indicate the population of the city (in thousands) and average sales (in 100 hectolitre/fortnight for France and in 1000 schäffel/year for Bavaria). *Sources: Drame et al (1991), Seuffert (1857).*

by the city's population, the second one by total sales. It seems that it is the supply side which is predominant. This view is supported by the example of Bordeaux and Nantes. Both cities have about the same population and both are important ports; sales, however, are much larger in Bordeaux than in Nantes. As a result, the influence of Bordeaux is largely predominant. For the three other market pairs examined in Table 6.7 the question is more controversial. Time averages are given in Table 6.7; the precise evolution in the course of time is as follows:

Bordeaux-Marseilles: from 1825 to 1870 Bordeaux is in the lead, thereafter it is Marseilles.

Lyons-Marseilles: from 1833 to 1847, Marseilles dominates, then from 1848 to 1880 it is Lyons and Marseilles again until 1913.

Munich and Lindau Analysing the interactions between Munich and Lindau was an interesting experience (Roehner 1991d). The strength of the Lindau → Munich interaction increased in the course of time (Fig.6.9); the Munich →

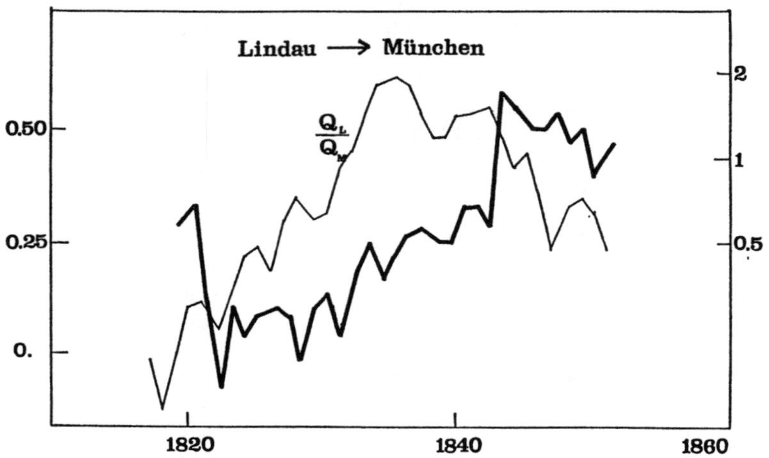

Fig.6.9 Direction of interaction between Lindau and Munich. Thick line: cross-regression coefficient of a bivariate autoregressive model; thin line: ratio of sales in Lindau to sales in Munich (right-hand scale). The coefficient characterizing the Munich → Lindau interaction on the contrary experienced a strong decrease from about 0.20 in 1820 to -0.30 in 1840; as a result the Lindau → Munich interaction became significantly predominant around 1835. *Source: Seuffert (1857).*

Lindau interaction on the contrary experienced a marked decrease. As a result the Lindau → Munich interaction became significantly predominant around 1835. This result appeared at first as rather surprising. Was it not clear, that Munich, by far the largest city, should be the dominant market throughout the whole period? Then, when examining sales figures (Seuffert 1857) we found out that sales in Lindau have been increasing during the whole period; after 1835, they even surpassed the sales in Munich. In the light of this evolution, the curve in Fig.6.9 becomes more plausible. In fact, there is a striking parallelism between the increase of sales in Lindau and the increase of the interaction parameter. Incidentally the fact that the interaction curve is ahead of the curve of sales is not really significant because Q_L/Q_M is an instantaneous value whereas the autoregressive modelling is carried out over a window of about 8 years; as is well known using such a window has the effect of shifting the resulting curve along the time axis.

3.2.2 Satellite markets

The correlation between two small markets may be artificially high if both of them are satellite markets of a nearby dominant market. The correlation then is not spurious from a statistical point of view but rather from an economic point of view. Let us examine whether the true interdependence may be uncovered by modelling these markets through a three variates autoregressive model. We shall analyse two triplets:

Bordeaux-Marans-Nantes and **Lyons-Albertville-Annecy**

The results are summarized in Figure 6.10. It can be seen that the true con-

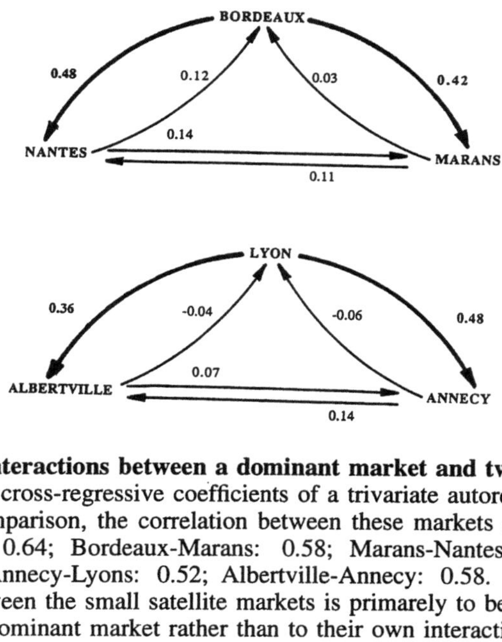

Fig.6.10 a,b Interactions between a dominant market and two satellite markets. The figures are cross-regressive coefficients of a trivariate autoregressive model. For the sake of comparison, the correlation between these markets are as follows: Bordeaux-Nantes: 0.64; Bordeaux-Marans: 0.58; Marans-Nantes: 0.58; Albertville-Lyons: 0.37; Annecy-Lyons: 0.52; Albertville-Annecy: 0.58. As can be seen the correlation between the small satellite markets is primarely to be attributed to the influence of the dominant market rather than to their own interactions. *Source: Drame et al (1991).*

nection between Nantes and Marans is indeed much smaller than correlation analysis would have suggested. The same observation also holds for Albertville and Annecy.

Remark Since vector autoregressive modelling appears to provide a more realistic picture of interdependence, one may well wonder why we did not use it from the very beginning. There are two reasons:

- Autoregressive analysis turns out to be much more sensitive to fluctuations than is correlation analysis, therefore it is more unstable in the course of time; this is the price one has to pay for improved accuracy.

• For the estimation of the correlation length (Section 2.3.1) it does not really matter whether the connections between markets are direct or indirect ones. In fact, the sample of markets at our disposal is anyway only a small fraction of all existing markets: 53 markets in a total of about 600.

4 Conclusion

Price series are the most reliable and abundant statistical source in economic history. The number of published price series has greatly increased in past decades. In this chapter we have tried to show that price series are able to provide a picture of the interdependence between market places. This image is economically meaningful in the sense that it is closely connected with the pattern of trade flows. Yet, this is by no means the only way in which market prices can be used. McCloskey and Nash (1984) for instance managed to relate corn prices to costs of grain storage. In this way, they were able to draw interesting conclusions about interest rates in Medieval England. In contrast to Medieval England a lot of statistical sources are available for the nineteenth century. Accordingly, one could well have the impression that nothing really new emerged from our analysis. Beyond the diversity of local situations our objective was to identify the basic trend toward more integrated markets. In particular, we have seen that at the level of international trade there has been a slowdown in market integration after World War II. In a sense there is a parallelism between these conclusions and the long term trend of American productivity growth (see for instance Williamson 1991).

A Appendix A: Technicalities of correlation analysis

Price series are "difficult" time series; at first sight they may appear as rather erratic, yet they greatly differ from white noise since their autocorrelation is on the contrary close to one. Moreover, they are from time to time marked by huge peaks that temporarily disturb their second order stationarity.

A.1 Prewhitening or not

Prewhitening of time series is a useful technique for many purposes such as for instance the determination of transfer function models or spectral analysis. In the perspective of correlation analysis it has both advantages and disadvantages. An approximate expression of the standard deviation of correlation estimates is given by Bartlett's formula (Bartlett 1955). From this formula, it can be inferred that, under some simplifying assumptions, the standard error is to increase when the (first lag) autocorrelation of the series goes to one. This is the main motivation for prewhitening since this operation sharply reduces the autocorrelation of the initial series. In particular, specific tests using the prewhitening technique are available to settle the question of whether or not there is a definite correlation between two series (Haugh 1976). Whereas the standard error of estimated correlation increases along with autocorrelation, it *decreases* when the (true) correlation between the series approaches one (remember that in Haugh's criterion for instance, the true correlation between the series is supposed to be equal to zero).
Let us illustrate these points with the curves in Figures 6.Aa,b. They show the fluctuations of the correlation between two simulated series, with given built in autocorrelations, respectively with and without prewhitening. It can be seen that the usefulness of the filtering falters as the true correlation between the series increases. In this example the filtering model is known exactly; in a real case, it is not; then, if inadequately specified, filtering may yield misleading results.

A.2 Differentiating or not

Differentiating can be considered as a crude form of prewhithening; its main purpose is to achieve second order stationarity and incidentally to reduce the autocorrelation. However, when a series displays sharp peaks (as is the case of price series) second order stationarity can be obtained only at the cost of high order differentiation. Moreover, differentiation also amplifies the repercussions of measurement errors. This is of particular importance for historic time series, in which errors resulting from miscalculations in averaging cannot be excluded.

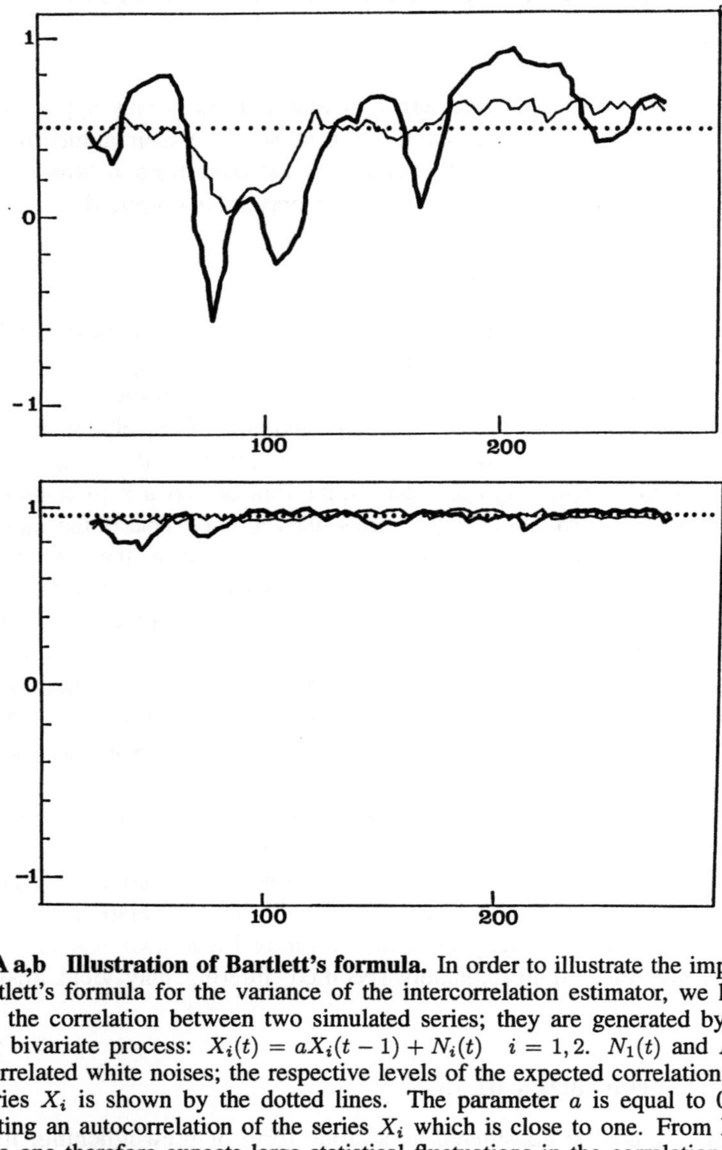

Fig.6.A a,b Illustration of Bartlett's formula. In order to illustrate the implications of Bartlett's formula for the variance of the intercorrelation estimator, we have displayed the correlation between two simulated series; they are generated by the following bivariate process: $X_i(t) = aX_i(t-1) + N_i(t) \quad i = 1, 2$. $N_1(t)$ and $N_2(t)$ are two correlated white noises; the respective levels of the expected correlation between the series X_i is shown by the dotted lines. The parameter a is equal to 0.95 thus generating an autocorrelation of the series X_i which is close to one. From Bartlett's formula one therefore expects large statistical fluctuations in the correlation between the X_i. In these figures the correlation has been computed on a moving window of width 41. The solid curves show the fluctuations of the correlation computed from the series X_i; the thin curves show the correlation computed from the pre-whitened series: $X_i'(t) = X_i(t) - aX_i(t-1)$. From these figures we draw the following lessons: 1) With an autocorrelation as high as 0.95, the intercorrelation fluctuates a great deal except when the true correlation between the series becomes close to 1. 2) Nonetheless, the correlation still remains a consistent, non biased estimator.

From the almost trivial example in Table 6.A it can be seen that an error of

Initial series										
X(t)	19	20	21	21	**21**	22	23	22	21	19
Y(t)	18	19	21	20	**21**	22	23	23	20	20
Modified series										
X'(t)	identical to X except for:				X'(4) = X(4) - c					
Y'(t)	identical to Y except for:				Y'(4) = Y(4) + c					

Magnitude of the error in the series		**c=0**	**c=1**	**c=2**	**c=3**
Relative error		0 %	5%	10%	15%
Correlation computed from:					
Series X',Y'	: r(X',Y')	0.88	0.87	0.69	0.44
First differences	: r(DX', DY')	0.60	0.59	0.23	-0.16
Second differences	: r(D^2X', D^2Y')	0.12	0.15	-0.16	-0.61

Table 6A The effect of measurement errors on the correlation between two series. The effect of simulated measurement errors is more important when the correlation is computed from first or second differences than it is when using the series themselves.

two francs (i.e. less than 10%) in only one entry has dramatic effects when the correlation is computed from first or second order differences. This may explain why differentiating often has the effect of increasing, rather than reducing, the standard deviation of correlations.

A.2.1 Confidence intervals and tests

Crude estimates for the correlation's confidence intervals have been obtained using Fisher's argth technique. We can note in passing that in this framework it becomes clear that the confidence interval becomes smaller as the correlation tends to 1.

B Appendix B: Technicalities of autoregressive modelling

B.1 Definition of the models

The class of discrete time series that we have considered is defined by:

$$X_i(t) = \sum_{i,j=1}^{n} a_{ij} X_j(t-1) + N_i(t) \qquad i = 1, 2, \ldots, n \qquad (B1)$$

with the following (zero lag) correlations between the disturbances $N_i(t)$:

$$E\left[N_i(t) N_j(t+k)\right] = \delta_{ij} \delta_{k0} c_{ij}$$

In this chapter we have stuck to model $(B1)$; indeed our aim was to compare the values of the parameters a_{ij} at different times and this can be done only by keeping the structure of the model unchanged.

B.2 Estimating the model

In contrast to the situation for moving average processes, the autoregressive parameters obtained from the Yule-Walker estimates approximate the fully efficient maximum likelihood estimators (Box and Jenkins 1976,p.244). However it is essential for this approximation to hold that no root of the autoregressive operator be near the unit circle. This requirement is easily met when using differentiated series.

To test the adequacy of the model we used two criteria: Akaike's information criterion (Priestley 1981,p.373) and a global Q-test for the autocorrelation of residuals.

For a bivariate model, the Yule-Walker estimates $\widehat{a}_{ij}$ are the solutions of the following systems of equations:

$$\begin{cases} \gamma_{11}(0)\,\widehat{a}_{11} + \gamma_{12}(0)\,\widehat{a}_{12} = \gamma_{11}(1) \\ \gamma_{21}(0)\,\widehat{a}_{11} + \gamma_{22}(0)\,\widehat{a}_{12} = \gamma_{21}(1) \end{cases}$$

$$\begin{cases} \gamma_{12}(0)\,\widehat{a}_{22} + \gamma_{11}(0)\,\widehat{a}_{21} = \gamma_{12}(1) \\ \gamma_{22}(0)\,\widehat{a}_{22} + \gamma_{21}(0)\,\widehat{a}_{21} = \gamma_{22}(1) \end{cases}$$

where the $\gamma_{ij}(k)$ are the coefficients of auto- $(i = j)$ and intercovariance.

The statistical properties of the disturbances $N_1(t)$ and $N_2(t)$ are given by:

$$\widehat{\sigma}_1^2 = \gamma_{11}(0)\,(1 - \widehat{a}_{11}^2) - \gamma_{22}(0)\,\widehat{a}_{12}^2 - 2\gamma_{12}(0)\,\widehat{a}_{11}\,\widehat{a}_{12}$$

$$\widehat{\sigma}_2^2 = \gamma_{22}(0)\,(1 - \widehat{a}_{22}^2) - \gamma_{11}(0)\,\widehat{a}_{21}^2 - 2\gamma_{12}(0)\,\widehat{a}_{21}\,\widehat{a}_{22}$$

$$\widehat{r}_{12} = [\gamma_{12}(0) \\ -\gamma_{11}(0)\ \widehat{a}_{11}\ \widehat{a}_{21} - \gamma_{22}(0)\ \widehat{a}_{12}\ \widehat{a}_{22} - \gamma_{12}(0)\ (\ \widehat{a}_{11}\ \widehat{a}_{22} + \ \widehat{a}_{12}\ \widehat{a}_{21})]\ /\widehat{\sigma}_1\widehat{\sigma}_2$$

These formulas may be easily generalized to more than two variates.

C Appendix C: Wheat prices in England, Finland, France, Germany and the United States: 1801-1913

Great Britain

1801	119	69	58	62	90	79	75	81	97	106
1811	95	126	109	74	65	78	96	86	74	67
1821	56	44	53	63	68	58	58	60	66	64
1831	66	58	52	46	39	48	55	64	70	66
1841	64	57	50	51	50	54	69	50	44	40
1851	38	40	53	72	74	69	56	44	43	53
1861	55	55	44	40	41	49	64	63	48	46
1871	56	57	58	55	45	46	56	46	43	44
1881	45	45	41	35	32	31	32	31	29	31
1891	37	30	26	22	23	26	30	34	25	26
1901	26	28	26	28	29	28	30	32	36	31
1911	31	34	31							

France

1801	2219	2514	2288	1836	2022	2000	1860	1667	1517	2026
1811	2633	3300	2282	1773	1953	2831	3616	2465	1842	1913
1821	1779	1549	1752	1622	1574	1585	1821	2203	2259	2239
1831	2210	2185	1662	1525	1525	1732	1853	1951	2214	2184
1841	1854	1955	2046	1975	1975	2405	2901	1665	1537	1432
1851	1448	1723	2239	2882	2932	3075	2437	1675	1674	2024
1861	2455	2324	1978	1758	1641	1959	2602	2608	2021	2048
1871	2665	2290	2570	2431	1938	2074	2342	2308	2192	2290
1881	2228	2151	1916	1776	1680	1694	1813	1887	1845	1905
1891	2058	1787	1655	1521	1440	1482	1885	1990	1535	1477
1901	1535	1654	1727	1663	1770	1778	1834	1751	1832	1951
1911	2023	2128	2166							

United States

1801	175	115	125	142	215	145	120	100	100	145
1811	200	178	195	142	138	181	300	200	182	108
1821	78	108	132	118	100	88	102	100	170	92
1831	123	108	115	114	106	132	225	168	176	113
1841	98	128	84	97	87	111	103	137	108	106
1851	103	87	112	158	200	195	151	112	129	133
1861	130	93	114	183	146	219	198	142	94	104
1871	125	124	115	94	100	103	108	77	110	95
1881	119	88	91	64	77	68	68	92	69	83
1891	83	62	53	49	50	72	80	58	58	61
1901	63	63	69	93	75	66	87	97	99	91
1911	87	81	79							

Germany

1801	111	112	118	121	169	146	126	135	91	70
1811	71	106	93	85	95	114	155	131	96	76
1821	73	67	68	54	50	54	64	78	93	89
1831	105	85	63	62	59	62	66	89	99	94
1841	88	102	77	78	76	108	139	87	86	83
1851	83	92	111	135	151	139	100	94	90	111
1861	114	108	94	82	84	94	131	126	100	100
1871	108	120	126	117	97	104	114	97	100	110
1881	110	103	94	82	81	76	83	87	94	98
1891	113	89	76	68	72	79	87	93	78	76
1901	82	82	81	88	88	90	104	106	118	106
1911	103	109	100							

Finland

1801	2556	1970	1278	1349	1420	1491	1811	2010	2625	2863
1811	3600	2867	3200	3367	3367	3517	3500	3700	3140	2993
1821	3680	3133	3000	2800	2800	2667	2400	2533	2560	2733
1831	2800	2667	2720	2800	3000	2934	2934	2933	2933	2620
1841	2720	2480	2600	2580	2700	2600	2560	2560	2720	2720
1851	2720	2720	2800	2800	2800	3000	3000	3000	3000	2900
1861	3250	3400	3175	3050	2876	2800	3200	3200	2800	2650
1871	2850	3075	3025	3200	3150	3250	3125	3000	2900	3025
1881	3475	3115	3075	3050	2975	2524	2376	2426	2437	2539
1891	3100	3237	2886	2584	2391	2300	2445	2556	2858	2914
1901										
1911										

Table 6.C Annual prices of wheat 1801-1913. Units: Finland: markka/tynnyri France: centimes/hectolitre; Germany: index: 1913=100=199, mark/ton; Great Britain: shilling/quarter; United States: cents/bushel. *Sources: Finland: Földes (1905); France: Földes (1905), Labrousse et al (1970); Germany: Jacobs and Richter (1935); Great Britain: Földes (1905), Mitchell (1978); United States: Cole (1938), Földes (1905), Historical Statistics of the US (1975).*

Chapter 7

Spatial and space-time autoregressive processes

In the preceding chapters we favoured economic investigation at the expense of mathematical thoroughness. In chapter 3 for instance we made use of the solution to spatial second order autoregressive processes but we postponed its derivation to latter examination. As the forthcoming analysis of the time dependent Enke-Samuelson model deeply relies on specific results about space-time autoregressive processes, it now is the time to tackle these mathematical issues. Basically, in this chapter we show how standard methods in autoregressive modelling have to be modified to fit to spatial and space-time processes. Although we shall give some attention to estimation problems at the end of the chapter, our general purpose is to focus on probabilistic issues rather than on statistical ones, our main objective being the discussion of stationarity conditions.

Spatial autoregressive processes have been introduced in the 1950's by Whittle (1954) and Bartlett (1955,1964,1975). They received renewed attention in the 1970's after maximum likelihood estimation procedures had been devised, in particular by Keith Ord (1975). In recent years they have been discussed in a number of books about spatial analysis; let us for instance mention the books by Cliff and Ord (1981), Upton and Fingleton (1985), Anselin (1988), Haining (1991). We can note in passing that our own approach heavily relies on spectral methods and is therefore much in line with those of Whittle (1954) and of Bartlett (1971). We should also mention a different approach, the so-called conditional models which constitute an attempt to transpose to spatial processes the concept of Markov processes. This approach has been developed in the 1970's especially by Besag (1972,1974).

So far spatial and space-time autoregressive processes have mainly been used in simulations and for estimation purposes; it is possible that their use as analytical tools has so far been hampered by the lack of a widespread understanding of some of their basic analytical properties. In the first section we recall a number of basic notions about spectral analysis of autoregressive processes and about their autocovariance functions. In section 2 we discuss stationarity conditions of spatial processes. In section 3, we develop maximum likelihood estimators for spatial processes. Finally, in section 4 we extend to space-time processes the methods previously developed for the spatial case. Throughout this chapter our objective is to present explicit formulas for subsequent use in specific applications rather than to establish general theorems.

1 Spectral functions and covariance functions of spatial processes

First of all, we shall in the following paragraph highlight the special features of spatial autoregressive processes as compared to time dependent autoregressive processes.

1.1 Spatial versus time dependent autoregressive processes

1.1.1 Causality condition

What differentiate a spatial autoregressive process from a time dependent process is not the form of its defining equation but rather the fact that in the later case the equation is supplemented by a causality condition. In intuitive terms, the causality condition means that if a perturbation affects a system described by a state function y_k at $k = 0$, then its effect will be restricted to the states $k \geq 0$; in that case k may be interpreted as being a time variable. To express this condition mathematically, it will be convenient to introduce the Green's function of a recurrence equation. To this end, we consider a recurrence equation of the general form:

$$H(B, F)y_k = g_k$$

supplemented by some boundary conditions on y_k. B, F are the backward and forward operators. H is a linear function of B and F. g_k is a given function of the integer k.

Definition 1 We say that G_k is the Green's function of the equation

$$H(B, F)y_k = g_k$$

if it satisfies:

$$H(B, F)G_k = \delta_{k,0} \qquad \delta_{k,0} : \text{ Kronecker delta}$$

together with the required boundary conditions.

Subsequently, Green's functions will also prove useful in the Fourier analysis of autoregressive processes. Together with the causality condition, this definition leads to the following distinction:

- Time dependent processes: $G_k = 0$ for $k < 0$
- Spatial processes: no condition imposed on G_k

In a sense, the class of time dependent processes can therefore be considered as a special case of the broader class of spatial processes.

1.1.2 Boundary conditions

When a spatial equation is used to model an empirical system it has to be supplemented by some kind of boundary conditions. For instance, one often has to impose that the solution should vanish on the boundaries of the domain on which it is defined. This condition is of special importance in the context of autoregressive processes for it will ensure stationarity. Of course the specific form of the boundary conditions depends on the order of the equation. To illustrate this point we consider the example of a second order equation. Throughout this chapter we shall often restrict our analysis to second or even first order equations; this usually gives the gist of the argument, the generalization to higher order processes being most often a straightforward matter.

A finite second order *time dependent* autoregressive process is ruled by the following equation and boundary conditions:

$$X_t + a_1 X_{t-1} + a_2 X_{t-2} = N_t \qquad t = 0, 1, \dots, N \qquad X_{-1} = X_{-2} = 0 \quad (1.1a)$$

or in matrix form:

$$\begin{pmatrix} 1 & 0 & 0 & \cdots & 0 & 0 & 0 \\ a_1 & 1 & 0 & \cdots & 0 & 0 & 0 \\ a_2 & a_1 & 1 & \cdots & 0 & 0 & 0 \\ \vdots & \vdots & \vdots & \cdots & \vdots & \vdots & \vdots \\ 0 & 0 & 0 & \cdots & a_2 & a_1 & 1 \end{pmatrix} \begin{pmatrix} X_0 \\ X_1 \\ X_2 \\ \vdots \\ X_N \end{pmatrix} = \begin{pmatrix} N_0 \\ N_1 \\ N_2 \\ \vdots \\ N_N \end{pmatrix} \qquad (1.1b)$$

A finite second order *spatial* autoregressive process is ruled by the following equation and boundary conditions:

$$X_x + a_{-1} X_{x-1} + a_1 X_{x+1} = N_x \qquad x = -N, \dots, N \qquad X_{-N-1} = X_{N+1} = 0 \quad (1.2a)$$

or in matrix form:

$$\begin{pmatrix} 1 & a_1 & 0 & \cdots & 0 & 0 & 0 \\ a_{-1} & 1 & a_1 & \cdots & 0 & 0 & 0 \\ 0 & a_{-1} & 1 & \cdots & 0 & 0 & 0 \\ \vdots & \vdots & \vdots & \cdots & \vdots & \vdots & \vdots \\ 0 & 0 & 0 & \cdots & 0 & a_{-1} & 1 \end{pmatrix} \begin{pmatrix} X_{-N} \\ X_{-N+1} \\ X_{-N+2} \\ \vdots \\ X_N \end{pmatrix} = \begin{pmatrix} N_{-N} \\ N_{-N+1} \\ N_{-N+2} \\ \vdots \\ N_N \end{pmatrix} \qquad (1.2b)$$

One may note that the same notation , N, is used for the number of states and for the stochastic noise; the context should prevent any confusion. Although the structure of equations (1.1a) and (1.2a) could appear rather similar (by an index change it is even possible to write equation (1.2a) in the form (1.1a)), they are essentially different for two (related) reasons:

1) **Form of the matrix**

The matrix of the system is triangular for the time dependent equation while it is tridiagonal for the spatial equation.

2) **Form of the boundary conditions**

In the time dependent case the boundary conditions refer to two successive states, while in the spatial case they pertain to states located at both ends of the domain.

1.2 Green's functions of recurrence equations

In this and in the following section our main purpose is to recall a number of basic formulas and to define the standard notations we shall use repeatedly in subsequent chapters.

1.2.1 Fundamental property

As is well known, the fundamental property of Green's functions is the fact that, by superposition, they permit to obtain the solution of the given equation with an arbitrary function in its right-hand side. Indeed, it is easy to check that u_t defined by:

$$u_k = \sum_{i=-\infty}^{\infty} G_{k-i} f_i \tag{1.3}$$

is a solution of $H(B,F)y_k = g_k$:

Needless to say, a necessary condition for the convergence of the series in equation (1.3) is that:

$$\lim_{k\to\infty} G_k = 0$$

1.2.2 Green's functions of first-order equations

We consider the first order process:

$$u_k - a u_{k-1} = f_k \qquad k = 0, 1, \ldots \qquad u_{-1} = 0 \tag{1.4a}$$

$$G_k - a G_{k-1} = \delta_{k,0} \qquad k = 0, 1, \ldots \qquad G_{-1} = 0 \tag{1.4b}$$

This will serve as an illustration of the difference between time dependent and spatial processes; moreover the results will be needed when discussing the stationary conditions in Section 2.

The solution of equation (1.4b) reads:

$$G_k = \begin{cases} 0 & k < 0 \\ a^k & k \geq 0 \end{cases} \tag{1.5}$$

G_k satisfies the causality condition; it can therefore be interpreted as the Green's function of a time dependent process. This is true whether $|a|$ is smaller or larger than one. If stationarity is required then the condition: $\lim_{k\to\infty} G_k = 0$ implies $|a| < 1$, which is the standard stationarity condition for a first order process. When $|a| > 1$, the equation:

$$G_k - aG_{k-1} = \delta_{k,0} \tag{1.6}$$

can be seen as defining a stationary *spatial* process, provided that we change the boundary condition into:

$$\lim_{k\to-\infty} G_k = 0$$

Indeed, we may rewrite (1.6) in the following form:

$$G_{k-1} = \frac{1}{a} G_k - \frac{1}{a} \delta_{k,0} \tag{1.7}$$

Whereas (1.4b) was (at least for $k > 0$) an ascending recurrence relation, (1.7) is a descending one; its solution reads:

$$G_k = \begin{cases} -(1/a)^{|k|} & k < 0 \\ 0 & k \geq 0 \end{cases} \tag{1.8}$$

This Green's function converges to zero as $|k| \to \infty$, but it does not satisfy the causality condition.

1.3 Spectral theory of autoregressive processes

1.3.1 The Fourier formalism

We consider the process:

$$H(B)X_k = N_k \qquad E(N_k) = 0 \tag{1.9}$$

where N_k represents white noise. In this paragraph we shall proceed formally and our derivations rather serve a mnemonic purpose. For more details, one could refer to Priestley (1981, Ch4).

First of all, we introduce the generating function of the G_k:

$$\widetilde{G}(\omega) = \mathcal{F}(G_k) \qquad \widetilde{G}(\omega) = \sum_{k=-\infty}^{\infty} G_k \, e^{-ik\omega} \tag{1.10a}$$

The inversion formula results from the orthogonality property:

$$\frac{1}{2\pi} \int_{-\pi}^{\pi} e^{i\omega l} d\omega = \delta_{l,0}$$

it reads:

$$G_k = \mathcal{F}^{-1}[G(\omega)] \qquad G_k = \frac{1}{2\pi}\int_{-\pi}^{\pi} \widetilde{G}(\omega)e^{i\omega k}d\omega \tag{1.10b}$$

From (1.10b), it results that:

$$G_{-k} = \frac{1}{2\pi}\int_{-\pi}^{\pi} \widetilde{G}(\omega)e^{-i\omega k}d\omega = \frac{1}{2\pi}\int_{-\pi}^{\pi} \widetilde{G}(-\omega)e^{i\omega k}d\omega = \mathcal{F}^{-1}[G(-\omega)] \tag{1.11}$$

Moreover, we can note that if G_k is real:

$$\widetilde{G}(-\omega) = \overline{\widetilde{G}(\omega)} \tag{1.12}$$

Next, let us introduce the autocovariance function of the stationary process X:

$$c_l = E(X_k X_{k+l})$$

From the fundamental property (1.3) of the Green's functions one has:

$$X_k = \sum_{i=-\infty}^{\infty} G_{k-i}N_i \qquad X_{k+l} = \sum_{i=-\infty}^{\infty} G_{k+l-i}N_i$$

Thus:

$$c_l = E(X_k X_{k+l}) = \sum_{i,j} G_{k-i}G_{k+l-j}E(N_iN_j)$$

If the N_i are white noise, they are uncorrelated: $E(N_iN_j) = \delta_{i,j}$, thus:

$$c_l = \sum_i G_{k-i}G_{l+k-i} = \sum_j G_jG_{l+j}$$

In order to write c_l in the form of a convolution product, we introduce: $\widehat{G}_j = G_{-j}$; thus:

$$c_l = \sum_j \widehat{G}_{-j}G_{l+j} = \widehat{G} * G \tag{1.13}$$

Going to Fourier transforms and taking into account (1.11) and (1.12) we obtain the spectral function:

$$\widetilde{c}_l(\omega) = \widetilde{G}(-\omega)\widetilde{G}(\omega) = |\widetilde{G}(\omega)|^2 \tag{1.14}$$

and going to the inverse Fourier transform, one obtains c_l:

$$c_l = \mathcal{F}^{-1}[\widetilde{G}(-\omega)\widetilde{G}(\omega)] = \frac{1}{2\pi}\int_{-\pi}^{\pi} |\widetilde{G}(\omega)|^2 e^{ik\omega}d\omega \tag{1.15}$$

In subsequent applications $\widetilde{G}(\omega)$ will actually be a function of $e^{i\omega}$: $|\widetilde{G}(\omega)|^2 = h(e^{i\omega})$. Therefore it is natural to change to the variable: $z = e^{i\omega}$. The integral from $-\pi$ to π then becomes an integral in the complex plane along the (positive) unit circle C:

$$c_l = \frac{1}{2i\pi}\int_C h(z)z^{l-1}dz \tag{1.16}$$

Using the theorem of residues, we obtain:

$$c_l = \sum_{\text{poles in } C} \text{Res}[h(z)z^{l-1}] \tag{1.17}$$

the summation extends to all poles of the function $h(z)z^{l-1}$ that are within the unit circle.

1.3.2 Applications

Just to show how the previous formalism works we shall apply it to the simple case of a first order process (1.4a).

Green's functions First of all, we shall reobtain the Green's function by Fourier analysis. To this end, we multiply both sides of its defining equation (1.4b) by $e^{-ik\omega}$ and we sum over k; this gives:

$$\sum_{k=-\infty}^{\infty} G_k e^{-ik\omega} - a \sum_{k=-\infty}^{\infty} G_{k-1} e^{-ik\omega} = 1 \tag{1.18}$$

In order to factorize out $\widetilde{G}(\omega)$, we perform a translation in the summation index of the second term: $j = k - 1$. If we assume, as we do here, that the process extends over $(-\infty, \infty)$, then the lower and upper summation limits remain unaffected; this, however, is no longer true for a finite process extending over $(-N, N)$; possible implications are discussed in Appendix A. From (1.18) we get:

$$\widetilde{G}(\omega) = \frac{1}{1 - ae^{-i\omega}}$$

Using (1.17) to express the inverse Fourier transform, we obtain:

$$G_k = \sum_C \text{Res}\frac{z^k}{z-a} \tag{1.19}$$

The actual calculation now depends on whether the pole $z = a$ is located inside or outside the unit disk.

- $|a| < 1$

a) $k \geq 0$

In this case $z = a$ is the only contributing pole; thus: $G_k = a^k$

b) $k < 0, \; k = -l$

In this case, there is in addition the contribution of the pole $z = 0$ which is of order $|k| = l$; thus:

$$G_k = (\frac{1}{a})^l + \frac{1}{(l-1)!}\frac{d^{l-1}}{dz^{l-1}}\left[\frac{1}{z-a}\right]\Big|_{z=0}$$

Since:

$$\frac{d^{l-1}}{dz^{l-1}}\left[\frac{1}{z-a}\right]\Big|_{z=0} = -\frac{(l-1)!}{a^l}$$

one obtains: $G_k = 0$

- $|a| > 1$

a) $k \geq 0$

There is no longer any pole inside the unit disk, thus: $G_k = 0$

b) $k < 0, \; k = -l$

The only pole inside the unit disk is the pole $z = 0$ of order l, the contribution of which is: $G_k = -(1/a)^{|k|}$

To sum up, we have obtained the following results:

$$|a| < 1 \qquad G_k = \begin{cases} 0 & k < 0 \\ a^k & k \geq 0 \end{cases} \tag{1.20}$$

$$|a| > 1 \qquad G_k = \begin{cases} -(1/a)^{|k|} & k < 0 \\ 0 & k \geq 0 \end{cases} \tag{1.21}$$

Seemingly these results are identical to our previous results (1.5) and (1.8); yet, there is an important difference: in contrast to (1.20), (1.5) holds true whatever the value of $|a|$. We shall elaborate further on this point in our discussion of stationarity (section 2).

In the same connection it should also be noticed that nowhere throughout the above calculation did we get any hint regarding stationarity requirements. For short, because the very definition of a Fourier series such as (1.10a) requires the coefficients G_k to decrease to zero for $k \to \pm\infty$, Fourier analysis always turns out solutions that decrease at infinity, regardless of their possible empirical meaning.

Autocovariance of a first order autoregressive process We now turn to the evaluation of the autocovariance function using formula (1.17). We have here:

$$h(z) = \frac{z^{l-1}}{(1-a/z)(1-az)} = \frac{z^l}{(z-a)(1-az)}$$

If we assume that $|a| < 1$, only $z = a$ is located inside the unit disk. Moreover, because the autocovariance is an even function of l, i.e. $c_l = c_{-l}$, we only need to consider the case $l \geq 0$; thus:

$$c_l = \frac{a^l}{1-a^2} \tag{1.22}$$

which is the standard expression for the autocovariance function of a first-order autoregressive process.

Remark The result (1.22) corresponds to the steady state behavior. One may wonder at which point in the derivation, the transient behavior has been lost. At some finite time t, one would actually have:

$$E(X_t X_{t+l}) = \sum_{k=0}^{t} G_k G_{l+k}$$

The lower limit can be extended to $k = -\infty$ because $G_k = 0$ for $k < 0$, but the upper limit cannot be extended to $k = \infty$ unless t truly tends to infinity. If we keep t as the upper limit, then:

$$\mathcal{F}[\sum_{k=-\infty}^{t} G_k G_{l+k}] \neq \tilde{G}(-\omega)\tilde{G}(\omega)$$

because:

$$\sum_{k=-\infty}^{t} e^{ik(\omega+\omega')} \neq \sum_{k=-\infty}^{\infty} e^{ik(\omega+\omega')} = \delta(\omega+\omega')$$

where $\delta(.)$ denotes Dirac's distribution.

Autocovariance of a spatial second order autoregressive process As a second example, we shall compute the Green's function and autocovariance of the following (symmetric) spatial process:

$$X_x - a(X_{x-1} + X_{x+1}) = N_x \qquad x = \ldots -1, 0, 1 \ldots \tag{1.23}$$

We shall carry out the calculation in some detail since the result is of central importance for the market-chain model in Chapter 3.

The Green's function is defined by:

$$G_x - a(G_{x-1} + G_{x+1}) = \delta_{x,0} \qquad G_{-\infty} = G_{\infty} = 0$$

For the spectral Green's function one has:

$$\tilde{G}(\omega) = \frac{1}{1 - a(e^{-i\omega} + e^{i\omega})}$$

Thus:

$$G_x = \frac{1}{\pi}\int_0^{\infty} \frac{\cos x\theta}{1-2a\cos\theta} = \frac{1}{2i\pi}\int_C \frac{z^{x-1}}{1-a(1/z+z)}dz \tag{1.24}$$

From the first integral, it is obvious that: $G_{-x} = G_x$. The integral may be evaluated in two ways.

1) As before it may be obtained from the theorem of residues. The zeroes of the denominator are the solutions of: $az^2 - z + a = 0$. Their product is equal to 1. If $|a| > 1/2$, the poles are complex and are both located *on* the unit circle; this leads to a singular integral which can only be defined by principal value. We shall leave this case aside, since it does not correspond to a stationary process. If, on the other hand, $|a| < 1/2$, there are two real poles of which only one, z_2 say, is located inside the unit disk. Thus, when $x > 0$ we have to compute one residue; one obtains:

$$G_x = \frac{1}{\sqrt{1-4a^2}}\left(\frac{1-\sqrt{1-4a^2}}{2a}\right)^{|x|} \qquad |a| < 1/2 \tag{1.25}$$

2) Alternatively, the real integral in (1.24) may be obtained, for $|a| < 1/2$ from Gradshteyn (1965, p.366: 3.613(1)).

We now turn to the covariance function:

$$c_x = \frac{1}{\pi}\int_0^{\infty} \frac{\cos x\theta}{(1-2a\cos\theta)^2} = \frac{1}{2i\pi}\int_C \frac{z^{x-1}}{[1-a(1/z+z)]^2}dz$$

There are again two ways to perform the calculation:

1) The integral may be calculated by the theorem of residues. This time, the pole z_2 which is located inside the unit disk is of order 2. The residue reads:

$$\mathrm{Res}(z_2) = \frac{d}{dz}\left[\frac{z^{x+1}}{a^2(z-z_1)^2}\right]\Bigg|_{z=z_2}$$

$$\mathrm{Res}(z_2) = \frac{z_2^x}{a^2}\frac{(x-1)z_2-(x+1)z_1}{(z_2-z_1)^3}$$

Finally, one obtains:

$$c_x = \frac{|x|\sqrt{1-4a^2}+1}{(1-4a^2)^{3/2}}\left(\frac{1-\sqrt{1-4a^2}}{2a}\right)^{|x|} \qquad |a| < 1/2$$

2) Alternatively, the previous result may be obtained by differentiation from an integral closely related to the Green's function; indeed with $\alpha = 1/a$:

$$\int_C \frac{z^{x-1}dz}{1-a(1/z+z)} = \frac{1}{a}\int_C \frac{z^{x-1}dz}{\alpha-(1/z+z)}$$

and:

$$\frac{d}{d\alpha}\int_C \frac{z^{x-1}dz}{\alpha-(1/z+z)} = -\int_C \frac{z^{x-1}dz}{[\alpha-(1/z+z)]^2} = -a^2\int_C \frac{z^{x-1}dz}{[1-a(1/z+z)]^2}$$

2 Stationarity conditions for spatial processes

First, we shall recall the standard reasonings and results for time dependent autoregressive processes; they will serve as our starting point for the study of spatial processes. As in the previous section, we shall for the sake of simplicity mainly confine our reasonings to second order processes.

2.1 Time dependent processes

2.1.1 Recurrence reasoning

We consider the following second order process:

$$X_t + a_1 X_{t-1} + a_2 X_{t-2} = N_t \qquad (2.1a)$$

Its Green's function satisfies:

$$G_t + a_1 G_{t-1} + a_2 G_{t-2} = \delta_{t,0} \qquad G_{-2} = G_{-1} = 0 \qquad (2.1b)$$

Using the backward operator B, (2.1b) may be rewritten:

$$(1 + a_1 B + a_2 B^2) G_t = \delta_{t,0} \qquad (2.2)$$

or:

$$(1 - s_1 B)(1 - s_2 B) G_t = \delta_{t,0} \qquad (2.3)$$

where s_1, s_2 are the roots of the equation:

$$s^2 + a_1 s + a_2 = 0 \qquad (2.4)$$

The operator $(1 - s_1 B)(1 - s_2 B)$ may be inverted in the following way:

$$\frac{1}{(1-s_1B)(1-s_2B)} = \frac{1}{s_1 - s_2}\left(\frac{s_1}{1-s_1B} - \frac{s_2}{1-s_2B}\right) \qquad (2.5)$$

Since the function G_t extends from $t = 0$ to $t = \infty$, both terms should be developed in series of B. Hence:

$$G_t = \frac{1}{s_1 - s_2}\left[s_1 \sum_{k=0}^{\infty} s_1^k B^k \delta_{t,0} - s_2 \sum_{k=0}^{\infty} s_2^k B^k \delta_{t,0}\right]$$

These developments require that:

$$|s_1| < 1, \qquad |s_2| < 1 \tag{2.6}$$

One obtains this way:

$$G_t = \frac{1}{s_1 - s_2} \sum_{k=0}^{\infty} (s_1^{k+1} - s_2^{k+1}) \delta_{t,k} = \frac{s_1^{t+1} - s_2^{t+1}}{s_1 - s_2}$$

Here, we are not particularly interested in the last result, but rather in the condition (2.6) which provides the well-known stationarity conditions for a second order time dependent process, namely, the moduli of the roots of the characteristic equation (2.4) have to be smaller than 1. We now have to express this condition in terms of the coefficients a_1, a_2. This is accomplished by the Schur theorem.

2.1.2 The Schur theorem

The Schur theorem (Chiang 1984, p.601) states the stationarity conditions for an autoregressive process of order n:

$$a_0 X_t + a_1 X_{t-1} + \ldots + a_n X_{t-n} = N_t$$

Schur's theorem The roots of the nth-degree polynomial equation:

$$a_0 s^n + a_1 s^{n-1} + \ldots + a_n = 0$$

will all be less (in modulus) than unity if and only if the following n determinants $\Delta_1, \Delta_2, \ldots, \Delta_n$ are all positive:

$$\Delta_1 = \begin{vmatrix} a_0 & a_n \\ a_n & a_0 \end{vmatrix}, \quad \Delta_2 = \begin{vmatrix} a_0 & 0 & a_n & a_{n-1} \\ a_1 & a_0 & 0 & a_n \\ a_n & 0 & a_0 & a_1 \\ a_{n-1} & a_n & 0 & a_0 \end{vmatrix}, \ldots$$

$$\Delta_n = \begin{vmatrix} a_0 & 0 & \ldots & 0 & a_n & a_{n-1} & \ldots & a_1 \\ a_1 & a_0 & \ldots & 0 & 0 & a_n & \ldots & a_2 \\ \vdots & \vdots & \vdots & \vdots & \vdots & \vdots & \vdots & \vdots \\ a_{n-1} & a_{n-2} & \ldots & a_0 & 0 & 0 & \ldots & a_n \\ a_n & 0 & \ldots & 0 & a_0 & a_1 & \ldots & a_{n-1} \\ a_{n-1} & a_n & \ldots & 0 & 0 & a_0 & \ldots & a_{n-2} \\ \vdots & \vdots & \vdots & \vdots & \vdots & \vdots & \vdots & \vdots \\ a_1 & a_2 & \ldots & a_n & 0 & 0 & \ldots & a_0 \end{vmatrix}$$

Application to $n = 2$. With $a_0 = 1$ and $n = 2$ one obtains:

$$\Delta_1 = 1 - a_2^2 \qquad \Delta_2 = -(a_1 + a_2 + 1)(a_1 - a_2 - 1)(a_2 - 1)^2$$

Thus the conditions: $\Delta_1 > 0$, $\Delta_2 > 0$ lead to :

$$|a_2| < 1 \qquad (a_1 + a_2 + 1)(a_1 - a_2 - 1) < 0$$

The second condition breaks up into two conditions:

$$a_1 + a_2 + 1 > 0 \qquad a_1 - a_2 - 1 < 0 \tag{2.7a}$$

$$a_1 + a_2 + 1 < 0 \qquad a_1 - a_2 - 1 > 0 \tag{2.7b}$$

Since the conditions (2.7b) are inconsistent with $|a_2| < 1$, we are finally left with the classical conditions (Priestley 1981, p.127):

$$|a_2| < 1 \qquad a_1 + a_2 + 1 > 0 \qquad a_1 - a_2 - 1 < 0$$

Geometrically they define the domain S_2 displayed in Fig.7.1a.

Application to $n = 3$. This case is of importance for the discussion of price stability in the time-dependent Enke-Samuelson model (Chapter 8). When $a_0 = 1$ and $n = 3$, the three Schur inequalities read:

$$\Delta_1 = 1 - a_3^2 > 0$$

$$\Delta_2 = -(-a_2 + a_1 a_3 + a_3^2 - 1)(-a_2 + a_1 a_3 - a_3^2 + 1) > 0$$

$$\Delta_3 = -(a_1 a_3 - a_2 - a_3^2 + 1)^2 (a_1 + a_2 + a_3 + 1)(a_1 - a_2 + a_3 - 1) > 0$$

The stationarity region is therefore defined by the following conditions:

$$|a_3| < 1 \tag{2.8a}$$

$$(a_1 + a_2 + a_3 + 1)(a_1 - a_2 + a_3 - 1) < 0 \tag{2.8b}$$

$$(-a_2 + a_1 a_3 + a_3^2 - 1)(-a_2 + a_1 a_3 - a_3^2 + 1) < 0 \tag{2.8c}$$

When $a_3 = 0$, the conditions (2.8b) and (2.8c) lead back to the stationarity region S_2. When $a_3 \neq 0$, the stationarity region S_3 is shown geometrically in Fig.7.1b.

There is a fundamental difference between S_2 and S_3: a straight line starting from the origin has only one intersection point with the frontier of S_2 while there may be two in the case of S_3. In other words, S_3 is a *non-convex* domain. Economic implications of this property will be discussed in chapter 8.

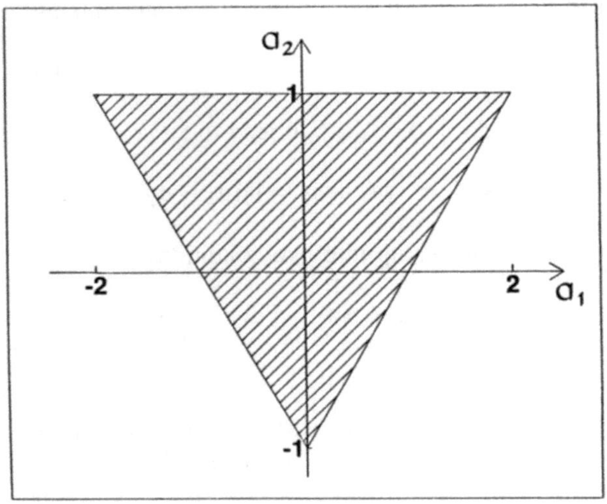

Fig.7.1 a Region of stationarity for a second order time dependent autoregressive process: $X_t + a_1 X_{t-1} + a_2 X_{t-2} = N_t$

Fig.7.1 b Region of stationarity for a third order time dependent autoregressive process: $X_t + a_1 X_{t-1} + a_2 X_{t-2} + a_3 X_{t-3} = N_t$. The region is a non-convex domain in (a_1, a_2, a_3) space. The figure shows horizontal (a_1, a_2) sections of this domain. The section $a_3 = 0$ is of course nothing else but the domain of Fig.7.1 a. The non-convex character of this domain is of importance in the time dependent analysis of interdependent markets (Chapter 8).

2.2 Spatial processes

For spatial processes, there are two different stationarity concepts. The first, which we shall call Fourier-stability, concerns the stationarity requirements for the process in its infinite dimensional setting; this was the point of view adopted by Whittle (1954). The second, which will be called matrix-stability, gives stationarity conditions for the process when it is written in its finite dimensional matrix representation. It is probably this point of view which proves most useful in the perspective of econometric modelling. More, specifically we shall set the following definition:

Definition 2 We consider a spatial autoregressive process of order $p+q$ defined by the infinite dimensional equation:

$$X_x - \sum_{k=-p}^{q} a_k X_{x+k} = N_x \qquad x = \ldots, -1, 0, 1, \ldots \tag{2.9a}$$

1) X_x is said to be Fourier-stationary if the Green's function of equation (2.9a) has a convergent Fourier series representation.
2) X_x is said to be matrix-stationary if the finite system of equations:

$$X_x - \sum_{k=-p}^{q} a_k X_{x+k} = N_x \qquad x = -N, \ldots, N \tag{2.9b}$$

with boundary conditions:

$$X_{-N-q} = \ldots = X_{-N-1} = 0 \qquad X_{N+p} = \ldots = X_{N+1} = 0 \tag{2.9c}$$

has a Green's function G_x which remains bounded when $N \to \infty$, that is if there exists a number A such that: $|G_x| < A \quad \forall x, \forall N$.

Let us already point out that the two concepts become identical for symmetrical processes, i.e. when:

- $p = q$
- $a_{x-k} = a_{x+k} \quad k = 1, 2, \ldots, p$

For time dependent processes the boundary conditions (the analog of (2.9c)) are anyway embedded in the causality condition; this is why the above distinction does not arise in that case.

In the following paragraph we analyse an example whose purpose it is to illustrate both stationarity notions.

2.2.1 An illustrative example

Fourier-stationarity We consider the second-order spatial process:

$$X_x + a_{-1} X_{x-1} + a_1 X_{x+1} = N_x \qquad x = \ldots, -1, 0, 1, \ldots \tag{2.10a}$$

We shall take here: $a_{-1} = 1 \quad a_1 = 1/2$. Thus the Green's function satisfies:

$$G_x + G_{x-1} + \frac{1}{2}G_{x+1} = \delta_{x,0} \qquad x = \ldots, -1, 0, 1, \ldots \tag{2.10b}$$

We now calculate G_x by Fourier transformation as in Section 1.3.2.

$$G_x = \frac{1}{2i\pi}\int_C \frac{z^x dz}{z^2/2 + z + 1}$$

Both poles:

$$s_1 = -1 + i = \sqrt{2}e^{i3\pi/4} \qquad s_2 = -1 - i = \sqrt{2}e^{-i3\pi/4}$$

are outside the unit disk; therefore:

$$G_x = 0 \qquad x \geq 0$$

For $x < 0$, there is the single pole $z = 0$ of order x. To compute its residue we decompose the fraction $1/(z^2/2 + z + 1)$ into simple elements; this way one obtains:

$$G_{-x} = \frac{1}{(x-1)!}\frac{2}{s_1 - s_2}\frac{d^{x-1}}{dz^{x-1}}\left[\frac{1}{z - s_1} - \frac{1}{z - s_2}\right]$$

$$G_{-x} = \frac{2}{s_1 - s_2}(-s_1^{-x} + s_2^{-x}) = \frac{2}{2^{x/2}}\sin\frac{3\pi x}{4} \tag{2.11}$$

The process is therefore Fourier stationary, a conclusion which could actually have been anticipated from the outset since the Fourier integral giving G_x is not singular.

Matrix-stationarity We now consider the same second order process written in its (finite dimensional) matrix form (1.2b). When going from the infinite form (2.9) to this finite form, a specific choice has to be made regarding the truncation of the infinite dimensional matrix. We shall come back to this point later on; for the time being we shall limit ourselves to calculating: G_{-N} and G_N.

G_N is the ratio of two determinants: at the denominator, there is the determinant D_{2N+1} of the system; at the numerator there is the determinant U_{2N+1} of the matrix of the system where the last column has been replaced by the column vector $\delta_{x,0}$. To obtain analytic expressions for the two determinants we use the following lemmas.

Lemma 1 The n-dimensional tridiagonal determinant:

$$K_n(a, b, c) = \begin{vmatrix} b & c & 0 & \ldots & 0 \\ a & b & c & \ldots & 0 \\ \vdots & \vdots & \vdots & \vdots & \vdots \\ 0 & 0 & 0 & \ldots & b \end{vmatrix}$$

has the expression:

$$K_n(a,b,c) = \frac{u^{n+1} - v^{n+1}}{u - v}$$

where u, v are the roots of the equation: $x^2 - bx + ac = 0$

Proof By developing K_n with respect to its first column, one notices that it satisfies the recurrence equation:

$$K_n = bK_{n-1} - acK_{n-2} \qquad K_1 = b \quad K_2 = b^2 - ac$$

By solving this recurrence equation, one obtains lemma 1.

Lemma 2 We consider the triangular block-matrix:

$$J = \begin{pmatrix} A_1 & B \\ 0 & A_2 \end{pmatrix}$$

where A_1 and A_2 are two square matrices respectively of dimensions p and q; B is a rectangular matrix of dimension $p \times q$. Then the determinant of J may be computed as if A_1, A_2, B were pure scalars, i.e.:

$$\det J = \det A_1 . \det \mathrm{A}_2$$

Proof The proof follows from the following obvious identity between block-matrices:

$$\begin{pmatrix} A_1 & B \\ 0 & A_2 \end{pmatrix} . \begin{pmatrix} I_p & -A_1^{-1}B \\ 0 & I_q \end{pmatrix} = \begin{pmatrix} A_1 & 0 \\ 0 & A_2 \end{pmatrix} \tag{2.12}$$

where I_p is the identity matrix of dimension p. In the left-hand side of relation (2.12), the second matrix is a true triangular matrix (whereas the first one is only triangular by blocks); its determinant is therefore equal to one. The determinant of the matrix on the left-hand side is simply $\det A_1 . \det A_2$.

With the help of these two lemmas, we obtain:

$$D_{2N+1} = K_{2N+1}(1, 1, 1/2)$$

The roots of the equation $x^2 - bx + ac = 0$ are here:

$$x_1 = \frac{1}{\sqrt{2}} e^{i\pi/4} \qquad x_2 = \frac{1}{\sqrt{2}} e^{-i\pi/4}$$

Thus:

$$D_{2N+1} = 2 \left(\frac{1}{\sqrt{2}} \right)^{2N+2} \sin[(N+1)\frac{\pi}{2}] \tag{2.13}$$

Moreover:

$$U_{2N+1} = \begin{pmatrix} A_1 & B \\ 0 & A_2 \end{pmatrix}$$

where:

$$A_1 = \begin{pmatrix} 1 & a_1 & 0 & \dots & 0 \\ a_{-1} & 1 & a_1 & \dots & 0 \\ \vdots & \vdots & \vdots & \vdots & \vdots \\ 0 & 0 & 0 & \dots & 1 \end{pmatrix} \qquad A_2 = \begin{pmatrix} a_{-1} & 1 & a_1 & \dots & 0 \\ 0 & a_{-1} & 1 & \dots & 0 \\ \vdots & \vdots & \vdots & \vdots & \vdots \\ 0 & 0 & 0 & \dots & a_{-1} \end{pmatrix}$$

$$B = \begin{pmatrix} 0 & \dots & 0 \\ \vdots & \vdots & \vdots \\ a_1 & \dots & 0 \end{pmatrix}$$

Hence:

$$U_{2N+1} = \det A_1 . \det A_2 = a_{-1}^N K_N(a_{-1}, 1, a_1) = 2\left(\frac{1}{\sqrt{2}}\right)^{N+1} \sin[(N+1)\frac{\pi}{4}] \tag{2.14}$$

Finally, we obtain for $N+1$ odd:

$$G_N = 2^{(N+1)/2} \frac{\sin[(N+1)\frac{\pi}{4}]}{\sin[(N+1)\frac{\pi}{2}]} \tag{2.15}$$

Similarly:

$$G_{-N} = G_N \frac{1}{2^N} = \frac{1}{2^{(N-1)/2}} \frac{\sin[(N+1)\frac{\pi}{4}]}{\sin[(N+1)\frac{\pi}{2}]} \tag{2.16}$$

Thus, G_N goes to infinity when $N \to \infty$; accordingly the process is not matrix-stationary.

Discussion The previous result could at first glance appear to be rather puzzling: the solution of the infinite process decreases to zero as $x \to \pm\infty$, while the finite process diverges as $x \to \infty$. The reason of this apparent paradox is that the infinite matrix may be truncated in three different ways (Fig.7.2), each of which corresponds to a different choice of boundary conditions. The Fourier method necessarily selects a solution G_x which converges to zero as $|x| \to \infty$; if, as in the previous case, G_N is not bounded, it selects the solution that is identically equal to zero for $x > 0$; in other words, it selects a descending time dependent solution. Another way to look at the connection between finite and infinite processes is developed in Appendix A.

There is still a question that remains unanswered, namely: does the fact that different truncations lead to different solutions mean that the infinite matrix equation has more than one solution? Formally the answer would be yes; however, for the uniqueness issue to have any meaning at all, one has to specify

$$G_{-N-2} = G_{-N-1} = 0 \Longrightarrow \begin{pmatrix} & \ddots & \ddots & \ddots & & \vdots & \vdots & \cdots & \vdots & \vdots & \vdots & \\ \cdots & 0 & a_{-1} & 1 & a_1 & 0 & 0 & \cdots & 0 & 0 & 0 & \cdots \\ \cdots & 0 & 0 & a_{-1} & 1 & a_1 & 0 & \cdots & 0 & 0 & 0 & \cdots \\ \vdots & \vdots & \vdots & & \ddots & \ddots & \ddots & & \vdots & \vdots & \vdots & \vdots \\ \cdots & 0 & 0 & \cdots & 0 & a_{-1} & 1 & a_1 & 0 & 0 & 0 & \cdots \\ \cdots & 0 & 0 & \cdots & 0 & 0 & a_{-1} & 1 & a_1 & 0 & 0 & \cdots \\ \vdots & \vdots & \vdots & \vdots & \vdots & \vdots & & \ddots & \ddots & \ddots & \vdots & \vdots \end{pmatrix}$$

Truncation of the first kind: ascending time-like solution

$$G_{-N-1} = G_{N+1} = 0 \Longrightarrow \begin{pmatrix} & \ddots & \ddots & \ddots & & \vdots & \vdots & \cdots & \vdots & \vdots & \vdots & \\ \cdots & 0 & a_{-1} & 1 & a_1 & 0 & 0 & \cdots & 0 & 0 & 0 & \cdots \\ \cdots & 0 & 0 & a_{-1} & 1 & a_1 & 0 & \cdots & 0 & 0 & 0 & \cdots \\ \vdots & \vdots & \vdots & & \ddots & \ddots & \ddots & & \vdots & \vdots & \vdots & \vdots \\ \cdots & 0 & 0 & \cdots & 0 & a_{-1} & 1 & a_1 & 0 & 0 & 0 & \cdots \\ \cdots & 0 & 0 & \cdots & 0 & 0 & a_{-1} & 1 & a_1 & 0 & 0 & \cdots \\ \vdots & \vdots & \vdots & \vdots & \vdots & \vdots & & \ddots & \ddots & \ddots & \vdots & \vdots \end{pmatrix}$$

Truncation of the second kind: space-like solution

$$G_{N+1} = G_{N+2} = 0 \Longrightarrow \begin{pmatrix} & \ddots & \ddots & \ddots & & \vdots & \vdots & \cdots & \vdots & \vdots & \vdots & \\ \cdots & 0 & a_{-1} & 1 & a_1 & 0 & 0 & \cdots & 0 & 0 & 0 & \cdots \\ \cdots & 0 & 0 & a_{-1} & 1 & a_1 & 0 & \cdots & 0 & 0 & 0 & \cdots \\ \vdots & \vdots & \vdots & & \ddots & \ddots & \ddots & & \vdots & \vdots & \vdots & \vdots \\ \cdots & 0 & 0 & \cdots & 0 & a_{-1} & 1 & a_1 & 0 & 0 & 0 & \cdots \\ \cdots & 0 & 0 & \cdots & 0 & 0 & a_{-1} & 1 & a_1 & 0 & 0 & \cdots \\ \vdots & \vdots & \vdots & \vdots & \vdots & \vdots & & \ddots & \ddots & \ddots & \vdots & \vdots \end{pmatrix}$$

Truncation of the third kind: descending time-like solution

Fig.7.2 Three possible truncations of the infinite matrix of a spatial second order process: $X_x + a_{-1}X_{x-1} + a_1X_{x+1} = N_x$. The Fourier solution (which corresponds to the infinite matrix) automatically selects the solution G_x which converge to zero (sufficiently fast to ensure convergence of the Fourier series) as $|x| \to \infty$.

the space of admissible solutions. A natural choice would be the space M of bounded real sequences: $(\ldots, x_{-1}, x_0, x_1, \ldots)$. The distance:

$$d(x,y) = \sup_k |x_k - y_k|$$

makes this space a complete (but not separable) metric space (Korn 1968 p.389). A matrix solution whose elements are not bounded therefore cannot converge towards a vector in M. It would converge towards an unbounded sequence the set of which cannot be given the structure of a metric space.

2.2.2 Stationarity conditions in terms of roots of the characteristic equation

In this paragraph, we express stationarity requirements in terms of the localization of the roots of the characteristic equation. Corresponding conditions in terms of the coefficients of the equation will be examined in the next paragraph.

Fourier-stationarity The only requirement for Fourier stationarity is that the poles of the Fourier transform $\tilde{G}(z)$ should not be located on the unit circle for this would result in a singular Fourier integral.

Matrix-stationarity The general result is summarized in:

Proposition 1 Stationarity of the spatial autoregressive process of order $2p$:

$$X_x + \sum_{k=-p}^{p} a_k X_{x+k} = N_x$$

$$X_{-N-p} = \ldots = X_{-N-1} = 0 \qquad X_{N+1} = \ldots = X_{N+p} = 0$$

requires that among the $2p$ roots of the characteristic equation:

$$\sum_{k=-p}^{p} a_k s^{p-k} = 0$$

p are inside the unit disk and p outside.

To begin with, let us again consider the finite second order process:

$$X_x + a_{-1}X_{x-1} + a_1 X_{x+1} = N_x \qquad X_{-N-1} = X_{N+1} = 0 \tag{2.17}$$

Since matrix methods are rather awkward to use, we shall discuss stationarity using the same kind of recurrence reasoning as we have already applied in Section 2.1.1 to time dependent processes. By introducing the backward operator B into the equation for the Green's function of (2.17) one obtains:

$$(a_{-1}B^2 + B + a_1)G_x = \delta_{x,1}$$

where both sides have been multiplied by B. Denoting by s_1, s_2 the roots of the equation:

$$a_{-1}s^2 + s + a_1 = 0 \tag{2.18}$$

one has:

$$G_x = \frac{1}{a_1(s_1 - s_2)}\left[s_1\frac{\delta_{x,1}}{1 - s_1 B} - s_2\frac{\delta_{x,1}}{1 - s_2 B}\right]$$

G_x may be rewritten by defining two auxiliary processes: P_x and Q_x:

$$G_x = \frac{1}{a_1(s_1 - s_2)}(s_1 P_x - s_2 Q_x) \tag{2.19a}$$

where:

$$P_x = \frac{\delta_{x,1}}{1 - s_1 B} \qquad Q_x = \frac{\delta_{x,1}}{1 - s_2 B} \tag{2.19b,c}$$

At this point one has to make specific assumptions about the positions of s_1 and s_2 with respect to the unit circle.

- $|s_1| < 1 \quad |s_2| > 1$

P_x in (2.19b) will be interpreted as an ascending recurrence relation:

$$P_x = s_1 P_{x-1} + \delta_{x,1}$$

With the notation: $P_{-N-2} = p$ one obtains:

$$P_{-N-1} = s_1 p,\ P_N = s_1^2 p,\ \ldots\ P_0 = s_1^{N+2} p,$$

$$P_1 = s_1^{N+3} p + 1,\ \ldots\ , P_{N+1} = s_1^N (s_1^{N+3} p + 1)$$

On the other hand, (2.19c) will be interpreted as a descending recurrence relation:

$$Q_{x-1} = \frac{1}{s_2}(Q_x - \delta_{x,1})$$

With the notation: $Q_{N+2} = q$, one obtains:

$$Q_{N+1} = \frac{q}{s_2},\ Q_N = \left(\frac{1}{s_2}\right)^2 q,\ \ldots\ , Q_0 = \frac{1}{s_2}\left[\left(\frac{1}{s_2}\right)^{N+1} q - 1\right]$$

$$Q_{-1} = \left(\frac{1}{s_2}\right)^2 \left[\left(\frac{1}{s_2}\right)^{N+1} q - 1\right],\ \ldots\ , Q_{-N-1} = \left(\frac{1}{s_2}\right)^{N+2} \left[\left(\frac{1}{s_2}\right)^{N+1} q - 1\right]$$

Now, one has to take into account the boundary conditions:

$$G_{-N-1} = G_{N+1} = 0$$

This gives rise to the following system of equations with respect to the unknown parameters p and q:

$$\begin{cases} s_1^2 p & - & (1/s_2)^{2N+2} q & = & (-1/s_2)^{N+1} \\ s_1^{2N+4} p & - & q & = & -s_1^{N+1} \end{cases}$$

Its solution reads:

$$p \simeq \left(-\frac{1}{s_2}\right)^{N+1} \frac{1}{s_1^2} \qquad q \simeq s_1^{N+1}$$

The solution is an approximation of the exact result in the sense that, for the sake of simplicity, we have considered $(s_1/s_2)^N$ to be negligibly small with respect to 1. Replacing p and q by their values gives the required solution; it goes to zero when $x \to \infty$. We therefore have matrix-stationarity.

- $|s_1| < 1, \; |s_2| < 1$

We assume that the numbering of s_1 and s_2 is such that: $|s_2| > |s_1|$. Both P_x and Q_x are now to be interpreted as ascending recurrence relations; by the same reasoning as before one obtains:

$$P_{-N} = s_1^2 p, \ldots, P_N = s_1^{N-1}(s_1^{N+3} p + 1)$$

$$Q_{-N} = s_2^2 q, \ldots, Q_N = s_2^{N-1}(s_2^{N+3} q + 1)$$

where:

$$p \simeq -\left(\frac{s_2}{s_1}\right)^2 \frac{1}{s_2^{N+3}}, \quad q \simeq -\frac{1}{s_2^{N+3}}$$

Now we have: $\lim_{N\to\infty} |G_{-N}| = \infty$ (although $G_{-N-1} = 0$) and $\lim_{N\to\infty} G_N = 0$: there is no matrix-stationarity.

The case $|s_1| > 1, \; |s_2| > 1$ which has already been treated matricially in Section 2.2.1 can be dealt with by the same method, with the result that:

$$\lim_{N\to\infty} G_{-N} = 0 \qquad \lim_{N\to\infty} |G_N| = \infty$$

The previous line of argument can be generalized to a process of order p; this leads to Proposition 1.

2.2.3 Stationarity conditions in terms of parameters of the process: second order processes

Let us first consider the spatial second-order process:

$$X_x + a_{-1} X_{x-1} + a_1 X_{x+1} = N_x \tag{2.20}$$

For which we shall determine the stationarity region in the a_{-1}, a_1 plane. We denote the characteristic equation by $f(x)$:

$$f(s) = a_{-1} s^2 + s + a_1$$

The product of its roots is equal to: a_1/a_{-1}

Fourier stationarity The non-stationarity region is composed of two parts:

1) When the roots are complex, that is when $\Delta = 1 - 4a_{-1}a_1 < 0$, it includes the lines where their modulus is equal to 1, i.e. the lines of equation: $|a_1| = |a_{-1}|$;

2) When the roots are real, it contains the lines where: $f(1) = f(-1) = 0$, i.e. the two lines of equation:

$$a_{-1} + a_1 + 1 = 0 \qquad a_{-1} + a_1 - 1 = 0$$

The non-stationarity region is depicted in Fig.7.3.

Matrix-stationarity The region in the (a_{-1}, a_1) plane where the roots are complex does not belong to the stationarity region for complex roots have same modulus. When the roots are real, i.e. when $\Delta > 0$, the stationarity condition can be written: $f(-1)f(1) < 0$; this result may be summed up in the following proposition:

Proposition 2 The region of matrix-stationarity of the finite second-order process:

$$X_x + a_{-1}X_{x-1} + a_1X_{x+1} = N_x \qquad X_{-N-1} = X_{N+1} = 0 \tag{2.21}$$

is defined by the conditions: $a_{-1} + a_1 + 1 > 0 \quad a_{-1} + a_1 - 1 < 0$

The stationarity region is depicted in Fig.7.4.

2.2.4 Stationarity conditions in terms of parameters of the process: symmetric processes

First we shall recall a result that has already been mentioned.

Proposition 3 For the spatial symmetric process of order $2p$:

$$X_x + \sum_{k=1}^{p} a_k(X_{x-k} + X_{x+k}) = N_x \tag{2.22}$$

the region of Fourier-stationarity coincides with the region of matrix-stationarity.

The proof is obvious. The roots of the characteristic equation of process (2.22) occur in reciprocal pairs: $s_k, s'_k \; : \; s'_k = 1/s_k$; hence, matrix stationarity is automatically ensured provided the roots are not located on the unit circle which is precisely the condition for Fourier-stationarity.

Next, we consider the symmetric process of order 4.

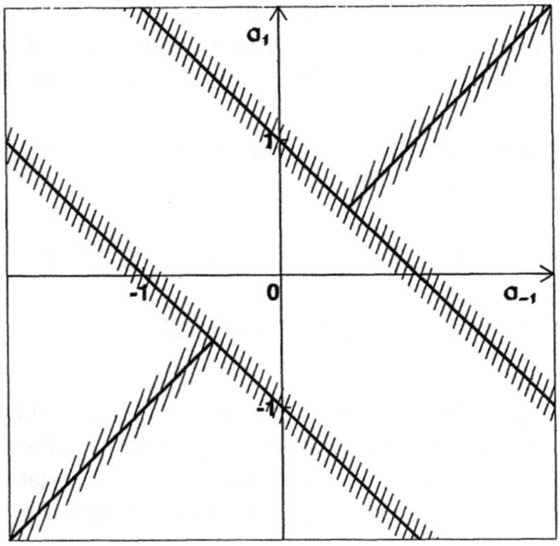

Fig.7.3 Region of Fourier-stationarity for a spatial second order autoregressive process: $X_x + a_{-1}X_{x-1} + a_1X_{x+1} = N_x$. The region of stationarity is the whole plane with the exception of the hatched lines.

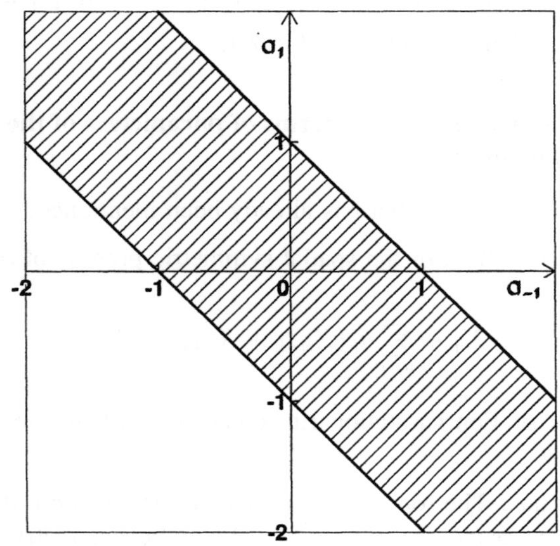

Fig.7.4 Region of matrix-stationarity for a spatial second order autoregressive process: $X_x + a_{-1}X_{x-1} + a_1X_{x+1} = N_x$. The region of stationarity is the hatched domain.

Proposition 4 The region of matrix stationarity of the fourth order symmetric process:

$$X_x + a_1(X_{x-1} + X_{x+1}) + a_2(X_{x-2} + X_{x+2}) = N_x$$

is defined by the inequalities (Fig.7.5):

$$a_1^2 + 4a_2(2a_2 - 1) > 0 \quad (2.23a)$$

$$(a_2 - a_1 + 1/2)(a_2 + a_1 + 1/2) > 0 \quad (2.23b)$$

$$-1/2 < a_2 < 1/6 \quad (2.23c)$$

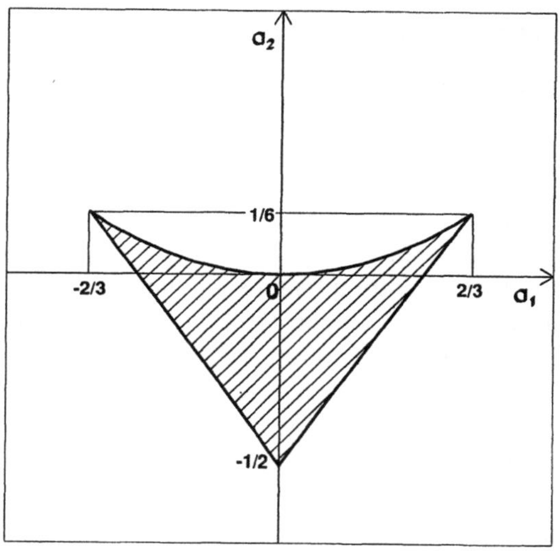

Fig.7.5 Region of stationarity for a fourth order (symmetric) spatial autoregressive process: $X_x + a_1(X_{x-1} + X_{x+1}) + a_2(X_{x-2} + X_{x+2}) = N_x$.

Proof In order to discuss the characteristic equation:

$$1 + a_1(z + 1/z) + a_2(z^2 + 1/z^2) = 0$$

we introduce the auxiliary variable: $y = z + 1/z$; therefore there are two steps in the discussion:

1) The solutions of the equation: $z^2 - yz + 1 = 0$ have to be real (otherwise $|z| = 1$), i.e.:

$$\Delta = y^2 - 4 > 0 \Longrightarrow |y| > 2$$

2) The solutions y_1, y_2 of the equation:

$$f(y) = a_2 y^2 + a_1 y + 1 - 2a_2 = 0$$

have to be real and larger than 2 in absolute value. The first condition leads to (2.23a). A necessary condition for $|y_k| > 2$ is that:

$$|y_1 y_2| > 4 \Longrightarrow |1 - 2a_2| > |a_2|$$

The discussion of this last inequality leads to (2.23c). A further necessary condition for $|y_k| > 2$ is that: $f(-2)f(2) > 0$ which leads to (2.23b). Together with the condition $|y_1 y_2| > 4$ the condition (2.23b) also proves to be sufficient.

3 Maximum likelihood estimation in spatial autoregressive processes

In the previous section, we have investigated in some detail the stationarity properties of spatial autoregressive processes for only little attention seems to have been given in the current literature to this important prerequisite. Much attention has, in contrast been given to the estimation problem of spatial processes. Among the major contributions to this field one should mention: Ord (1975), Cliff and Ord (1981), Guyon (1982), Anselin (1988, 1990). In this section, our scope will be limited to rather practical issues.

1) We shall examine to which extent maximum likelihood estimation (MLE) can be carried out analytically. This is important in applications for it may save a good deal of computing time.

2) We shall propose a comparison of the estimation procedures both for time dependent and for spatial processes.

3.1 Time dependent processes

First let us briefly recall the different steps in the estimation procedure for the standard case of time dependent processes (Priestley 1981, p.346). For the sake of simplicity we shall consider a process of second order, namely the following finite process:

$$X_t + a_1 X_{t-1} + a_2 X_{t-2} = N_t \quad t = 0, 1, \ldots, N \quad X_{-2} = X_{-1} = 0 \tag{3.1}$$

If the uncorrelated disturbances $N_0, N_1, \ldots$ have a multivariate normal distribution then their joint probability density function reads:

$$f_{\overrightarrow{N}}(n_0, n_1, \ldots, n_N) = \left(\frac{1}{2\pi\sigma_N^2}\right)^{N/2} \exp\left[-\frac{1}{2\sigma_N^2}\sum_{t=0}^{N} n_t^2\right] \tag{3.2}$$

Relation (3.1) defines a linear change of variables of the form:

$$\vec{n} = \vec{n}(\vec{x})$$

Thus, using the standard theorem for functions of random variables (Papoulis 1965, p.201) we may obtain from (3.2) the joint probability density function of the variables $X_k, k = 0, \ldots, N$:

$$f_{\vec{X}}(x_0, x_1, \ldots, x_N) = |\partial\vec{n}/\partial\vec{x}| \left(\frac{1}{2\pi\sigma_N^2}\right)^{N/2} \exp\left[-\frac{1}{2\sigma_N^2}\sum_{t=0}^{N} n_t^2(\vec{x})\right]$$

where $\partial\vec{n}/\partial\vec{x}$ denotes the Jacobian of the transformation:

$$|\partial\vec{n}/\partial\vec{x}| = \begin{vmatrix} \partial n_0/\partial x_0 & \partial n_1/\partial x_0 & \ldots & \partial n_N/\partial x_0 \\ \vdots & \vdots & \vdots & \vdots \\ \partial n_0/\partial x_N & \partial n_1/\partial x_N & \ldots & \partial n_N/\partial x_N \end{vmatrix}$$

$$|\partial\vec{n}/\partial\vec{x}| = \begin{vmatrix} 1 & a_1 & a_2 & \ldots & 0 \\ 0 & 1 & a_1 & \ldots & 0 \\ \vdots & \vdots & \vdots & \vdots & \\ 0 & 0 & 0 & \ldots & 1 \end{vmatrix}$$

The Jacobian turns out to be the determinant of a triangular matrix:

$$|\partial\vec{n}/\partial\vec{x}| = 1$$

The log-likelihood function: $L(a_1, a_2) = \ln(f_{\vec{X}}(\vec{x}))$ thus takes the simple form:

$$L(a_1, a_2) = (\frac{-N}{2})\ln(2\pi\sigma_N^2) - \frac{1}{2\sigma_N^2}\sum_{t=0}^{N}(x_t + a_1x_{t-1} + a_2x_{t-2})^2 \qquad (3.3)$$

If σ_N^2 is assumed to be known, the ML estimates of a_1 and a_2 are obtained by minimizing the second term in (3.3), i.e. by maximizing:

$$Q(a_1, a_2) = \sum_{t=0}^{N}(x_t + a_1x_{t-1} + a_2x_{t-2})^2 \qquad (3.4)$$

The expression $x_t - (-a_1x_{t-1} - a_2x_{t-2})$ in (3.4) represents the residuals between the observed variables x_t and the assumed model:

$$y_t = -a_1x_{t-1} - a_2x_{t-2}$$

$Q(\widehat{a}_1, \widehat{a}_2)$ therefore is identical with the sum of squares of residuals; accordingly, under the normal assumption, ML estimators can also be interpreted as being least-squares estimators.

Differentiating with respect to a_1 and a_2 leads to the following set of linear equations for the estimates $\widehat{a}_1, \widehat{a}_2$:

$$\begin{cases} \widehat{a}_1 c_0 & + & \widehat{a}_2 c_1 & = & -c_1 \\ \widehat{a}_1 c_1 & + & \widehat{a}_2 c_0 & = & -c_2 \end{cases} \tag{3.5}$$

where the c_k denote the statistical autocovariance coefficients.

Remark It is obvious from (3.1) that the variables x_{-1} and x_{-2} which occur in (3.3) do not have the same status as the other variables since $x_{-1} \equiv 0, \quad x_{-2} \equiv 0$. Such an assumption cannot hold true for real observations. Accordingly, (3.3) rather represents the joint *conditional* density function:

$$f_{\overrightarrow{X}}(\overrightarrow{x}/X_{-2} = 0, X_{-1} = 0)$$

But, provided N is large enough, this modification has only a small "end effect" so that we may consider (3.3) as an adequate approximation to the exact likelihood function.

3.2 Spatial processes

3.2.1 The nonlinear equations for the estimates

We now consider a spatial second order process:

$$X_x - aX_{x-1} - bX_{x+1} = N_x \qquad X_{-N-1} = X_{N+1} = 0 \tag{3.6}$$

Our previous argument may be transposed to this case but for one modification: the Jacobian $\partial\overrightarrow{n}/\partial\overrightarrow{x}$ is no longer triangular; in fact, it is tridiagonal:

$$|\partial\overrightarrow{n}/\partial\overrightarrow{x}| = \begin{vmatrix} 1 & -a & 0 & \dots & 0 \\ -b & 1 & -a & \dots & 0 \\ \vdots & \vdots & \vdots & \vdots & \vdots \\ 0 & 0 & 0 & \dots & 1 \end{vmatrix} \tag{3.7}$$

This has two important implications:

1) ML estimates are no longer equivalent to least-square estimates.

2) The minimization of the likelihood function leads to a nonlinear problem.

Let us now go through this derivation in some detail. Our first task is to express the Jacobian in closed form. This can be done with the help of Lemma 1 (Section 2.2.1). We thus obtain:

$$|\partial\overrightarrow{n}/\partial\overrightarrow{x}| = \frac{s_1^{2N+2} - s_2^{2N+2}}{s_1 - s_2} \tag{3.8}$$

where s_1, s_2 ($|s_1| > |s_2|$) are the roots of the equation:

$$s^2 - s + ab = 0$$

Because of the stationarity condition one necessarily has : $1 - 4ab > 0$.

The second step is to write out the minimization conditions:

$$\frac{\partial L}{\partial a} = \frac{\partial L}{\partial b} = 0 \tag{3.9}$$

The first condition reads:

$$\frac{\partial L}{\partial a} = \frac{1}{2N+1} \sum_{j=-N}^{N} (x_j - \widehat{a}x_{j-1} - \widehat{b}x_{j+1})x_{j-1} + \sigma_N^2 \frac{\frac{\partial s_1}{\partial a} s_1^{2N+1} - \frac{\partial s_2}{\partial a} s_2^{2N+1}}{s_1^{2N+2} - s_2^{2N+2}} = 0 \tag{3.10}$$

Introducing the statistical autocovariance coefficients:

$$c_k = \frac{1}{2N+1} \sum_{j=-N}^{N} x_j x_{j-k}$$

one obtains:

$$\widehat{a}c_0 + \widehat{b}c_2 + \widehat{b}\frac{\sigma_N^2}{\sqrt{1-4\widehat{a}\widehat{b}}} \frac{s_1^{2N+1} + s_2^{2N+1}}{s_1^{2N+2} - s_2^{2N+2}} = c_1 \tag{3.11}$$

We have already used the assumption $N \gg 1$, when we approximated the exact likelihood function by the conditional likelihood function; once again we take advantage of this assumption by writing:

$$\frac{s_1^{2N+1} + s_2^{2N+1}}{s_1^{2N+2} - s_2^{2N+2}} \simeq \frac{1}{s_1}$$

The second condition $\partial L / \partial b = 0$ can be handled in the same way and we obtain finally:

Proposition 5 When the variance of the disturbances is known, the estimates $\widehat{a}, \widehat{b}$ of the parameters of the spatial second-order process:

$$X_x - aX_{x-1} - bX_{x+1} = N_x$$

are the solutions of the following set of nonlinear equations:

$$\begin{cases} f(\widehat{a}, \widehat{b}) & = & c_1 \\ f(\widehat{b}, \widehat{a}) & = & c_1 \end{cases} \tag{3.12a, b}$$

where:

$$f(\widehat{a}, \widehat{b}) = \widehat{a}c_0 + \widehat{b}c_2 + \frac{2\sigma_N^2}{\delta(1+\delta)}\widehat{b} \qquad \delta = \sqrt{1-4\widehat{a}\widehat{b}} \tag{3.12c}$$

c_0, c_1, c_2 are the statistical autocovariance coefficients.

From the standard relation (Priestley, 1981, p.308):

$$\mathrm{Var}(\widehat{a}) \sim -\frac{1}{E[\partial^2 L/\partial \widehat{a}^2]}$$

it is also possible to obtain confidence intervals for the estimates $\widehat{a}, \widehat{b}$.

3.2.2 Discussion

The equations (3.12 a,b) may be represented in the $(\widehat{a}, \widehat{b})$ plane (see Fig.7.6b). Because of the nonlinearity of the equations the system has more than one

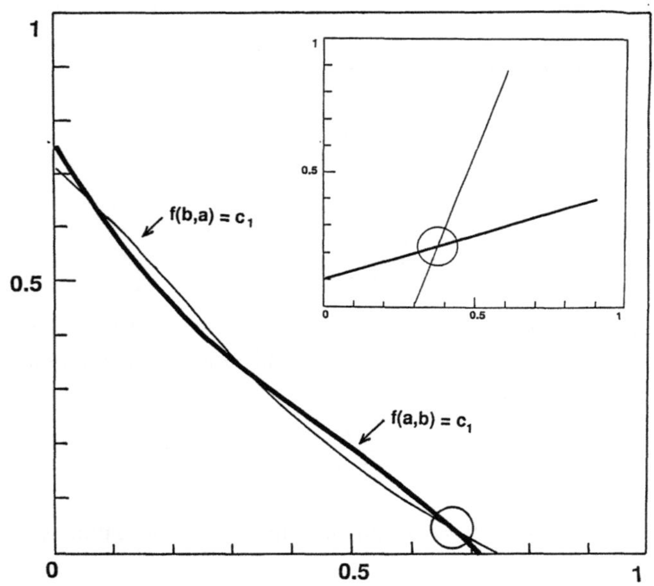

Fig.7.6 a,b Comparison of parameter estimation for time dependent versus spatial processes. Fig.7.6a in the upper right corner shows the solution of the Yule-Walker equations for the second order process: $X_t + a_1 X_{t-1} + a_2 X_{t-2} = N_t \quad a_1 = 0.4, a_2 = 0.2$ The figure in the lower left corner shows the solution of the nonlinear equations: $f(a,b) = c_1;\ f(b,a) = c_1$ for a second order spatial process: $X_x - aX_{x-1} - bX_{x+1} = N_x$; The values of the (exact) parameters: $a = 0.6,\ b = 0.1$ have been chosen in order to make the correct solution to be clearly distinguishable from the spurious solution $a = b$ (which is always present). The fact that the estimates are obtained as intersections of two curves which are almost parallel remains true whatever parameters are selected.

solution; the solution of the likelihood problem is of course given by the root which yields the largest likelihood. However, because the curves turn out to be almost parallel there is some inaccuracy in the determination of the right solution; this remains true whatever minimization procedure is used and it comes very much in contrast to the estimation problem for the time dependent process (Fig.7.6a) in which case there is neither ambiguity nor imprecision (provided the autocorrelation r_1 does not become close to one which is merely the stationarity condition). For short, one may say that the estimation problem is much more tricky for spatial processes than for time dependent processes. This motivates the development of more sophisticated estimation methods, as are for instance those based on the bootstrap technique for systems of simultaneous equations which have been developed by Anselin (1990 p.158).

3.2.3 The variance of the disturbances is unknown

If in addition one wants to estimate the variance σ_N^2, one has to differentiate the likelihood function with respect to σ_N^2; since $|\partial \overrightarrow{n} / \partial \overrightarrow{x}|$ does not contain σ_N^2 this derivative will be the same as for the time dependent process; it is therefore possible to make use of the result (Priestley 1981, p.352):

$$\widehat{\sigma}_N^2 = \frac{1}{2N-3} Q(\widehat{a}, \widehat{b})$$

Expressing $Q(\widehat{a}, \widehat{b})$ in terms of the statistical covariance function, one obtains:

Proposition 6 When the variance of the disturbances is unknown, the estimates $\widehat{a}, \widehat{b}$ of the parameters of the spatial process:

$$X_x - aX_{x-1} - bX_{x+1} = N_x$$

are given by the same equations as in Proposition 5, with σ_N^2 replaced by $\widehat{\sigma}_N^2$. Moreover, the estimate of the variance is:

$$\widehat{\sigma_N^2} = (1 + \widehat{a}^2 + \widehat{b}^2)c_0 - 2(\widehat{a} + \widehat{b})c_1 + 2\widehat{a}\widehat{b}c_2$$

3.2.4 Simulation

In this paragraph we shall put to work the results in Propositions 5 and 6 to estimate the parameters of a simulated spatial second order process. The results are summarized in Table 7.1. At the same time the simulation gives a realistic evaluation of the confidence intervals of the estimates. In particular, it can be observed that the variance of $\widehat{\sigma}_N^2$ becomes fairly large as the process comes closer to its stationarity frontier.

Exact value of a	σ_N^2 known: Estimates of a mean	st.dev	st.dev %	σ_N^2 unknown: Estimates of a mean	st.dev	st.dev %	Estimates of σ_N^2 mean	st.dev	st.dev %
0.05	0.056	0.03	53	0.057	0.03	54	0.98	0.11	11
0.10	0.099	0.03	31	0.099	0.03	31	1.00	0.10	10
0.20	0.195	0.03	15	0.196	0.03	31	0.99	0.10	10
0.30	0.298	0.02	6	0.300	0.02	7	0.97	0.11	11
0.40	0.395	0.01	3	0.397	0.02	4	0.96	0.12	12
0.45	0.446	0.06	1.3	0.448	0.07	1.6	0.97	0.12	12
0.47	0.465	0.06	1.3	0.469	0.06	1.3	0.90	0.12	14
0.48	0.473	0.05	1	0.477	0.07	1.4	0.87	0.16	18
0.485	0.479	0.04	0.9	0.484	0.06	1.3	0.81	0.24	29
0.490	0.482	0.04	0.8	0.488	0.05	1	0.74	0.41	55

Table 7.1 Estimates of the parameters of the spatial autoregressive process:
$X_k - a(X_{k-1} + X_{k+1}) = N_k \qquad \mathrm{Var}(N_k) = \sigma_N^2$

100 simulations have been run for each value of the parameter a. The variance of the white noise was taken equal to 1. The estimates have been obtained through the formulas of propositions 5 and 6. The table also shows the standard deviation of statistical fluctuations. When the parameter a tends towards the value 0.5 located at the edge of the stationarity domain, there is a slight bias due to the fact that the approximation: $s_1^N >> s_2^N$ becomes less acceptable. The most dramatic effect, however, is the increase in the standard deviation of the statistical fluctuations of the estimates of σ_N^2 .

4 Space-time autoregressive processes

In this section, we generalize to space-time processes many of the results obtained so far. We shall distinguish between multivariate time dependent processes for which the number of spatial localizations is basically finite and bidimensional processes for which this number is infinite. We shall take the same steps as in Section 1,2,3. To begin with, we define the Green's matrix of a multivariate recurrence equation and we present the formalism of spectral theory. Then we discuss stationarity conditions; finally we examine parameter's estimation.

4.1 Multivariate autoregressive processes

Multivariate autoregressive processes constitute one of the major tools in multiple time series modelling. In their application to spatial problems there are two specificities.

1) The number of variates to be taken into account is usually fairly large (of the order of 15-20 for instance).

2) One would expect the matrix of the system to exhibit some regular patterns for all variables play similar roles.

4.1.1 The Green's matrix of a system of recurrence equations

The Green's matrix, also known as the resolvent kernel (Cartan 1967 p.129), of a system of recurrence relations:

$$H(B)\overrightarrow{y}(t) = \overrightarrow{g}(t) \tag{4.1}$$

is defined as follows:

Definition 3 The Green's matrix $R(t) = [R_{i,j}(t)]$ of the system (4.1) is the solution of:

$$H(B)[R_{i,j}(t)] = [\delta_{i,j}]\delta_{t,0}$$

The fundamental property of the Green's matrix is that, as in the univariate case, it permits by superposition to write the solution of the given equation with an arbitrary function in its right-hand side.

$$\overrightarrow{y}(t) = \sum_i R(t-i)\overrightarrow{g}(i)$$

Examples

The following systems will play a significant role in the Enke-Samuelson model (Chapter 8).

$$H_2(B) = \begin{pmatrix} 1+A(B) & -1 \\ -1 & 1+A(B) \end{pmatrix} \tag{4.2a}$$

$$H_3(B) = \begin{pmatrix} 1+A(B) & -1 & 0 \\ -1 & 1+A(B) & -1 \\ 0 & -1 & 1+A(B) \end{pmatrix} \tag{4.2b}$$

where $A(B)$ is some linear function of the backward operator.

The coefficients R_{kl} of the Green's matrix for operator H_2 are the solutions of:

$$\begin{cases} [1+A(B)]R_{11}(t) & - & R_{21}(t) & = & \delta_{t,0} \\ -R_{11}(t) & + & [1+A(B)]R_{21}(t) & = & 0 \end{cases} \tag{4.3a}$$

$$\begin{cases} [1+A(B)]R_{12}(t) & - & R_{22}(t) & = & 0 \\ -R_{12}(t) & + & [1+A(B)]R_{22}(t) & = & \delta_{t,0} \end{cases} \tag{4.3b}$$

Solving these systems yields:

$$R(t) = D^{-1}(B)\begin{pmatrix} 1+A(B) & 1 \\ 1 & 1+A(B) \end{pmatrix}\delta_{t,0} \qquad D(B) = A(B)[A(B)+2] \tag{4.4}$$

The Green's matrix of operator H_3 is obtained similarly:

$$R(t) = D^{-1}(B)\begin{pmatrix} [1+A(B)]^2-1 & 1+A(B) & 1 \\ 1+A(B) & [1+A(B)]^2 & 1+A(B) \\ 1 & 1+A(B) & [1+A(B)]^2-1 \end{pmatrix}\delta_{t,0} \tag{4.5a}$$

where:

$$D(B) = (1+A(B))^3 - 2(1+A(B)) \tag{4.5b}$$

4.1.2 Spectral theory: from Green's matrices to covariance functions

This paragraph parallels the discussion of the univariate case in Section 1.3.1; here, however, we shall in addition have to deal with intercovariance functions. We consider the autoregressive process:

$$H(B)\overrightarrow{X}(t) = \overrightarrow{N}(t) \qquad E(\overrightarrow{N}(t)) = 0$$

The vector $\overrightarrow{X}(t)$ is given in terms of the Green's matrix R by:

$$\overrightarrow{X}(t) = \sum_i R(t-i)\overrightarrow{N}(i) \tag{4.6}$$

The covariance matrix is defined as:

$$c_{ij}(l) = E[X_i(t)X_j(t+l)] \tag{4.7}$$

The spectral matrix is defined as the Fourier transform of the covariance matrix:

$$\widetilde{c}_{ij}(\omega) = \mathcal{F}[c_{ij}(l)] \tag{4.8}$$

From (4.6) one derives the expression of the spectral matrix in terms of the Fourier transform $\widetilde{R}_{ij}(\omega)$ of the Green's matrix:

$$\widetilde{c}_{ij}(\omega) = \sum_{l=1}^{n} \widetilde{R}_{il}(-\omega)\widetilde{R}_{jl}(\omega) = [\widetilde{R}(-\omega)\widetilde{R}(\omega)]_{ij} \tag{4.9}$$

Application to a bivariate process

Let us apply (4.9) to the bivariate process defined by $H_2(B)$ in (4.2); here, one has:

$$R_{11}(k) = R_{22}(k) \qquad R_{12}(k) = R_{21}(k)$$

As a result, the spectral matrix has the same symmetric structure:

$$\begin{pmatrix} \widetilde{c}_{11}(\omega) & \widetilde{c}_{12}(\omega) \\ \widetilde{c}_{21}(\omega) & \widetilde{c}_{22}(\omega) \end{pmatrix} = \begin{pmatrix} \widetilde{c}_{11}(\omega) & \widetilde{c}_{12}(\omega) \\ \widetilde{c}_{12}(\omega) & \widetilde{c}_{11}(\omega) \end{pmatrix}$$

where:

$$\widetilde{c}_{11}(\omega) = |\widetilde{R}_{11}(\omega)|^2 + |\widetilde{R}_{12}(\omega)|^2$$

$$\widetilde{c}_{12}(\omega) = \widetilde{R}_{11}(-\omega)\widetilde{R}_{12}(\omega) + \widetilde{R}_{12}(-\omega)\widetilde{R}_{11}(\omega)$$

4.1.3 Stationarity conditions

In principle, one could contemplate the possibility of multivariate spatial processes. However in the perspective of modelling interdependent markets, we shall rather be concerned with multivariate time dependent processes; the variable $X_k(t)$ then describes the evolution of the kth market. Implicitly, we have already made this assumption in the foregoing paragraphs. Stationarity conditions for such multivariate processes are the same as those for univariate time dependent processes, namely all the roots of the characteristic equation must lie inside the unit disk.

Example By way of illustration, let us again consider the process $H_2(B)$. The denominator in the Fourier transform of the Green's matrix is (see equation (4.4)):

$$D(B) = D(e^{-i\omega}) = D(1/z) = A(1/z)[A(1/z) + 2]$$

In the special case when $A(B) = aB$, the poles of the denominator are: $z_1 = 0 \quad z_2 = -a/2$. Thus, the stationarity condition is: $|a| < 2$

4.2 Bidimensional processes

Multidimensional processes (Priestley 1981, Chapter 9) are the discrete analogs of partial differential equations. Clearly, this is a very broad subject. We shall here limit our attention to a few illustrative examples selected among those we shall meet in Chapter 8.

4.2.1 Definitions

First we state a few definitions.

Definition 4 The process defined by the following equation, where $N(x_1, x_2, t)$ represents random disturbances:

$$\sum_{k_1=-p}^{p} \sum_{k_2=-p}^{p} \sum_{j=1}^{q} a_{k_1 k_2 j} X(x_1 + k_1, x_2 + k_2, t + j) = N(x_1, x_2, t) \qquad (4.10a)$$

$$t = 0, 1 \ldots \qquad x_1 = \ldots -1, 0, 1 \ldots \qquad x_2 = \ldots -1, 0, 1 \ldots \tag{4.10b}$$

is called a space-time autoregressive process of order p with respect to the space variables x_1, x_2 and of order q with respect to time; in short STAR$[p, p; q]$.

Moreover, we shall, by analogy with the corresponding partial differential equations (see Chapter 9), propose the following definitions:

Definition 5
a) The STAR$[1, 2]$ process defined by the equation:

$$X(x,t) + aX(x,t-1) + b[X(x-1,t) + X(x+1,t)] = N(x,t) \tag{4.11}$$

is called a diffusion process.
b) The STAR$[2, 2]$ process defined by the following equation:

$$X(x,t) + a_1X(x,t-1) + a_2X(x,t-2)$$
$$+b[X(x-1,t) + X(x+1,t)] = N(x,t) \tag{4.12}$$

is called a propagation or wave process.

Remark (4.11) and (4.12) are not the only possible ways to write the equations for diffusion and propagation processes. This question is discussed in Appendix B in connection with the crucial stability problem.

4.2.2 Stationarity of diffusion and propagation processes

Proposition 7 The stationarity region of the diffusion process (4.11) is given by:

$$|b| < 1/2 \qquad |a| < 1 - 2|b|$$

Proof By going to Fourier transforms with respect to the space variables, the stationarity problem for both equations (4.11) and (4.12) may be reduced to analysing the stationarity of a time dependent process. For equation (4.11) we get:

$$\widetilde{X}(\theta,t) + a\widetilde{X}(\theta,t-1) + b[e^{-i\theta t}\widetilde{X}(\theta,t) + e^{i\theta t}\widetilde{X}(\theta,t)] = \widetilde{N}(\theta,t)$$

that is:

$$\widetilde{X}(\theta,t) + A(\theta,b)\widetilde{X}(\theta,t-1) = \widetilde{N}'(\theta,t)$$

where:

$$A(\theta,b) = \frac{a}{1+2b\cos\theta} \qquad \widetilde{N}'(\theta,t) = \frac{\widetilde{N}(\theta,t)}{1+2b\cos\theta}$$

First, for $A(\theta)$ not to diverge one should have: $|b| < 1/2$. Then, for a given value of b, the stationarity problem boils down to the stationarity of the time dependent process:

$$\widetilde{X}(\theta,t) + \overline{A}(b)\widetilde{X}(\theta,t-1) = \widetilde{N}'(\theta,t) \tag{4.13}$$

where:

$$\overline{A}(b) = \sup_{\theta\in[0,2\pi]} A(\theta,b) = \frac{a}{1-2|b|}$$

The stationarity condition for process (4.13) is:

$$|\overline{A}(b)| < 1 \Longrightarrow |a| < 1-2|b|$$

In short, the stationarity region in time domain narrows as $|b|$ tends to $1/2$.

Similarly, equation (4.12) leads to:

$$\widetilde{X}(\theta,t) + \overline{A}_1(b)\widetilde{X}(\theta,t-1) + \overline{A}_2(b)\widetilde{X}(\theta,t-2) = \widetilde{N}'(\theta,t) \tag{4.14}$$

where:

$$\overline{A}_i(b) = \frac{a_i}{1-2|b|}$$

The stationarity region in the space of the parameters (a_1, a_2, b) is shown in Fig.7.7.

4.2.3 Maximum likelihood parameter estimation for space-time processes

Here, we extend our approach in Section 3 to space-time processes. By way of illustration, we consider the diffusion process (4.11). The same argument could easily be extended to propagation processes.

The variables x and t are supposed to take the following values:

$$x = -N,\ldots,0,\ldots,N \qquad t = 0,\ldots,M-1$$

In order, to be able to write equation (4.11) in matrix form, we must choose a specific arrangement order for the components $X(x,t)$; we shall take:

$$X_{-N,0},\ldots,X_{-N,M-1};X_{-N+1,0},\ldots,X_{-N+1,M-1};\ldots;X_{N+1,0},\ldots,X_{N,M-1}$$

Next, we shall evaluate the Jacobian of the transformation:

$$N(x,t) \longrightarrow X(x,t)$$

The Jacobian matrix can be written in block-form:

$$\partial\overrightarrow{n}/\partial\overrightarrow{x} = \begin{pmatrix} A & B & \ldots & 0 \\ 0 & A & \ldots & 0 \\ \vdots & \vdots & \vdots & \vdots \\ 0 & 0 & \ldots & A \end{pmatrix}$$

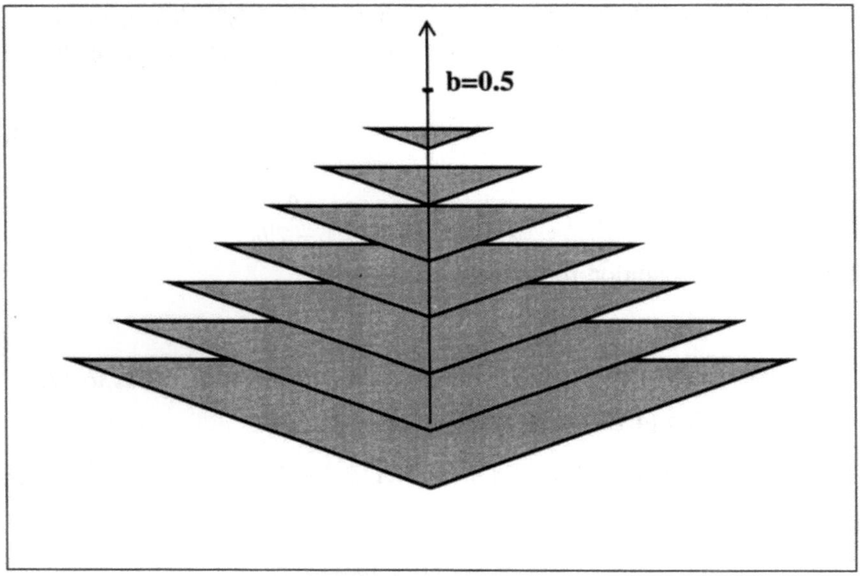

Fig.7.7 Region of stationarity for the second order wave equation:

$$X(x,t) + a_1 X(x,t-1) + a_2 X(x,t-2) + b(X(x-1,t) + X(x+1,t)) = N(x,t)$$

The vertical axis corresponds to b. The figure shows sections that are parallel to the (a_1, a_2) plane. Only positive values of b are shown; actually the domain is symmetric with respect to the plane $b = 0$.

where A and B are matrices of dimension $2N+1$:

$$A = \begin{pmatrix} 1 & a & \dots & 0 \\ 0 & 1 & a \dots & 0 \\ \vdots & \vdots & \vdots & \vdots \\ 0 & 0 & \dots & 1 \end{pmatrix} \qquad B = bI_{2N+1}$$

I_n denotes the identity matrix of dimension n.

If A and B were scalars instead of matrices, the Jacobian matrix would be triangular and its determinant would be simply A^M. The following lemma shows that this property holds true even when A and B are matrices.

Lemma 3 We consider the triangular block-matrix:

$$T = \begin{pmatrix} D_1 & B_{12} & \dots & B_{1n} \\ 0 & D_2 & \dots & B_{2n} \\ \vdots & \vdots & \vdots & \vdots \\ 0 & 0 & \dots & D_n \end{pmatrix}$$

where the D_i and the B_{ij} are square matrices of dimension h. The determinant of T can be evaluated as if the D_i and the B_{ij} were scalars, i.e.:

$$\det T = \det D_1 \det D_2 \ldots \det D_n$$

Proof The proof merely requires an application of lemma 2 in Section 2.2.1. Indeed let us define:

$$A_1^{(1)} = \begin{pmatrix} D_1 & B_{12} & \ldots & B_{1,n-1} \\ 0 & D_2 & \ldots & B_{2,n-1} \\ \vdots & \vdots & \vdots & \\ 0 & 0 & \vdots & D_{n-1} \end{pmatrix} \qquad A_2^{(1)} = D_n \qquad B_2^{(1)} = \begin{pmatrix} B_{1n} \\ B_{2n} \\ \ldots \\ B_{n-1,n} \end{pmatrix}$$

$A_1^{(1)}$ and $A_2^{(1)}$ are two square matrices respectively of dimensions $(n-1)h$ and h; $B_2^{(1)}$ is a rectangular $(n-1)h \times h$ matrix. By applying lemma 2 with $p = (n-1)h,\ q = h$ one obtains:

$$\det T = \det A_1^{(1)} \det D_n$$

Accordingly, we have shown that $\det T$ does not depend upon the column vector $B_2^{(1)}$. We may now repeat the same argument for $A_1^{(1)}, A_1^{(2)}, \ldots$ until we are left with $A_1^{(n-1)} = D_1$.

Remark Lemma 3 actually is somewhat more general than required for the evaluation of $|\partial \overrightarrow{n} / \partial \overrightarrow{x}|$. In this special case, a more direct argument results from the following identity between block-matrices:

$$\begin{pmatrix} A & B & 0 & \ldots & 0 \\ 0 & A & B & \ldots & 0 \\ \vdots & \vdots & \vdots & \vdots & \vdots \\ 0 & 0 & 0 & \ldots & A \end{pmatrix} \begin{pmatrix} I & -C & C^2 & -C^3 & \ldots \\ 0 & I & -C & C^2 & \ldots \\ \vdots & \vdots & \vdots & \vdots & \vdots \\ 0 & 0 & 0 & 0 & \ldots \end{pmatrix} = \begin{pmatrix} A & \ldots & 0 \\ 0 & \ldots & 0 \\ \vdots & \vdots & \vdots \\ 0 & \ldots & A \end{pmatrix}$$

where: $C = A^{-1}B$. Whereas $\partial \overrightarrow{n} / \partial \overrightarrow{x}$ is only triangular by blocks, the second matrix on the left-hand side is a true triangular matrix. Taking determinants on both sides gives the required result. This special case can also be derived from a lemma given in Magnus (1982,p.243).

Once we know that $|\partial \overrightarrow{n} / \partial \overrightarrow{x}| = A^M$, the ML condition:

$$\frac{\partial L}{\partial a} = \frac{\partial L}{\partial b} = 0$$

can be written out explicitly. In the same way as in Section 3, we are thus led to the following result:

Proposition 8 The estimates $\widehat{a}, \widehat{b}$ of the parameters of the diffusion process:

$$X(x,t) + aX(x,t-1) + b[X(x-1,t) + X(x+1,t)] = N(x,t)$$

where the variance σ_N^2 is known, are the solutions of the following set of nonlinear equations:

$$\widehat{b}c_{00} + 2\widehat{a}c_{11} = c_{01}$$

$$\widehat{b}c_{11} + \widehat{a}[c_{00} + c_{20} + \frac{2\sigma_N^2}{(\delta+1)\delta}] = c_{10}$$

where: $\delta = \sqrt{1-4\widehat{a}^2}$ and where c_{kj} denotes the statistical covariance of order k in x and of order j in t.

In line with Proposition 6 a similar result can be stated when the variance σ_N^2 is unknown.

A Appendix A: Validity of Fourier expansion for a system of finite size

Suppose, by way of illustration, that we want to solve the following finite spatial second-order process ($|a| < 1/2$):

$$G_x^{(N)} + a(G_{x-1}^{(N)} + G_{x+1}^{(N)}) = \delta_{x,0} \quad x = -N, \ldots, N \quad G_{-N-1}^{(N)} = G_{N+1}^{(N)} = 0 \quad \text{(A1)}$$

We introduce the generating function:

$$\widetilde{G}(\theta) = \sum_{x=-N}^{N} e^{-ix\theta} G_x^{(N)} \quad \text{(A2)}$$

Multiplying both sides of (A1) by $e^{-ix\theta}$ and summing leads to:

$$\widetilde{G}(\theta) + a \sum_{x=-N}^{N} G_{x-1}^{(N)} e^{-ix\theta} + a \sum_{x=-N}^{N} G_{x+1}^{(N)} e^{-ix\theta} = 1$$

Now, because of the boundary conditions on $G^{(N)}$ one has:

$$\sum_{x=-N}^{N} G_{x-1}^{(N)} e^{-ix\theta} = e^{-i\theta}[\widetilde{G}(\theta) - G_N^{(N)} e^{-iN\theta}]$$

$$\sum_{x=-N}^{N} G_{x+1}^{(N)} e^{-ix\theta} = e^{i\theta}[\widetilde{G}(\theta) - G_{-N}^{(N)} e^{iN\theta}]$$

Substituting and inverting, one obtains:

$$G_x^{(N)} = G_x^{(\infty)} + \frac{G_N^{(N)}}{2\pi} \int_0^{2\pi} \frac{e^{-i(N+1-x)\theta}}{1 + 2a\cos\theta} + \frac{G_{-N}^{(N)}}{2\pi} \int_0^{2\pi} \frac{e^{i(N+1+x)\theta}}{1 + 2a\cos\theta}$$

Since both integrals are bounded in the stationarity region, it is clear that when $\lim_{N\to\infty} G_{\pm N}^{(N)} = 0$, i.e. when the solution $G_x^{(N)}$ decreases to zero as $x \to \infty$, then:

$$\lim_{N\to\infty} G_x^{(N)} = G_x^{(\infty)}$$

On the contrary, when either $G_{-N}^{(N)}$ or $G_N^{(N)}$ diverges, then there is no longer any connection between $G_x^{(N)}$ and $G_x^{(\infty)}$. This is precisely what has been observed in Section 2.2.1.

B Appendix B: Stability of partial difference equations

The discussions of stationarity in Sections 2 and 4.3 are closely related to the general stability problem for finite difference equations and for partial difference equations. The central question which is of crucial importance in numerical analysis can be formulated as follows: how should a given partial differential equation be represented at the level of discrete variables in order to achieve:

1) Stability of the solutions
2) Convergence of the discrete solutions towards the continuous solution
3) The best accuracy for a given amount of computation.

In this Appendix we shall focus on the first of these three issues and limit ourselves to a few important definitions and properties (Garabedian 1964, Strang 1986)

B.1 Stability threshold in forward Euler's method

To start with, we consider the simple equation:

$$\frac{du}{dt} = au \qquad a < 0 \tag{B1}$$

Euler's finite difference approximation to this equation is:

$$\frac{u_{n+1} - u_n}{\Delta t} = au_n \tag{B2}$$

If the solution remains bounded for all n (as does the continuous solution for all t) we say that we have absolute stability; this notion is closely connected with the stationarity requirement that we have discussed previously.
The solution to the discrete equation $(B2)$ is:

$$u_n = G^n u_0 \qquad G = 1 + a\Delta t \tag{B3}$$

G is called the growth factor.
The discrete equation cannot in general be more stable than the continuous one, but it can certainly be less stable. This may happen here when:

$$1 + a\Delta t \leq -1$$

The stability threshold of Euler's method is therefore:

$$1 + a\Delta t \geq -1 \tag{B4}$$

B.2 Stiff systems

Euler's method can also be used for a differential system:

$$u' = Au$$

In this case, the growth factor is the matrix:

$$G = I + A\Delta t$$

If G has a diagonal representation: $G^n = PD^nP^{-1}$ where D is the diagonal representation of G. According to the stability criterion $(B4)$, the discrete equation is stable if:

$$1 + \lambda_j \Delta \geq -1 \qquad \forall j \tag{B5}$$

where λ_j denotes the eigenvalues of A.
Suppose now that A has negative eigenvalues of very different magnitude. Such systems are called stiff systems. Assume for instance that $\lambda_1 = -1$ and $\lambda_2 = -100$. Thus we have the paradoxical situation that the behaviour of the continuous solution is governed by $\lambda_1 = -1$, while the stability of the discrete approximation is governed by $\lambda_2 = -100$. In other words, Δt has to be much smaller than mere accuracy would require. This is an obvious drawback of Euler's method.

B.3 The diffusion equation

The continuous diffusion equation reads:

$$\frac{\partial u}{\partial t} = \frac{\partial^2 u}{\partial x^2}$$

(The coefficients of the derivatives can always be taken equal to one by renormalizing t and x).
By Euler's method it gives rise to the discrete equation:

$$\frac{u(x,t+1) - u(x,t)}{\Delta t} = \frac{u(x+1,t) - 2u(x,t) + u(x-1,t)}{h^2} \tag{B6}$$

Introducing the vector:

$$U(t) = \begin{pmatrix} u(-N,t) \\ \dots \\ u(N,t) \end{pmatrix}$$

$(B6)$ may be written:

$$\frac{1}{\Delta t}[U(t+1) - U(t)] = AU(t) \tag{B7}$$

where:

$$A = \frac{1}{h^2}\begin{pmatrix} -2 & 1 & 0 & \dots & 0 \\ 1 & -2 & 1 & \dots & 0 \\ \vdots & \vdots & \vdots & \vdots & \vdots \\ 0 & 0 & 0 & \dots & -2 \end{pmatrix}$$

The matrix A has negative eigenvalues lying between $-4/h^2$ and 0 (see chapter 8). Thus A is an exceedingly stiff matrix. The stability threshold is obtained by applying the condition $(B5)$:

$$1 + (\frac{-4}{h^2})\Delta t > -1 \Longrightarrow \frac{\Delta t}{h^2} < \frac{1}{2} \qquad (B8)$$

The numerical consequences of this condition are very serious: it means that, as h is reduced to improve accuracy in the x direction, the time steps has to be drastically reduced solely to ensure stability.

Apart from Euler's forward method there are other discretization procedures; for instance, Euler's backward method is unconditionally stable, but this has a cost in extra computation time since it is no longer possible to solve the equation merely by recurrence.

B.4 The wave equation: Von Neumann's method and Courant ratio

We consider the one-way wave equation:

$$\frac{\partial u}{\partial t} = c\frac{\partial u}{\partial x} \qquad u(x,0) = u_0(x) \qquad c > 0 \qquad (B9)$$

In Euler's form, the corresponding difference equation is:

$$\frac{u(x,t+\Delta t) - u(x,t)}{\Delta t} = c\frac{u(x+h,t) - u(x,t)}{h} \qquad (B10)$$

To test the stability we shall not use the same argument as before. As an alternative method, known as Von Neumann's method, we shall separately examine the behavior of each frequency component; this yields more detailed information than the global growth factor method. The principle of the method is to introduce a test function of spatial frequency f:

$$u(l,0) = e^{ilfh}$$

and to examine how this test function is amplified in the first step.

First we apply the method to the previous diffusion equation. It leads to:

$$u(l,1) = G(f)u(l,0) \qquad G(f) = 1 - \frac{2(1-\cos(fh))}{h^2}\Delta t$$

$G(f)$ is the growth factor at frequency f. Stability requires (see $(B4)$):

$$\frac{\Delta t}{h^2} < \frac{1}{1 - \cos(fh)} \qquad \forall f$$

The most "dangerous" frequency, i.e. the frequency for which the right-hand side is smallest occurs when: $f = \pi/h$. The stability condition is therefore given by:

$$\frac{\Delta t}{h^2} < \frac{1}{2}$$

For short, Von Neumann's method yields the same stability criterion already obtained in the previous section, but with an extra insight into the stability behaviour at each frequency.

Let us now apply the same argument to the wave-equation $(B10)$:

$$u(l,1) = G(f)u(l,0) \qquad G(f) = 1 + \frac{c}{h}(e^{ifh} - 1)\Delta t$$

The most "dangerous" frequency still occurs when $e^{ifh} = -1$ and the stability condition becomes:

$$\frac{c\Delta t}{h} < 1$$

The dimensionless ratio $c\Delta t/h$ is called the Courant ratio.

Chapter 8
Time dependent Enke-Samuelson trade models

In this chapter we resume the task of constructing a theory of spatial arbitrage that has been undertaken for the equilibrium case in Chapter 3. While time already played a major role in Chapter 6, we yet have to examine the implications of its introduction in the arbitrage models of Chapter 3. Another way to put it, is to say that our objective is to extend the dynamic models considered in chapter 2 to spatially separated markets. In Chapter 6 we have been mainly concerned with the spatial properties of *price* series. In arbitrage models, however, trade flows and price levels are conjugate variables; accordingly, the predictions of such models not only concern prices but also inter-market trade; they also predict cross relations between trade and prices. This is a distinctive feature of the models to be developed here as compared to standard dynamic price models.

Some of the topics we shall develop in this chapter are a continuation of the spatial analysis in Chapter 3; for instance, we already know that a decrease in transportation costs has the twofold consequence of decreasing the variance of prices and of increasing average trade. While the first consequence is rather obvious intuitively, the second is less evident. Most of the results we shall come by in this chapter could hardly be anticipated merely by common sense reasoning for they concern stochastic properties of price patterns. We shall for instance address the following questions:

1) What is the impact of a variation in transportation costs on the autocorrelation of prices or of trade?

2) How is the autocorrelation of prices on a single market to be modified by the opening of trade relations with a number of other markets?

These questions will be answered in the framework of stationary processes. Some of the most interesting issues in price analysis concern transient behaviour. For instance, what is the effect on the trade between two markets of a sudden price boost at one of the marketplaces?

May be the reader will be disappointed not to find in this chapter the straight confrontation with empirical evidence that we tried to provide in previous chapters.

The reason is the following. In the course of time many variables (transportation rates, average prices, excess-supply functions, standard deviation of local shocks, etc) change simultaneously. To control these changes requires extensive statistical information which may not be available. By stating a number of basic mathematical results, our general strategy in this chapter is to smooth the way to subsequent statistical investigations. In the next chapter, when dealing with large networks of markets (for which local parameter changes are to some extent averaged out), we shall again be able to make contact with empirical evidence.
In the first section, we present the general equations of the time dependent Enke-Samuelson model. Section 2 provides solutions to these equations and draws some economic implications. This section uses different results established in chapter 7; it also paves the way for the continuous-time model to be developed in chapter 9. Section 3 is devoted to transient phenomena. Finally, in section 4 we discuss ergodicity. Interpreting time series on spatially separated markets as a set of different realizations of the same stochastic process enables us to test the ergodic hypothesis.

1 The equations of the dynamic Enke-Samuelson arbitrage models

In this section we display the equations of the dynamic Enke-Samuelson model within the framework set up in Chapter 3; it involves the following assumptions:

1) We assume linear supply and demand functions $S(t)$ and $D(t)$:

$$S(t) = \gamma_1 p_t^e - c \qquad D(t) = -\beta_1 p(t) + b \tag{1.1}$$

p_t^e is the price expected by the producer at the time when decision has to be made about what output should be planned (see Chapter 3).

2) For simplicity, we suppose the market clearance condition:

$$S(t) = D(t) \tag{1.2}$$

to hold at any time. This is equivalent to the assumption that there are no inventories.

3) We shall assume that the expected price p_t^e is a function of past prices: $p_{t-1}, p_{t-2}, \ldots$:

$$p_t^e = e(B)p_t \tag{1.3}$$

where $e(B)$ is some function of the backward operator: $Bp_t = p_{t-1}$. If the dynamics of the model is formulated in the framework of rational expectations, the assumption (1.3) simply means that the model has been solved for an explicit form of the expected price.

4) The model will be made stochastic by interpreting $b+c$ as a white noise $a(t)$:

$$b + c = a(t) \tag{1.4}$$

The local disturbance $a(t)$ can for instance be considered as a climatic factor whose effect it is to increase or to decrease the local supply; alternatively, it can be interpreted as reflecting modifications in local demand. The function of excess-supply $s(t) = S(t) - D(t)$ then takes the form:

$$s(t) = (\gamma_1 e(B) + \beta_1)p(t) - a(t) \tag{1.5}$$

Introducing the operator: $s(B) = \gamma_1 e(B) + \beta_1$ we have:

$$s(t) = s(B)p(t) - a(t) \tag{1.6}$$

or:

$$p(t) = s^{-1}(B)[s(t) + a(t)] \tag{1.7}$$

The assumption about inventories is clearly unrealistic at least at the level of international trade (see Table 2.2 in chapter 2); so is the assumption about linear demand and supply functions. Our philosophy here is the same as in chapter 3. In Chapter 9 we shall examine how some of the implications of the model are matched by statistical evidence.

Four particular forms of the expectation operator $e(B)$ should be mentioned which are of special interest:

- $$e(B) = 1 \tag{1.8}$$

  which leads back to the equilibrium model of Chapter 3.

- $$e(B) = B \tag{1.9}$$

  which corresponds to the conservative anticipation assumption (see Chapter 2, Section 1.1.1): the price expectation at time $t-1$ is based on the then prevailing price: $p_t^e = p_{t-1}$

- In Muth's rational expectations model (Chapter 2, Section 2.2) the price expectation takes the form:

$$p_t^e = e(B)p_t \qquad e(B) = \frac{\beta_1}{\gamma_1}\sum_{j=1}^{\infty}\left(\frac{\gamma_1 B}{\beta_1 + \gamma_1}\right)^j \tag{1.10}$$

This is the price expectation derived from the assumption of random walk disturbances. Convergence requires that: $\rho = \gamma_1/(\beta_1 + \gamma_1) < 1$ which is ensured if β_1 is positive. With t_1 denoting transport costs one has:

$$t_1 s(B) = t_1(\beta_1 + \gamma_1 e(B)) = \theta[1 + \sum_{j=1}^{\infty}(\rho B)^j]$$

where: $\theta = t_1\beta_1$. If ρ is not close to one, a reasonable approximation is provided by the second order model:

$$t_1 s(B) = \theta(1 + \rho B + \rho^2 B^2) \tag{1.11}$$

• The previous second order process has an oscillatory behaviour with a rather small period. We may also want to consider the general second order process:

$$e(B) = e_1 B + e_2 B^2$$

1.1 Equations for two markets

We consider two markets with the following excess-supply functions:

$$s_1(t) = s_1(B)p_1(t) - a_1(t) \qquad s_2(t) = s_2(B)p_2(t) - a_2(t)$$

The arbitrage condition is expressed as in Chapter 3 by the relation:

$$\Delta p = p_2(t)|_{s_2(t)=-s(t)} - p_1(t)|_{s_1(t)=s(t)} = t_1\varphi_c(s) \tag{1.12}$$

where we have made the convention that exchanges are counted positively when they flow from market 1 to market 2; t_1 is the transportation cost (per unit of weight) between both markets. $\varphi_c(s)$ is a continuous function such that:

$$\lim_{c\longrightarrow\infty} \varphi_c(s) = Y(s)$$

where $Y(s)$ has the same meaning as in Chapter 3.

1.1.1 The nonlinear model

Substituting in (1.12) the expressions (1.7) for $p_1(t)$ and $p_2(t)$, we obtain:

$$[-s_1^{-1}(B) - s_2^{-1}(B)]s(t) + s_2^{-1}(B)a_2(t) - s_1^{-1}(B)a_1(t) = t_1\varphi_c(s(t)) \tag{1.13}$$

If the excess-supply functions of the two markets are different, that is if $s_1(B) \neq s_2(B)$, this equation can hardly be simplified further. Then, in order to write it out explicitly, s_1^{-1} and $s_2^{-1}(B)$ have to be expanded in series with respect to

B. The time t being a discrete variable: $t = 0, 1, 2, \ldots, n$, (1.13) represents a system of n nonlinear equations which may be solved numerically.

Things become simpler when $s_1(B) = s_2(B) = s(B)$; multiplying both sides of the equation by $s(B)$ we obtain:

$$-2s(t) + a_2(t) - a_1(t) = t_1 s(B)\varphi_c(s(t))$$

$s(B)$ being a polynomial in B:

$$s(B) = \beta_1 + \gamma_1 \sum_{k=1}^{n} e_k B^k$$

the previous equation can be written:

$$-2s(t) + a_2(t) - a_1(t) = \theta[1 + \gamma \sum_{k=1}^{n} e_k \varphi_c(s(t-k)] \quad \gamma = \beta_1/\gamma_1 \tag{1.14}$$

an equation which is substantially simpler then (1.13) although it is still nonlinear.

A comment is in order concerning the definition of its steady-state. In the case of a *linear* autoregressive process, stability is governed by the position of the characteristic roots with respect to the unit circle; for a stable system the transient behaviour decays at a rate determined by the logarithm of the root whose modulus is closest to one; thus, there is a definite distinction between transient and steady-state behaviour. In the case of nonlinear autoregressive processes we cannot rely on general theorems for the discussion of stability. It is well known, for instance, that Lyapounoff's theorems which constitute one possible tool for the analysis of nonlinear stability do not always apply (Minorsky 1947, p.55).

1.1.2 The linear model

General case As in Chapter 3, we consider the linear approximation: $\varphi_c(s) \simeq s$; then due to the relation:

$$s(t) = (p_2(t) - p_1(t))/t_1 \tag{1.15}$$

$s(t)$ can be eliminated and the equations for the prices $p_1(t), p_2(t)$ take the following form:

$$\begin{cases} [1 + t_1 s_1(B)]p_1(t) & - & p_2(t) & = & t_1 a_1(t) \\ -p_1(t) & + & [1 + t_2 s_2(B)]p_2(t) & = & t_1 a_2(t) \end{cases} \tag{1.16}$$

Conservative anticipation Let us consider a special case of the above equations which will enable us to make contact with an empirical observation made in Chapter 6. We consider a symmetrical first order process:

$$s_1(B) = s_2(B) = \beta_1 + \gamma_1 B$$

We introduce the notations:

$$\theta = t_1\beta_1 \quad \gamma = \gamma_1/\beta_1 \quad b_1 = a_1/\beta_1 \quad b_2 = a_2/\beta_1 \tag{1.17a}$$

θ and γ are dimensionless parameters; the equations (1.16) become:

$$\begin{cases} (1+\theta+\theta\gamma B)p_1(t) & - & p_2(t) & = & \theta b_1 \\ -p_1(t) & + & (1+\theta+\theta\gamma B)p_2(t) & = & \theta b_2 \end{cases} \tag{1.17b}$$

In order to allow a comparison of (1.17) with the phenomenological equations used in Chapter 6 (Section 1.3.1) we solve (1.17) with respect to $p_1(t)$ and $p_2(t)$; one obtains:

$$\begin{cases} p_1(t) & = & \frac{1}{\theta+2}[-\gamma(\theta+1)p_1(t-1) - \gamma p_2(t-1) & + & (\theta+1)b_1 + b_2] \\ p_2(t) & = & \frac{1}{\theta+2}[-\gamma(\theta+1)p_2(t-1) - \gamma p_1(t-1) & + & b_1 + (\theta+1)b_2] \end{cases} \tag{1.18}$$

Identifying with equation (1.1) in Chapter 6, we get:

$$a_{11} = a_{22} = -\gamma\frac{\theta+1}{\theta+2} \qquad a_{12} = a_{21} = \frac{-\gamma}{\theta+2} \tag{1.19}$$

$$N_1(t) = \frac{(\theta+1)b_1 + b_2}{\theta+2} \qquad N_2(t) = \frac{b_1 + (\theta+1)b_2}{\theta+2} \tag{1.20a}$$

$$r_{N_1,N_2} = 2\frac{\theta+1}{\theta^2+2\theta+2} \sim \begin{cases} 2/\theta & \theta \longrightarrow \infty \\ 1-\theta^2/2 & \theta \longrightarrow 0 \end{cases} \tag{1.20b}$$

$$\text{Var }(N_1) = \text{Var }(N_2) = \frac{\theta^2+2\theta+2}{(\theta+2)^2}\sigma^2 \sim \begin{cases} \sigma^2 & \theta \longrightarrow \infty \\ \sigma^2/2 & \theta \longrightarrow 0 \end{cases} \tag{1.20c}$$

where σ^2 denotes the variance of b_1 and b_2.

As transportation costs diminish, the correlation between the noises N_1, N_2 becomes larger and at the same time the variance of the noises decreases from σ^2 to $\sigma^2/2$. The curve of the variance of disturbances (dotted line in Fig.6.5a) shows such a long range decrease.

A part of the decrease in the variance of N_1 and N_2 should probably be attributed to the reduction of the variance σ^2 itself; this reduction can be traced back to progressive diversification of the diet which had the effect of smoothing out the fluctuations in demand, and to the fact that, due to improved agricultural techniques, yields became less dependent on meteorological factors.

Through the relations (1.19) it should in principle be possible to estimate the parameter γ. Yet the coefficients a_{ij} turn out to be rather fluctuating in the course of time. This points to rather changing anticipation patterns and constitutes one of the most serious difficulties in time dependent analysis.

1.2 Equations for market networks

As a matter of fact each market does business with several others. In this section, we focus on two extreme situations: firstly, we examine the case where each market is in relation but with its nearest neighbours; secondly, we briefly consider the case of long-range interdependence. Real markets are somewhere in between these extremes.

1.2.1 Connection to nearest neighbours

In this and in the next paragraph, we consider three cases of increasing complexity: a set of three markets, a chain of markets, a two-dimensional network of markets.

Three markets We consider three markets having the same excess-supply function; furthermore, we assume that relative distances between them are almost equal. The continuity equations read (Fig.8.1):

$$j_1 + s_1 = s_2 \qquad j_2 + s_2 = s_3 \qquad j_3 + s_3 = s_1$$

(the directions of j_1, j_2, j_3 in Fig.8.1 are of course a matter of convention). Replacing the j_k and the s_k by their expressions:

$$j_k = -s(B)p_k + a_k \qquad s_k = \frac{p_{k+1} - p_k}{t_1}$$

one obtains the following system of equations:

$$\begin{pmatrix} H & -1 & -1 \\ -1 & H & -1 \\ -1 & -1 & H \end{pmatrix} \begin{pmatrix} p_1(t) \\ p_2(t) \\ p_3(t) \end{pmatrix} = \begin{pmatrix} t_1 a_1 \\ t_1 a_2 \\ t_1 a_3 \end{pmatrix} \tag{1.21}$$

where: $H = 2 + t_1 s(B)$

Chain of markets We consider a chain of markets as depicted in Fig.3.7. The conservation equation of the flow of goods at market-node x reads: $j_x = s_{x-1} - s_x$; with:

$$j_x = -s(B)p(x,t) + a(x,t) \qquad s_x(t) = \frac{p(x+1,t) - p(x,t)}{t_1}$$

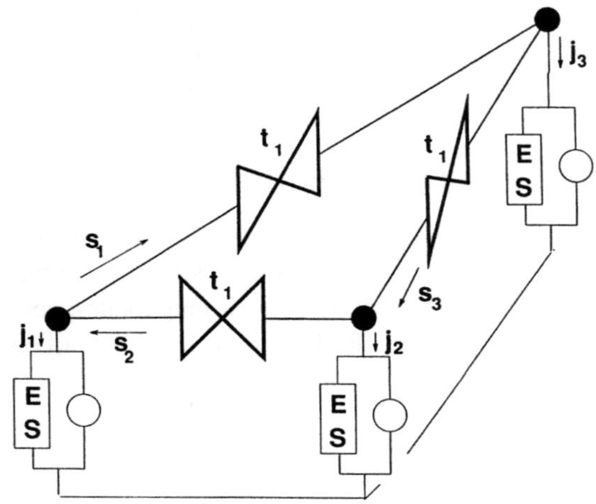

Fig.8.1 Schematic representation of the arbitrage equations for three interdependent markets. The ES blocks contain the excess-supply information for each market. The circles symbolize the stochastic noise terms. Directions of flows are conventional; the variables s_k represent the amounts that are exchanged; j_k represents excess-supply at market k.

This leads to the following space-time autoregressive process:

$$\left[2+\theta[1+\frac{\gamma_1}{\beta_1}e(B)]\right]p(x,t)-[p(x-1,t)+p(x+1,t)]=\theta b(x,t) \quad (1.22)$$

the definitions of $\beta_1, \gamma_1, \theta, e(B)$ and $b(x,t)$ can be summarized as follows:

$$D(t)=-\beta_1 p(t)+b \qquad S(t)=\gamma_1 p^e(t)-c \quad p^e(t)=e(B)p(t)$$

$$\theta=t_1\beta_1 \qquad b(x,t)=a(x,t)/\beta_1$$

In the notations of Chapter 7, (1.22) is a STAR[2,n] process, where n is the order of the dynamic pricing model defined by the expectation operator $e(B)$.

Network of markets As in Chapter 3, the previous equation may easily be generalized to a two-dimensional network of markets where exchanges are assumed to take place with nearest neighbours only. Thereby, one obtains:

$$\left[2+\theta[1+\frac{\gamma_1}{\beta_1}e(B)]\right]p(x_1,x_2;t)-\mathcal{S}p(x_1,x_2;t)=\theta b(x_1,x_2;t) \quad (1.23)$$

where the spatial operator $\mathcal{S}$ is defined as:

$$\mathcal{S}p(x_1,x_2;t) = p(x_1-1,x_2;t)+p(x_1+1,x_2;t)+p(x_1,x_2-1;t)+p(x_1,x_2+1;t)$$

1.2.2 Long range interdependence

As far as primary commodities are concerned the natural assumption about transportation costs is that they are roughly proportional to distance (at least for long distances). Yet such an assumption no longer holds for financial products. In this case, provided there are no restrictive regulations, transactions can be carried out in a way which is almost distance-independent. Intuitively, it is fairly obvious that this possibility could bring about important changes in the market's dynamics. However, it is not clear whether this will increase stability or on the contrary destabilize the market. This issue provides a strong motivation for examining the case of long range interdependence between markets.

Arbitrage models This paragraph only provides some introductory remarks; it shows how the issue can be discussed in the framework of the Enke-Samuelson model and it mentions some convergence problems which may be encountered. Equation (3.1) of Chapter 3 pertaining to a chain with p neighbours provides a first step in the modelling of long range interaction. In the context of a dynamic system, it reads:

$$[2\sum_{l=1}^{p} c_l + t_1 s(B)]p(x,t) - \sum_{l=1}^{p} c_l[p(x-l,t)+p(x+l,t)] = t_1 a(x,t) \quad (1.24)$$

where: $c_l = t_1/t_l \quad t_l =$ transportation costs from market k to market $k+l$. The option $c_l = 1/l$ has been considered in Chapter 3; it corresponds to the standard case of transportation charges that are proportional to distance. In the case of financial products, one would rather have:

$$c_l = 1/l^\alpha \qquad 0 \le \alpha < 1$$

Furthermore, the hypothesis of long range interdependence means that p should be allowed to go to infinity. Taken together, these two requirements imply the divergence of the series $\sum^\infty c_l$; they are therefore incompatible with the form of equation (1.24). Accordingly, long range dependence has in this framework to be analysed as a limiting process. This limit can be taken in a number of different ways:

- One may consider (as we have done in equation (1.24)) an infinite chain with an interaction restricted to a finite range p; long range interaction then corresponds to the limit $p \to \infty$.
- Alternatively, one may consider a finite chain of N markets all of which are interdependent; long range interaction then corresponds to the limit

$N \to \infty$.
It is not obvious whether these limiting processes will lead to identical results.

Haining's models of retail outlets At this point, two classes of models should be mentioned that have been put forward by R. Haining at the beginning of the eighties in a series of pioneering papers (1983,1984) which have become classic references in spatial analysis of price patterns. Haining's objective was to describe price interactions between urban retail outlets. This problem bears a resemblance with the above problem of price interaction between financial markets in so far as transmission of information plays a key role in both cases. Each retailer sets his own price in a way which takes into account:

1) The prices charged at neighbouring, competing markets
2) The pricing strategy of the company to which it may belong.

Distance does not play an important role because, in Haining's words (1984, p.576), "retailers may be well aware of their competitor's prices and purchasers are able to obtain relative price information at almost no cost."

The first model belongs to the class of Ising models (Kindermann and Snell 1980). The first step is to transform the price p_i charged by the ith outlet into a binary variable X_i:

$$X_i = I(p_i; s_1, s_2) = \begin{cases} 1 & \text{if } p_i \in [s_1, s_2] \\ 0 & \text{if } p_i \notin [s_1, s_2] \end{cases}$$

Then, one defines the probability that $X_i = x_i$ (assuming other variables to be in a fixed state $x_j,\ i \neq j$) as being of the form:

$$P(X_i = x_i) = C \exp[x_i(\alpha + \sum_{j \neq i}^{n} \beta_{ij} x_j] \qquad (1.25)$$

where C is a normalization constant. To see how (1.25) should be interpreted let us for a moment drop the term α which is merely a drift coefficient and consider the case $n = 2$. Then:

$$\frac{P(X_1 = 1)}{P(X_1 = 0)} = \exp(\beta_{12} x_2)$$

There are two possibilities:

- $\beta_{12} > 0$: one has an imitative behaviour (ferromagnetism in the vocabulary of Ising models)
- $\beta_{12} < 0$: one has a behaviour with a tendency to opposition and counteraction (antiferromagnetism)

When estimated for a set of petrol retail outlets, the β_{ij} mostly turn out to be positive (Haining 1984, p.581).

Remark The form (1.25) of the stationary probabilities can also de derived from a set of spatial-interacting equations (Haining 1984,p.580; Roehner 1983,p.1200).

The second model belongs to the class of autoregressive models. It uses the conservative price assumption (as defined above) and its function of excess-supply is of the form:

$$\vec{s}_t = A\vec{p}_t - B\vec{p}_{t-1} + \vec{c} + \vec{e} - \vec{u} \tag{1.26}$$

where:

- A is an $n \times n$ matrix with diagonal entries less than zero and off-diagonal entries greater than or equal to zero.
- B is an $n \times n$ diagonal matrix with positive entries in the diagonal
- $\vec{c}$ and $\vec{e}$ are constant vectors
- $\vec{u}$ is a random vector with independent components.

The number of free parameters is clearly too large to be estimated. It could be reduced by assuming them to be of a pre-determined form: ρw_{ij} where only ρ is a free parameter. The weights w_{ij} are selected is a way which describes the assumed interaction pattern between the outlets. Estimated values of ρ turn out to be rather fluctuating; nonetheless, they are significant especially in periods when prices show a marked increase or decrease trend.

2 Stationary solutions of the Enke-Samuelson model

2.1 Stability in a set of spatially interdependent markets

Mathematically, the lack of stability results in divergence of the variance of prices. Economically, it will show up as an unexpected "price bubble". In principle, instability may even occur at the level of a single market (see Chapter 2). As far as spatial interdependence is concerned an important issue is to examine whether it raises or lowers stability bounds. The answer is provided by the following proposition:

> **Proposition 1** We consider a chain of spatially interdependent markets, each of which obeys (when isolated) a pricing model described by an autoregressive process of order n. When $n \leq 2$, spatial interaction improves stability; on the contrary, when $n \geq 3$ it may either decrease or increase stability.

Proof Our starting point will be equation (1.22) for a chain of markets. Needless to say, since real market sets are always finite, the kind of stability we are concerned with is matrix-stability (see chapter 7). Let us denote by:

$$A(B) = 1 + \gamma e(B) \quad \gamma = \beta_1/\gamma_1$$

the operator of an isolated market. The poles z_i of the market chain are the solutions of the equation:

$$2 + \theta A(1/z) = h_k \tag{2.1a}$$

where h_k is a zero of the determinant:

$$D_N = \begin{vmatrix} h & -1 & 0 & \dots & 0 \\ -1 & h & -1 & \dots & 0 \\ \vdots & \vdots & \vdots & & \vdots \\ 0 & 0 & 0 & \dots & h \end{vmatrix} \tag{2.1b}$$

Using Lemma 1 of Chapter 7, and introducing an auxiliary variable α such that: $h = 2\cos\alpha$, the zeroes of (2.1b) turn out to be of the form:

$$h_k = 2\cos\alpha_k \qquad \alpha_k = k\frac{\pi}{N+1} \qquad k = 1, 2, \dots, N \tag{2.2}$$

We successively examine the cases $n = 1, n = 2$ and $n \geq 3$.

- $n = 1$

For a first order process, $A(B)$ is of the form: $A(B) = 1 + \gamma B$ and equation (2.1a) reads:

$$\theta(1 + \frac{\gamma}{z_k}) = h_k - 2 \Longrightarrow z_k = \frac{-\gamma}{1 + (2 - h_k)/\theta}$$

When the markets are isolated $z_k(\theta = \infty) = -\gamma$; stability would be decreased whenever z_k becomes closer to one than $|\gamma|$; this would require $h_k > 2$ which is impossible.

- $n = 2$

For a second order process, $A(B)$ is of the form:

$$A(B) = 1 + aB + bB^2$$

and equation (2.1a) leads to:

$$z^2 + a'z + b' = 0 \qquad a' = \frac{a}{1 + (2 - h_k)/\theta} \quad b' = \frac{b}{1 + (2 - h_k)/\theta}$$

The stationarity region S($\theta = \infty$) of an isolated market is given in the (a, b) plane by Fig.7.1a. Since $r = 1 + (2 - h_k)/\theta > 1$ the point (a', b') derives from (a, b) by a homotethy of center O and of ratio $r < 1$. The fact that S($\theta = \infty$) is a convex set ensures that the stationarity region S(θ) will be larger or at least equal to S($\theta = \infty$).

- $n \geq 3$

For a process of order n, $A(B)$ is of the form:

$$A(B) = 1 + \sum_{l=1}^{n} a_l B^l$$

and equation (2.1a) leads to:

$$z^n + \sum_{l=1}^{n} a'_{n-l} z^l = 0 \qquad a'_l = \frac{a_l}{1 + (2 - h_k)/\theta} \tag{2.3}$$

In the parameter space $(a_1, \ldots, a_n)$ we consider the cross-section of the stability region by the hyperplane:

$$a_4 = a_5 = \ldots = a_n = 0$$

In this plane, stability is ruled by the third order equation:

$$z^3 + a'_1 z^2 + a'_2 z + a'_3 = 0$$

It is known (Chapter 7, Section 2.1.2) that the stability region of such an equation is a non-convex set. Therefore, by decreasing θ from ∞ to 0, one may have the following sequence: stability, instability, stability. Fig.8.2 gives an estimate of the size of each region in a specific case.

2.2 Two markets

In this and in the following section, we obtain analytical solutions for the two- and three-market models. This allows some qualitative insight into the behaviour of trade and prices. We shall study the two-market case in some details, for it is the archetype of more complicated situations. To be specific, we consider that each market taken apart undergoes a second order process defined by:

$$p^e(t) = e(B)p(t) \qquad e(B) = e_1 B + e_2 B^2$$

Such a process encompasses as special cases the conservative anticipation model and the rational expectations model discussed in Section 1. The prices $p_1(t)$ and $p_2(t)$ are ruled by the equations:

$$\begin{cases} [1 + \theta A(B)]p_1(t) & - & p_2(t) & = & \theta b_1 \\ & & -p_1(t) + [1 + \theta A(B)]p_2(t) & = & \theta b_2 \end{cases}$$

where:

$$\theta = \beta_1 t_1 \qquad A(B) = 1 + aB + bB^2 \quad a = \gamma_1 e_1/\beta_1 \quad b = \gamma_1 e_2/\beta_1$$

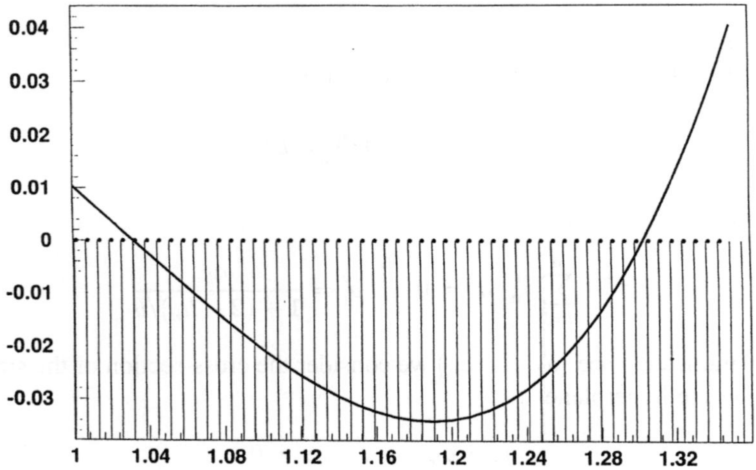

Fig.8.2 Sign of Schur's determinant for a process of third order. Schur's stationarity conditions for a process of third order:

$$p_t + (a_1/d)p_{t-1} + (a_2/d)p_{t-2} + (a_3/d)p_{t-3} = N_t$$

are of the form: $\Delta_1 > 0$, $\Delta_2 > 0$, $\Delta_3 > 0$. Within the interval under consideration, Δ_1 and Δ_3 are positive; the curve represents Δ_2 as a function of d. The hatched region corresponds to nonstationarity. The point $d = 1$ corresponds to the case of infinte transportation costs; one then has the following (stationary) roots: $z_1 = 0.80$, $z_2 = 0.90$, $z_3 = 0.95$ (that is: $a_1 = -2.65$, $a_2 = 2.33$, $a_3 = -0.68$). Obviously there is also stationarity when d tends to infinity. The excursion into the nonstationarity region between $d = 1.03$ and $d = 1.30$ is a consequence of the fact that the stationarity region in (a_1, a_2, a_3) space is non-convex.

2.2.1 General expressions

For the analysis of the auto- and intercovariance functions of prices, our starting points are the results (1.17) and (4.9) of chapter 7. They give:

$$c_{p_1p_1}(t) = \theta^2\sigma^2 \sum_{\text{Res}} z^{t-1} \frac{[\theta\overline{A}(z)+1][\theta A(z)+1]+1}{[\theta\overline{A}(z)-a_0][\theta\overline{A}(z)-a_1][\theta A(z)-a_0][\theta A(z)-a_1]} \tag{2.4a}$$

$$c_{p_1p_2}(t) = \theta^2\sigma^2 \sum_{\text{Res}} z^{t-1} \frac{\theta[\overline{A}(z)+A(z)]+2}{[\theta\overline{A}(z)-a_0][\theta\overline{A}(z)-a_1][\theta A(z)-a_0][\theta A(z)-a_1]} \tag{2.4b}$$

where the notations: a_j, $A(z)$ and $\overline{A}(z)$ have the following meanings:

- a_0, a_1 are the zeroes of the determinant:

$$D = \begin{vmatrix} 1+a & -1 \\ -1 & 1+a \end{vmatrix} \Longrightarrow a_0 = 0,\ a_1 = -2$$

- $A(B)p(t) = b(t)$ is the equation obeyed by an isolated market.
- $\overline{A}(z) = A(1/z)$

Fortunately, the expressions (2.4a,b) can be simplified. Two poles z_j and z'_j are associated to each value of a_j through the relation $\theta\overline{A}(z) = a_j$. Because stationarity is guaranteed by Proposition 1, each of these poles will be in the unit disk. Moreover, $A(z)$ can be expressed in terms of z_j, z'_j as follows:

$$\theta\overline{A}(z) - a_j = \frac{(z-z_j)(z-z'_j)}{z^2}(\theta - a_j) \tag{2.5}$$

indeed the numerators in each side are second degree polynomials which are identical since they have same zeroes and same leading terms. Substituting (2.5) in (2.4a) leads to the following expression for the residue at z_j:

$\text{Res}(z_j) =$

$$\theta z_j^{t-1} \frac{(a_j+1)[\theta A(z_j)+1]+1}{(a_j-a_k)(\theta-a_j)[(z_j-z'_j)/z^2][\theta A(z_j)-a_0][\theta A(z_j)-a_1]} \qquad k \neq j \tag{2.6}$$

Repeating this operation for each residue and summing up, one obtains finally:

$$c_{p_1p_1}(t) = (\frac{F_0}{2} + \frac{F_1}{2})\sigma^2 \tag{2.7a}$$

where, for $t \geq 0$:

$$F_0 = \frac{1}{z_0 - z'_0}\left[\frac{{z_0}^{t+1}}{A(z_0)} - \frac{{z'_0}^{t+1}}{A(z'_0)}\right] \tag{2.7b}$$

$$F_1 = \frac{\theta^2}{(\theta+2)(z_1-z'_1)}\left[\frac{{z_1}^{t+1}}{\theta A(z_1)+2} - \frac{{z'_1}^{t+1}}{\theta A(z'_1)+2}\right] \tag{2.7c}$$

and similarly:

$$c_{p_1p_2}(t) \equiv c_{p_2p_1}(t) = \left(\frac{F_0}{2} - \frac{F_1}{2}\right)\sigma^2 \tag{2.8}$$

Taking for the trade T between two markets the same definition as in Chapter 3, one has (for Gaussian disturbances):

$$T = \frac{1}{2}E(|s|) = \frac{1}{2t_1}E(|p_2 - p_1|) = \frac{\sigma_p}{t_1\sqrt{\pi}}\sqrt{1 - r_{p_1p_2}} \tag{2.9}$$

where $r_{p_1p_2}$ denotes the coefficient of correlation between the two markets. Moreover, the autocorrelation of order t of the trade flow s is given by:

$$c_{ss}(t) = \frac{1}{t_1^2}[2c_{p_1p_1}(t) - c_{p_1p_2}(t) - c_{p_2p_1}(t)] \tag{2.10}$$

In the three subsequent paragraphs we shall discuss special cases and qualitative implications of the results (2.7)-(2.10).

2.2.2 Variance and coefficient of correlation

For $t = 0$, (2.7) and (2.8) respectively give the variance and the coefficient of correlation. They can be expressed in closed form because F_1 and F_2 are symmetric functions of the roots z_j, z'_j. The results are summarized in the following proposition:

Proposition 2 For a system of two interdependent markets, each of which is ruled by a second order pricing model: $(1 + aB + bB^2)p(t) = b(t)$, the variance, the coefficient of correlation and the trade have the following expressions:

- $$\sigma_{p_1}^2 = \sigma_{p_2}^2 = \left(\frac{F_0}{2} + \frac{F_1}{2}\right)\sigma^2 \tag{2.11a}$$

where:

$$F_0 = \frac{1+b}{(1-b)(1-a+b)(1+a+b)} \tag{2.11b}$$

$$F_1 = \frac{\theta^2}{\theta+2}\frac{1-b^2q}{1-a^2q+bq[a^2(1+q)-2b]-b^2q^2(a^2-b^2)} \tag{2.11c}$$

with: $q = 1/(1+2/\theta)$

- $r_{p_1p_2} = \dfrac{F_0 - F_1}{F_0 + F_1}$ (2.12)
- $T = (\sigma/t_1)\sqrt{F_1/\pi}$ (2.13)

2.2.3 Behaviour of prices and of trade for large, respectively small transportation costs

Developments to zero order

- **Large transportation costs** The limit $\theta \longrightarrow \infty$ leads back to the results for a single market, namely:

$$\lim_{\theta\to\infty} F_1 = F_0 \Longrightarrow \lim_{\theta\to\infty} \sigma_p^2 = F_0 \quad \lim_{\theta\to\infty} r_{p_1p_2} = 0 \quad \lim_{\theta\to\infty} T = 0$$

• **Small transportation costs** In Proposition 2 the limit $\theta \longrightarrow 0$ corresponds to:

$$q \longrightarrow 0 \qquad F_1 \sim \theta^2/2$$

thus:

$$\sigma_p^2(\theta = 0) = F_0/2 \qquad r_{p_1p_2}(\theta = 0) = 1 \qquad T(\theta = 0) = \frac{\beta_1}{\sqrt{2\pi}}\sigma$$

Developments to first and second order
It is interesting to examine higher order corrections for they give the behaviour in the vicinity of $\theta = \infty$ and $\theta = 0$; also it permits a comparison with the results obtained for equilibrium prices in Chapter 3. For the sake of simplicity, we shall limit ourselves to giving results for the case $(b = 0)$ of a process of first order; generalizations to higher orders can be obtained similarly. With the help of a software for symbolic computation, one obtains:

$\theta \to 0$	$\theta \to \infty$
• $\sigma_p^2 \sim \frac{\sigma^2}{2(1-a^2)} + \frac{\sigma^2}{8}\theta^2$	• $\sigma_p^2 \sim \frac{\sigma^2}{1-a^2}(1 - \frac{2}{1-a^2}\frac{1}{\theta})$
• $r_{p_1p_2}(0) \sim 1 - \frac{1-a^2}{2}\theta^2$	• $r_{p_1p_2}(0) \sim \frac{2}{1-a^2}\frac{1}{\theta}$
• $\Delta \sim \frac{\theta\sigma}{\sqrt{\pi}}(1 - \frac{\theta}{2})$	• $\Delta \sim \frac{2\sigma}{\sqrt{\pi(1-a^2)}}(1 - \frac{2}{1-a^2}\frac{1}{\theta})$
• $\sigma_s^2 \sim \frac{\beta_1^2\sigma^2}{2}(1 - \frac{\theta}{2} + \frac{3+a^2}{4}\theta^2)$	• $\sigma_s^2 \sim O(1/\theta^2)$
∘ $r_{p_1p_1}(1) \sim (-a)(1 - \frac{1-a^2}{4}\theta^2)$	∘ $r_{p_1p_1}(1) \sim (-a)(1 - \frac{1}{\theta})$
∘ $r_{p_1p_2}(1) \sim (-a)(1 - \frac{1-a^2}{4}\theta^2)$	∘ $r_{p_1p_2}(1) \sim (-a)\frac{3-a^2}{1-a^2}\frac{1}{\theta}$
∘ $r_{ss}(1) \sim (-\frac{a}{2})(\theta - \frac{\theta^2}{2})$	∘ $r_{ss}(1) \sim (-a)(1 - \frac{2}{\theta})$

where Δ denotes the price differential: $\Delta = E(|p_1 - p_2|)$. Similarly, one could obtain cross correlations between prices and trade. It can be noticed that the autocorrelation $r_{p_1p_1}(1)$ has the same limit $-a$ either for $\theta \to 0$ or for $\theta \to \infty$.

2.2.4 Graphical representation

The above results already provide some insight into the behaviour of trade and prices at least for low covariance orders. Yet, we still have to investigate the behaviour of auto-and inter-correlations of higher orders. This is summarized in Fig.8.3a,b,c. Three interesting features emerge:

1) Because the limits of autocorrelation coefficients are the same for either $\theta \to 0$ or $\theta \to \infty$, these coefficients remain confined within a rather narrow interval whatever the values of θ.

2) The general shape of the intercorrelation curves $r_{p_1p_2}(t)$ is primarily determined by the stochastic behaviour of the isolated markets; namely, they are either steadily decreasing or oscillatory according to the form of the single market's autocorrelation curve.

3) When comparing the evolution of trade (Fig.8.3c) with the corresponding curve in the equilibrium case (Fig.3.6b), it can be observed that the former is somewhat lower. Moreover, in the non equilibrium case trade seems to be highest when prices behave smoothly (dashed curve). On the contrary, rapid oscillations (dotted curve) yield low trade levels.

2.3 Three markets

In the three-market model, there is a pole of multiplicity 2. It is this rather technical feature which makes its investigation worthwhile; we shall see that using a limiting process, poles of multiplicity higher than one can be handled much in the same way as simple poles.

2.3.1 General expressions

We consider the model of Fig.8.1. One has:

$$c_{p_1p_1}(t) = \theta^2\sigma^2 \sum_{\text{Res}}$$

$$z^{t-1}\frac{[\overline{H}(z)^2-1][H^2(z)-1]+2[\overline{H}(z)+1][H(z)+1]}{[\overline{H}(z)-h_0][\overline{H}(z)-h_1][\overline{H}(z)-h_2][H(z)-h_0][H(z)-h_1][H(z)-h_2]} \tag{2.14}$$

where the notations $h_j, H, \overline{H}$ have the following definitions:

- h_0, h_1, h_2 are the zeroes of the determinant:

$$D = \begin{vmatrix} h & -1 & -1 \\ -1 & h & -1 \\ -1 & -1 & h \end{vmatrix} \Longrightarrow h_0 = 0 \quad h_1 = -1 \quad h_2 = -1$$

Instead of $h_2 = -1$ we take $h_2 = -1+\eta$; at the end of the calculation (namely in the evaluation of F_2) we shall go to the limit: $\eta \longrightarrow 0$.

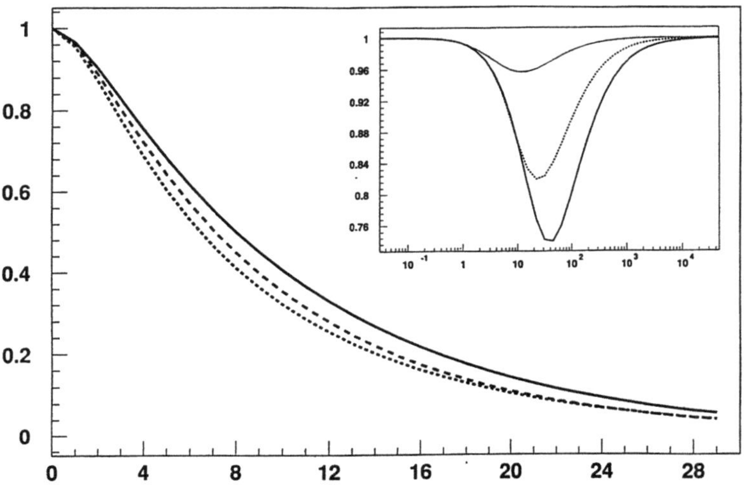

Fig.8.3 a Autocorrelation $r_{11}(k,\theta)$ of the price $p_1(t)$ in the case of two markets. Horizontal scale: order of the autocorrelation coefficient. The three curves correspond to different transportation costs: solid curve: $\theta = 10^5$ and $\theta = 10^{-3}$ (the curves are almost identical); dashed curve: $\theta = 100$; small dashes: $\theta = 30$. The dynamic pricing model on both markets is of second-order: $p_t + ap_{t-1} + bp_{t-2} = N_t$ with: $a = -1.4, b = 0.45$. The Figure in the upper right corner shows $r_{11}(k,\theta)$ as a function of θ for three values of k: $k = 2, k = 8, k = 16$ (from top to bottom). The curves have been normalized to one for the levels $r_{11}(k,0) = r_{11}(k,\infty)$.

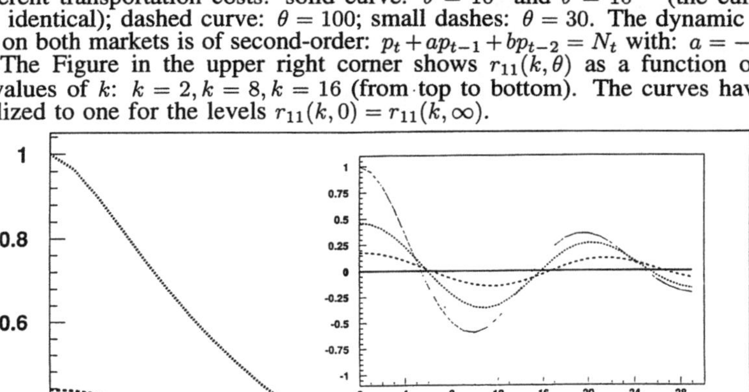

Fig.8.3 b Intercorrelation $r_{12}(k,\theta)$ of the prices $p_1(t)$ and $p_2(t)$ in the case of two markets. Horizontal scale: order of the autocorrelation coefficient. The four curves correspond to different transportation costs: from bottom to top: $\theta = 10^5, \theta = 100, \theta = 30, \theta = 10^{-3}$. Same pricing model as in the previous figure. The Figure in the upper right corner shows the same curves in the case of an oscillatory pricing model on both markets. Under the assumption of different pricing models on each market (exponential decay at one market and oscillatory decay at the other for instance) the interaction would bring about a mix-up of both dynamics.

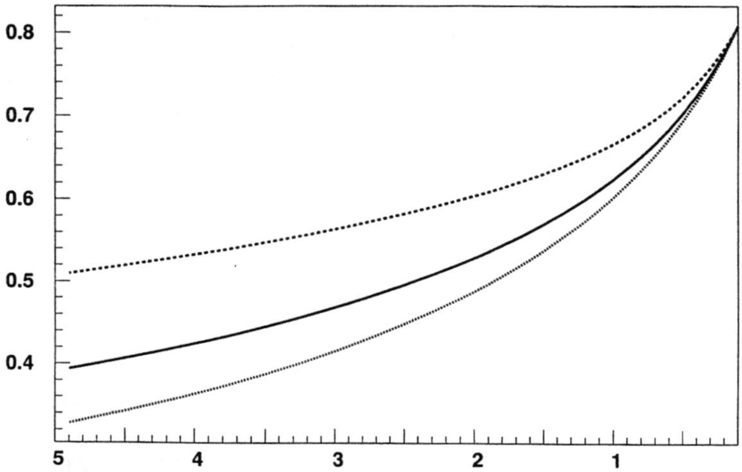

Fig.8.3 c Trade as a function of transportation costs in the case of two markets. Horizontal scale: transportation costs (in decreasing order). Vertical scale: trade between both markets. The three curves correspond to different second order pricing models: solid curve: exponential decay ($a = -1.4, b = 0.45$); dashed curve: large period oscillations ($a = -1.8, b = 0.90$); dotted curve: small period oscillations ($a = 0.9, b = 0.81$). The smoother the oscillations, the larger the trade. These curves can also be compared to the solid curve in Fig.3.6b: trade is somewhat lower here than in the equilibrium model.

- $H(z) = 2 + \theta A(z)$ where $A(B)p(t) = b(t)$ is the equation obeyed by an isolated market.

- $\overline{H}(z) = H(1/z)$

The calculation can then be carried out in the same way as in the previous paragraph. One obtains:

$$c_{p_1p_1}(t) = \left(\frac{1}{3}F_0 + \frac{2}{3}F_2\right)\sigma^2 \tag{2.15a}$$

where:

$$F_0 = \frac{1}{z_0 - z_0'}\left[\frac{z_0^{t+1}}{A(z_0)} - \frac{{z_0'}^{t+1}}{A(z_0')}\right] \tag{2.15b}$$

$$F_2 = \frac{\theta^2}{\theta + 3}\frac{1}{z_2 - z_2'}\left[\frac{z_2^{t+1}}{\theta A(z_2) + 3} - \frac{{z_2'}^{t+1}}{\theta A(z_2) + 3}\right] \tag{2.15c}$$

and:

$$c_{p_1p_2}(t) = \left(\frac{1}{3}F_0 - \frac{1}{3}F_2\right)\sigma^2 \tag{2.16}$$

$$T = \frac{2\sigma}{t_1}\sqrt{\frac{F_2(t=0)}{\pi}} \tag{2.17}$$

2.3.2 Developments to first and second order

The results given here parallel those given above for the two-market case. Again we shall limit ourselves to a first order process, i.e. $b = 0$. One obtains:

$\theta \to 0$	$\theta \to \infty$
• $\sigma_p^2 \sim \frac{\sigma^2}{3(1-a^2)} + \frac{2}{27}\theta^2\sigma^2$	• $\sigma_p^2 \sim \frac{\sigma^2}{1-a^2}(1 - \frac{4}{1-a^2}\frac{1}{\theta})$
• $r_{p_1p_2}(0) \sim 1 - \frac{1-a^2}{3}\theta - \frac{1-a^4}{9}\theta^2$	• $r_{p_1p_2}(0) \sim \frac{1}{1-a^2}\frac{1}{\theta}$
∘ $r_{p_1p_1}(1) \sim (-a)[1 - \frac{2}{9}(1-a^2)\theta^2]$	∘ $r_{p_1p_1}(1) \sim (-a)[1 - \frac{2}{\theta}]$
∘ $r_{p_1p_2}(1) \sim (-a)[1 - \frac{1}{3}(1-a^2)\theta^2]$	∘ $r_{p_1p_2}(1) \sim (-a)\frac{2-a^2}{1-a^2}\frac{1}{\theta}$

2.3.3 Comment

The three-market model with equal inter-market distances: $d_{23} = d_{31} = d_{12}$ that we considered in this section could seem to be rather unrealistic. It is clear that this requirement regarding distances will never be *exactly* satisfied. If it is not, the roots h_j are the solutions of a third order equation of general form and one has to resort to numerical calculation. However, there are cases where the conditions $d_{23} = d_{31} = d_{12}$ are a reasonable approximation; let us mention for instance nineteenth century wheat trade between France, Germany, and Great Britain or between France, Great Britain and the Netherlands or, at a regional level, between Bordeaux, Lyon, and Rouen.

Throughout our discussion so far, we have stressed qualitative implications of the Enke-Samuelson model. Up to now however, we did not try (with one exception in Section 1) to confront them to empirical evidence. There are two reasons for this:

1) Statistical testing will be postponed until Chapter 9 because space-time models become simpler in a continuous setting. In Chapter 9 we shall take advantage of this simplification to carry out statistical estimations.

2) In general a country does business with a large body of foreign markets[1]; thus a test restricted to two or three markets would be of little significance.

2.4 Chain of markets

We consider the model of a chain of markets that has been introduced in Section 1.2.1. By Fourier transformation, the space-time covariance function can be written in the form:

$$c(x,t) = \frac{\theta^2\sigma^2}{(2\pi)^2}\int_0^{2\pi}\int_0^{2\pi}\frac{e^{i\omega t}e^{iqt}d\omega dq}{D\,\overline{D}} \tag{2.18a}$$

where:

$$D = 2 - (e^{iq} + e^{-iq}) + \theta[1 + \gamma e(e^{-i\omega})] \qquad \gamma = \frac{\gamma_1}{\beta_1} \tag{2.18b}$$

This is a rather intricate integral; in Chapter 9 we shall see that the covariance function $c(x,t)$ can be obtained in a much simpler way for a *continuous* space-time process. Here, we shall limit ourselves to establishing two results:

- The first one emphasizes the qualitative similarity between the discrete covariance function (2.18) and the continuous covariance function to be obtained in Chapter 9: both of them show a sort of plateau in the vicinity of $t = 0$ and this plateau becomes more pronounced as x becomes larger.
- The second provides the explicit form of the development to first order of $c(x,t)$ with respect to $1/\theta$.

2.4.1 Slope of the covariance function in the vicinity of $t = 0$

Proposition 3 The covariance function of the STAR$[2,n]$ process defined by (2.18) satisfies:

$$c(x,0) - c(x,1) \underset{\theta\to\infty}{\sim} \frac{d(x)}{\theta^x}$$

The difference $c(x,0)-c(x,1)$ is proportional to the slope of the autocovariance function $c(x,t)$ (with respect to t) in the vicinity of $t = 0$

Proof $c(x,t)$ being analytic in the vicinity of $\theta = \infty$, we may write the development:

$$c(x,t) = \sum_{n=0}^{\infty} c_n(x,t)(\frac{1}{\theta})^n \tag{2.19}$$

[1] Nonetheless it may be possible to select special circumstances (regarding products, countries and time periods) in which the two- or three-market models provide reasonable approximations.

First, we shall obtain the expression of $c_n(x,t)$. In the denominator of (2.18) we factorize:

$$\theta\left[1+\gamma e(e^{-i\omega})\right]=\theta E(\omega)$$

$$c(x,t)=\frac{\sigma^2}{\pi^2}\int_0^\pi\int_0^\pi\frac{\cos\omega t\cos qx d\omega dq}{|E(\omega)|^2(1+aw)(1+\bar{a}w)} \tag{2.20}$$

where: $a=2(1-\cos q)/E(\omega)$ and $w=1/\theta$. The denominator may be developed with respect to w:

$$\frac{1}{(1+aw)(1+\bar{a}w)}=\frac{1}{a-\bar{a}}\sum_{n=0}^{\infty}(-1)^n\left[a^{n+1}-\bar{a}^{n+1}\right]w^n$$

Developing, one has:

$$\frac{a^{n+1}-\bar{a}^{n+1}}{a-\bar{a}}=\sum_{k=0}^{n}a^{n-k}\bar{a}^k$$

Hence:

$$c_n(x,t)=(-1)^n2^n\frac{\sigma^2}{\pi^2}\left(\int_0^\pi(1-\cos q)^n\cos(xq)\,dq\right) \tag{2.21a}$$

$$\left(\int_0^\pi\frac{\cos t\omega}{|E(\omega)|^2}\sum_{k=0}^{n}\frac{1}{E^n(\omega)\overline{E}^k(\omega)}\right) \tag{2.21b}$$

We now make use of the following easy lemma:

Lemma 1 Let $P_n(u)$ be a polynomial of degree n; then for any integer x such as $|x|\geq n+1$ one has:

$$\int_0^\pi P_n(\cos q)\cos(qx)dq=0$$

It is sufficient to show that:

$$\int_0^\pi\cos^n q\cos(qx)dq=0 \qquad |x|=n+1,n+2,\ldots$$

One has (Gradshteyn 1965, p.25):

$$\cos^n q=\frac{\cos(nq)}{2^{n-1}}+R(q)$$

where R contains the terms $\cos kq, \quad k\leq n-1$.
Hence:

$$\int_0^\pi\cos^n q\cos(qx)dq=$$

$$\frac{1}{2^n}\left[\int_0^\pi\cos((n+x)q)dq+\int_0^\pi\cos((n-x)q)dq\right]+\int_0^\pi R(q)\cos(qx)dq$$

The first term on the right-hand side is simply:

$$\frac{\pi}{2^n}(\delta_{x,-n}+\delta_{x,n})$$

while the second term is non-zero only for $|x|=0,1,\ldots,n-1$.

Applying this lemma to (2.21) shows that $c_n(x,t)$ is equal to zero for $n\le|x|-1$; in other words $c_x(x,t)$ is the first term in the development (2.19) to be different from zero; thus:

$$c(x,t) \underset{\theta\to\infty}{\sim} c_x(x,t)(\frac{1}{\theta})^x$$

Proposition 3 follows with $d(x)=c_x(x,0)-c_x(x,1)$. In fact, we did not show that $d(x)\neq 0$; would this be the case, then the slope of the covariance function would be even lower than claimed in Proposition 3.

2.4.2 Development to first order of the covariance function

For the sakė of simplicity we shall consider that the dynamic pricing model at each isolated market is of first order; however, the subsequent analysis can be generalized to higher orders. We shall establish the following result.

Proposition 4 Under the assumption of a conservative pricing model $e(B)=B$, the covariance function $c(x,t)$ of a chain of markets has the following development for large transportation costs:

$$c(x,t) \underset{\theta\to\infty}{\sim} \frac{(-\gamma)^t}{1-\gamma^2}\sigma^2[\delta_{x,0}-d_1(x,t)\frac{1}{\theta}]$$

where:

$$d_1(x,t)=2[2+t(1-\gamma^2)][\delta_{x,0}-\frac{1}{2}(\delta_{x,1}+\delta_{x,-1})]$$

Moreover, the trade T has the following development:

$$T \underset{\theta\to\infty}{\sim} \frac{\beta_1\sigma}{\theta\sqrt{\pi(1-\gamma^2)}}(1-\frac{1}{\theta})$$

Proof First, we rewrite the development given by (2.21) in the following explicit form:

$$c(x,t)=c_0(x,t)+c_1(x,t)\frac{1}{\theta}+O(\frac{1}{\theta}) \tag{2.22}$$

$$c_0(x,t)=\frac{\sigma^2}{\pi^2}\left(\int_0^{\pi}\cos qx dq\right)\left(\int_0^{\pi}\frac{\cos\omega t}{|E(\omega)|^2}d\omega\right) \tag{2.23}$$

$$c_1(x,t) = (-2)\frac{\sigma^2}{\pi^2}\left(\int_0^{\pi}(1-\cos q)\cos xq dq\right)$$
$$\left(\int_0^{\pi}\frac{E(\omega)+\overline{E}(\omega)}{|E(\omega)|^4}\cos\omega t\; d\omega\right) \tag{2.24}$$

Taking into account Lemma 1, these expressions become:

$$c_0(x,t) = \frac{\sigma^2}{\pi}\delta_{x,0}I_1^{(t)}$$

$$c_1(x,t) = (-4)\frac{\sigma^2}{\pi}[\delta_{x,0} - \frac{1}{2}(\delta_{x,1}+\delta_{x,-1})][I_2^{(t)} + \frac{\gamma}{2}(I_2^{(t+1)} + I_2^{(t-1)})] \tag{2.25}$$

where:

$$I_n^{(t)} = \int_0^{\pi}\frac{\cos\omega t}{(1+2\gamma\cos\omega+\gamma^2)^n}d\omega \tag{2.26}$$

The integral $I_n^{(t)}$ is given in Gradshteyn (1965, p.369); a tedious but straightforward calculation then leads to the expression given in Proposition 4. Substituting the development of the covariance function in the expression of trade:

$$T = \frac{1}{2(N+1)}\sum E(|s_x|) = \frac{1}{t_1\sqrt{\pi}}[c(0,0)-c(1,0)]^{1/2}$$

gives the expression of trade in Proposition 4.

Remark In contrast to theorems 1 and 3 of chapter 3, Proposition 4 does not give the developments for $\theta \to 0$. The covariance function is not analytic in the vicinity of $\theta = 0$; as in Chapter 3 one therefore has to "extract" the singular terms. This would be somewhat useless here, since in the next chapter we shall obtain the covariance function of a continuous process in closed form.

3 Transient behaviour of trade and prices

What was the effect of the Great Depression (1929-1933) on international trade? Because of the sharp decrease in price levels, trade has plummeted in *value*; here, however, we shall be interested in the *volume* of trade. In Chapter 4, we have studied the effect on trade of a strong decline in transportation costs; we have seen that it experienced an amazing increase (even under fixed production). Here we shall analyse the effect of a sharp decline in prices.

3.1 Evolution of trade during the Great Depression

In which country did the Great Depression begin? Broadly speaking, the answers to this question seem to fall into two categories (Eichengreen 1990, p.4). According to one thesis, it first started in the US and afterwards spread to Europe and to the rest of the world. In Eichengreen's words:

> "Friedman and Schwartz share with Temin the view that the events which converted a garden-variety recession into a Great Depression originated primarily in the United States. They attribute to feedbacks from overseas at most a subsidiary role in the Depression's depth and duration."

Alternatively one may argue that the depression broke out simultaneously in Europe and in the US. Such an opinion is expressed for instance by C.Kindleberger (1978, p.137):

> "I find it impossible to understand the view that the 1929 depression was of domestic origin in the U.S."

Within the framework of the Enke-Samuelson model, we shall discuss two models based on either of these conceptions. We are aware of the fact that this is merely an exercise about "stylized facts" (Granger 1992); our main objective is to show that, although the Enke-Samuelson model has primarily been designed to model spatial patterns, it can also be fruitfully applied to yet other problems, for instance to the analysis of trade.

3.1.1 Qualitative discussion

Before formalizing the problem, let us describe the possible models qualitatively. From this discussion, it will become clear that even for such a simple model there is a fairly large number of possible options.

For simplicity we consider a two-market model. Let us first recall that in our model, the steady-state trade arises as a result of price differentials due to local, more or less random fluctuations (of variance σ) in supply and demand.

We now suppose that a sudden downturn occurs at one of the markets or at both markets. What are the possible scenarios?

1) If the price fall exclusively takes place at market 1 (and if transportation costs and σ remain constant) there will be an increase in the price differential and thereby an increase in the volume of trade.

2) If the price fall hits both markets at the same time (and if transportation costs and σ remain constant), trade will remain unchanged.

3) If the evolution of prices are part of a general deflation mouvement, transportation costs are likely to fall in about the same proportion as prices of goods; then (if σ nevertheless remains constant), trade will increase.

4) Up to now, σ has been assumed unchanged. However, it could reasonably be argued that for wheat for instance σ is likely to experience an even

larger decrease than p_1 or p_2. Indeed during a serious recession wheat and bread again become *essential* staples; thereby fluctuations in demand are likely to be drastically reduced; as a result trade is expected to drop off. A similar argument may hold for other commodities too.
One could proceed with this discussion and consider still other combinations of assumptions. Some of them are summarized in Table 8.1.

	p_1	p_2	t_1	σ	**Effect on trade**
1)	↓	-	-	-	increase
2)	↓	↓	-	-	statu quo
3)	↓	↓	↓	-	increase
4)	↓	↓	↓	↓	statu quo
5)	↓	↓	-	↓	decrease
6)	↓	↓	↓	↓↓	decrease

Table 8.1 Effect on the trade between two markets of a decrease in some of the variables of the two-market model. t_1 denotes the transportation costs and σ the standard deviation of local disturbances.

To sum up, one may say that, simple as it is (it contains only four parameters), the present model has sufficient flexibility to describe a great variety of situations. In the following, we shall limit ourselves to comparing scenarios 1 and 2. In paragraph 3.1.2 we consider the deterministic evolution; in paragraph 3.1.3 we outline the solution of the transient stochastic model. Once again, we emphasize that this should be considered merely as an example of how the model can be put to use.

3.1.2 Evolution of prices and trade expectations

We consider a two-market model, one of which can be thought of as representing Europe and the other the United States. The equations of the model are (see Section 1):

$$\begin{cases} [1+\theta A(B)]p_1(t) & - & p_2(t) & = & \theta b_1(t) + h_1\delta_{t,t_1} \\ -p_1(t) & + & [1+\theta A(B)]p_2(t) & = & \theta b_2(t) + h_2\delta_{t,t_1} \end{cases} \tag{3.1}$$

$A(B)$ is an operator describing the dynamic pricing model at each market (for the sake of simplicity the pricing models are assumed to be identical at each market). θ as usually represents transportation costs. h_1 and h_2 are two random variables; the terms $h_i\delta_{t,t_1}$ describe the exogenous shocks occurring at time t_1. In the first conception one has:

$$|E(h_1)| \gg |E(h_2)|$$

one could take for instance: $E(h_1) = 1, \quad E(h_2) = 0$.
In the second conception, one has:

$$E(h_1) \simeq E(h_2)$$

Taking expectations on both sides of (3.1) gives (assuming that $E(b_1) = E(b_2) = 0$):

$$\begin{cases} [1+\theta A(B)]\bar{p}_1(t) & - & \bar{p}_2(t) & = & \bar{h}_1\delta_{t,t_1} \\ -\bar{p}_1(t) & + & [1+\theta A(B)]\bar{p}_2(t) & = & \bar{h}_2\delta_{t,t_1} \end{cases} \tag{3.2}$$

where the bar denotes expectation. With the definitions and notations of Chapter 7 (Section 4.1) one has:

$$\begin{array}{rcrcl} \bar{p}_1(t) & = & \bar{h}_1 R_{11}(t-t_1) & + & \bar{h}_2 R_{12}(t-t_1) \\ \bar{p}_2(t) & = & \bar{h}_1 R_{21}(t-t_1) & + & \bar{h}_2 R_{22}(t-t_1) \end{array}$$

Thus, with trade between both markets given by $T = (\bar{p}_1 - \bar{p}_2)/2t_1$, and taking into account that: $R_{11} = R_{22} \quad R_{12} = R_{21}$ one has:

$$T = \frac{\bar{h}_1 - \bar{h}_2}{2t_1}[R_{11}(t-t_1) - R_{21}(t-t_1)] \qquad \bar{h}_1 > \bar{h}_2 \tag{3.3}$$

In the notations of section 2.2.1 one has:

$$R_{11}(t-t_1) = \frac{1}{2i\pi}\int_C \frac{1+\theta\overline{A}(z)}{\theta\overline{A}(z)(\theta\overline{A}(z)+2)} z^{t-t_1-1}dz$$

$$R_{21}(t-t_1) = \frac{1}{2i\pi}\int_C \frac{1}{\theta\overline{A}(z)(\theta\overline{A}(z)+2)} z^{t-t_1-1}dz$$

Substituting into (3.3) leads to:

$$T = \frac{\bar{h}_1 - \bar{h}_2}{2i\pi(2t_1)}\int_C \frac{z^{t-t_1-1}}{\theta\overline{A}(z)+2}dz$$

At this point, a specific assumption has to be made regarding the dynamic pricing model. We shall here consider a process of second order; it should however be clear that the conclusions we shall draw are largely independent of this specific assumption. One obtains in the same way as in Section 2.2.1:

$$T = (\bar{h}_1 - \bar{h}_2)\frac{z_1^{t-t_1+1} - z_1'^{\,t-t_1+1}}{2t_1(\theta+2)(z_1 - z_1')} \tag{3.4}$$

where z_1, z_1' are the roots of the characteristic equation $\theta\overline{A}(z) + 2 = 0$

The evolutions of the prices $\bar{p}_1$ and $\bar{p}_2$ after the occurrence of the shock at time $t_1 = 4$ is represented in Figures 8.4a,b under the assumption $\bar{h}_1 = 1, \quad \bar{h}_2 = 0$. The evolution of trade is shown in Fig.8.4c. The effect of the shock in

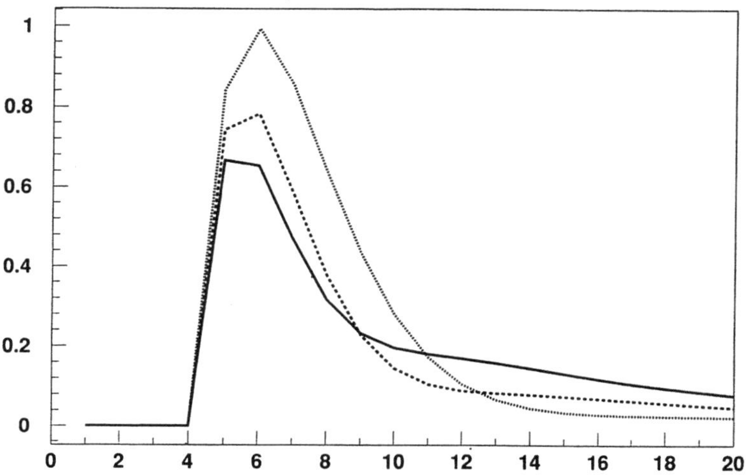

Fig.8.4 a Transient behaviour of $p_1(t)$ in the two-market model. Market 1 has been subject to a price shock of magnitude 1 at time $t_1 = 4$. Horizontal scale: time; vertical scale: $p_1(t)$. The three curves correspond to different transportation costs: solid curve $\theta = 3$; dashed curve: $\theta = 5$; dotted curve $\theta = 10$. The dynamic pricing model is given by: $p_t + ap_{t-1} + bp_{t-2} = N_t$ with: $a = -1.4, b = 0.45$

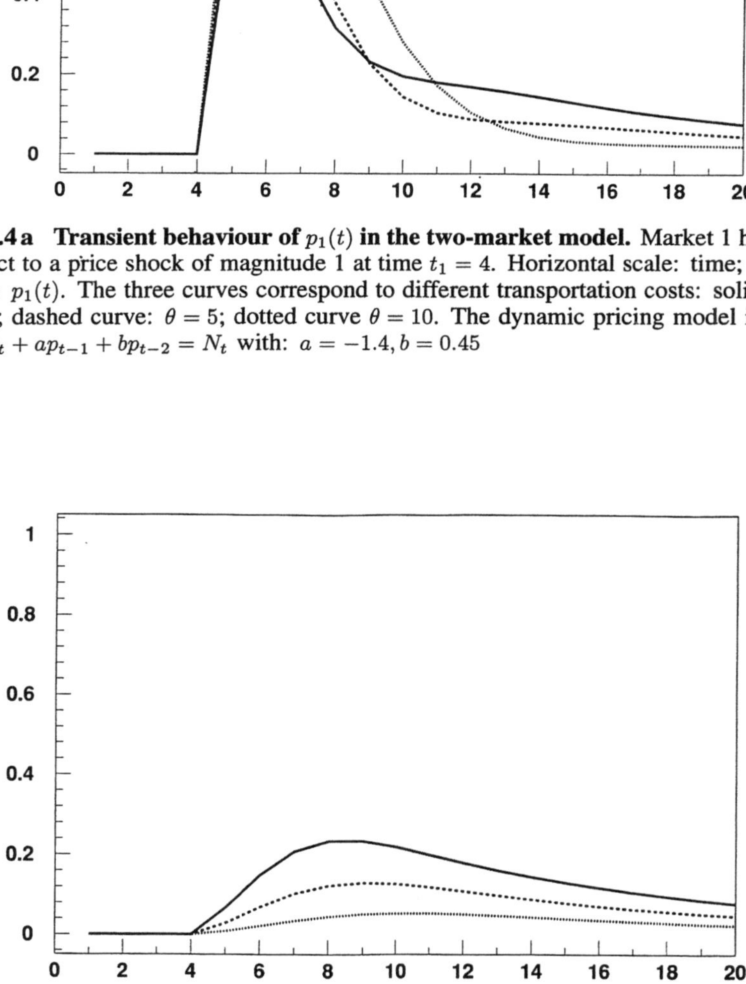

Fig.8.4 b Transient behaviour of $p_2(t)$ in the two-market model. Vertical scale: $p_2(t)$. The figure shows the contagion of price increase on market 2. Same caption as for the previous figure.

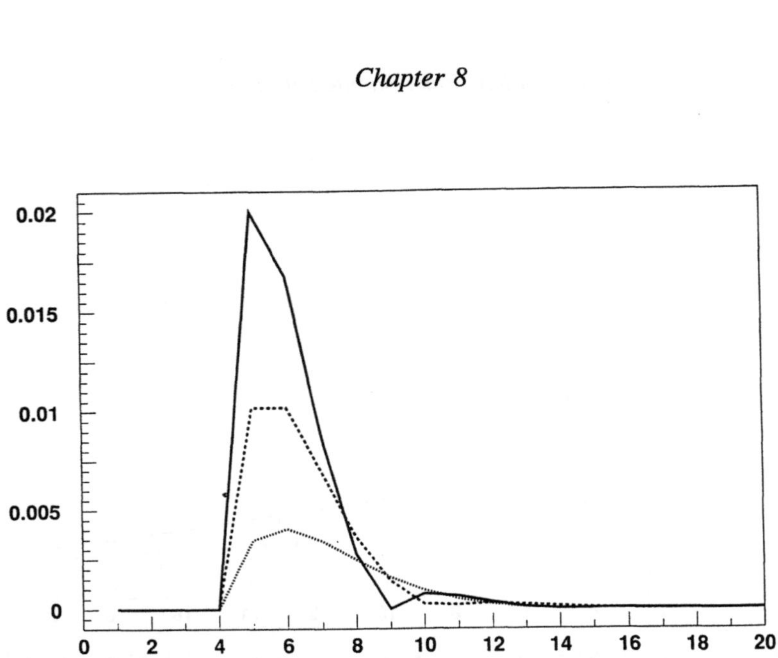

Fig.8.4 c Transient behaviour of trade in the two-market model. Vertical scale: trade between both markets; same caption as for the two previous figures.

market 1 is greatest when transportation costs are large; on the contrary, when transportation costs are small, the shock can, to a large extent, be "exported away" to market 2. The resulting trade bubble is largest in this case, though rather short-lived.
Under the assumption $\bar{h}_1 \simeq \bar{h}_2$ of scenario 2 it is clear from (3.4) that transient trade is almost negligible.

3.1.3 The transient stochastic model

The transient behaviour of the correlation function cannot be obtained through Fourier analysis; it has to be worked out from the solutions $p_1(t)$ and $p_2(t)$ of equation (3.1); one has:

$$p_k(t) = \theta \sum_{j=0}^{t} [R_{k1}(t-j)b_1(j) + R_{k2}(t-j)b_2(j)] + R_{k1}(t')h_1 + R_{k2}(t')h_2$$

where: $k = 1, 2$ and $t' = t - t_1$. The first term in the right-hand side corresponds to the stationary solution; the second contains the "innovations". We assume the shocks h_1 and h_2 to be correlated with covariance h_{12}. The stationary noises b_1 and b_2 still are supposed to be independent.

Let us compute the covariances:

$$c_{p_i p_j}(0) = E[p_i(t)p_j(t)] - \bar{p}_i(t)\bar{p}_j(t)$$

One obtains: $c_{p_1 p_1}(0) =$

$$c^{\mathrm{st}}_{p_1 p_1} + R^2_{11}(t')\sigma^2_{h_1} + 2R_{11}(t-t_1)R_{12}(t')h_{12} + R^2_{12}(t')\sigma^2_{h_2}\bar{p}_i(t)\bar{p}_j(t) \quad \text{(3.5a)}$$

$c_{p_1 p_2}(0) =$

$$c^{\mathrm{st}}_{p_1 p_2} + R_{11}(t')R_{12}(t')\sigma^2_{h_1} + 2R^2_{11}(t')h_{12} + R_{11}(t')R_{12}(t')\sigma^2_{h_2}\bar{p}_i(t)\bar{p}_j(t) \quad \text{(3.5b)}$$

c^{st} denotes the stationary component corresponding to $h_1 = h_2 = 0$. Now, these covariances enter into the expression of the variance of the trade flow s in the usual way:

$$\sigma^2_s = \frac{1}{t_1^2}[c_{p_1 p_1}(0) + c_{p_2 p_2}(0) - 2c_{p_1 p_2}(0)] \quad \text{(3.6)}$$

Once σ_s is known, the trade $T = \frac{1}{2}E(|s|)$ is given by the following lemma:

Lemma 2 If X is a normal N(m, σ^2) random variable one has:

$$E(|X|) = \sigma\sqrt{\frac{2}{\pi}}\exp(-m^2/2\sigma^2) + \frac{m}{2}\left[\mathrm{Erfc}(\frac{-m}{\sigma\sqrt{2}}) - \mathrm{Erfc}(\frac{m}{\sigma\sqrt{2}})\right] \quad \text{(3.7)}$$

where the complementary error function is defined by:

$$\mathrm{Erfc}(x) = \frac{2}{\sqrt{\pi}}\int_x^\infty e^{-u^2}du$$

(3.7) is a straightforward consequence of:

$E(|X|) =$

$$\frac{1}{\sigma\sqrt{2\pi}}\int_0^\infty x\exp[-(x+m)^2/2\sigma^2]\,dx + \frac{1}{\sigma\sqrt{2\pi}}\int_0^\infty x\exp[-(x-m)^2/2\sigma^2]\,dx \quad \text{(3.8)}$$

When $m = 0$, (3.7) leads back to the special result: $E(|X|) = \sigma\sqrt{2/\pi}$ and when $\sigma = 0$, it gives as expected: $E(|X|) = |m|$

When applying (3.7) to $E(|s|)$, $m(t)$ will be given by the deterministic solution obtained in the previous paragraph; then, from (3.5),(3.6) and (3.7), one obtains the transient evolution of trade in the stochastic model.

WHEAT

Year	**28**	**29**	**30**	**31**	**32**	**33**	**34**	**35**	**36**	**37**
Price	100	100	71	42	36	42	57	63	70	100
Trade		100	84	104	90	80	66	76	73	79
Prod.		100	108	107	106	102	97	99	97	105
Tr / Pr		18%	14%	18%	15%	14%	12%	14%	13%	14%

COFFEE

Year	**28**	**29**	**30**	**31**	**32**	**33**	**34**	**35**	**36**	**37**
Price	105	100	58	40	48	41	50	40	43	50
Trade		100	107	115	90	107	90	117	116	116
Prod.	60	100	102	87	102	110	106	88	109	106
Tr / Pr		58%	60%	76%	51%	60%	50%	77%	61%	63%

SUGAR

Year	**28**	**29**	**30**	**31**	**32**	**33**	**34**	**35**	**36**	**37**
Price	126	100	71	64	41	56	69	92	100	102
Trade		100	84	72	74	62		71	75	77
Prod.	99	100	102	94	85	90	92	98	107	109
Tr / Pr		44%	36%	34%	57%	30%		32%	31%	31%

COTTON

Year	**28**	**29**	**30**	**31**	**32**	**33**	**34**	**35**	**36**	**37**
Price	111	100	74	45	38	52	67	69	70	62
Trade		100	90	89	95	100	89	93	104	108
Prod.		100	98	104	89	97	89	100	119	144
Tr / Pr		54%	50%	46%	58%	55%	54%	50%	47%	40%

ALUMINIUM

Year	**28**	**29**	**30**	**31**	**32**	**33**	**34**	**35**	**36**	**37**
Price	100	100	89	82	79	65	51	52	52	52
Trade		100	75	63	40	56	60			
Prod.	88	100	97	79	56	52	62	95	133	181
Tr / Pr		33%	25%	26%	23%	35%	32%			

LEAD

Year	**28**	**29**	**30**	**31**	**32**	**33**	**34**	**35**	**36**	**37**
Price	92	100	89	82	79	65	51	52	52	52
Trade		100	75	63	40	56	60			
Prod.	88	100	97	79	56	52	62	95	133	181
Tr / Pr		37%	36%	43%	43%	46%	45%			

ZINC

Year	**28**	**29**	**30**	**31**	**32**	**33**	**34**	**35**	**36**	**37**
Price	93	100	71	58	47	50	39	40	45	59
Trade		100	96	107	84	73	93			
Prod.	97	100	96	69	54	68	81	92	100	112
Tr / Pr		21%	21%	33%	33%	23%	24%			

Table 8.2a Evolution of prices, world production and world trade during the years of the Great Depression 1928-1937. The price indexes refer to prices expressed in dollars. In our perpective products which can be produced almost everywhere (such as wheat or sugar) are the most representative; in contrast the trading structure of tropical goods is lacking flexibility. *Sources: Prices: World Bank (personal communication) and Statistical Yearbook of the League of Nations. Production: Statistical Yearbook of the League of Nations 1937/38. Trade: 1929-1934: Hickmann and Ricker (1936); 1935-1938: Commerce international de certaines matières premières et denrées mondiales par pays d'origine et de consommation. Société des Nations 1937,1939.*

3.1.4 Statistical evidence

Table 8.2a summarizes the evolution of prices, production and trade between 1929 and 1937. Regarding the evolution of trade three categories of goods may be distinguished

1) Tropical goods such as coffee and cotton do not show any substantial decrease: the index remains above 89.

2) Sugar, wheat and zinc experienced a decrease of about 35%.

3) Aluminium and lead experienced a sharp fall (of more than 40%)

Accordingly, the products in the first category seem to follow scenario 2 of Table 8.1 (or any of the other scenarios leading to a quasi status quo for trade) while the products in categories 2 and 3 can be thought of as following scenarios 5 or 6. Analysing the possible impact on trade of variations in freight rates is

Year	**28**	**29**	**30**	**31**	**32**	**33**	**34**	**35**	**36**	**37**
Freight	96	100	93	103	102	98	95	96	102	137

Table 8.2b Deflated ocean freight index. During the period 1928-1936 freight rates on average followed the variations in the general price level. *Source: The Economist freight index (tramp charter).*

made tricky by the fact that freight rates more or less followed the evolution of the general price level (Table 8.2b); in other words freight was rather neutral with respect to the evolution of trade.

Evolutions of lead prices respectively in Germany, in the United Kingdom and in the United States are shown in Fig.8.5. It can be seen that, in their downward trend, prices in Europe rather are ahead of prices in the United States.

Remark So far we have assumed fixed excess-supply functions. In the nineteenth century (see Chapter 4), during a period of several decades there was a steady increase in production accompanied by almost unchanged prices. This clearly points to a global upward shift in demand as well as in supply functions. In the case of the Great Depression there was a fall in production *and* in prices; in other words the downward shift of the demand function predominated.

3.1.5 Clark's analysis of spatial price dispersion before and after the crash of 1929

Most of this section has dealt with the impact of a sudden disequilibrium on the spatial distribution of prices. In 1983, G.Clark made a thorough examination of this question in examining spatial price patterns in the United States before and after the Great Depression. More specifically he addressed the following three questions:

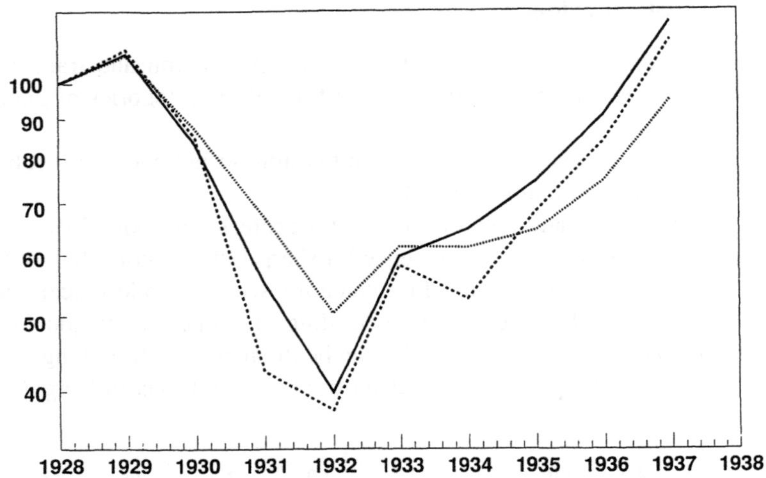

Fig.8.5 Evolution of the price of lead in Germany, in the United Kingdom and in the United States. Prices, expressed in dollar/ton, have been normalized to 100 in 1928. Solid curve: Germany; dashed curve: United Kingdom; dotted curve: United States. The price decrease actually began in 1925. These curves do not support the idea of a shock (or of a succession of shocks) that would have originated in the US and spread over to Europe. On the contrary (and there are similar curves for copper, zinc and tin), the price shock appears to have been largest in Europe. *Sources: Prices: Schmitz(1979); Exchange rates: Statistical Yearbook of the League of Nations 1938/39.*

1) How responsive were local prices to changes in national economic performances?

2) How variable were these responses over space and time?

3) How spatially integrated was the US economy over this period of time?

The empirical part of his paper relies upon a data set of semiannual consumer price indexes covering the period 1918-1941 and extending to 32 cities. During this period there have been three major transients: the end of the First World War, the crash of 1929-1933 and the beginning of the Second World War. A response to question 2 is provided by Table 8.3 (Clark 1983, p.29-30). Is is particularly interesting to compare periods during which the inflation rates were of the same order of magnitude but of a different sign: 1920/1921; 1927,1937/1938. The general conclusion is that variability is lower in through periods than in peak periods (of similar amplitude). We refer to Clark's paper for a number of other interesting conclusions.

	Mean		Variance		Coeff. of var.	
	Total	Food	Total	Food	Total	Food
	%	%				
1919 T	11,3	7,3	2,7	10,4	14	44
1920 P	10,5	16,7	4,6	24,3	20	29
1921 T	-8,5	-17,2	1,5	3,2	14	10
1923 P	1,1	2,0	1,3	7,7	103	132
1924 T	-1,5	-3,0	0,9	5,0	63	66
1927 P	-0,1	1,5	1,2	10,0	799	210
1927 T	-2,1	-5,3	1,9	12,2	67	66
1929 P	-0,2	0,9	0,5	2,8	342	171
1932 T	-6,4	-11,3	1,4	7,9	19	25
1937 P	2,7	3,8	1,5	5,2	45	60
1938 T	-2,7	-4,9	13,2	14,9	133	79
1940 P	0,7	0,4	0,8	4,8	120	598

Table 8.3 Spatial dispersion of inflation in 32 US cities by economic episode 1919-1940. T: Through; P: Peak. The table gives the variations of the genreral price index (total) and of the index of food prices. *Source: Adapted from Clark (1985).*

4 The ergodic assumption: ensemble averages versus time averages

This section does not specifically pertain to the Enke-Samuelson model, but it is of general significance to stochastic models especially in so far as they aim at describing transient behaviour. Probabilistic and stochastic models refer to ensemble averages; yet the statistic of a process is usually derived from the observation of a *single* time series. The question of whether parameters (i.e. mean, autocorrelation, distribution function, etc) determined from a single time series are identical to those obtained from ensemble averages is referred to as the ergodic problem. Although of major importance, this question usually cannot be tested empirically. However, in some conditions, averages of time series on spatially separated markets can be identified with ensemble averages; this gives us the opportunity of testing the ergodic hypothesis as will be seen in the second paragraph of this section. In the first paragraph, we define ergodicity and we state several ergodicity criteria. Finally, in the last paragraph, we discuss the link between Mandelbrot's scaling principle and ergodicity of the distribution function.

4.1 Definitions and criteria of ergodicity

One is usually interested not in all but only in certain parameters of a process. Clearly a process might be ergodic for certain parameters, but not for others. Three kinds of ergodicity are of special importance: ergodicity of the mean, ergodicity of the autocorrelation (which includes ergodicity of the variance) and ergodicity of the distribution function. Ergodicity of the mean for instance is defined in the following way:

Definition A process $X(t)$ is ergodic with respect to the mean if:

$$\lim_{T\to\infty} \frac{1}{2T} \int_{-T}^{T} X(t)dt = E[X(t)] \tag{3.9}$$

There are similar definitions for each of the aforementioned notions of ergodicity. More interesting are the statements of ergodicity criteria. Some of these are summarized below (Papoulis 1965, p.328-331).

Ergodicity criteria Let $X(t)$ be a stochastic process which is stationary to first and second order and also for the distribution function.

- One has ergodicity of the mean if and only if:

$$\lim_{T\to\infty} \frac{1}{2T} \int_{0}^{2T} (1 - \frac{\tau}{2T}) c_1(\tau) d\tau = 0$$

where $c_1(\tau)$ denotes the autocovariance of the process $X(t)$.

- One has ergodicity of the autocorrelation if and only if:

$$\lim_{T\to\infty} \frac{1}{2T} \int_{0}^{2T} (1 - \frac{\tau}{2T}) c_2(\tau;\lambda) d\tau = 0$$

where $c_2(\tau;\lambda)$ denotes the autocovariance of the process:

$$P_2(\lambda) = X(t+\lambda)X(t)$$

- One has ergodicity of the distribution function if and only if:

$$\lim_{T\to\infty} \frac{1}{2T} \int_{0}^{2T} (1 - \frac{\tau}{2T}) [F_2(x,x;\tau) - F_1^2(x)] d\tau = 0$$

$F_1(x)$ denotes the one-point distribution function of the process $X(t)$: $F_1(x) = P\{X(t) \le x\}$ and $F_2(x_1,x_2;\tau)$ denotes the two-point distribution function of the process $X(t)$:

$$F_2(x_1,x_2;t_1-t_2) = P\{X(t_1) \le x_1,\ X(t_2) \le x_2\}$$

The previous statements are made for the case of a continuous time variable; they can without much difficulty be transposed to the case of a discrete time variable.

Application to autoregressive processes The condition concerning ergodicity of the mean is trivially satisfied for any autoregressive process. Indeed, the covariance function of an autoregressive process behaves (for $t \to \infty$) as a decreasing exponential.
This result becomes even more obvious when the previous criteria are restated in terms of spectral functions; one has the following results (Priestley 1981, p.342-343):

- One has ergodicity of the mean if and only if the spectral density function $f(\omega)$ exists for $\omega = 0$.
- One has ergodicity of the autocorrelation if and only if the spectral density function exists everywhere and is square integrable.

The first condition obviously holds for an autoregressive process. The second holds too; indeed, among autoregressive processes it is the process of first order which has the spectral density function with slowest decrease (for $\omega \to \infty$); in this case one has $f(\omega) \underset{\infty}{\sim} 1/\omega^2$; thus $f(\omega)$ is square integrable even in this case.

Regarding ergodicity of the distribution function, one has the following sufficient condition in terms of the autocorrelation function $\rho(t)$.

Proposition 5 For a Gaussian stochastic process ergodicity of the distribution function is ensured by the following two conditions:

$$\circ \quad \rho(t) \underset{t \to 0}{\sim} 1 - 1/t^{2-\epsilon} \qquad \epsilon > 0$$

$$\circ \quad \lim_{T \to \infty} \frac{1}{T} \int_1^{2T} (1 - \frac{\tau}{2T}) \rho(\tau) dt < \infty$$

The proof which is purely technical and rather straightforward will be omitted. These conditions can be seen to be fulfilled for a Gaussian autoregressive process.

4.2 Ergodicity and non stationarity

The concept of ergodicity and its definition (3.9) has its origin in statistical mechanics. However, (3.9) is somewhat too restrictive for many situations which are of interest in economics. For one thing a time average which runs from $-\infty$ to ∞ clearly is not well adapted to economic problems. In economics the horizon very much depends upon the specific problem under investigation: of the order of a few years for short run investigations, it may broaden to several decades when long term evolutions are considered. A second and even more crucial problem concerns stationarity. This is an essential assumption in the standard definition of ergodicity, yet many of the most important phenomena in economics are of the transient type; a generalization of the concept of ergodicity to non stationary time series would therefore be appropriate. Tentatively, one may propose the following generalization of ergodicity (of the mean):

$$\frac{1}{2\Delta T}\int_{t_0-\Delta T}^{t_0+\Delta T} X(t)dt - E[X(t_0)] = O(1/\Delta T) \qquad (3.10)$$

where $O(1/\Delta T)$ denotes a term of the order of $1/\Delta T$. However heuristic this definition may be, let us nevertheless test it in the case of a typically non stationary phenomenon, namely the occurrence of a huge price peak. This test is summarized in Fig.8.6a for the mean and in Fig.8.6b for the variance. In each case the solid curve shows the time average ($\Delta t = 15$ months) while the broken curve corresponds to a spatial average over eleven other marketplaces where the same phenomenon occurred. Time averages and spatial averages appear to be closely connected in the case of the mean; in the case of the variance they are completely different however. Whether this should be attributed to the fact that the time series we considered do not constitute *independent* realizations (as required for an ensemble average) will be left as an open question.

4.3 Ergodicity and Mandelbrot's scaling principle

This paragraph gives us the opportunity to pay tribute to Benoit Mandelbrot. Although his ideas about chaos and fractals have had tremendous repercussions in many fields, his economic work did probably not receive the attention it deserved. One reason for this may be traced to the fact that it had no direct implication for policy purposes. B. Mandelbrot made important contributions to the study of price distributions. Among these we shall here be interested in the scaling property of price distributions for, as will be seen, it is directly connected with the ergodic problem. Let us first recall the statement of this principle (Mandelbrot 1963; 1982, p.337).

> **Scaling principle of price change** When $X(t)$ is a price, $\ln X(t)$ has the property that its increment over an arbitrary time lag d, namely $\ln X(t+d) - \ln X(t)$ has a statistical distribution independent of d except for a scale factor.

Mandelbrot provides three cotton price series in support of this principle:

1) A series of *daily* closing prices at the New York Cotton Exchange (1900-1905).

2) The variations of an index of *daily* closing prices on various Exchanges in the United States (1944-1958).

3) A series of *monthly* closing prices at the New York Cotton Exchange (1880-1940).

When represented on a log-log plot, the tails of the cumulative distribution

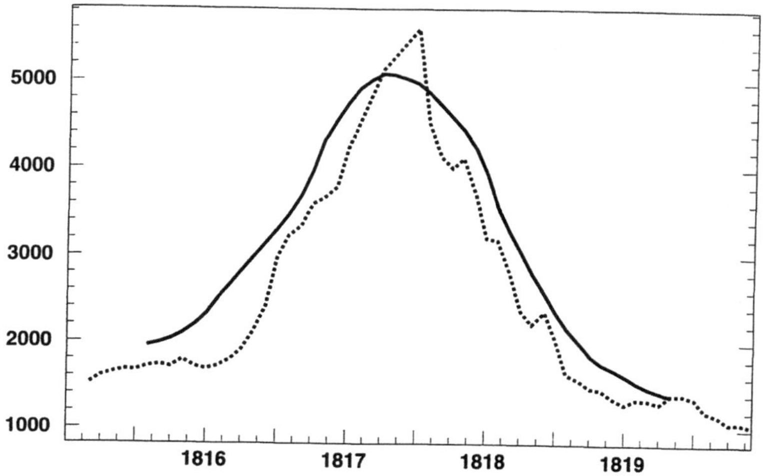

Fig.8.6a Time averages versus ensemble averages for the mean in the case of a non stationary process. Between January 1815 and June 1817 wheat prices in Bavaria have been multiplied by a factor of four. The solid curve shows the mean as computed from the price series in Munchen by moving average (window of 15 months). In this case ensemble and time averages lead to very similar results.

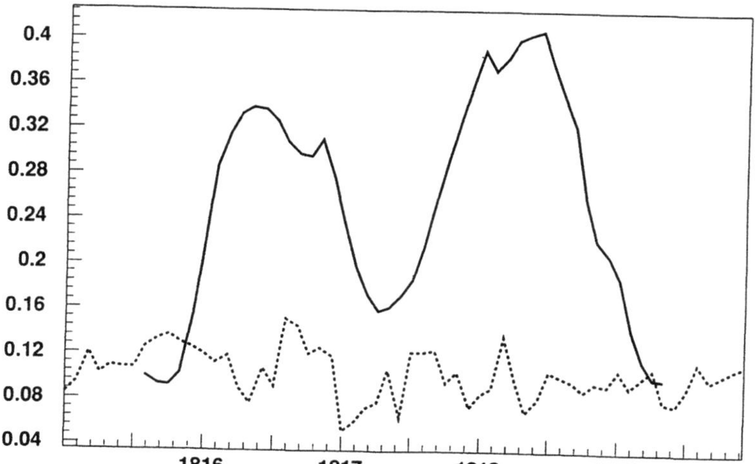

Fig.8.6b Time averages versus ensemble averages for the coefficient of variation in the case of a nonstationary process. The solid curve shows the coefficient of variation (square root of variance / mean) as computed from the price series in Munchen by moving average (window of 15 months); the trough corresponds to the maximum of the price peak. The ensemble average, on the contrary, shows almost perfect stationarity.

of changes in the logarithms of daily prices are almost identical in spite of the fact that the periods considered are about forty years apart. Furthermore the curve of monthly price changes can be deduced from the daily curves by an horizontal translation (see Fig.8.7a); all three curves can be derived by horizontal translation from the tail of a stable[2]distribution.

There are in fact two different parts in Mandelbrot's statement.

1) Distributions corresponding to different time lags can be deduced one from another by horizontal translations.

2) The distributions are parallel to the distribution of a stable law.

Our own contribution to the problem consists in showing that these statements are in fact disconnected. Indeed, the first property is not peculiar to stable laws; provided prices are ergodic, it can be shown to hold even under the (more standard) assumption of lognormal price distributions. Under this assumption, pairs of logarithms of prices are described by a bidimensional Gaussian distribution. For the sake of simplicity we assume this distribution to be normalized to zero mean; it reads then:

$$f(p_1', p_2'; \tau) = \frac{1}{2\pi\sigma^2\sqrt{1-r^2(\tau)}} \exp\left[-\frac{p_1'^2 - 2rp_1'p_2' + p_2'^2}{2\sigma^2(1-r^2(\tau))}\right] \qquad (3.11)$$

where $r(\tau)$ denotes the coefficient of correlation between:

$$p_1' = \ln p_t \quad \text{and} \quad p_2' = \ln p_{t+\tau}$$

If prices are ergodic for the distribution function it is equivalent to pick out pairs of prices from a time series or to generate them as dependent Gaussian variates. Mandelbrot's scaling property refers to the distribution function $G(x)$ of positive differences[3]; this distribution can be readily derived from (3.11) (see chapter 3 section 2.1). The distribution G reads:

$$G(z; \tau) = 1 - \frac{1}{2\sigma\sqrt{\pi(1-r(\tau))}} \int_0^z \exp\left[-\frac{x^2}{4\sigma^2(1-r(\tau))}\right] dx$$

Making the change of variable:

$$u = \frac{x}{2\sigma\sqrt{1-r(\tau)}}$$

[2]Let us recall that the family of stable distributions has the property that a sum of random variables identically distributed with a given distribution is a distribution of the same family. With the exception of the Gaussian distribution, stable distributions have an infinite variance.

[3]One could equivalently consider absolute values of differences since both distributions are identical but for a factor $1/2$.

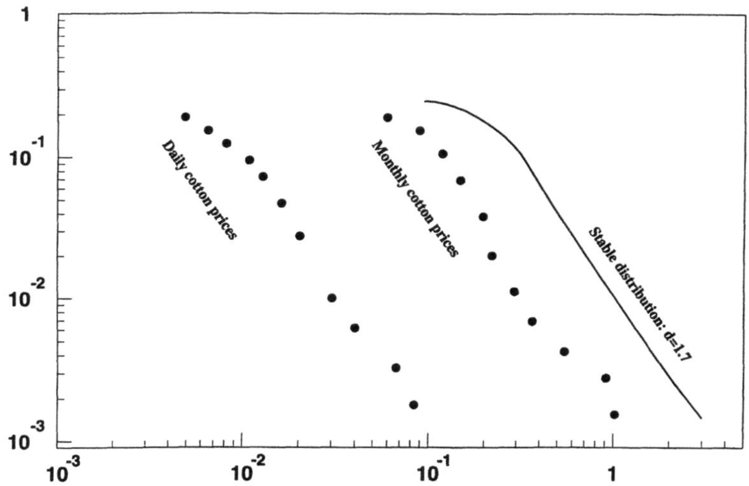

Fig.8.7 a Illustration of Mandelbrot's scaling principle. Horizontal scale: positive changes of logarithms of prices. Vertical scale: tail of the cumulated distribution function. The daily prices refer to an average index of closing prices on various Cotton Exchanges in the US for the period 1944-1958. The monthly prices refer to closing prices on the 15th of each month at the New York Cotton Exchange for the period 1880-1940. *Source: adapted from Mandelbrot (1982).*

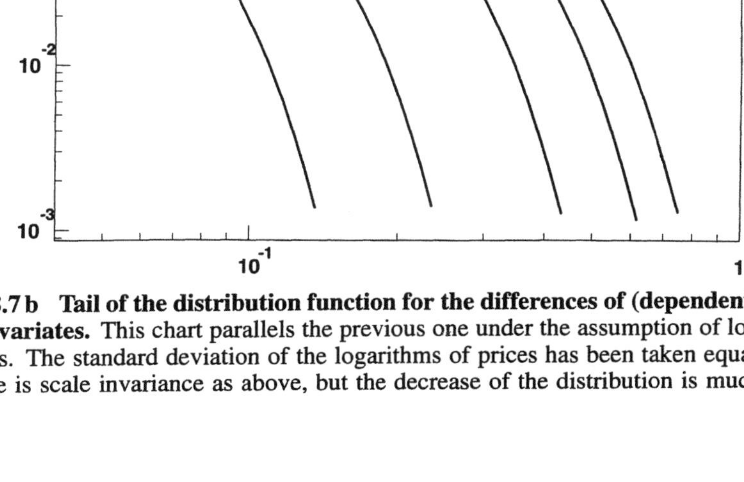

Fig.8.7 b Tail of the distribution function for the differences of (dependent) Gaussian variates. This chart parallels the previous one under the assumption of lognormal prices. The standard deviation of the logarithms of prices has been taken equal to 0.4. There is scale invariance as above, but the decrease of the distribution is much faster.

we obtain:

$$G(z;\tau) = \frac{1}{2}\mathrm{Erfc}\left[\frac{z}{2\sigma\sqrt{1-r(\tau)}}\right] \qquad (3.12)$$

Our objective is to study the tail of the distribution (3.12); this can hardly be done analytically however. Indeed, because z is a difference of logarithms the significant part of the distribution corresponds to fairly *small* values of z (see Fig.8.7a). Thus, one has to rely on numerical computation. This has been done in Fig.8.7b in which the parallelism of various curves appears clearly. Fig.8.7b has been drawn for realistic estimates of the parameters σ and $r(\tau)$ (see Roehner 1990b, p.12).

Let us now come to the second part of Mandelbrot's statement. Fig.8.7a and Fig.8.7b greatly differ in the slopes of the tails; one has respectively:

- Cotton prices slope $= 2.0$
- Lognormal prices slope $\simeq 6.5$

Remark Another difference between the two figures is the fact that the tails in Fig.8.7b are but poorly approximated by straight lines. For really large values of z, one has the following asymptotic development (Magnus et al 1966, p.352):

$$\ln[\mathrm{Erfc}(x)] \underset{\infty}{\sim} -x^2 - \ln(2x)$$

Thus the tails in Fig. 8.7b become steeper and steeper as $z \to \infty$.

The observation regarding the slopes strongly supports Mandelbrot's hypothesis that high volatility commodities are best described by stable laws. Fama (1965) reached a similar conclusion for stock prices. One should bear in mind, however, that this conclusion specifically concerns the tails of the distributions. As long as small samples[4] are considered the lognormal law provides a reasonable (and simple) approximation.

[4]Mandelbrot used large samples containing several thousand prices.

Chapter 9

Dynamic random field models

Spatial equations in which the variables are real continuous variables are known as field equations. It turns out that continuous field models possess definite mathematical advantages (in terms of tractability in particular). This may explain why, in spite of the fact that statistical records are of discrete form, such models have been used for some time in transportation and in space economics (Beckmann 1952, Isard 1952,1956).

In this chapter there are basically two different, though interconnected, parts. The first part deals with second order random fields the potential usefulness of which goes beyond their application to arbitrage models which is the theme of the second part. In fact, second order random fields can be used every time there is a need to describe spatial (or functional) connections between several time-dependent phenomena. A classical example is the propagation of innovations or of epidemics. Because of its potential widespread applicability we develop the theory of random fields in some detail at least as far as their space-time correlations are concerned. One striking feature which turns up in this framework is the plateau displayed by the correlation functions $\rho(x,t)$ in the region $x < ct$, where c is a positive parameter which may be interpreted as the velocity of price waves.

We do not in this chapter consider the so-called Ising's models of random fields (which are continuous in time but discrete with respect to spatial variables); an introduction to these topics can be found in Kindermann and Snell (1980) and also, as far as symmetrical interactions are concerned, in Roehner (1983).

In section one we first establish the equations of the Enke-Samuelson model in continuous space-time variables. Then we present the essential features of second order random fields in a simple case. In section 2 we recall some general properties of deterministic diffusion and propagation equations. In section 3 we derive the analytical expression of the covariance functions for stochastic diffusion and propagation equations. Section 4 is devoted to the application of the solutions obtained in section 3 to the Enke-Samuelson model. In particular we estimate the parameters of the model and analyse their evolution in the course of time. This provides a space-time picture of market integration.

1 Introduction

1.1 From discrete to continuous space-time equations

1.1.1 The continuous Enke-Samuelson model

Given the following demand and supply functions:

$$S(t) = \gamma_1 e(B)p(t) - c \qquad D(t) = \beta_1 p(t) + b$$

the equation obeyed by the distribution of prices $p(x,t)$ in a chain of markets is (Chapter 8, Section 1.2):

$$[\frac{2}{\theta} + 1 + \gamma e(B)]p(x,t) - \frac{1}{\theta}[p(x-1,t) + p(x+1,t)] = b(x,t) \tag{1.1}$$

with transportation costs denoted by t_1 and:

$$\theta = t_1 \beta_1 \qquad \gamma = \gamma_1/\beta_1$$

When the dynamic pricing model $e(B)$ is of second order: $\gamma e(B) = w_1 B + w_2 B^2$, (1.1) becomes a second order space-time process. Its continuous version reads:

$$\gamma \partial^2_{t^2} p(x,t) + 2\beta \partial_t p(x,t) + \alpha p(x,t) - k\partial^2_{x^2} p(x,t) = N(x,t) \tag{1.2}$$

Using an heuristic argument, we are able to establish a connection between the parameters in equations (1.1) and (1.2); indeed, for small increments h and q, (1.2) can be developed as:

$$\frac{\gamma}{h^2}[p(x,t) - 2p(x,t-h) + p(x,t-2h)] + \frac{2\beta}{h}[p(x,t) - p(x,t-h)] +$$

$$\alpha p(x,t) - \frac{k}{q^2}[p(x-q,t) - 2p(x,t) + p(x+q,t)] = N(x,t) \tag{1.3}$$

Identification between (1.1) and (1.3) leads to:

$$k = 1/\theta \quad \gamma = w_2 \quad \alpha = 1 + w_1 + w_2 \quad \beta = -w_1/2 - w_2 \tag{1.4}$$

where the time and distance units have been chosen in such a way that $h = q = 1$.

There is an alternative form of equation (1.2) which turns out to be useful; it is obtained by dividing both sides by k:

$$(1/c^2)\partial^2_{t^2} p(x,t) + 2b\partial_t p(x,t) + a^2 p(x,t) - \partial^2_{x^2} p(x,t) = N_1(x,t) \tag{1.5}$$

where:

$$c = \sqrt{k/\gamma} \qquad b = \beta/k \qquad a^2 = \alpha/k \tag{1.6}$$

The parameter c in equation (1.5) can be interpreted as the wave velocity (see Section 2.3).

There is of course an obvious generalization of the above argument to the case of a two-dimensional network of markets. One should also mention that the very definition of a random process by a stochastic partial differential equation such as (1.2) raises some non trivial mathematical problems. This question will be taken up again in Section 1.2.

1.1.2 Trade and price differentials

In Chapter 3 and 8 the trade T for a chain of N markets has been defined as:

$$T = \frac{1}{2N}\sum_x E(|s_x|) \underset{N\to\infty}{\sim} \frac{1}{2}E(|s_x|) \tag{1.7}$$

where:

$$s_x = \frac{p(x,t) - p(x-1,t)}{t_1} \qquad t_1 : \text{ cost of transportation between } x-1 \text{ and } x$$

This definition has an obvious generalization to the continuous case:

$$s(x) = \frac{p(x,t) - p(x-h,t)}{t_1 h}$$

where t_1 now represents the transportation costs per unit of distance. In the limit $h \to 0$, $s(x)$ becomes the spatial derivative of $p(x,t)$ with respect to x. Thus (Papoulis 1965, p.317):

$$\sigma_s^2 = -\frac{1}{t_1^2}\partial^2_{x^2} c\ (0,0) \tag{1.8}$$

where $c(x,t)$ denotes the covariance function of $p(x,t)$. Accordingly:

$$T = \frac{1}{t_1\sqrt{2\pi}}\sqrt{-\partial^2_{x^2} c\ (0,0)} \tag{1.9}$$

The extension to the case of a two-dimensional network of markets reads:

$$T = \frac{1}{t_1\sqrt{2\pi}}\sqrt{-\partial^2{}_{x_1{}^2} c\ (0,0;0) - \partial^2{}_{x_2{}^2} c\ (0,0;0)} \tag{1.10}$$

where $c(x_1, x_2; t)$ denotes the covariance function of $p(x_1, x_2; t)$

We have here implicitly assumed that the covariance function is differentiable to second order; however, as we shall see subsequently, this condition is not fulfilled when the disturbances $N(x,t)$ consist of pure white noise. Spatial autocorrelation of $N(x,t)$ is required in order to smooth out the process.

The price differential $\Delta(d)$ between two markets a distance d apart reads:

$$\Delta(d) = E[|p(x+d,t) - p(x,t)|] \tag{1.11}$$

In term of the covariance function $c(x,t)$, $\Delta(d)$ becomes:

$$\Delta(d) = \frac{2}{\sqrt{\pi}}[c(0,0) - c(d,0)]^{1/2} \tag{1.12}$$

From the previous formulas, it becomes clear that, as in Chapter 3 and 8, the economic implications of the model are to be derived from the covariance functions.

1.1.3 Generalizations and comments

The argument in the former paragraph can be generalized to a pricing model of higher order, thus leading to an equation of the form:

$$\gamma e(\partial_t)p(x,t) - k\partial^2_{x^2}p(x,t) = N(x,t) \tag{1.13}$$

where $e(\partial_t)$ denotes the nth order differential operator of the pricing model. In this chapter, however, we shall limit ourselves to discussing equations of order less or equal to two with respect to time. While this could appear somewhat restrictive, one should also notice that the dynamic models delineated in Chapter 2 do no longer apply here anyway. The reason is that we are here interested in sampling times that are much shorter than one year. Indeed, in order to investigate in some detail the covariance function of prices one has to use sampling times which are as short as possible.

The transition from the discrete model to the continuous equation which has been discussed in an heuristic way can be made rigorous. More specifically, one can prove that the solution of the discrete problem converges, as $q = h \to 0$ towards the corresponding solution of Cauchy's problem for the wave equation (Garabedian 1964, p.464).

- From Chapter 8, one may recall that the *nonlinear* Enke-Samuelson model of a chain of markets is ruled by the following equations:

$$\theta[1+\gamma e(B)]\varphi_c[s_k(t)] + 2s_k(t) - s_{k-1}(t) - s_{k+1}(t) = a_{k+1}(t) - a_k(t) \tag{1.14a}$$

where $s_k(t)$ denotes the trade flow (at time t) between markets k and $k+1$; the price $p_k(t)$ is given in terms of the trade flows $s_k(t)$ by the expression:

$$p_k(t) = \frac{1}{\theta}[1+\gamma e(B)]^{-1}[s_k(t) - s_{k-1}(t) + a_k(t)] \tag{1.14b}$$

The formal generalization of (1.14a,b) to the case of continuous variables leads to equations of the form:

$$\theta[1+\gamma e(\partial_t)]\varphi_c[s(x,t)] - \frac{\partial^2 s(x,t)}{\partial x^2} = \frac{\partial a(x,t)}{\partial x} \tag{1.15a}$$

and:

$$p(x,t) = \frac{1}{\theta}[1+\gamma e(\partial_t)]^{-1}[\frac{\partial a(x,t)}{\partial x} + a(x,t)] \tag{1.15b}$$

In contrast with the linear case, it is no longer possible to develop the nonlinear partial differential equation (1.15) and to perform a term to term identification with the discrete equation.

1.2 The spectral theory in the continuous case

Formally, the spectral theory outlined in Chapter 7 (Section 4) can be generalized to the continuous case without difficulty, with Fourier series replaced by Fourier transforms. The relevant steps and definitions are given below:

1) We consider an equation of the form:

$$L(\partial_x, \partial_t)X(x,t) = N(x,t) \tag{1.16}$$

where x denotes a vector $(x_1, \ldots, x_n)$ and $L(\partial_x, \partial_t)$ is a second-order differential operator with respect to $(\partial_{x_1}, \ldots, \partial_{x_2})$ and t.

We introduce the solution $G(x,t;x',t')$ of the equation:

$$L(\partial_x, \partial_t)G(x,t;x',t') = \delta(x-x')\delta(t-t') \tag{1.17}$$

where $\delta(x)$ denotes Dirac's distribution. Different names have been given to the function G according to the context in which it occurs. Mathematicians call it the fundamental solution of the operator L (Hörmander 1983), or the Green's function of equation (1.17) (Morse and Feshbach 1953, p.795). In the context of signal theory it is known as the impulse response (Papoulis 1962, p.82).

2) Assuming translational invariance with respect to time the solution $X(t)$ is given in term of G by:

$$X(x,t) = \int G(x,x';t-t')X(x',t')dx'dt' \tag{1.18}$$

3) The Fourier transformation $\mathcal{F}(.)$ is defined by the pairs of formulas:

$$\widetilde{A}(q) = \int d^n x e^{iqx} A(x) \tag{1.19a}$$

$$A(x) = \frac{1}{(2\pi)^n} \int d^n q e^{-iqx} \widetilde{A}(q) \tag{1.19b}$$

4) The spectral function $\widetilde{c}(q;\omega)$ is the Fourier transform of the covariance function $c(x;t)$; it is given in terms of the Fourier transform of the Green's function by:

$$\widetilde{c}(q;\omega) = \widetilde{G}(-q;-\omega)\widetilde{G}(q;\omega)\widetilde{c}_N(q;\omega) \tag{1.20}$$

where $\widetilde{c}_N(q;\omega)$ denotes the covariance function of the disturbances $N(x;t)$.

5) The mathematical definition of a stochastic process such as (1.16) is considered in Gaveau (1989) in the case of a wave equation: it is shown that under certain conditions the argument leading to the definition of Ito's equation can be extended to a partial differential equation. Here, however, since we are interested in the covariance function rather than in sample functions it is natural, in view of (1.20), to adopt the following definition:

Definition 1 Given the random field defined by the equation:

$$L(\partial_x, \partial_t)X(x,t) = N(x,t)$$

we define the covariance function $c(x;t)$ of the field $X(x;t)$ as the solution of the equation:

$$L(\partial_x, \partial_t)L(-\partial_x, -\partial_t)c(x;t) = c_N(x;t) \tag{1.21}$$

where $c_N(x;t)$ denotes the covariance function of the disturbances $N(x;t)$. The boundary conditions are such that $c(x;t)$ vanishes, as well as its first three derivatives, on the boundaries of the domain.

Remark In contrast to the case of second order linear partial differential equations for which there is a general theory (Hörmander 1983), a general theory does not seem to exist for fourth order equations such as (1.21).

1.3 A special case

Before we discuss the general case, let us consider a special form of equation (1.2). It will give an introductory insight into the main features of hyperbolic random fields with technicalities kept at the minimum.

1.3.1 The covariance function

We are interested in the covariance function of the process defined by equation (1.2) where $N(x,t)$ consists of continuous "white noise", the covariance of which reads (Priestley 1981, p.163):

$$c_N(x,t) = \sigma_W^2 \delta(x)\delta(t) \tag{1.22}$$

where σ_W^2 denotes the rate of increase of the variance of the Wiener process:

$$W(x,t) = \int_0^t \int_{-\infty}^{x} N(x',t')dx'dt' \tag{1.23}$$

According to (1.20) and (1.19b), the covariance function of prices is given by the integral:

$$c(x,t) = \frac{\sigma_W^2}{(2\pi)^2} \int\int \frac{e^{-i(qx+\omega t)}}{\widetilde{L}(q,\omega)\widetilde{L}(-q,-\omega)} dq d\omega \tag{1.24}$$

where:

$$\widetilde{L}(q,\omega) = -\gamma\omega^2 - 2i\beta\omega + \alpha + kq^2$$

Because $\widetilde{L}(q,\omega)$ is an even function of q, it is obvious that $c(x,t)$ will be an even function of x; accordingly, x may thereafter be assumed to be positive. We rewrite $\widetilde{L}(q,\omega)$ in the following form:

$$\widetilde{L}(q,\omega) = \gamma(-\omega^2 + 2i\beta_1\omega + \alpha_1 + q_1^2)$$

where:

$$\beta_1 = \beta/\gamma \qquad \alpha_1 = \alpha/\gamma \qquad q_1 = q\sqrt{k/\gamma}$$

In the special case: $\alpha_1 = \beta_1^2$ (that is to say: $\beta^2 = \alpha\gamma$)), $\widetilde{L}(q,\omega)$ factorizes in the following way:

$$\widetilde{L}(q,\omega)/\gamma = [\beta_1 + i(\omega - q_1)][\beta_1 + i(\omega + q_1)] \tag{1.25}$$

Therefore:

$$L(iq,i\omega)L(-iq,-i\omega)/\gamma^2 = [\beta_1^2 + (q_1-\omega)^2][\beta_1^2 + (q_1+\omega)^2]$$

Thus, by performing in the integral the following change of variables:

$$u = q_1 - \omega \qquad v = q_1 + \omega$$

the double integral becomes a product of two simple integrals with respect to u and v:

$$c(x,t) = \frac{\sigma_W^2}{2(2\pi)^2\gamma^2\sqrt{k/\gamma}} \left(\int_{-\infty}^{\infty} \frac{e^{-iu(x_1-t)/2}}{u^2+\beta_1^2} du\right) \left(\int_{-\infty}^{\infty} \frac{e^{-iv(x_1+t)/2}}{v^2+\beta_1^2} dv\right)$$

where: $x_1 = x/\sqrt{k/\gamma}$.

The simple integrals are given by Gradshteyn (1965, p.406):

$$\int_0^{\infty} \frac{\cos ua}{u^2+\beta_1^2} du = \frac{\pi}{2\beta_1} e^{-|a|\beta_1} \qquad \beta_1 > 0 \tag{1.26}$$

Thus, one obtains finally:

$$c(x,t) = \begin{cases} \dfrac{\sigma_W^2}{8\beta^2\sqrt{k/\gamma}} \exp(\dfrac{-\beta}{\sqrt{\gamma k}}|x|) & |x| > t\sqrt{k/\gamma} > 0 \\ \dfrac{\sigma_W^2}{8\beta^2\sqrt{k/\gamma}} \exp(-\dfrac{\beta}{\gamma}t) & |x| < t\sqrt{k/\gamma} \end{cases} \tag{1.27}$$

At this point, it can be of interest to note that (see Section 2) a deterministic field ruled by equation (1.2) propagates with a velocity $c = \sqrt{k/\gamma}$.
The solution $|x| > t\sqrt{k/\gamma}$ in (1.27) will be called the space-like section of the covariance function; the solution $|x| > t\sqrt{k/\gamma}$ will be referred to as its time-like section.
The variance $\sigma_p^2 = c(0,0)$ of the process turns out to be finite:

$$\sigma_p^2 = \frac{1}{8\beta^2\sqrt{k/\gamma}}$$

Thus one may define a correlation function:

$$\rho(x,t) = \begin{cases} \exp(-\dfrac{\beta}{\sqrt{\gamma k}}|x|) & |x| > t\sqrt{k/\gamma} \\ \exp(-\dfrac{\beta}{\gamma}t) & |x| < t\sqrt{k/\gamma} \end{cases}$$

On the contrary, for a two-dimensional market network the covariance function will be seen to diverge at $x_1 = x_2 = t = 0$.

1.3.2 Qualitative features of the covariance function

Most of the following features are common to all covariance functions to be derived throughout this chapter.

- The space-like section of the correlation function has an exponential decrease. This is the generalization to dynamic processes of the result obtained in Chapter 3 (Section 3.1) in the static case. One can therefore define a *correlation length* δ by:

$$\delta = \sqrt{\gamma k}/\beta \tag{1.28}$$

The correlation length goes to infinity along with $k \sim 1/\theta$, that is when transportation costs vanish.
Remark Such a correlation length has been introduced empirically in Chapter 6. In the general case, the decrease of the spatial section of the correlation

function is no longer purely exponential; the correlation length may then be defined more generally as (Rebuffet 1945, p.30; Tritton 1977, p.249):

$$\delta_t = \int_0^{\infty} \rho(x,t)dx \tag{1.29}$$

In other words, the correlation length is defined as the area under the curve $\rho_t(x)$, a definition which coincides with (1.28) in the special case of an exponential decrease.

- In the limit $k \to 0$, one expects the markets to become independent; this should result in a limiting form of the covariance function that is proportional to $\delta(x)$. In fact, one obtains from the space-like section:

$$\lim_{k\to 0} c(x,t) = \frac{\gamma\sigma_W^2}{4\beta^3}\delta(x)$$

- It is interesting to check (1.27) from the point of view of dimensions. From equations (1.2) and (1.22) one has, with obvious notations:

$$[k]=[L]^2 \quad [\beta]=[T] \quad [\gamma]=[T]^2 \quad [\sigma_W^2]=[P]^2[L][T]$$

and therefore: $[c(x,t)] = [P]^2$ as expected.

- The covariance function is not differentiable at the following points:

$$x=t=0 \qquad |x| = \sqrt{k/\gamma}t$$

As a result, $p(x,t)$ is not stochastically differentiable at these points. This prevents us from computing the trade expectation (1.9). The introduction of spatially autocorrelated noise remedies this difficulty as we shall see shortly.

- Finally, Figure 9.1 shows the evolution of $\rho_x(t)$. The most interesting feature is the plateau at the left-hand side of the curve for such a shape may be easily identified when occurring in empirical correlation curves; as we shall see in Section 4, empirical curves do indeed display plateaus of this kind. One should also remember that Proposition 3 in Chapter 8 points to a similar configuration in the case of a discrete chain of markets. In more general cases (Section 3), the decreasing part of the curve will not necessarily be of exponential form; the plateau, however, will still be present. When the noise is autocorrelated, the covariance function becomes differentiable and thereby the sharp edges disappear; there is still a kind of plateau however.

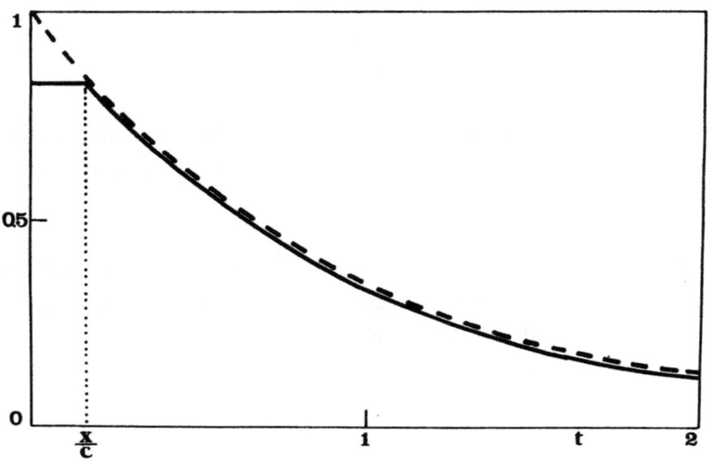

Fig.9.1 Intercorrelation $\rho_x(t)$ between two markets a distance x apart. The two markets belong to an infinite chain of markets. Horizontal scale: t. Solid curve: $x = 0$; dashed curve: $x = 0.17$. The price fluctuations are ruled by the random wave equation (1.5) where $a = bc$. The length of the plateau is proportional to the distance x between the markets.

1.3.3 Covariance function of regional price averages

So far prices have been assumed to be well localized spatially. Most often, however, prices are recorded as regional *averages*. What will be the effect of such an averaging process upon the former correlation pattern? To get at least a schematic insight, we define:

$$\bar{p}_1(t) = \int_0^\infty p(x,t)dx \qquad \bar{p}_2(t) = \int_{-\infty}^0 p(x,t)dx$$

and we compute the covariance function of $\bar{p}_1(t)$ and $\bar{p}_2(t)$:

$$c_{12}(t) = \int_0^\infty dx' \int_{-\infty}^0 dx'' c(x'' - x', t)$$

where $c(x,t)$ denotes the covariance function (1.27). The above integral is easily obtained:

$$c_{12}(t) = e^{-act}[\frac{c^2t^2}{2} - \frac{ct}{a} - \frac{1}{a^2}]$$

where:

$$a = \beta/\sqrt{k\gamma} \qquad c = \sqrt{k/\gamma}$$

There is no longer a plateau, since as expected, the averaging process has smoothed out the covariance function; nevertheless, one observes that $c'_{12}(0) = 0$; this horizontal tangent is, so to say, a vestige of the former plateau. The lesson of this paragraph is that in order to analyse spatial covariance patterns it is most important to use well localized price series.

2 Field equations

2.1 Classification of spatial differential equations of the second order

As a field equation, (1.2) could seem to be of rather special form; however, we shall see presently that it can be derived from the general second order equation under a few natural assumptions: invariance by translation, isotropy and causality requirement.

The most general linear second order equation can be written in the following form:

$$a_{11}(x,t)\partial^2_{t^2}X + 2a_{12}(x,t)\partial^2_{xt}X + a_{22}(x,t)\partial^2_{x^2}X +$$

$$b_1(x,t)\partial_t X + b_2(x,t)\partial_x X + c(x,t)X = N(x,t) \tag{2.1}$$

If we impose to the process $X(x,t)$ the requirement of being invariant by translation (i.e. stationary) with respect to x and t, the coefficients have to be constants. Furthermore, the equation can be of three different types according to the sign of:

$$\Delta = a_{12}^2 - a_{11}a_{22}$$

$$\Delta < 0 : \quad \text{elliptic equation} \tag{2.2a}$$

$$\Delta = 0 : \quad \text{parabolic equation} \tag{2.2b}$$

$$\Delta > 0 : \quad \text{hyperbolic equation} \tag{2.2c}$$

If we impose the causality condition (i.e. that an impulse applied at $t = 0$ cannot be observed for $t < 0$), it can be shown (Heine 1955, p.174) that the elliptic case has to be excluded.

Furthermore, by a change of variables (and of the function on the left-hand side) equation (2.1) can be reduced to the following canonical forms (Tychonov and Samarski 1964, p.5):

$$\text{Hyperbolic equation:} \quad \partial_{\alpha\alpha}u - \partial_{\beta\beta}u = \phi$$

$$\text{Parabolic equation:} \quad \partial_{\alpha\alpha}u = \phi$$

Instead of these canonical forms, we prefer to write out explicitly the terms arising from the pricing model. Therefore, we shall use the following forms:

1) Hyperbolic (wave) equation:

$$\frac{1}{c^2}\partial^2_{t^2}p(x,t) + 2b\partial_t p(x,t) + a^2 p(x,t) - \partial^2_{x^2}p(x,t) = N(x,t) \tag{2.3}$$

2) Parabolic (diffusion) equation:

$$b\partial_t p(x,t) + a^2 p(x,t) - \partial^2_{x^2}p(x,t) = N(x,t) \tag{2.4}$$

2.2 Source terms and boundary conditions

For the solution of a partial differential equation (with given source terms in the right-hand side) to be completely defined, one has to specify the initial state and the boundary conditions. These have been left implicit in foregoing paragraphs since, by using spectral methods, we have limited ourselves to solutions that vanish at infinity. In this paragraph we emphasize that there is an equivalence (under some conditions) between source terms on one hand and initial conditions on the other.

We shall take the following result as our starting point (Morse and Feshbach 1953, p.837).

The solution of the equation:

$$\frac{1}{c^2}\partial^2_{t^2}p + 2b\partial_t p + a^2 p - \partial^2_{x^2}p = n(x,t)$$

$$p(x,t=0) = p_0(x) \qquad \partial_t p|_{t=0} = p_0'(x)$$

can be written in the form:

$$p(x,t) = \int\int n(x',t')G(x,t;x',t')dx'dt' +$$

$$\int_{-\infty}^{\infty} dx' \left[p_0(x')\partial_{t'} G(x,t;x',t')|_{t'=0} - p_0'(x')G(x,t;x',0)\right] \tag{2.5}$$

The first term takes into account the source term $n(x,t)$, while the second represents the contribution of initial conditions. One therefore has the rule:

The source term $n(x,t)$ required to duplicate the initial conditions:

$$p(x,t=0) = p_0(x) \qquad \partial_t p|_{t=0} = p_0'(x)$$

is:

$$n(x,t) = p_0(x)\delta'(t) + p_0'(x)\delta(t)$$

where $\delta(t)$ and $\delta'(t)$ stand for Dirac's distribution and its derivative.

A similar rule holds for the diffusion equation (Morse and Feshbach 1953, p.859); in this case only a single initial condition can of course be specified.

2.3 Diffusion versus wave equations

It is the objective of this paragraph to provide a qualitative insight into the behaviour of a field of prices subject to an initial disequilibrium either in prices or in demand and supply conditions. The main message is that there is a smooth transition between diffusion behaviour and wave behaviour. This can already been inferred from the definitions (2.2b) and (2.2c) from which it is clear that parabolic equations are a limiting case of hyperbolic equations; for short, a diffusion equation can be considered as the limit of a wave equation when wave-velocity goes to infinity.

2.3.1 Linear equations

The similarities between equations (2.3) and (2.4) are illustrated in Figures 9.2a,b,a',b'. The economic rationale of these figures is the following. Let us consider a set of markets that is brought into disequilibrium by a shock occurring in one market which we assume to be located at $x = 0$. Such a perturbation may come about in two ways, either as a shock in price levels (as a result of increasing production costs for instance) or as a shock on the supply and demand side. The relation between price levels and excess-supply levels may in first approximation be written as (Beckmann and Ryder 1969, p.471):

$$\frac{dp(x=0,t)}{dt} = \lambda Q_e(t) \qquad Q_e = D - S$$

where D and S respectively denote demand and supply. As a result, a short lived peak in excess-supply could be seen as an impulse p'_0 in the time-derivative of the price. Taking into account the rule stated in the former paragraph, one has the following connection between initial disequilibria and corresponding responses in price levels:

Disequilibrium at market $x = 0$	**Response induced in the set of markets**
price disequilibrium	$p(x,t) = \partial_t G(x,t)$
excess-supply disequilibrium	$p(x,t) = G(x,t)$

Qualitatively, as may be observed from Fig.9.2, the diffusion solution bears a strong likeness to the wave solution. The main difference concern the intensity of dumping. Dumping is clearly largest in the diffusion case because the friction term $\partial_t p$ cannot in this case be offset by a second order derivative. There is also a difference in velocity of propagation: in the diffusion case, it is in a sense proportional to $\sqrt{t}$, whereas it is proportional to t in the wave equation.

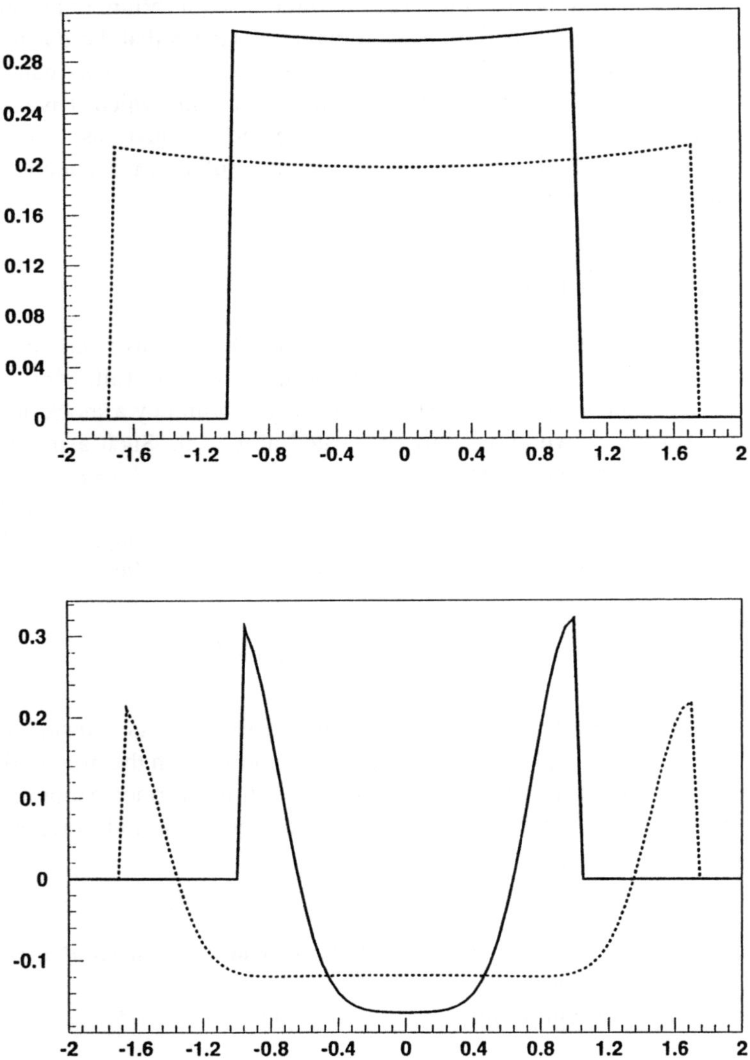

Fig.9.2 a,b Comparison of wave and diffusion models: wave solutions. Horizontal scale: x. Upper figure: response (at two instants t_1, t_2) of a chain of markets to an initial disequilibrium in excess-supply: $a = 0.6, b = 0.5, c = 1$; solid curve: $t_1 = 1$; dashed curve: $t_2 = 1.7$. Lower figure: response (at two instants t_1, t_2) of a chain of markets to an initial price disequilibrium. Same parameters.

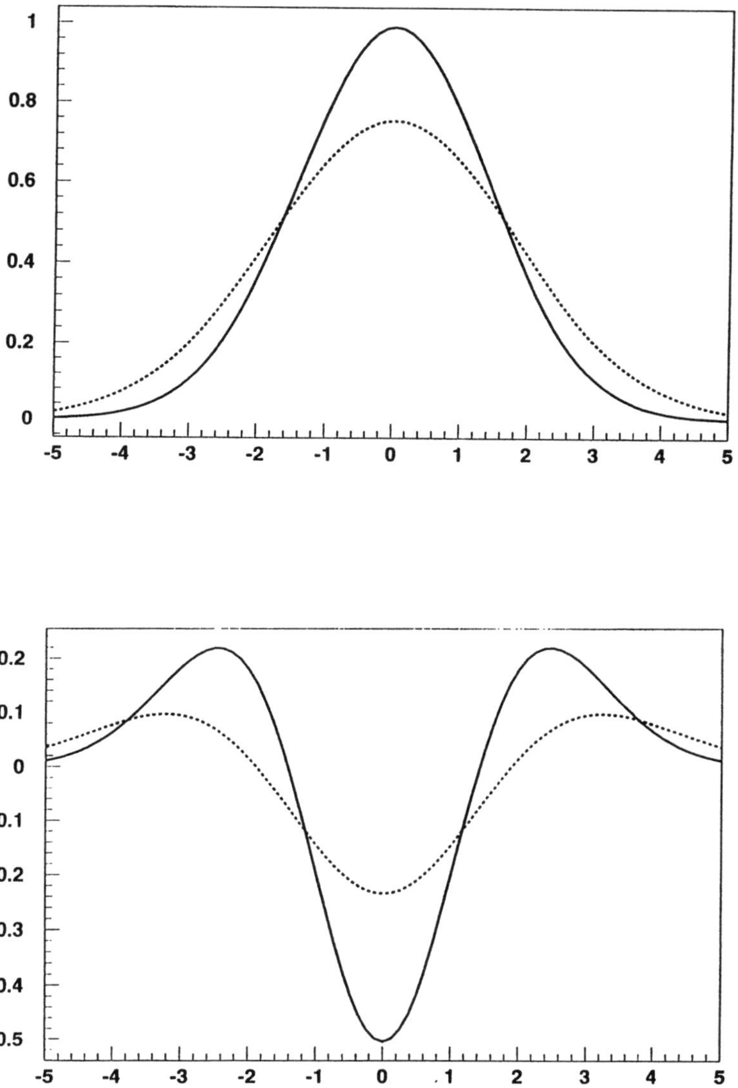

Fig.9.2 a',b' Comparison of wave and diffusion models: diffusion solutions. Horizontal scale: x. Upper figure: response (at two instants t_1, t_2) of a chain of markets to an initial disequilibrium in excess-supply: $a = 0.1, b = 0.5$ solid curve: $t_1 = 1$; dashed curve: $t_2 = 1.7$. Lower figure: response (at two instants t_1, t_2) of a chain of markets to an initial price disequilibrium. Same parameters as above.

2.3.2 Nonlinear diffusion: the porous media equation

One could think that it is the existence of a wave front which is the most distinctive feature of wave fields. However, in this paragraph we shall see that some *nonlinear* diffusion equations exhibit wave fronts too. We consider the following equation (Murray 1989, p.238):

$$\partial_t p = \partial_x (p^\alpha \partial_x p) \qquad \alpha > 0 \tag{2.6}$$

It is known as the porous media equation. Its solution for an initial value $p(x, t = 0) = 1$ reads:

$$p(x,t) = \begin{cases} \dfrac{1}{\lambda(t)} \left[1 - \left(\dfrac{x}{\gamma \lambda(t)} \right)^2 \right]^{1/\alpha} & |x| \le \gamma \lambda(t) \\ 0 & |x| > \gamma \lambda(t) \end{cases} \tag{2.7a}$$

where:

$$\gamma = \frac{\Gamma(1/\alpha + 3/2)}{\sqrt{\pi}\Gamma(1/\alpha + 1)} \qquad t_0 = \frac{\alpha \gamma^2}{2(\alpha + 2)} \qquad \lambda(t) = \left(\frac{t}{t_0} \right)^{1/(2+\alpha)} \tag{2.7b}$$

The solution represents a wave with the front at $x_f = \gamma \lambda(t)$ (Fig.9.3a,b). Furthermore, there is a smooth transition between equation (2.6) and the linear diffusion equation:

$$\partial_t p = \partial_{x^2}^2 p \quad \Longrightarrow \quad p(x,t) = \frac{1}{\sqrt{4\pi t}} e^{-x^2/4t} \tag{2.8}$$

Indeed, taking the limit $\alpha \to 0$ in (2.7) leads to the solution (2.8); in the derivation one has to use the developments:

$$\frac{\Gamma(n + b)}{\Gamma(n + a)} \underset{n \to \infty}{\sim} n^{b-a} \qquad (1 + \frac{x}{n})^n \underset{n \to \infty}{\sim} e^x$$

3 Correlation function of hyperbolic and parabolic random fields

In this section we take up the problem of obtaining the covariance function for the wave equation (2.3) and for the diffusion equation (2.4). In Yadrenko (1983), one may find the spectral theory of *static* random fields in Euclidian space and on the sphere; the subsequent developments constitute a generalization to *dynamic* random fields. First, we shall prove a relation between Green's functions and covariance functions which will be of great utility in the rest of the chapter.

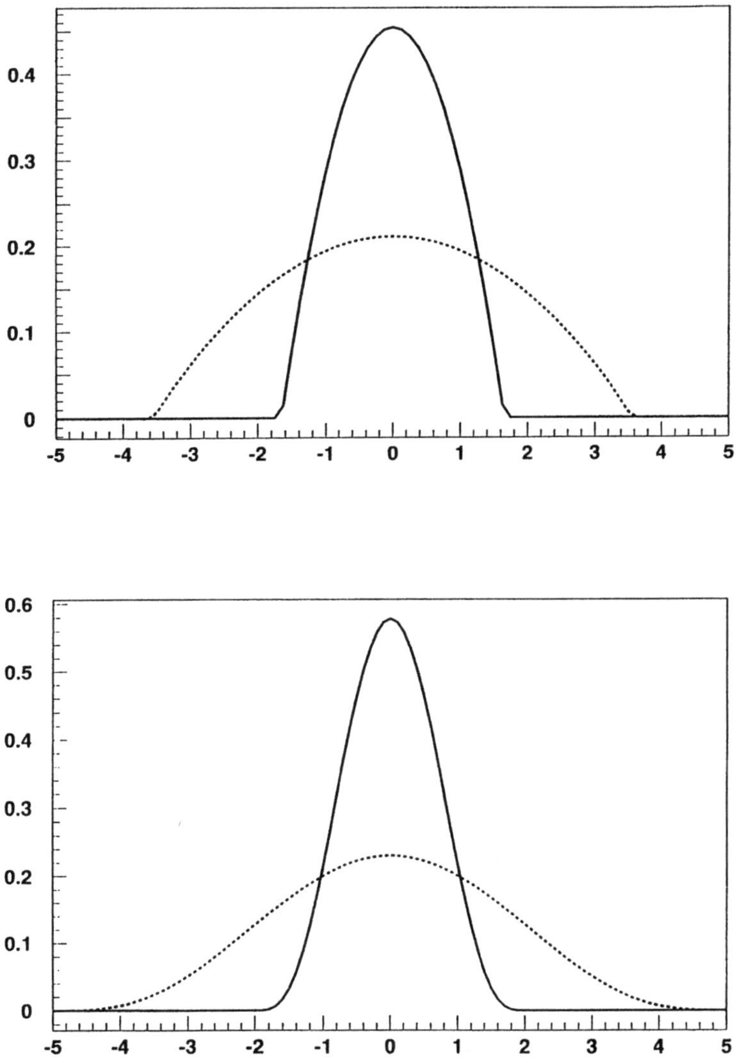

Fig.9.3 a,b Green's function $G_x(t)$ of the porous media equation. Horizontal scale: x. The porous media equation (2.6) is a nonlinear diffusion equation. Yet, its Green's function displays a wave front. When the parameter α goes to zero, the equation becomes identical with the standard diffusion equation. Upper figure: $\alpha = 1$; solid curve: $t_1 = 1$; dashed curve: $t_2 = 10$. Lower figure: $\alpha = 0.3$; solid curve: $t_1 = 0.3$; dashed curve: $t_2 = 2.5$.

3.1 The passage theorems

First we state the theorem for the case of white noise. Subsequently, it will be extended to the case where the noise is spatially autocorrelated.

3.1.1 White noise

Theorem 1 We consider the random field $p(x,t)$ defined by:

$$Lp(x,t) = N(x,t) \qquad L(x,t) = (1/c^2)\partial^2_{t^2} + 2b\partial_t + a^2 - k\sum_{j=1}^{n}\partial^2_{x_j^2}$$

where the source term $N(x,t)$ has a white noise covariance function of the form:

$$c_N(x,t) = \sigma^2_W \delta(x)\delta(t)$$

Then the covariance function $c(x,t)$ of the field $p(x,t)$ is given by:

$$c(x,t) = \begin{cases} c(x,0) & r \geq c_1 t > 0 \\ \left(-\frac{1}{4b}\right)\int_{r/c_1}^{t} G(x,t')dt' + c(x,0) & r \leq c_1 t \end{cases}$$

where:

$$c_1 = c/\sqrt{k} \quad r = \|x\|$$

$$c(x,0) = \frac{(a/r)^{n/2-1}\sigma^2_W}{(2\pi)^{n/2}(4b)k^{n/4+1/2}} K_{n/2-1}(ar/\sqrt{k}) \tag{3.1}$$

K_ν: modified Bessel function of the second kind.
$G(x,t)$: Green's function of the operator L

Proof The proof is carried out in two steps; in the first one, we proceed formally; in the second (Appendix B) we shall examine the convergence of the Fourier integrals and justify their differentiation.
From (1.20) results that:

$$c(x,t) = \frac{1}{(2\pi)^{n+1}}\int_{\mathbf{R}^n} e^{-iqx}dq \int_{-\infty}^{\infty} \frac{e^{-i\omega t}}{\widetilde{L}(q,\omega)\widetilde{L}(q,-\omega)} d\omega \tag{3.2}$$

where:

$$\widetilde{L}(q,\omega) = -\omega^2/c^2 - 2ib\omega + a^2 + q^2$$

In the integral with respect to ω we perform the following decomposition:

$$\frac{-i\omega}{\widetilde{L}(q,\omega)\widetilde{L}(q,-\omega)} = \left(-\frac{1}{4b}\right)\left[\frac{1}{\widetilde{L}(q,\omega)} - \frac{1}{\widetilde{L}(q,-\omega)}\right] \tag{3.3}$$

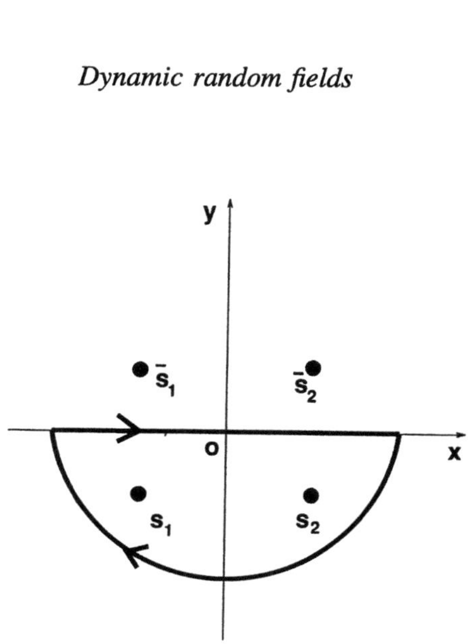

Fig.9.4 Integration contour. $\omega = s_1, s_2$ are the zeroes of $L(q, \omega)$.

We now apply the theorem of residues to the decomposition (3.3). Because $L(x, t)$ is assumed to be a causal operator, its zeroes s_1 and s_2 are necessarily in the lower half-plane Im$s < 0$. Since t is assumed to be positive, we shall use the contour shown in Fig.9.4. Therefore, the term $1/\widetilde{L}(q, -\omega)$ will not contribute to the integral. The term $1/\widetilde{L}(q, \omega)$ on the other hand merely corresponds to the definition of the Green's function. Furthermore, it is shown in Appendix B, that:

$$\mathcal{F}_\omega^{-1}[-i\omega\widetilde{c}(x, \omega)] = \partial_t c(x, t)$$

One has therefore:

$$\partial_t c(x, t) = (-1/4b)G(x, t) \tag{3.4}$$

Since the Green's function of the wave operator L vanishes for $r \geq c_1 t$, $c(x, t)$ is, in this domain, a function of x only which we denote by: $c(x, 0)$:

$$r \geq c_1 t \quad c(x, t) = c(x, 0) \tag{3.5}$$

In the domain $r < c_1 t$ one has on the other hand:

$$c(x, t) = (-1/4b) \int_{r/c_1}^{t} G(x, t')dt' + C(x) \tag{3.6}$$

where $C(x)$ is an arbitrary function of x. If the integral (3.2) is summable (a point which is discussed in Appendix B), then $c(x, t)$ is a continuous function of x and t; if so, it is in particular continuous on the cone $r = c_1 t$ which implies that:

$$C(x) = c(x, 0)$$

To close the proof, it remains to obtain $c(x, 0)$; this is done in Appendix A.

3.1.2 Comments

What are the essential "ingredients" in the proof of theorem 1? The decomposition (3.3) clearly is of fundamental importance. However, its validity as an algebraic identity is in itself far from being sufficient. Algebraically, the fraction in the left-hand side may be decomposed in a number of different ways, for instance:

$$\frac{1}{\tilde{L}(q,\omega)\tilde{L}(q,-\omega)} = \frac{A\omega + B}{\tilde{L}(q,\omega)} + \frac{-A\omega + B}{\tilde{L}(q,-\omega)}$$

where:

$$A = \frac{ib}{4c^2(a^2 + q^2k^2)} \qquad B = \frac{1}{2(a^2 + q^2k^2)}$$

Yet, the terms in the right-hand side lead to integrals with respect to ω which are not even convergent.
Another factor of key importance is the fact that the numerators in the decomposition (3.3) do not depend upon q. This would for instance no longer be true for a dynamic pricing model of third order. Finally, the causality condition plays a crucial role.

3.1.3 Spatially autocorrelated noise

Theorem 1 can be extended to spatially correlated noise in the following form:

Theorem 2 We consider the random field $p(x, t)$ defined by:

$$Lp(x,t) = N(x,t) \qquad L(x,t) = (1/c^2)\partial^2_{t^2} + 2b\partial_t + a^2 - k\sum_{j=1}^{n} \partial^2_{x_j^2}$$

where the source term $N(x, t)$ is spatially autocorrelated:

$$c_N(x,t) = c_N(r)\delta(t) \qquad r = \|x\|$$

Then the covariance function $c(x, t)$ of the field $p(x, t)$ is given by:

$$c(x,t) = \begin{cases} (-1/4b)\int_0^t H_1(x,t')dt' + c(x,0) & r \geq c_1 t > 0 \\ (-1/4b)\int_{r/c_1}^t H_2(x,t')dt' + c(x,r/c_1) & r \leq c_1 t \end{cases} \tag{3.7a}$$

where:

$$c_1 = c/\sqrt{k}$$

$$c(x,0) = \frac{1}{(2\pi)^{n/2}(4b)k^{n/4+1/2}r^{n/2-1}} \int_0^\infty q^{n/2}\frac{J_{n/2-1}(qr/\sqrt{k})}{q^2+a^2}\widetilde{c}_N(q/\sqrt{k})dq \tag{3.7b}$$

J_ν: Bessel function of order ν.
H_1, H_2: solutions (vanishing at infinity) of the equation:

$$L(x,t)H(x,t) = c_N(x)\delta(t) \tag{3.8}$$

respectively in the region $r \geq c_1 t$ and $r \leq c_1 t$

Proof One has:

$$c(x,t) = \frac{1}{(2\pi)^{n+1}} \int_{\mathbf{R}^n} e^{-iqx}\widetilde{c}_N(q)dq \int_{-\infty}^{\infty} \frac{e^{-i\omega t}}{\widetilde{L}(q,\omega)\widetilde{L}(q,-\omega)}d\omega \tag{3.9}$$

The proof goes along the same lines as the proof of theorem 1 with the difference that in (3.4) the Green's function is to be replaced by the solution $H(x,t)$ of equation (3.8). Since $H(x,t)$ does *not* vanish for $r > c_1 t$, (3.5) should be replaced by (3.7a); because of the factor $\widetilde{c}_N(q,\omega)$ the integral over q can no longer be evaluated explicitly and one has to content oneself with the expression (3.7b) which is derived in Appendix A.

3.1.4 Numerical computation

For the space-like segment of the covariance function, theorem 1 gives a closed-form expression; for the time-like part one still has to compute the integral of the Green's function (over a finite interval). Why is this expression more convenient from the point of view of numerical computation than the initial Fourier integral? Numerically, Fourier integrals are rather tricky to evaluate for the following reasons:

1) Since the integration interval is infinite, it has to be truncated; for slowly decreasing functions, the truncated interval may still be rather large.

2) As ω (or q) becomes large, $e^{-i\omega t}$ (or e^{-iqx}) oscillates more and more rapidly thereby requiring smaller and smaller subdivisions.

These are rather conflicting conditions and may lead to extensive computation times.

Remark FFT (Fast Fourier Transform) algorithms are designed for the *discrete* Fourier transformation. Due to aliasing and to leakage they are not really suited to the computation of continuous Fourier transforms.

Another possibility one could think of would be to use the convolution integral. Table 9.1 summarizes the number of integrations that are required in each of these approaches.

	Convolution integral	Fourier transform	Passage theorem
Integration interval	infinite	infinite	finite
One spatial dimension			
White noise $C_N = \delta(x)\delta(t)$	2	2	1
Autocorrelated noise $C_N = \mathrm{f(x)}\delta(\mathrm{t})$	3	2	1
Autocorrelated noise $C_N = \mathrm{f(x)g(t)}$	4	2	does not apply
Two spatial dimensions			
White noise $C_N = \delta(x)\delta(t)$	3	2	1
Autocorrelated noise $C_N = \mathrm{f(x)}\delta(\mathrm{t})$	5	2	1
Autocorrelated noise $C_N = \mathrm{f(x)g(t)}$	6	2	does not apply

Table 9.1 Comparison of the number of numerical integrations that are required in order to compute the covariance function in three different approaches.

3.2 One and two-dimensional hyperbolic fields

3.2.1 White noise

• $n = 1$ For the application of the first passage theorem, two steps have to be taken:

1) Replace $K_{-1/2}$ by its expression in terms of exponentials, namely (Spiegel 1978, p.139):

$$K_{-1/2}(x) = \sqrt{\frac{\pi}{2x}}e^{-x}$$

2) Replace the Green's function by its explicit expression (Van der Pol 1950, p.348).

Thereby, one obtains (with $k = 1,\ \sigma_W^2 = 1$):

$$c(x,t) = \begin{cases} (1/8ab)e^{-a|x|} & |x| \geq ct > 0 \\ (-1/4b)\displaystyle\int_{|x|/c}^{t} G^{(1)}(x,t')dt' + \frac{1}{8ab}e^{-a|x|} & |x| \leq ct \end{cases} \tag{3.10a}$$

where:

$$G^{(1)}(x,t) = \begin{cases} \frac{c}{2}e^{-bc^2t}J_0\left[\sqrt{(a^2-b^2c^2)(c^2t^2-x^2)}\right]Y(ct-|x|) & a \geq bc \\ \frac{c}{2}e^{-bc^2t}I_0\left[\sqrt{(b^2c^2-a^2)(c^2t^2-x^2)}\right]Y(ct-|x|) & a \leq bc \end{cases} \tag{3.10b}$$

Y is the Heaviside function; I_0 is the modified Bessel function of first kind.

We note that the variance of prices is finite: $\sigma_p^2 = 1/8ab$.
As a result of Lebesgue's theorem, one should have the following limiting properties:

$$\lim_{|x|\to\infty} c(x,t) = 0 \qquad \lim_{t\to\infty} c(x,t) = 0$$

Let us check that these limits hold. The first one is obviously satisfied. In order to check the second, one has to evaluate the integral:

$$I = (-c/8b) \lim_{t\to\infty} \int_{x/c}^{t} = (-c/8b) \int_{x/c}^{\infty} J_0 \left[\sqrt{(a^2 - b^2c^2)(c^2t^2 - x^2)}\right] e^{-bc^2} dt$$

From Gradshteyn (1965, p.710), one obtains: $I = -e^{-ax}/8ab$ and thus:

$$\lim_{t\to\infty} c(x,t) = 0$$

The Figure 9.5 gives an illustration of the correlation function $\rho_x(t)$

• $n = 2$ In two dimensions, the Bessel function K_0 can no longer be expressed in terms of elementary functions. One obtains (with $k = 1$, $\sigma_W^2 = 1$):

$$c(x,t) = \begin{cases} \dfrac{1}{8\pi b} K_0(ar) & r \geq ct \\ \left(\dfrac{-1}{4b}\right) \displaystyle\int_{r/c}^{t} G^{(2)}(r,t')dt' + \dfrac{1}{8\pi b} K_0(ar) & r < ct \end{cases} \tag{3.11}$$

where:

$$G^{(2)}(r,t) = \begin{cases} \dfrac{c}{2\pi} e^{-bc^2 t} \dfrac{\cos\left[\sqrt{(a^2 - b^2c^2)(c^2t^2 - r^2)}\right]}{\sqrt{c^2t^2 - r^2}} Y(ct - r) & a \geq bc \\ \dfrac{c}{2\pi} e^{-bc^2 t} \dfrac{\cosh\left[\sqrt{(b^2c^2 - a^2)(c^2t^2 - r^2)}\right]}{\sqrt{c^2t^2 - r^2}} Y(ct - r) & a \leq bc \end{cases} \tag{3.12}$$

The variance $\sigma_p = c(0,0)$ is no longer finite for $K_0(ar)$ diverges as $r \to 0$.

Non-isotropic plane Throughout our discussion so far, we have made the assumption of isotropy. This condition is somewhat unrealistic, especially at small distances; it could be easily relaxed, however, by replacing $\partial_{x_1^2}^2 + \partial_{x_2^2}^2$ by a term: $k_1^2\partial_{x_1^2}^2 + k_2^2\partial_{x_2^2}^2$. The two constants k_1, k_2 may be absorbed in a redefinition of x_1 and x_2; the previous formulas thus remain valid provided r is replaced by: $r = \sqrt{(x_1/k_1)^2 + (x_2/k_2)^2}$.

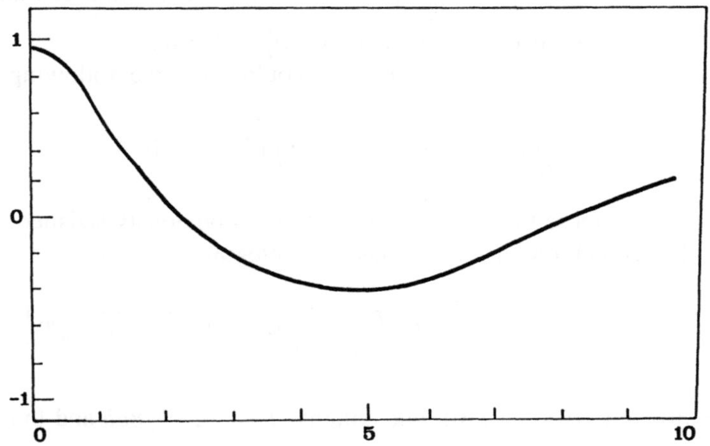

Fig.9.5 a autocorrelation $\rho_{x=0}(t)$ of prices within a chain of markets ruled by an hyperbolic equation with a white noise source term. Horizontal scale: t; $a = 1, b = 0.1, c = 0.5$.

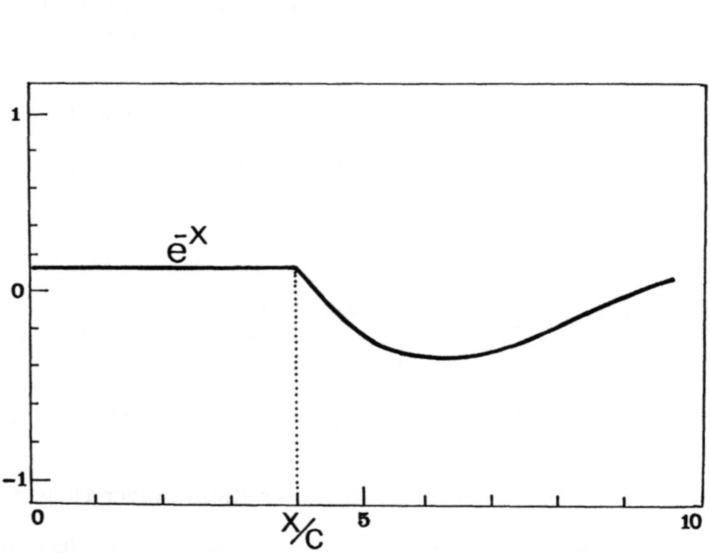

Fig.9.5 b Intercorrelation $\rho_x(t)$ between two markets a distance x apart (white noise). The two markets belong to an infinite chain of markets. Horizontal scale: t; $x = 2$. Prices on both markets are ruled by an hyperbolic equation with a white noise source term: $a = 1, b = 0.1, c = 0.5$. This figure should be compared to Fig.9.1. The decrease is no longer purely exponential but there is still a plateau.

3.2.2 Spatially autocorrelated noise

The source term may display an autocorrelation in time as well as in space. Yet, since the second passage theorem does not apply to time-autocorrelated noise, we shall in this paragraph restrict ourselves to spatial autocorrelation. An example of time-autocorrelated noise will be given below in the section about diffusion models.

More specifically, we shall in one dimension assume the following spatial autocorrelation function:

$$c_N(x) = \sigma^2 \frac{e^{-|x|/\lambda}}{2\lambda} \quad \Longrightarrow \quad \tilde{c}_N(q) = \frac{\sigma^2}{(\lambda q)^2 + 1} \tag{3.13}$$

The white noise case corresponds to the limit: $\lambda \to 0$.
Applying theorem 2, one obtains:

$$c(x,t) = \begin{cases} (-1/4b) \int_0^t H_1(x,t')dt' + c(x,0) & |x| \geq ct \\ (-1/4b) \int_{|x|/c}^t H_2(x,t') + c(x,x/c) & |x| \leq ct \end{cases} \tag{3.14}$$

where H_1, H_2 are the solutions of:

$$[(1/c^2)\partial_{t^2}^2 + 2b\partial_t - a^2 - \partial_{x^2}^2]H(x,t) = c_N(x)\delta(t) \tag{3.15}$$

respectively in the regions $|x| \geq ct$ and $|x| \leq ct$.
By Fourier transformation, one obtains $H(x,t)$ in the form

$$H(x,t) = \sigma^2 \frac{c}{\pi} e^{-bc^2 t} \int_0^\infty \frac{\cos(qx/\lambda) \sin\left[\frac{ct}{\lambda}\sqrt{q^2 + (h\lambda)^2}\right]}{(q^2+1)\sqrt{q^2 + (h\lambda)^2}} \tag{3.16}$$

In the general case there is no explicit expression for the integral in the region $t > x/c$. Therefore, let us first discuss the special case $a = bc$ for which a solution can be obtained in both regions. One obtains:

$$\rho(x,t) = \begin{cases} \dfrac{e^{-ax}}{1 - a\lambda} - \dfrac{a\lambda}{2} e^{-act} \left[e^{-(|x|+ct)/\lambda} + \dfrac{1 + a\lambda}{1 - a\lambda} e^{-(|x|-ct)/\lambda} \right] & |x| \geq ct \geq 0 \\ e^{-act} \left[1 + a\lambda(1 - e^{-ct/\lambda} \cosh(|x|/\lambda))\right] & |x| \leq ct \end{cases}$$

As expected, for $\lambda = 0$, the spatial segment of $\rho(x,t)$ is a function only of x; if λ is different from zero but remains small, we still have a plateau. This is illustrated in Fig.9.6a.

In the general case, the integral (3.16) may be obtained in the region $|x| \geq ct$ from Gradshteyn (1965, p.472):

$$H(x,t) = \frac{c^2}{2\lambda\beta} e^{-t\alpha} e^{-|x|/\lambda} \sin(t\beta) Y(t) \qquad |x| \geq ct \tag{3.17}$$

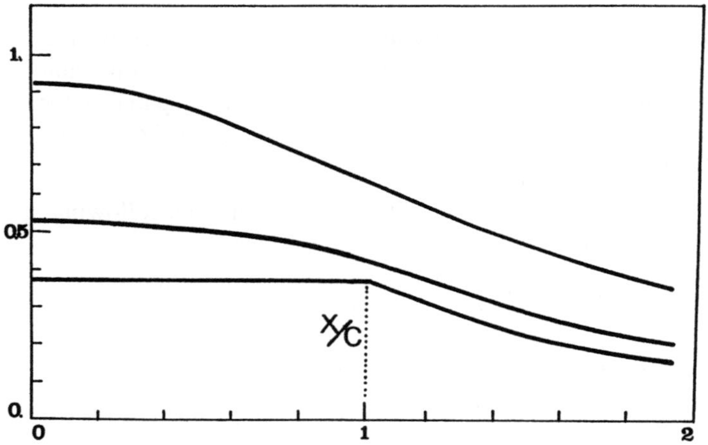

Fig.9.6 a Intercorrelation $\rho_x(t)$ **between two markets a distance** x **apart (non-white noise).** The two markets belong to an infinite chain of markets. Horizontal scale: t; $x = 1$. Prices on both markets are ruled by an hyperbolic equation: $a = 1, b = 1, c = 1, (a = bc)$; the source term consists of spatially autocorrelated noise. From bottom to top: $\lambda = 0$ (white noise), $\lambda = 0.35$, $\lambda = 4.1$. As λ becomes large, the plateau becomes less apparent.

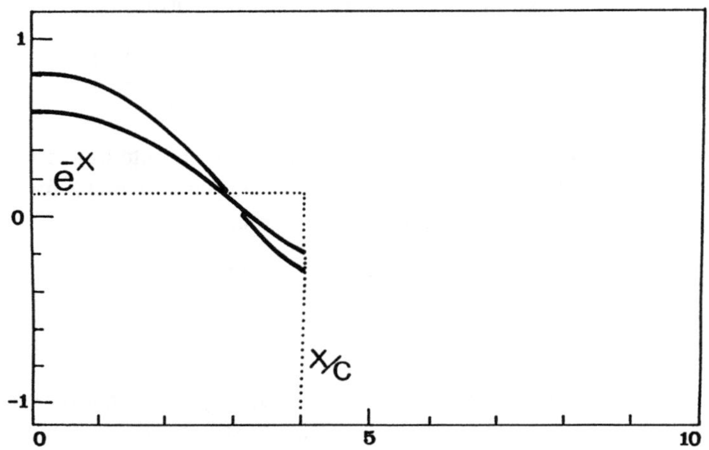

Fig.9.6 b Intercorrelation $\rho_x(t)$ **between two markets a distance** x **apart (non-white noise).** The two markets belong to an infinite chain of markets. Horizontal scale: t; $x = 2$. Prices on both markets are ruled by an hyperbolic equation: $a = 1, b = 0.1, c = 0.5, (a \neq bc)$; the source term consists of spatially autocorrelated noise. The curve starting from $\rho = 0.6$ corresponds to $\lambda = 2$, the curve starting from $\rho = 0.8$ corresponds to $\lambda = 5$.

where:

$$\alpha = bc^2 \qquad \beta = (c/\lambda)\sqrt{(h\lambda)^2 - 1}$$

In (3.17) it has been assumed that $h\lambda \geq 1$; for $h\lambda < 1$, there is a similar expression with the sinus replaced by sinh. From (3.14) one obtains:

$$c(x,t) = \frac{\sigma^2}{8b(1 - a^2\lambda^2)}\left[\frac{e^{-a|x|}}{a} - \frac{\lambda}{\beta}e^{-x/\lambda - \alpha t}(\alpha \sin\beta t + \beta\cos\beta t)\right] \qquad |x| \geq ct \tag{3.18}$$

Fig.9.6b shows that for $\lambda = 2$ or $\lambda = 5$, the curve of $c_x(t)$ does no longer exhibit any plateau.

Trade

In contrast to the white noise case $\partial_x c(x,t)$ is differentiable with respect to x at $x = t = 0$; therefore we are able to compute the trade expectation as given by (1.9); one obtains:

$$T = \sqrt{1/[8b(1 + a\lambda)]}$$

Trade decreases as exogenous shocks become more intercorrelated (i.e. when $\lambda \to \infty$). In the perspective of international trade this happens when all countries experience similar business fluctuations at the same time.

3.3 One and two dimensional parabolic fields

In this section, we have three objectives:

1) We show that parabolic fields can be considered as a limiting case of hyperbolic fields and that they can be treated by similar methods.

2) We emphasize that, as far as covariance functions are concerned, there is a marked similarity between hyperbolic fields with autocorrelated noise on one hand and parabolic fields on the other.

3) We provide an example of how a two-dimensional field may be "regularized" by the use of a time-autocorrelated source term.

The Green's function of an n-dimensional parabolic field is the solution of:

$$(\partial_t + a^2 - k^2\Delta_n)G(x,t) = \delta(x)\delta(t) \tag{3.19}$$

It is given by (Van der Pol 1950, p.323):

$$G(x,t) = \frac{e^{-a^2 t}}{k(4\pi t)^{n/2}}e^{-r^2/4k^2 t}Y(t) \qquad r = \|x\| \tag{3.20}$$

Two conclusions can be drawn from this expression:

1) $G(x,t)$ is different from zero everywhere for any $t > 0$; in other words, we have a signal which, strictly speaking, travels with infinite speed. This is consistent with the fact that (3.19) may be interpreted as the limit when $c \to \infty$

of a wave equation of the form (2.3). The increase rate of the width of the Gaussian curve (3.20) namely:

$$w = 2k\sqrt{t}$$

should however be considered as a more realistic estimate of the diffusion velocity.

2) Although the passage theorems apply, they are less useful here than in the hyperbolic case for the indefinite integral of (3.20) is rather awkward.

From the spectral function, one obtains directly the following expression of the covariance function:

$$c(x,t) = \frac{1}{(2\pi)^n}\frac{e^{-a^2t}}{2k}\int_{\mathbf{R}^n}\frac{e^{iqx/k-q^2t}}{q^2+a^2}dq \tag{3.21}$$

We shall now consider the cases $n = 1$ and $n = 2$.

3.3.1 One spatial dimension

(3.21) becomes:

$$c(x,t) = \frac{e^{-a^2t}}{2\pi}\int_0^\infty e^{-q^2t}\frac{\cos(qx/k)}{q^2+a^2}dq$$

From Erdéleyi (1954, p.15) one obtains for $t > 0$:

$$c(x,t) = \frac{1}{8ak}\left[e^{-a|x|/k}\mathrm{Erfc}\left(a\sqrt{t} - \frac{|x|}{2k\sqrt{t}}\right) + e^{a|x|/k}\mathrm{Erfc}\left(a\sqrt{t} + \frac{|x|}{2k\sqrt{t}}\right)\right] \tag{3.21}$$

where the function Erfc is defined as:

$$\mathrm{Erfc}(x) = \frac{2}{\sqrt{\pi}}\int_x^\infty e^{-t^2}dt$$

The following comments are in order:

• Let us consider the limit of large transportation costs, that is: $k \to 0$. From:

$$\mathrm{Erfc}(-\infty) = 2 \qquad \mathrm{Erfc}(\infty) = 0$$

one obtains:

$$c(x,t) \underset{k\to 0}{\sim} \frac{1}{8ak}e^{-|x|/k} \to \delta(x)/4a$$

• The covariance exists at the origin: $\lim_{t\to 0^+} c(0,t) = 4ak$; the derivative $\partial_x c(x,t)|_{x=t=0}$ diverges however.

• It is obvious that $c(x,t)$ does not display any oscillations. It is somewhat less apparent, but nevertheless true, that $c(x,t)$ is in fact monotonously decreasing with respect to both x and t. The two following special cases are typical of the general case:

$$c(x,0) = e^{-a|x|/k} \qquad c(0,t) = \text{Erfc}(a\sqrt{t}) \quad t > 0$$

3.3.2 Two spatial dimensions

In order to ensure continuity of $c(x,t)$ at the origin the source term should have an autocorrelation either in x or in t. One may take for instance:

• Autocorrelation in t:

$$c_N(x,t) = K\delta(x)c_N(t) \qquad c_N(t) = \frac{\nu}{2}e^{-\nu t} \Longrightarrow \tilde{c}_N(\omega) = \frac{\nu^2}{\omega^2+\nu^2}$$

• Autocorrelation in x:

$$c_N(x,t) = Kc_N(x)\delta(t) \qquad c_N(x) = \frac{\nu}{2}\frac{e^{-\nu r}}{r} \Longrightarrow \tilde{c}_N(q) = \frac{\nu}{\sqrt{q^2+\nu^2}}$$

Let us consider the autocorrelation in t; it leads to an expression of $c(x,t)$ which is rather involved; for the sake of simplicity, we shall rather discuss the special form $c(x,0)$ obtained from Gradshteyn (1965, p.678):

$$c(r,0) = \frac{1}{4\pi k^2}\left[K_0(\frac{a}{k}r) - K_0(\frac{\sqrt{a^2+\nu}}{k}r)\right] \tag{3.22}$$

Since $K_0(\infty) = 0$, $c(r,0)$ becomes in the white noise limit $\nu \longrightarrow \infty$:

$$c(r,0) = (1/4\pi k^2)K_0(\frac{a}{k}r)$$

As $r \longrightarrow 0$, it diverges along with $K_0(ar/k)$. On the contrary, for $\nu \neq 0$ and $r \longrightarrow 0$, one obtains:

$$c(r,0) \underset{r\rightarrow 0}{\sim} \frac{1}{8\pi k^2}\ln(1+\nu a^2)$$

where we used the following development of $K_0(x)$ about $x = 0$:

$$K_0(x) = -(\ln(x/2)+\gamma)I_0(x) + O(x^2) \quad \gamma : \text{Euler's constant}$$

Regarding differentiability, it can be shown that: $\partial^2_{x_1^2} + \partial^2_{x_2^2}\Big|_{r=t=0}$ diverges. In the previous section, we have seen that a regularization using spatial autocovariance was sufficient to ensure second order differentiability. It is not really surprising that a regularization using time-dependent autocovariance is found to be less effective in securing differentiability with respect to *space* variables.

3.4 Random fields on one and two-dimensional spheres

3.4.1 Economic rationale of the introduction of fields on compact manifolds

There are two main motivations for studying random fields on compact manifolds such as the circle S_1 or the sphere S_2:

1) The surface of the earth is a compact manifold. Locally an euclidian model may provide an adequate approximation. However, when studying markets all around the world, the natural framework is the surface of the sphere. This is inescapable.

2) Throughout our discussions so far, we have considered spatially separated markets. Another possible application would be the analysis of intersectorial interactions. The spatial distance would then be replaced by an intersectorial distance which could for instance be estimated from input-output tables. Very often, such interactions turn out to be cyclical; accordingly they have to be described as occurring on a compact manifold. This is illustrated in Fig.9.7.

3.4.2 Dynamic random field on the circumference of a circle

The field equation on the one-dimensional sphere S_1 reads:

$$L(\theta, t)p(\theta, t) = N(\theta, t) \tag{3.23a}$$

$$L(\theta, t) = (1/c^2)\partial^2_{t^2} + 2b\partial_t + a^2 - L_1(\theta) \tag{3.23b}$$

$$L_1(\theta) = \partial^2_{\theta^2} \qquad -\pi \leq \theta < \pi \tag{3.23c}$$

Formally, this equation is similar to the equation on the line. The difference comes from the parametrization by a closed interval $[-\pi, \pi]$. The Fourier transforms with respect to x, t that we have used previously are here replaced by "mixed" Fourier transforms: Fourier series with respect to θ, Fourier transforms with respect to t:

$$\widetilde{F}_n(\omega) = \int_{-\pi}^{\pi} e^{in\theta} d\theta \int_{-\infty}^{\infty} e^{i\omega t} F(\theta, t) dt \tag{3.24a}$$

The inverse transformation is:

$$F(\theta, t) = \frac{1}{(2\pi)^2} \sum_{n=-\infty}^{\infty} e^{-in\theta} \int_{-\infty}^{\infty} e^{-i\omega t} \widetilde{F}_n(\theta) d\omega \tag{3.24b}$$

The passage theorems apply. Our first task therefore is to calculate the Green's function.

	A	B	C	D	E	F
A	*	*				
B	*	*	*			
C		*	*	*		
D			*	*	*	
E				*	*	*
F					*	*

A $\longleftrightarrow$ B $\longleftrightarrow$ C $\longleftrightarrow$ D $\longleftrightarrow$ E $\longleftrightarrow$ F

Fig.9.7a Inter-sectorial interactions without cyclical interaction

	A	B	C	D	E	F
A	*	*				*
B	*	*	*			
C		*	*	*		
D			*	*	*	
E				*	*	*
F	*				*	*

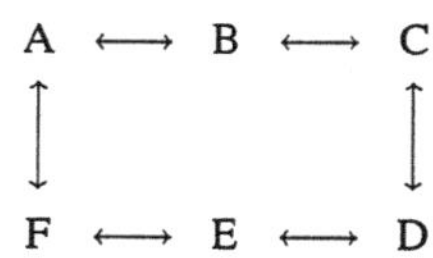

Fig.9.7b Inter-sectorial interactions with cyclical interaction

Green's function The Green's function is worked out in Appendix C. One obtains:

$$G(\theta, t) = \frac{c}{2} e^{-bc^2 t} \sum_{-(ct+\theta)/2\pi \leq n \leq (ct-\theta)/2\pi} J_0 \left[\sqrt{(a^2 - b^2c^2)[c^2t^2 - (\theta + 2n\pi)^2]} \right] \tag{3.25}$$

Fig.9.8a displays the function $G(\theta, t)$ with respect to θ. It can be interpreted in the following way:
At $t = 0$, two impulses C^+ and C^- start from $\theta = 0$: C^+ moves anti-clockwise, while C^- moves in a clockwise way. At $t = \pi/c$, the wave-front of C^+ and the wave-front of C^- overlap in the vicinity of $\theta = \pi$; such a superposition repeats itself again and again at times: $t = n\pi/c, \quad n = 2, 3, \ldots$. These successive superpositions eventually result in quite complicated patterns.
In intersectorial interactions, one direction of propagation may be favoured. Nevertheless, the wave front will repeatedly overlap (at times $t = 2n\pi/c$) with its own tail; the resulting pattern can be almost as chaotic as in Figure 9.8a.

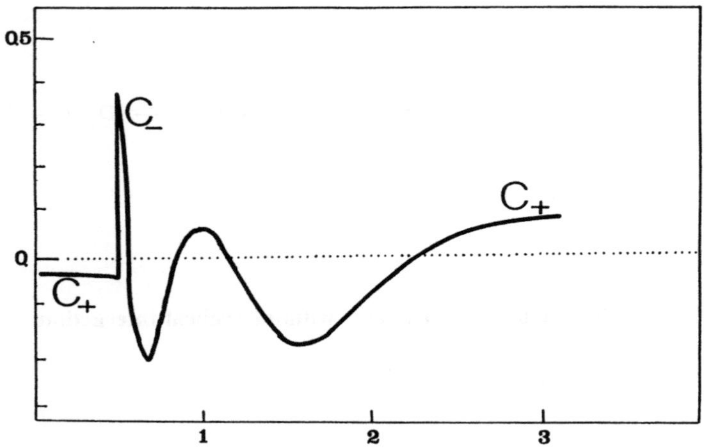

Fig.9.8 a Green's function $G_t(\theta)$ of an hyperbolic equation on the circle. Horizontal scale: angle θ; $a = 3, b = 1, c = 1,\ t = 5.7$. The curve is the superposition of two waves respectively propagating clockwise and anti-clockwise.

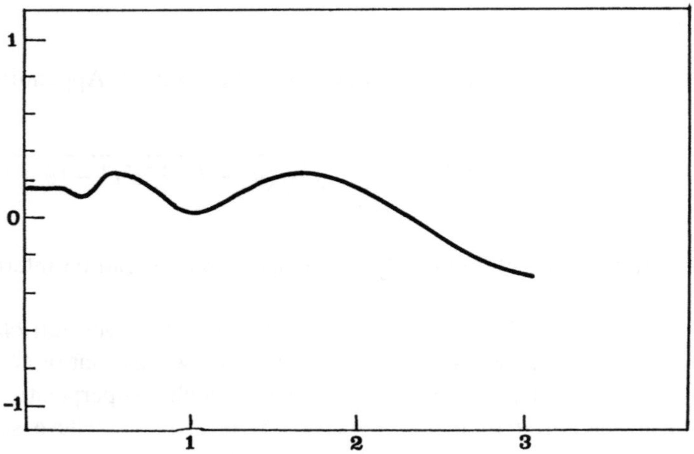

Fig.9.8 b Correlation function $\rho_t(\theta)$ of an hyperbolic field on the circle. Horizontal scale: angle θ. Parameters: $a = 3, b = 1, c = 1; t = 6$.

Correlation function For $c(\theta,0)$ one obtains:

$$c(\theta,0)=\frac{1}{8\pi b}\sum_{n=-\infty}^{\infty}\frac{e^{-in\theta}}{n^2+a^2} \tag{3.26}$$

The sum of the Fourier series is well known (Gradshteyn 1965, p.40).

$$c(\theta,0)=\frac{1}{8ab}\frac{\cosh[a(\pi-\theta)]}{\sinh(a\pi)} \qquad 0\leq\theta<2\pi \tag{3.27}$$

The first passage theorem therefore leads to the following correlation function:

$$\rho(\theta,t)=\begin{cases}\dfrac{\cosh[a(\pi-\theta)]}{\cosh(a\pi)} & 2\pi>\theta>ct\\ (-2a)\sinh(a\pi)\displaystyle\int_{\theta/c}^{t}G(\theta,t')dt'+\dfrac{\cosh[a(\pi-\theta)]}{\cosh(a\pi)} & ct>\theta\end{cases} \tag{3.28}$$

Fig.9.8b shows the function $\rho(\theta,t)$ with respect to θ.

3.4.3 Dynamic random field on the sphere

In this paragraph, we shall restrict ourselves to indicating the great lines of the calculation. The reason why we do not try to work out full expressions of the covariance function is that we have not been able to find satisfactory data concerning a worldwide set of markets. An adequate data set should give weekly prices for about 10 or 15 markets all around the world.

The field equation and the spherical harmonics The field equation reads:

$$L(\theta,\varphi;t)p(\theta,\varphi;t)=N(\theta,\varphi;t) \tag{3.29a}$$

$$L(\theta,\varphi;t)=(1/c^2)\partial^2_{t^2}+2b\partial_t+a^2-L_2(\theta,\varphi) \tag{3.29b}$$

$$L_2(\theta,\varphi)=\frac{1}{\sin\theta}\partial_\theta(\sin\theta\partial_\theta)+\frac{1}{\sin^2\theta}\partial^2_{\varphi^2} \tag{3.29c}$$

In the previous paragraph, we have introduced the eigenfunctions of the operator $L_1(\theta)$, namely:

$$L_1(\theta)=\lambda y \quad y(0)=y(2\pi) \quad\Longrightarrow\quad y_n(\theta)=\frac{e^{in\theta}}{\sqrt{2\pi}} \tag{3.30}$$

The development of a function defined on S_1 in terms of the $y_n(\theta)$ constitutes the Fourier series of a periodic function; the orthonormality and completeness relations are:

$$\int_{-\pi}^{\pi}y_n(\theta)y_m(\theta)=\delta_{nm} \qquad \sum_{n=-\infty}^{\infty}y_n(\theta)y_n(\theta')=2\pi\delta(\theta-\theta') \tag{3.31}$$

In the same way, we shall here introduce the eigenfunctions of $L_2(\theta, \varphi)$:

$$L_2 Y(\theta, \varphi) = \lambda Y(\theta, \varphi) \qquad Y(\theta, \varphi) = Y(\theta + \pi, \varphi + 2\pi) \tag{3.32}$$

These eigenfunctions are the spherical harmonics (Hobson 1965):

$$\lambda = -l(l+1) \qquad l : \text{non negative integer}$$

$$Y(\theta, \varphi) = Y_{lm}(\theta, \varphi) \quad -l \leq m \leq l \quad 0 \leq \theta \leq \pi \quad 0 \leq \varphi \leq 2\pi$$

The development of a function defined on S_2 in terms of the Y_{lm} constitutes the generalization of Fourier series to the sphere S_2. The development reads:

$$F(\theta, \varphi) = \sum_{l=0}^{\infty} \sum_{m=-l}^{l} \widetilde{F}_{lm} Y_{lm}(\theta, \varphi) \quad \widetilde{F}_{lm} = \int_0^{\pi} d\theta \int_0^{2\pi} d\varphi \sin\theta F(\theta, \varphi) \bar{Y}_{lm}(\theta, \varphi) \tag{3.33}$$

The orthonormality and completeness relations are:

$$\int_0^{2\pi} d\varphi \int_0^{\pi} d\theta \sin\theta \bar{Y}_{l'm'}(\theta, \varphi) Y_{lm}(\theta, \varphi) = \delta_{ll'} \delta_{mm'} \tag{3.34}$$

$$\sum_{l=0}^{\infty} \sum_{m=-l}^{l} \bar{Y}_{lm}(\theta, \varphi) Y_{lm}(\theta', \varphi') = \delta(\theta, \varphi; \theta', \varphi') \tag{3.35}$$

where $\delta(\theta, \varphi; \theta', \varphi')$, the Dirac's distribution on the sphere S_2, is defined by:

$$< \delta, f >= \int_0^{2\pi} d\varphi' \int_0^{\pi} d\theta' \sin\theta' \delta(\theta, \varphi; \theta', \varphi') f(\theta', \varphi') = f(\theta, \varphi) \tag{3.36}$$

Moreover, there is an additional summation formula which will prove useful subsequently:

$$\sum_{m=-l}^{l} \bar{Y}_{lm}(\theta', \varphi') Y_{lm}(\theta, \varphi) = \frac{2l+1}{4\pi} P_l(\cos\gamma) \tag{3.37}$$

where P_l is the Legendre polynomial of order l; the angle γ is defined by the relation:

$$\cos\gamma = \cos\theta\cos\theta' + \sin\theta\sin\theta'\cos(\varphi - \varphi') \tag{3.38}$$

Covariance function In order to apply the first passage theorem, we need the Green's function and $c(\theta, \varphi; \theta', \varphi'; t = 0)$. The calculation of the Green's function is given in Appendix C; the covariance function at $t = 0$ is obtained very much in the same way. The result is:

$$c(\theta, \varphi; \theta', \varphi'; t = 0) = -\frac{\pi}{8b\sin(\alpha'\pi)} P_{\alpha'}(-\cos\gamma) \tag{3.39}$$

where $P_{\alpha'}$ denotes the Legendre function of the first kind and:

$$\alpha' = -1/2 + \sqrt{1/4 - a^2}$$

4 Estimating the random field model

4.1 Selecting appropriate price data

The price data we are looking for are prices for a commodity of major economic importance at different market places and with a sampling time of the order of one week. Let us make some comments about these requirements:

- In contrast to Clark (1986) (see Chapter 8, Section 3.1.5) we cannot use local consumer price indexes. Such indexes may be appropriate on an annual basis; however, they are basically biased in so far as they reflect the composition of the index as well as the shifts in each of the components.
- The spatial localization of prices should be as precise as possible; accordingly market prices (or city averages as used in Clark 1986) should be preferred to regional averages.
- In our model we did not take into account (except at the level of the noise term) the impact of price changes in other products. This impact should therefore be kept as small as possible. In other words, the selected product should be one of major economic importance in such a way that its price fluctuations govern business fluctuations rather than being conditioned by them. Nineteenth century wheat prices fulfill this requirement especially before 1850.
- Our estimation procedure is based on the intercovariance functions; for these functions to be defined with adequate accuracy, the sampling time of the series should be as small as possible. The series we have selected have a sampling time of two weeks; if available, data with an even shorter sampling time would be preferable .

4.2 Identification: qualitative analysis of statistical evidence

In this paragraph, we describe some salient features of the price-covariance functions; this may in a sense be considered as the identification stage in our analysis.

4.2.1 Modifications of intercorrelation functions with distance

The curves in Fig.9.9 a,b,c show the intercorrelation (as a function of time-lag) for a number of market pairs corresponding to increasing inter-market distances. Three comments are in order:

1) In a perfectly integrated market all curves would be identical. Obviously, this is not the case.

2) The correlation between markets decreases with distance, a result which has already been established in Chapter 6.

3) The duration of the plateau increases with distance, a property which points to a wave equation model.

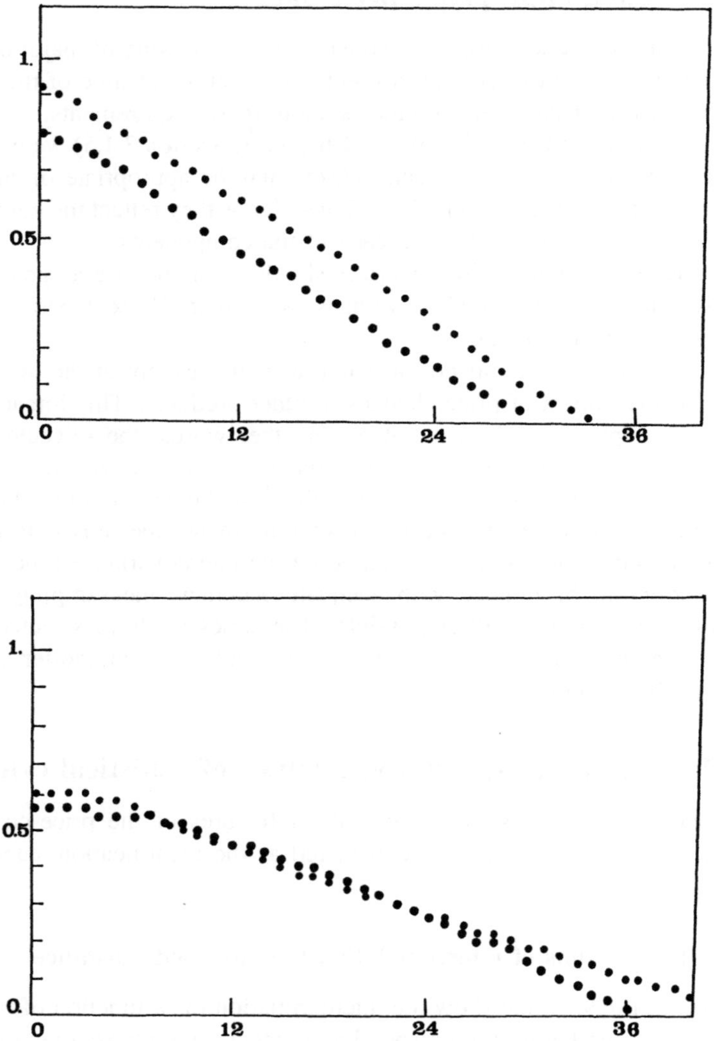

Fig.9.9 a,b Correlation functions $\rho_x(t)$ between wheat markets. Horizontal scale: fortnights. Upper figure: small dots: Albi-Montauban (64 km) 1825-1841; large dots: Mende-Albi (120 km) 1825-1841. Lower figure: small dots: Beaugency-Mende (390 km) 1833-1850; large dots: Clermont-Pau (390 km) 1825-1841.

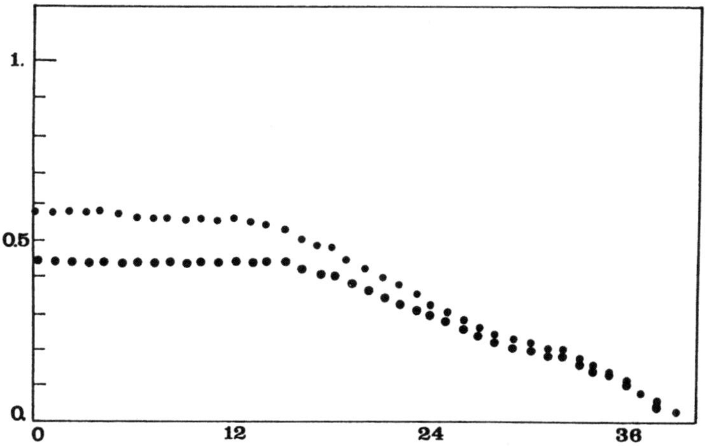

Fig.9.9 c Correlation functions $\rho_x(t)$ between wheat markets. Horizontal scale: fortnights. Small dots: Douai-Montauban (720km) 1830-1846; large dots: Arras-Albi (710 km) 1830-1846.

Confidence intervals for the intercovariance functions

Each correlation is computed from 400 (fortnight) prices. In spite of this rather large number, confidence intervals certainly cannot be considered as being negligible especially for large time-lags. The use of Bartlett's formula (Bartlett 1955, Box and Jenkins 1976) requires (even in its asymptotic form) a number of assumptions about the statistical properties of each series. As a crude order of magnitude, one could take the standard estimate: $\sigma(\hat{\rho}(r)) \sim 1/\sqrt{N}$ where N is the length of the series. This gives here: $\sigma(\hat{\rho}(r)) \simeq 0.05$; with $\hat{\rho}(r)$ of the order of 0.5 one obtains $\sigma(\hat{\rho}(r))/\hat{\rho}(r) \simeq 10\%$.

4.2.2 Wave models versus diffusion models

Regarding the choice between a wave equation and a diffusion model, the mere occurrence of plateaus in the correlation function is not conclusive for, as we have seen in Section 3, there is no clear distinction between a wave equation with an autocorrelated source term on one hand and a diffusion equation on the other. One could of course argue that since the wave equation includes the diffusion equation as a special case ($c = \infty$), the present discussion is rather pointless. This argument would be relevant if maximum likelihood estimates were separately available for each parameter. On the contrary, if one has to

rely on a global (mean square) fit, then estimating an additional parameter may affect all of them.
The question may be settled by examining whether there is evidence of an oscillatory behaviour in the correlation function. The conclusion is that, at least during specific periods, there is clear evidence of pseudo-periodic oscillations. Two examples pertaining to the autocorrelation $\rho(0,t)$ are shown in Fig.9.10. Another example referring to the intercorrelation function $\rho(x,0)$ is shown in

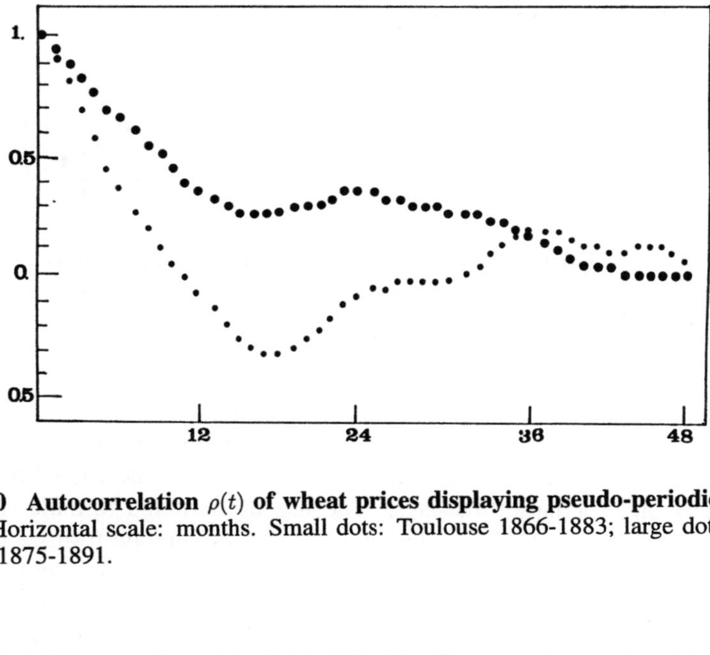

Fig.9.10 Autocorrelation $\rho(t)$ of wheat prices displaying pseudo-periodic oscillations. Horizontal scale: months. Small dots: Toulouse 1866-1883; large dots: Saint-Brieuc 1875-1891.

Fig.6.7b,d (Chapter 6) and in Table 9.2. The linear estimates in table 9.2 give the slope of the tangent to the curve $\rho(x, t = 0)$ in the vicinity of $x = 0$.

4.2.3 Specifying the disturbance term

It would of course be unrealistic to pretend that the disturbances occurring in the pricing process can strictly be described by white noise. For instance, the correlation length of climatic fluctuations is not equal to zero (see chapter 6, Section 2.3.2); the important point, however, is that it is much smaller than the correlation length of prices. Therefore, the white noise assumption constitutes a reasonable approximation; besides it is in line with our general option of keeping the number of free parameters as small as possible.

Lag (months)	Linear coefficient of correlation	Slope of the correlation function in the vicinity of $x = 0$ $(\times 10^2)$
0	-0.91	**-1.7**
2	-0.47	**-0.4**
4	0.31	**0.5**
6	0.51	**1.3**
8	0.55	**1.8**
10	0.56	**2.0**
12	0.50	**1.8**
14	0.47	**1.6**
16	0.44	**1.4**
18	0.38	**1.2**
20	0.30	**0.9**

Table 9.2 Slope of the correlation function $\rho_t(x)$ in the vicinity of $x = 0$. These results concern the group B, (i.e. the markets in an area surrounding Paris) and the period: 1841-1858.

4.3 Estimating a random wave equation

4.3.1 Procedure

At this stage we shall not embark on an attempt to propose maximum likelihood estimators; instead we shall use the method of moments which constitutes a rather cautious estimating approach, though probably not the most efficient.

Selection of market sets We have at our disposal about 50 price series. These data (published in Drame et al 1991) have specifically been compiled from the French Archives Nationales in order to comply with the requirements listed above in Section 4.1.

Treating a market set of 50 markets would require extensive computation without being very informative. Alternatively, we may select different subsets in the following way.
Firstly, we have selected two subsets *at random* among those series which have almost no gaps:
1) The first subset, which will be referred to as group 1, includes 14 markets: BAYEUX, BERNAY, BLOIS, BORDEAUX, CARCASSONNE, CHATEAUROUX, EVREUX, MARANS, MARSEILLE, PEYREHORADE, PONT L'ABBE, SAINT-BRIEUC, TOULOUSE, VITRE.

2) The second subset, referred to as group 2, includes 11 markets:
ALBI, ARRAS, BEAUGENCY, DOUAI, CLERMONT, LE MANS, LYON, MACON, MONTAUBAN, ROUEN, VANNES.

The second collection of subsets have been formed with a concern about homogeneity:
1) The first subset, referred to as group A, includes 11 ports:
BAYEUX, BORDEAUX, DIEPPE, CHERBOURG, MARANS, MARSEILLE, NANTES, PONT-L'ABBE, ROUEN, SAINT-BRIEUC, VANNES.

2) The second subset includes 11 markets of the wheat plains of Normandy and Beauce; it will be referred to as group B:
AUXERRE, BEAUGENCY, BERNAY, BLOIS, BOURGES, CHARTRES, CHATEAUDUN, CHATEAUROUX, EVREUX, LOUVIERS, ROUEN.

Intercorrelation for given inter-market distances We shall follow a procedure which is similar to the one described in Chapter 4 (Section 4.1). The market in the former subsets are arranged into pairs corresponding to inter-market distances ranging from 0 to about 800 km; for distances x in a given interval $x, x + \Delta x$ the function $\rho_x(t)$ is then obtained by averaging over market pairs belonging to this interval of distances.

Spatial dimension of the model As a first approximation, we have used a one-dimensional model. The rationale behind this choice is the following:

- A two-dimensional field would require a regularization; yet, this condition comes in conflict with our preference for white noise.
- The subsets 1,2 and B are rather stripe-shaped areas, which makes a one-dimensional model not unrealistic.

The question of stationarity Although the series are not stationary over the whole period 1825-1913, they may be quasi-stationary (to second order) in subintervals. Actually, the discussion of stationarity in Chapter 6 (Appendix A and B) applies here again without significant changes.

4.3.2 Hypothesis tests of the model

Apart from assessing the quality of the fit (see also Fig.9.11a,b), we shall have to check that the parameters of the model remain the same (in the limit of statistical fluctuations):

- within the whole range of inter-market distances.
- within the different subsets 1,2,A,B

These conditions are to some extent related. For to get large inter-market

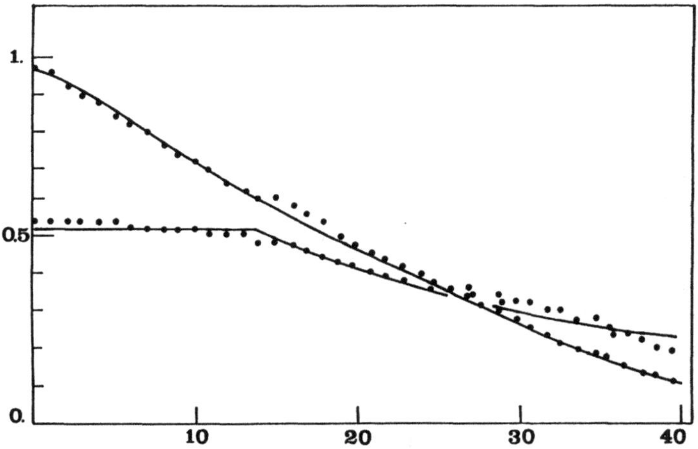

Fig.9.11 a Comparison of the estimated model to observations. The curve without a plateau is the average intercorrelation for the pairs: Bernay-Evreux and Carcassonne-Toulouse in the period 1825-1841. Average distance=64 km. Estimated parameters: $a = 5.6\ 10^{-4}$, $b = 3.6\ 10^{-6}$, $c = 48$; $Q = 1.1\%$. The curve with the plateau is the average intercorrelation for the pairs: Carcassonne-Evreux and Carcassonne-Bernay in the period 1825-1841. Average distance=655 km. Estimated parameters: $a = 9.2\ 10^{-4}$, $b = 2.6\ 10^{-5}$, $c = 48$; $Q = 4.0\%$.

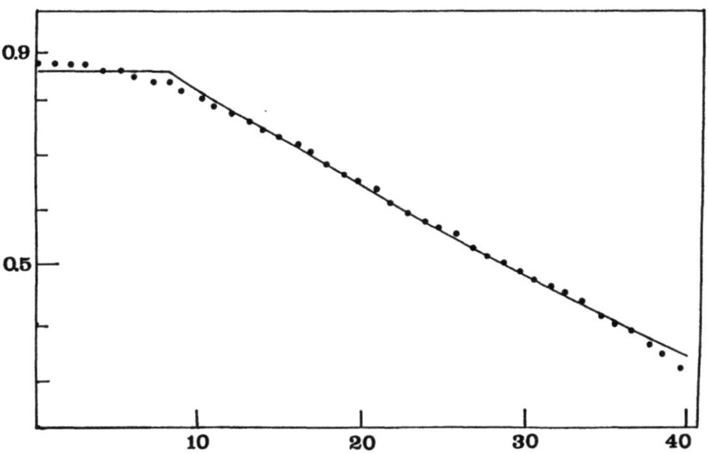

Fig.9.11 b Comparison of the estimated model to observations. The curve is the average intercorrelation for the pairs: Rouen-Albi, Arras-Montauban, Douai-Montauban, Douai-Albi in the period 1845-1861. Average distance=720 km. Estimated parameters: $a = 2.2\ 10^{-4}$, $b = 1.6\ 10^{-6}$, $c = 82$; $Q = 1.4\%$.

distances one has to put together in the same sample markets from distant regions which the effect of increasing sample heterogeneity.

From Table 9.3 we observe that:

- The factor Q[1]is almost always less than 5%.
- The coefficients of variation of the parameters a and c are of the order of 15%; the coefficient of variation of b is not really meaningful since this parameter is very small.

An additional comment is in order regarding the wave velocity c. Its estimates which is of the order of 100 km/month could seem to be rather small in comparison to average speeds of transportation in the nineteenth century. Two comments may clarify this point:

1) The most accurate estimates of c come from large inter-market distances ($d > 500$ km). Now, one should recall from Chapter 4, that even by 1850, transportation by road over such long distances were almost negligible. Thus the velocity c rather measures the speed of a contagion process of the kind shown in Fig.9.12: shipments are made to nearby markets with in each case stocking delays.

2) On top of transportation time, one should take into account the inertia of each market (stocking time for instance), that is to say its response delay to a given price shift. An analogy may help at this point: the velocity of sound in a gas is smaller than the velocity of the molecules: for a monoatomic gas the ratio of both velocities is equal to:$\sqrt{5/3} = 0.74$; moreover, in a mixture of gases the velocity of sound v_s is determined by the velocity V of the *slowest* molecules; in air $v_s = 330\ m/s$ while:

$$V = \sqrt{2kT/m} \Longrightarrow V_{O_2} = 660 \text{ m/s} \quad V_{N_2} = 500 \text{ m/s}$$

4.3.3 Time evolution of estimated parameters

Table 9.4 gives the evolution of the model's parameters during the period 1825-1913. Let us focus our attention on the parameter c. Between 1833 and 1891, there is a dramatic increase. We can note in passing that, as c increases, its measure becomes less accurate; to keep accuracy unchanged would require price series with smaller and smaller sampling times.

This process of increasing market integration has already been described in chapter 4 and in chapter 6; our main purpose here is not to describe this process which can be done with simpler analytical means. The increase of c merely provides a consistency test of the estimation procedure.

---

[1]Q denotes the residual normalized squares i.e. the ratio of the sum of squared residuals to the sum of squared observations.

Region	Group 1	Group 2	Group A Ports	Group B Around Paris	Average over 4 regions
Number of markets	14	14	10	11	
Max. distance between markets	700 km	680 km	520 km	270 km	
a: average	$7.74\ 10^{-4}$	$1.02\ 10^{-3}$	$7.39\ 10^{-4}$	$1.03\ 10^{-3}$	$8.9\ 10^{-4}$
coefficient of variation	24%	22%	15%	8%	17%
b: average	$1.44\ 10^{-5}$	$2.58\ 10^{-5}$	$2.22\ 10^{-5}$	$6.00\ 10^{-6}$	$1.7\ 10^{-5}$
coefficient of variation	80%	60%	24%	139%	75%
c: average	48	36	35	31	37
coefficient of variation	0.3%	23%	31%	11%	16%
Goodness fit (Q)	3.8%	5.3%	4.3%	1.7%	3.7%

Table 9.3 Estimating a random wave equation. The period is: 1825-1841. The index Q gives the residual normalized squares, i.e. the ratio of the sum of squared residuals to the sum of squared observations

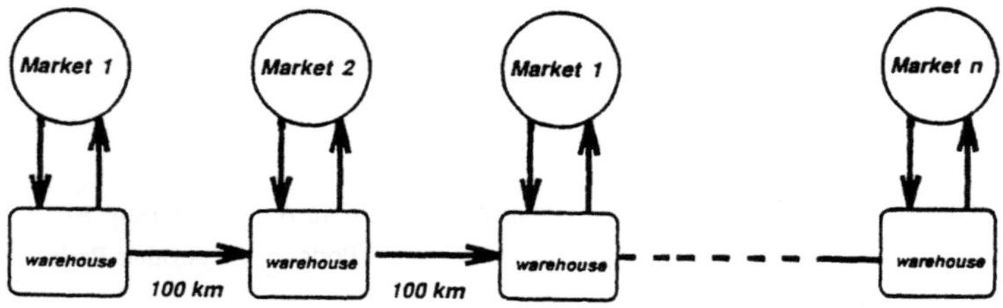

Fig.9.12 Contagion model of wheat prices transmission. Before 1850, shipments by road were rarely made over distances exceeding 100 - 200 km. Long range transportation thus took the form of a contagion process; this may explain the low wave velocities that have been observed.

In August 1936, with the creation of the "Office National Inter-professionnel du Blé", a single price of wheat was set up all over the country. Subsequently, in 1962, price controls have been lifted again with the result of restoring inter-regional price differentials.

4.3.4 Epidemic velocities

Let us compare the velocities estimated above to observed epidemic velocities. Table 9.5 gives approximate velocities for three epidemics: plague, Asiatic cholera and influenza. Since the contamination risk is usually highest at the end of the incubation period, incubation times provide an estimate of how fast contamination of susceptibles occurs. Epidemics usually do no propagate with a well defined wave front; the propagation is rather of mixed hierarchical/contagious type (Cliff et al 1981, p.9). Plague may be an exception[2]. The figures in Table 9.5 should be considered as orders of magnitude rather than as precise estimates.

Another possible application of the diffusion and propagation models developed in this chapter concern the diffusion of collective violence; see for instance in this respect Bishop (1974), Burbeck et al (1978), Pitcher et al (1978).

[2]Plague is primarily a disease of rodents and man enters only accidentally into the usual cycle; the disease originates from contact with the fleas of infected rodents. While the cycle rodent-flea-rodent is potentially present in animal communities at all times it is only in special circumstances that it reaches epizootic proportions.

		1 1833	2 1841	3 1850	4 1858	5 1866	6 1875	7 1883	8 1891
1	a 10^4	8.0	5.7	3.1	1.6	3.0	7.6	6.3	1.3
1	b	1.5 10^{-5}	1.2 10^{-5}	8.3 10^{-7}	3.9 10^{-11}	2.0 10^{-11}	1.9 10^{-6}	2.1 10^{-5}	1.4 10^{-6}
1	c	46	76	88	129	114	92	100	228
1	Q	4%	2%	2%	4%	7%	5%	2%	6%
2	a 10^4	10.	7.7	3.7	1.9	2.2	4.1	3.8	2.2
2	b	2.0 10^{-5}	6.0 10^{-6}	2.0 10^{-7}	4.9 10^{-12}	3.6 10^{-10}	1.3 10^{-5}	1.2 10^{-5}	1.1 10^{-7}
2	c	36	51	58	100	120	124	281	125
2	Q	6%	5%	2%	5%	8%	7%	3%	5%
A	a 10^4	9.7	3.2	2.0	1.7	2.3	5.6		
A	b	2.0 10^{-5}	1.9 10^{-6}	7.2 10^{-7}	3.6 10^{-12}	1.4 10^{-11}	1.8 10^{-6}		
A	c	24	69	63	40	41	56		
A	Q	2%	5%	3%	6%	8%	7%		
B	a 10^4	8.2	4.0	3.2	4.5	7.3	9.0	6.5	
B	b	2.0 10^{-6}	6.5 10^{-7}	1.7 10^{-9}	4.9 10^{-8}	3.7 10^{-8}	3.1 10^{-6}	1.7 10^{-5}	
B	c	24	69	63	40	41	56	74	
B	Q	2%	5%	3%	6%	8%	7%	4%	
AVERAGE	a 10^4	**9.0**	**5.2**	**3.0**	**2.4**	**3.7**	**6.6**	**5.5**	**1.8**
AVERAGE	c	**35**	**82**	**81**	**93**	**96**	**56**	**151**	**176**

Table 9.4 Estimating a random wave equation for different time periods. There is a marked tendency to increased market integration. The period around 1875 is somewhat atypical: this should probably be attributed to the depression of 1873-1880, rather than to the short war between France and Prussia (1870)

Disease	Incubation time	Velocity	Source
Plague	3 to 10 days	100 km/month	Fossier (1983, p.60)
Asiatic cholera	1 day	800 km/month	Cliff et al (1981, p.28-30)
Influenza	a few hours to 2 days	180 km/month	Cliff et al (1981, p.14)

Table 9.5 Approximate velocities of epidemics. Incubation times provide an estimate of how fast contamination occurs for the contamination risk is usually highest at the end of the incubation period.

A Appendix A: Expression of $c(x,0)$ for a wave equation

From (3.9) one has:

$$c(x,0) = \frac{1}{(2\pi)^{n+1}} \int_{\mathbf{R}^n} e^{-iqx} \widetilde{c}_N(q) I(t,q) dq \qquad \text{(A1a)}$$

where:

$$I(t,q) = \int_{-\infty}^{\infty} \frac{e^{-i\omega t}}{\widetilde{L}(q,\omega)\widetilde{L}(q,-\omega)} d\omega \qquad \text{(A.1b)}$$

First, we prove the following result:

Lemma A If:

$$J(t) = \int_{-\infty}^{\infty} \frac{e^{-i\omega t}}{D(\omega)} d\omega$$

where: $D(\omega) = d(\omega)\bar{d}(\omega)$ $d(\omega) = \omega^2 - 2i\omega\beta - A^2$, then, for $A > |\beta|$:

$$J(t) = \frac{\pi}{2} \frac{e^{-t|\beta|}}{|\beta| A^2 a} [a\cos(ta) + |\beta| \sin(ta)] \quad t \geq 0$$

where: $a = \sqrt{A^2 - \beta^2}$. In particular:

$$J(0) = \frac{\pi}{2} \frac{1}{|\beta| A^2}$$

Proof First we factorize $D(\omega)$; introducing the parameter: $a = \sqrt{A^2 - \beta^2}$ one has:

$$D(\omega) = \omega^2 - 2i\omega\beta - (a^2 + \beta^2) = (\omega - s_1)(\omega - s_2)$$

where: $s_1 = -a - i\beta, \qquad s_2 = a - i\beta$
hence:

$$D(\omega) = (\omega - s_1)(\omega - \bar{s}_1)(\omega - s_2)(\omega - \bar{s}_2)$$

Next, we carry out the integration by the theorem of residues; since $t > 0$, the contour will be closed in the lower half plane so that only the poles s_1 and s_2 are to contribute when $\beta > 0$. This leads for $\beta > 0$ to the result given in the lemma. Furthermore, $D(\omega)$ can also be written:

$$D(\omega) = (\omega^2 - 2\omega a + a^2 + \beta^2)(\omega^2 + 2\omega a + a^2 + \beta^2)$$

which shows that $J(t)$ only depends on the absolute value of β.

Before applying Lemma A, we perform two obvious variable changes in (A.1), namely: $\omega' = \omega/c \quad q' = \sqrt{k}q$. Then, applying the lemma with: $A^2 = a^2 + q'^2$ and $\beta = bc$, one obtains:

$$c(x,0) = \frac{1}{4b}\frac{k^{-n/2}}{(2\pi)^n}\int_{\mathbf{R}^n} e^{-iq'x\sqrt{k}}\frac{\widetilde{c}_N(q'/\sqrt{k})}{q'^2+a^2}dq' \qquad \text{(A.2)}$$

Since $c_N(x,t)$ is assumed to be a function only of $r = \|x\|$, $\widetilde{c}(q')$ will be a function of the norm of q'; this norm, we denote by q' (no confusion should arise in a given context). As a result the Fourier transform can be expressed as a simple integral (Schwartz 1961, p.224-225):

$$c(x,0) = \frac{1}{(2\pi)^{n/2}(4b)k^{n/4+1/2}r^{n/2-1}}\int_0^\infty q'^{n/2}\frac{J_{n/2-1}(q'r/\sqrt{k})\widetilde{c}_N(q'/\sqrt{k})}{q'^2+a^2}dq' \qquad \text{(A.3)}$$

This is the expression given in theorem 2.

Under the white noise assumption, one has $\widetilde{c}_N(q) = \sigma_W^2$ and the integral (A.3) can be evaluated explicitly by using the following result from Gradshteyn (1965, p.686):

$$\int_0^\infty q^{n/2}\frac{J_{n/2-1}(qr)}{q^2+a^2}dq = a^{n/2-1}K_{n/2-1}(ar) \qquad 1 \leq n \leq 4 \qquad \text{(A.4)}$$

This leads to the result given in theorem 1.

At this point, it is appropriate to carry out the two following verifications:

Limit of $c(x,0)$ when $k \to 0$ As $k \to 0$, one expects that:

$$\lim_{k\to 0} c(x,0) = K\delta(x) = K'\frac{\delta(r)}{r^{n-1}}$$

In order to prove this limit, it is sufficient to show that (Schwartz 1961, p.104, Papoulis 1962 p.280):

1) $\lim_{k\to 0} c(x,0) = 0$
2) $\int_0^\infty c(r,0)r^{n-1}dr$ is independent of k.

The first property results from the asymptotic behaviour of K_n:

$$K_n(x) \underset{x\to\infty}{\sim} \frac{e^{-x}}{\sqrt{2\pi x}}$$

The second property results from the following formula (Gradshteyn 1965, p.684):

$$\int_0^\infty r^\mu K_\nu(ar)dr = \frac{C(\mu,\nu)}{a^{\mu+1}}$$

where $C(\mu, \nu)$ is independent of a.

Dimensional verification Let us here extend the dimensional verification that has been carried out in Section 1.2.2. Substituting the following dimensions:

$$[k] = [L]^2 \quad [b] = [T] \quad a : \text{without dimension} \quad [\sigma_W^2] = [P]^2[L]^n[T]$$

in $c(x, 0)$ as given in theorem 1, one obtains: $[c(x, 0)] = [P]^2$. Furthermore, if one takes into account that:

$$[c_N(x)] = [P]^2[T] \Longrightarrow [\tilde{c}(q)] = [P]^2[T][L]^n$$

one obtains from the expression of $c(x, 0)$ given in theorem 2: $[c(x, 0)] = [P]^2$.

B Appendix B: Existence, continuity and differentiability of the Fourier integral

In this Appendix, we discuss the continuity and differentiability of the inverse Fourier integral (3.2) according to the number of spatial dimensions.

B.1 Continuity

One has the obvious inequality:

$$|c(x,t)| = \left| \int \frac{e^{-i(qx+\omega t)}}{\widetilde{L}(q,\omega)\widetilde{L}(q,-\omega)} dq d\omega \right| < \int \frac{dq d\omega}{|\widetilde{L}(q,\omega)|^2} = I$$

Thus, according to Lebesgue's theorem, $c(x,t)$ is continuous (with respect to x, t) if the function $1/|L(q,\omega)|^2$ is integrable. We shall show that I exists when calculated by successive integrations; integrability then results by the converse of Fubini's theorem for positive functions.

$$I = K_1 \int_0^\infty q^{n-1} dq \int_0^\infty \frac{d\omega}{|L(q,\omega)|^2}$$

Applying lemma A (Appendix A), one obtains:

$$I = K_2 \int_0^\infty \frac{q'^{n-1}}{q'^2 + a^2} dq'$$

The integral in the right-hand side converges when $n = 1$; it diverges when $n \geq 2$. In the last case, however we may still have continuity, and even differentiability, in $\mathbf{R}^{n+1}$ deprived of the origin.

B.2 Continuity and differentiability in $\mathbf{R}^{n+1} - (0,0)$

We first consider the case $n = 2$. We again apply lemma A, but this time with $t \neq 0$; the covariance function becomes:

$$c(x,t) = \int_0^\infty \frac{qJ_0(qr)}{q^2+a^2} \left[\cos(t\sqrt{q^2+\beta}) + \frac{\sin(t\sqrt{q^2+\beta})}{\sqrt{q^2+\beta}} \right] \quad \beta = a^2 - b^2c^2 \tag{B.1}$$

For definiteness we assume that $\beta > 0$ but this assumption is not essential. Now, it is sufficient to discuss the integral corresponding to the first term, since the integral with the sinus converges more rapidly; thus, we consider:

$$I(\nu; r, t) = \int_0^\nu \frac{qJ_0(qr)\cos(t\sqrt{q^2+\beta}\,)}{q^2+a^2} dq \tag{B.2}$$

To prove the continuity of $c(x,t)$, one has to show that, as $\nu \to \infty$, $I(\nu; r, t)$ converges uniformly in the region $r \geq \delta_2 > 0, \quad t \geq \delta_2 > 0$. Since $|J_0(x)| \leq 1$ and since $q/(q^2 + a^2)$ is integrable on $[0, \nu]$, we obviously have convergence; in order to have uniform convergence, one has to show that: $R_\nu = \int_\nu^\infty$ is bounded by a sequence u_ν converging to zero and independent of r and t. To this end, we use the asymptotic development (Magnus 1966, p.139):

$$J_0(x) = \sqrt{\frac{2}{\pi x}}[\cos(x - \pi/4) + O(x)] \tag{B.3}$$

R_ν comprises two terms, each of which corresponds to a function which is integrable over $(0, \infty)$.

For the discussion of differentiability of $c(x,t)$ with respect to t, the argument is essentially the same. Now, however, the substitution of (B3) in R_ν does no longer lead to integrals which converge over $(0, \infty)$. One therefore has to resort to Abel's theorem (Schwartz 1961,p.44); accordingly, one has to find an upper bound for the integral

$$\int_c^d \cos(qr - \pi/4)\cos(t\sqrt{q^2 + \beta}\,)dq$$

that is independent of c, d, r, t. This is easily done by first transforming the product into a sum and then by changing the argument of $\cos f(q)$ into $u = f(q)$ where $f(q)$ is a bounded function.

The foregoing proof for $n = 2$ can be adapted to $n = 3, 4, 5$; the results are summarized in Table 9.B.

Number of spatial dimensions	Existence of $C_X(x,t)$ $(\vec{x},t) \neq (\vec{0},0)$	Continuity of $C_X(x,t)$ $(\vec{x},t) \neq (\vec{0},0)$	Derivability of $C_X(x,t)$ $(\vec{x},t) \neq (\vec{0},0)$	Existence of $C_X(0,0)$
1	yes	yes	yes	yes
2	yes	yes	yes	no
3	yes	yes	no	no
4	yes	yes	no	no
5	yes	no	no	no

Table 9.B Existence, continuity and derivability of the inverse Fourier integral of the covariance function of an hyperbolic equation

C Appendix C: Green's functions of wave equations on one and two dimensional spheres

C.1 Green's function on S_1

We have to solve the equation:

$$[(1/c^2)\partial^2_{t^2} + 2b\partial_t + a^2 - \partial^2_{\theta^2}]G(x,t) = \delta(x)\delta(\theta) \tag{C.1}$$

First we eliminate the term $2b\partial_t$ by the change of function:

$$G(\theta,t) = ce^{-bc^2t}g(\theta,\tau) \qquad \tau = ct \tag{C.2}$$

$g(\theta,\tau)$ is the solution of:

$$(\partial^2_{\tau^2} + \alpha^2 - \partial^2_{\theta^2})g(\theta,\tau) = \delta(\theta)\delta(\tau) \qquad \alpha^2 = a^2 - b^2c^2 \tag{C.3}$$

Using the transformation (3.24) we are led to the following Fourier series:

$$g(\theta,\tau) = \frac{1}{2\pi}\sum_{n=-\infty}^{\infty} e^{-in\theta}\frac{\sin(\tau\sqrt{n^2+\alpha^2}\,)}{\sqrt{n^2+\alpha^2}} \tag{C.4}$$

where we have used the formula:

$$\text{v.p.}\int_{-\infty}^{\infty}\frac{e^{-i\omega t}}{a^2-\omega^2} = \frac{2\pi}{a}\sin(ta)$$

In order to obtain a summation formula for the series (C.4) we introduce an integral representation of the function $\sin(\tau\sqrt{n^2+\alpha^2})/\sqrt{n^2+\alpha^2}$ (Gradshteyn 1965, p.737):

$$\frac{\sin(\tau\sqrt{n^2+\alpha^2}\,)}{\sqrt{n^2+\alpha^2}} = \int_0^\tau J_0(\alpha\sqrt{\tau^2-\lambda^2}\,)\cos n\lambda d\lambda \tag{C.5}$$

Formally exchanging the summation and the integration, one obtains:

$$g(\theta,\tau) = \frac{1}{2\pi}\int_0^\tau d\lambda J_0(\alpha\sqrt{\tau^2-\lambda^2}\,)\sum_{n=\infty}^{\infty}\cos(n\lambda)\cos(n\theta) \tag{C.6}$$

The series in (C.6) only converges in the space of distributions (Schwartz 1961,p.171):

$$\sum_{n=-\infty}^{\infty}\cos(n\lambda)\cos(n\theta) =$$

$$\frac{1}{2}\Re\sum_{n=-\infty}^{\infty}\left[e^{in(\theta+\lambda)} + e^{in(\theta-\lambda)}\right] = \pi\sum_{n=-\infty}^{\infty}[\delta(\theta+\lambda+2n\pi) + \delta(\theta-\lambda+2n\pi)]$$

Substituting into (C.6), one obtains:

$$g(\theta,\tau) = (1/2) \sum_{-(\tau+\theta)/2\pi \leq n \leq (\tau-\theta)/2\pi} J_0\left[\alpha\sqrt{\tau^2 - (\theta + 2n\pi)^2}\right] \tag{C.7}$$

When either $(\tau + \theta)/2\pi$ or $(\tau - \theta)/2\pi$ is an integer, the corresponding term should be multiplied by $1/2$; this comes from the fact that for an even function:

$$\int_0^\infty \delta(x)f(x)dx = f(0)/2 \tag{C.8}$$

In fact, the summation formula (C.7) is given in Hansen (1975, p.268) with, however, a misprint in the summation bounds. When $a^2 - b^2c^2$ is negative, the function J_0 has to be replaced by I_0. The result (C.7) bears a resemblance to the Green's function on **R**; this is not surprising since the circle can locally be approximated by its tangent.

C.2 Green's function on $\mathbf{S}_2$

The field equation for the Green's function on the two-dimensional sphere reads:

$$L(\theta,\varphi;t)G(\theta,\varphi;\theta',\varphi';t) = \delta(\theta,\varphi;\theta',\varphi')\delta(t) \tag{C.9}$$

Since we do no longer have translational invariance as in the Euclidian case the Green's function depends on the *two* points (θ,φ) and (θ',φ') and not only on the differences $\theta - \theta'$ and $\varphi - \varphi'$.
Transforming equation (3.29) by the spherical harmonics transformation and by a Fourier transformation with respect to t, one obtains ($g = cG$):

$$[-\omega - 2ibc\omega + a^2 + l(l+1)]\tilde{g}_{lm}(\omega) = \tilde{\delta}_{lm} \tag{C.10}$$

where:

$$\tilde{\delta}_{lm} = \int_0^\pi d\theta \int_0^{2\pi} d\varphi \sin\theta\delta(\theta,\varphi;\theta',\varphi')\bar{Y}_{lm}(\theta,\varphi) = Y_{lm}(\theta',\varphi')$$

Using (3.33) one obtains:

$$\tilde{g}(\theta,\varphi;\theta',\varphi';\omega) = \sum_{l=0}^\infty \frac{1}{-\omega^2 - 2ibc\omega + a^2 + l(l+1)} \sum_{m=-l}^{l} \bar{Y}_{lm}(\theta',\varphi')Y_{lm}(\theta,\varphi) \tag{C.11}$$

Using (3.37) one obtains:

$$\tilde{g}(\theta,\varphi;\theta',\varphi';\omega) = \frac{1}{4\pi}\sum_{l=0}^\infty \frac{1}{-\omega^2 - 2ibc\omega + a^2 + l(l+1)} P_l(\cos\gamma) \tag{C.12}$$

Summing up the series (Hansen 1975, p.301) one obtains:

$$\tilde{g}(\theta, \varphi; \theta', \varphi'; \omega) = -\frac{P_\alpha(-\cos\gamma)}{4\sin(\alpha\pi)} \tag{C.13}$$

where:

$$\alpha = -1/2 + \sqrt{\omega^2 + 2ibc\omega - a^2 + 1/4}$$

P_α denotes the Legendre function of the first kind; both determinations of the square root lead to the same function P_α. Finally, one obtains the Green's function:

$$G(\theta, \varphi; \theta', \varphi'; t) = \frac{c}{8\pi}\int_{\infty}^{\infty} \frac{e^{-i\omega t}}{\sin(\pi\alpha)} P_\alpha(-\cos\gamma)d\omega \tag{C.14}$$

Stereographic coordinates The stereographic projection (see Fig.9.C)

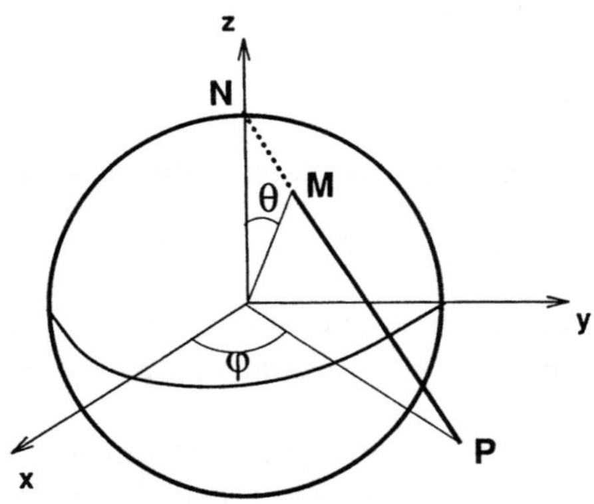

Fig.9.C Stereographic projection of a point M of the sphere $S_2 - N$ onto the plane: $M \rightarrow P$.

is an application P:

$$P: \quad S_2 - (0,0,1) \longrightarrow \mathbf{R}^2$$

where $(0,0,1)$ represents the North Pole of S_2. More specifically, the application P is defined by the relation:

$$(\theta, \varphi) \longrightarrow z = x + iy = \frac{e^{i\varphi}}{\tan(\theta/2)}$$

This gives:

$$\partial_\varphi = i(z\partial_z - \bar{z}\partial_{\bar{z}}) \quad \partial_\theta = (-1/2)(1 + z\bar{z})(e^{i\varphi}\partial_z + e^{-i\varphi}\partial_{\bar{z}})$$

and:

$$L_2 = \frac{1}{\sin\theta}(\partial_\theta(\sin\theta\partial_\theta)) + \frac{1}{\sin^2\theta}\partial^2_{\varphi^2} = (1 + z\bar{z})^2\partial^2_{z\bar{z}} \tag{C.15}$$

Because of the simplicity of (C.15) stereographic coordinates could appear as the "natural" coordinates on S_2. There is a snag, however; for, in the coordinates $(z, \bar{z})$, infinity corresponds to the image of the North Pole. This introduces a rather unusual boundary condition which makes the solution of the field equation in $(z, \bar{z})$ coordinates somewhat tricky.

D Appendix D: Checking the correlation function as a solution of the field equation

Let us prove that the correlation function in the case $a = bc$:

$$c(x,t) = e^{-a|x|}Y(|x| - |t|) + e^{-a|t|}Y(|t| - |x|)$$

satisfies the following partial differential equation (Definition 1, Section 1.2)

$$(\frac{1}{c^2}\partial^2_{t^2} + 2b\partial_t + a^2 - \partial^2_{x^2})(\frac{1}{c^2}\partial^2_{t^2} - 2b\partial_t + a^2 - \partial^2_{x^2})c(x,t) = \delta(x)\delta(t)$$

Absorbing the factor $1/c^2$ in a redefinition of t; the equation becomes:

$$L^+L^-c(x,t) = \delta(x)\delta(t)$$

$$L^+ = (a + \partial_t)^2 - \partial^2_{x^2} \qquad L^- = (a - \partial_t)^2 - \partial^2_{x^2}$$

We shall use the three following lemmas whose demonstration is straightforward.

Lemma D1 $(\alpha \pm \partial_t)^n e^{-at} f(t) = e^{-at}(\alpha - a \pm \partial_t)^n f(t) \quad n = 1, 2, \ldots$

Lemma D2 $Y(x)Y(|x| - |t|) = Y(x - |t|) = Y(x-t)Y(x+t) \quad \forall\, x, t$

Lemma D3 $(\partial^2_{x^2} - \partial^2_{t^2})Y(x-t)Y(x+t) = \delta(x)\delta(t)$

One has the following decomposition:

$c(x,t) = e^{-ax}Y(x)Y(x - |t|) +$

$$e^{ax}Y(-x)Y(-x - |t|) + e^{-at}Y(t)Y(t - |x|) + e^{at}Y(-t)Y(-t - |x|)$$

Using the lemmas one obtains:

$$L^+L^-e^{-ax}Y(x)Y(x - |t|) = [(a - \partial_x)^2 - \partial^2_{t^2}]\delta(x)\delta(t)$$

Similar relations hold for the other terms; summing up one obtains:

$L^+L^-c(x,t) =$

$$[(a - \partial_x)^2 - \partial^2_{t^2} + (a + \partial_x)^2 - \partial^2_{t^2} + (a - \partial_t)^2 - \partial^2_{x^2} + (a + \partial_t)^2 - \partial^2_{x^2}]\delta(x)\delta(t)$$

Thus:

$$L^+L^-c(x,t) = 4a^2\delta(x)\delta(t)$$

Chapter 10
Conclusion and perspectives

As indicated in the title there are two separate parts in this last chapter. The first part is a methodological reflection on previous chapters' objectives. We shall in particular try to give a more specific content to the book's subtitle: "A study in analytical economics". In the second part we discuss possible goals for future research in two different perspectives:

- In-depth studies relying on more precise or more adequate statistical material.
- Theoretical investigation of the role of economic interdependence in shaping differentiated evolutions.

1 "A study in analytical economics"

Let us open this section with an anecdote. I remember having been asked by colleagues who had but a vague notion of my research interests: "In which kind of prices are you particularly interested". Partly for fun, partly because it was the truth and partly because I was curious about my colleagues' reactions, I used to answer: "I am studying potato prices". Reactions ranged from amusement to consternation and dismay. Had I answered "Well, I am analysing stock prices", certainly the effect would have been very different. Accordingly, one has to admit that, at least in the opinion of a number of people, some subjects are not really worth being investigated at length. Yet (as we tried to show in previous chapters) potatoes are a commodity of the greatest importance for the spatial analysis of markets.

1.1 The two purposes of economics

The point we would like to emphasize in this paragraph can be summarized in the following way. Although there is a general consensus of opinion among leading economists to make a clear distinction between fundamental economics and applied economics, it seems that this distinction has so far remained rather formal, in other words it has had but a negligible influence on the development of economic research. Let us now develop this argument. Among the many quotations which could illustrate its first part we selected the following three.

- The first quotation is taken from a paper by Joseph Schumpeter (1933) which appeared in the first issue of Econometrica; it can in a sense be considered as defining the objectives of the journal.

> "No science thrives in the atmosphere of direct practical aim, and even practical results are but the by-products of disinterested work at the problem for the problem's sake. We should still be without most of the conveniences of modern life if physicists had been as eager for immediate applications as most economists are and always have been."
>
> J. Schumpeter (1933, p.6)

- The second quotation is taken from a book by Milton Friedman (1953). In fact, it illustrates and supports a view expressed by J.N.Keynes[1]some fifty years before.

> "In his admirable book on 'The scope and methods of political economy' John Neville Keynes distinguishes among a positive science, a body of systematized knowledge concerning what is; a normative or regulatrice science, a body of criteria of what ought to be; an art, a system of rules for the attainment of a given end. He comments that confusion between them is common and has been the source of many mischievous errors."
>
> M. Friedman (1953, p.3)

- The third quotation is taken from a recent methodological paper by Edmond Malinvaud (1990)[2]

> "Economics has a double purpose: to understand and to advise. The search for objective explanations of economic phenomena corresponds to the first objective. The second consists in providing policy makers with objective assessments of the consequences to be expected from alternative contemplated decisions."
>
> E. Malinvaud (1990, p.115-121)

It is really surprising that an opinion that has been held so constantly throughout a century has had so little influence on the shaping of the economic science. The

---

[1]John Neville Keynes (1852-1949) was the father of John Maynard Keynes (1883-1946). His most important contributions to economics were as a methodologist. His chief work on economic methodology: "The scope and methods of political economy" was published in 1891 at a time when the German-speaking world was engaged in the Methodenstreit ("battle of method"). The debate was on the classical question of deductive versus inductive approach; the latter was advocated by the German economist Gustav Schmoller. J.N. Keynes by contrast insisted that both deduction and induction were required.

[2]Here is the original text in French from which the above quotation has been translated: "Notre discipline a un double objectif: comprendre et conseiller. Comprendre, c'est-à-dire établir objectivement une explication des phénomènes économiques. Conseiller, c'est-à-dire apporter aux décideurs un témoignage objectif sur les conséquences à attendre des décisions alternatives entre lesquelles ils devront choisir."

reactions we reported in the introduction to this section already are revealing in this respect. Nevertheless one would like some more objective pieces of evidence. To this end we tried to compare the annual number of newly published books on the subject of inflation[3]to the evolution of the inflation rate itself. The results are summarized in Fig.10.1. Because of the time it takes to write a

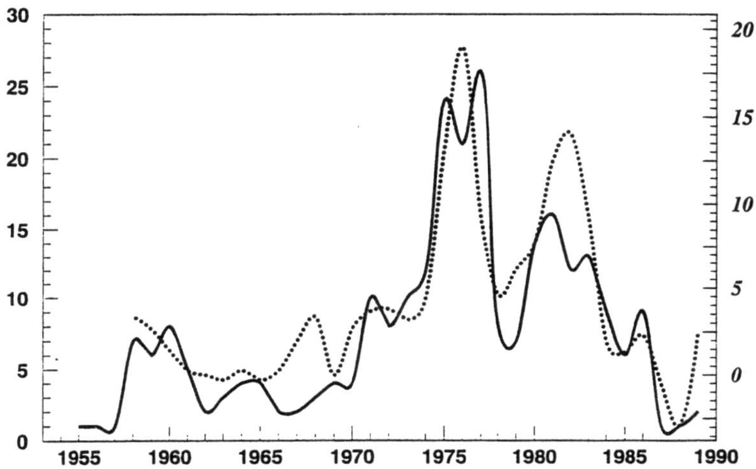

Fig.10.1 Comparison between numbers of yearly published books about inflation and inflation rates. Solid curve: number of books, left-hand scale; dotted curve: inflation rate, right-hand scale in per cent. In order to get rid of any subjective assessment, we considered the number of books under the heading "inflation" in the subject catalogue of an important economic library (Fondation Nationale des Sciences Politiques, Paris). Regarding the inflation curve, a three-year shift to the right has been performed which takes into account the delay between the decision to write a book and its actual publication. This brings both curves into close coincidence.

book, one expects the curve of new books to lag behind the curve of inflation rates. This is indeed the case and motivated a shift of the later three years ahead. This brings both curves in close coincidence. There would be nothing amiss with this parallelism if it could be argued that times of inflation are more appropriate for the investigation of inflation than are times of stable prices. This is not obvious however. For instance, it could be just as instructive to explain why inflation remained moderate in industrialized countries during the decade 1984-1993 in spite of growing public deficits. Furthermore, during the same decade a number of developing countries experienced very large inflation rates.

During the nineteenth century French economists (and also the general public) were engaged in a tumultuous debate on the question of whether trade and es-

[3]In practice we counted the books listed under the heading "inflation" in the subject classification of one of the major French libraries, namely the library of the "Fondation Nationale des Sciences Politiques." Paris VIe.

pecially grain trade should be deregulated (Modeste 1862; Biollay 1885,1886; Afanassiev 1894; new editions of Herbert 1755, Abeille 1764, Dupont de Nemours 1764). At that time the questions of spatial price differences, of transport costs and of transportation delay were at the centre of the controversy. These questions no longer are of crucial importance at least in industrialized countries. Other issues have been brought to the fore: in the decades before and after World War II the role of public expenditure received considerable attention in the framework of Keynesian and neo-Keynesian theories; in the seventies the main concern was about inflation; then there was a come-back of neo-liberal theories in the wake of the great deregulation wave that swept the eighties.

1.2 "Collectors of facts"

In order to test the models developed in previous chapters we relied on statistics which are taken from the 20th, the 19th or even from the 18th century. What matters is the reliability of the data and the fact they are appropriate for the planned investigation; whether they are taken from present day statistics or from historic records is irrelevant. On many occasions, however, we had to complain that by lack of proper statistics our models could not be tested as thoroughly as required. Regarding the general problem of data availability one has to recognize that only scarce attention has been given to the publication of original statistical series[4]. It was one of the objectives of the founders of Econometrica to contribute to this task. In Ragnar Frisch's words (1933, p.3): "In statistical and other numerical work presented in Econometrica the original raw data will, as a rule, be published, unless their volume is excessive". He continues: "The aim will be to present this kind of paper in a condensed form with a brief precise description of:

(1) the theoretical setting (2) the data (3) the method (4) the results.

Only few empirical papers of this kind ever appeared in economic journals[5]. J.Schumpeter in the paper we mentioned above (1933, p.11) distinguishes three sorts of economists: theorists, statisticians and collectors of facts; the last variety of economists simply failed to come into existence.

How we understand the term "analytical economics" can be inferred from our previous observations as well as from the methodology used in previous chapters: a particular concern for fundamental economics and a special emphasis on comparative statistical studies.

[4]Let us mention for instance the construction of consistent and reliable long run statistical series or the publication of comparable series for different countries. Such undertakings require great ingenuity and rigour and a lot of time.

[5]Papers of this kind can be found in the Journal of the Statistical Society (1838-1889) and in the Journal of the Royal Statistical Society.

2 Perspectives

2.1 Tests of quantitative models

Different empirical tests have been left pending in previous chapters due to lack of statistical evidence. Let us consider a specific example. In chapter 8 we were unable to provide but qualitative tests for our time dependent models. A potentially interesting application would concern the pork (hog) market in the CEE during the last two decades. This problem has several interesting features from the point of view of spatial analysis.

1) In every country, hogs are traded on *several* spatially separated markets.

2) Pork prices more or less display a characteristic cyclical behaviour (see chapter 2, section 1.2.3).

3) Between 1972 and 1992 Common Market agricultural agreements brought about substantial integration between various national pork markets. Provided appropriate data could be found[6]it would be very interesting to analyse this evolution.

2.2 Construction of qualitative models

Throughout this book one of our main concern was the analysis of spatial economic connections. Clearly interdependence between agents is a crucial feature in the evolution of an economy. While basic properties have been studied a long time ago (see for instance models of international trade) more "exotic" features such as multiple equilibria, nonergodicity (Durlauf 1993) still remain largely unexplored. Let us in this respect mention a mathematical theory which may be of great significance in analysing the evolution of interdependent systems, namely the theory of evolution of random graphs. It was founded by Erdös and Rényi in the early 1960s. A graph basically describes the interdependence between different vertices by the introduction of edges drawn between pairs of vertices. The theory of random graphs distinguishes itself from the theory of graphs in the sense that one is no longer interested in properties of individual graphs but only in probabilistic properties; in other words, classes of graphs which are sufficiently exceptional to be of measure zero can be altogether ignored. This results in greater relevance of the theory as to potential applications for instance in economics. By progressively increasing the number of edges one is able to model a system whose parts become more and more interdependent. The amazing discovery of the theory of random graphs is that the evolution regarding certain structural features (such as for instance the number of isolated

[6] Not only prices are required but also data about excess-supply functions, tariffs and transportation costs.

vertices) displays abrupt transitions (Palmer 1985). Clearly such a theory and the random field model (see chapter 9) complement one another. In the first case there are only two levels in the coupling between two edges (0: no connection; 1: connection); but there is the possibility of describing complex spatial patterns (in this respect see for instance Quah 1993a,b), including qualitative transitions. Whereas the second description is more appropriate for quantitative modelling, it is not well suited for the description of intricate spatial patterns.

References

ABDEL-RAHMAN (H.), FUJITA (M.) 1990: Product variety, marshallian externalities and city sizes. Journal of Regional Science 30, 2,165-183.

ABEILLE (L.P.) 1764,1910: *Réflexions sur la police des grains en France et en Angleterre.* Librairie Geuthner. Paris.

ABEL (W.) 1935: *Agrarkrisen und Agrarkonjunkturen.* Paul Harey. Berlin.

ACHILLES (W.) 1959: Getreidepreise und Getreidehandelsbeziehungen europäischer Räume im 16. und 17. Jahrhundert. Zeitschrift für Agrargeschichte und Agrarsoziologie 7, 32-53.

AFANASSIEV (G.) 1894: *Le commerce des céréales en France au 18e siècle. Etude historique traduite du russe.* Alphonse Picard et Fils. Paris.

AFTALION (F.) 1988: Le prix du blé à Pontoise en 1789. Histoire, Economie et Société 1, 107-115.

AKAIKE (H.) 1969: Fitting autoregressive models for predictions. Am. Inst. Statist. Math. 21,243,7.

ALBUM DE STATISTIQUE AGRICOLE 1887: Résultats généraux de l'enquête décennale de 1882. Ministère de l'Agriculture. Paris.

ALEXANDERSSON (G.), NORSTRÖM (G.) 1963: *World shipping.* Almqvist and Wiksell. Stockholm.

ANSELIN (L.) 1988: *Spatial econometrics: methods and models.* Kluwer. Dordrecht.

ANSELIN (L.) 1990: Some robust approaches to testing and estimation in spatial econometrics. Regional Science and Urban Economics 20, 141-163.

ARBIA (G.) 1989: *Spatial data configuration in statistical analysis of regional economic and related problems.* Kluwer. Dordrecht.

ATKINSON (A.B.) 1975: *The economics of inequality.* Clarendon Press. Oxford.

ATLAS UNIVERSALIS 1978: Encyclopedia Universalis. Paris.

AUERBACH (F.) 1913: Das Gesetz der Bevölkerungskonzentration. Petermans Mitteilungen 59, 1, 44-76.

BADILLO (D.), DALLOZ (J.-P.) 1985: *Marché, spéculation, stabilisation.* Economica. Paris.

BAIROCH (P.) 1976: *Commerce extérieur et développement économique de l'Europe au XIXe siècle.* Mouton. Paris.

BALL (R.), BROWN (P.) 1968: An empirical evaluation of accounting income numbers. Journal of Accounting Research 6.

BANK OF JAPAN 1966: *Hundred-year statistics of the Japanese economy.* Statistics Dept of the Bank of Japan. Tokyo.

BARTLETT (M.S.) 1955: *Stochastic processes.* Cambridge University Press. Cambridge.

BARTLETT (M.S.) 1964: The spectral analysis of two-dimensional point processes. Biometrika 51, 299-311.

BARTLETT (M.S.) 1971: Physical nearest neighbour models and non linear time series. Journal of Applied Probability 8,2,222-232.

BARTLETT (M.S.) 1975: *The statistical analysis of spatial pattern.* Chapman and Hall. London.

BATEMAN (H.) 1953: *Higher transcendental functions Vol II.* McGraw-Hill. New York.

BATES (T.H.), SCHMITZ (A.) 1969: A spatial equilibrium analysis of the world sugar economy. Gianini Foundation Monograph No23. California Agricultural Experiment Station. Berkeley.

BATTEN (D.), MARTELLATO (D.) 1988: Modelling interregional trade within input-output systems. Ricerche Economiche 42,2,204-221.

BATTEN (D.), WESTIN (L.) 1990: Modelling commodity flows on trade networks: retrospect and prospect. in *New frontiers in regional science* ed. by Chatterji (M.), Kuenne (R.E.), Macmillan Press.

BAUCHET (P.) 1991: *Le transport international dans l'économie mondiale.* Economica. Paris.

BAULANT (M.), MEUVRET (J.) 1960: *Prix des céréales extraits de la mercuriale de Paris.* S.E.V.P.E.N. Paris.

BAUMOL (W.J.) 1952: Spatial equilibrium with supply points separated from markets and with supplies predetermined. Report of the Bureau of Agricultural Economics, US Department of Agriculture.

BAWDEN (D.L.) 1966: A spatial price equilibrium model of international trade. Journal of Farm Economics 48, 862-874.

BECKMANN (M.) 1952: A continuous model of transportation. Econometrica 20,643-660.

BECKMANN (M.J.), RYDER (H.E.) 1969: Simultaneous price and quantity adjustment in a single market. Econometrica 37,3,470-484.

BECKMANN (M.J.), PUU (T.) 1985: *Spatial economics: density, potential and flow.* North Holland. Amsterdam.

BEGG (D.K.) 1982: *The rational expectations revolution in economics.* Philip Allen. Oxford.

BENGTSSON (T.), JÖRBERG (L.) 1975: Market integration in Sweden during the 18th and 19th centuries. Spectral analysis of grain prices. Economy and History 17,8,93-106.

BENNET (R.) 1979: *Spatial time series.* Pion. London.

BESAG (J.E.) 1972: Nearest neighbour systems and the auto-logistic model for binary data. Journal of the Royal Society. Series B, 34, 75-83.

BESAG (J.) 1974: Spatial interactions and the statistical analysis of lattice systems. Journal of the Royal Statistical Society B, 36, 192-236.

BEVERIDGE (W.H.) 1921: Weather and harvest cycles. Economic Journal 31,429-452.

BEVERIDGE (W.H.) 1922: Wheat prices and rainfall in western Europe. Journal of the Royal Statistical Society 85,412-459.

BHATIA (B.M.) 1967: *Famines in India. A study in some aspects of the economic history of India (1860-1965).* Asia Publishing House. Bombay.

BILLINGSLEY (P.) 1979: *Probability and measure.* Wiley. New York.

BIOLLAY (L.) 1885: *Le pacte de famine.* Guillaumin. Paris.

BIOLLAY (L.) 1886: *Les prix en 1790.* Guillaumin. Paris.

BISHOP (V.) 1974: *Summary information on the strive events data sets.* Northwestern University.

BLUM (A.), BONNEUIL (N.), BLANCHET (D.) ed. 1992: Modèles de a démographie historique. INED. Presses Universitaires de France. Paris.

BOX (G.E.P.), JENKINS (G.M.) 1976: *Time series analysis, forecasting and control.* Holden Bay. San Francisco.

BRAUDEL (F.) 1967: *Civilisation matérielle et capitalisme.* Armand Colin. Paris.

BRESSLER (R.G.), KING (R.A) 1970: *Markets, prices and interregional trade.* John Wiley. New York.

BRONARS (S.G.), JANSEN (P.W.) 1987: The geographic distribution of unemployment rates in the U.S.: a spatial-time series analysis. Journal of Econometrics, 36, 251-279.

BROZE (L.), SZAFARZ (A.) 1991: *The econometric analysis of non-uniqueness in rational expectations models.* North Holland. Amsterdam.

BURBECK (S.L.), RAINE (W.J.), ABUDU-STARK (M.J.) 1978: The dynamics of riot growth: an epidemiological approach. Journal of Mathematical Sociology 6,1-22.

CAPOZZA (D.R.), VAN ORDER (R.) 1977: Pricing under spatial competition and spatial monopoly. Econometrica 43,1329-1338.

CAPOZZA (D.R.), VAN ORDER (R.) 1978: A generalized model of spatial competition. American Economic Review 68,896-908.

CARTAN (H.) 1967: *Calcul différentiel.* Hermann. Paris.

CASSELS (J.M.) 1937: *Study of fluid milk prices.* Harvard University Press. Cambridge.

CHALMIN (Ph.) 1983: *Tate and Lyle, géant du sucre.* Economica. Paris.

CHALMIN (Ph.) 1991: *Cyclope. Les marchés mondiaux.* Economica. Paris.

CHAMBERLAIN (G.) 1982: Panel data. In *Handbook of Econometrics Vol II* Edited by Griliches and Intriligator (M.) pp.1247-1318. North Holland. Amsterdam.

CHARTRES (J.A.) 1977: *Internal trade in England.* London.

CHARTRES (J.) ed. 1990: *Agricultural markets and trade 1500-1750.* Cambridge University Press. Cambridge.

CHARTRES (J.) 1991: City and towns, farmers and economic change in the eighteenth century. Historical Research (Bulletin of the Institute of Historical Research) 64,154,138-155.

CHARTRES (J.) 1993: Market integration and agricultural output in seventeenth, eighteenth, and early nineteenth-century England. European Historical Economics Workshop on Market Integration (Lerici).

CHARVET (J.-P.) 1990: *Le blé.* Economica. Paris.

CHEVET (J.M.), SAINT AMOUR (P.) 1991: Sens probable de la causalité pour les prix du blé. Histoire et Mesure 6, 93-119.

CHIANG (A.C.) 1967,1984: *Fundamental methods of mathematical economics.* McGraw Hill.

CLARK (C.) 1968: *Population growth and land use.* Macmillan. London.

CLARK (G.L.) 1986: Dimensions of spatial price dispersion before and after the crash of 1929. Geographical Analysis 18,1,19-47

CLAYTON (H.H.) 1944: *World weather records.* Smithsonian Institution. Washington D.C.

CLIFF (A.D.), HAGGET (P.), ORD (J.K.), VERSEY (G.R.) 1981: *Spatial diffusion. An historical geography of epidemics in an island community.* Pion. London.

CLIFF (A.D.), HAGGET (P.) 1988: *Atlas of disease distributions: analytical approaches to epidemiological data.* Blackwell Reference. Oxford.

CLIFF (A.), ORD (J.) 1973: *Spatial autocorrelation.* Pion. London.

CLIFF (A.), ORD (J.) 1981: *Spatial processes, models and applications.* Pion. London.

COALE (A.J.), ZELNICK (M.) 1963: *New estimates of fertility and population in the United States* Princeton University Press. Princeton.

COASE (R.H.), FOWLER (R.F.) 1937: The pig-cycle in Great Britain: an explanation. Economica 4,55-82.

COLE (A.H.) 1938: *Wholesale commodity prices in the United States 1700-1861. Statistical Supplement.* Harvard University Press. Cambridge.

CROUHY-VEYRAC (L.), CROUHY (M.), MÉLITZ (J.) 1982: More about the law of one price. European Economic Review 18,325-344.

D'AGOSTINO (R.B.) 1986: Tests for the normal distribution in *Goodness of fit techniques.* Edited by d'Agostino (R.B.) and Stephens (M.A.). Marcel Dekker. New York.

DAS GETREIDE IM WETVERKEHR 1900: Ackerbauministerium. Vienna.

DAVIS (H.T.) 1941: *The theory of econometrics.* Principia Press. Bloomington, Indiana.

DEAKIN (B.M.), LIESNER (Th.) 1969: *Productivity in transport.* Cambridge University Press. Cambridge.

DEATON (A.), LAROQUE (G.) 1992: On the behavior of commodity prices. Review of Economic Studies. 59,1-23.

DEARDORFF (A.V.) 1984: *Testing trade theories and predicting trade flows.* in *Handbook of international economics, Vol.I* edited by Jones (R.W.), Kenen (P.B.). Elsevier. Amsterdam.

DEMOGRAPHIC YEARBOOK OF THE UNITED NATIONS. United Nations. New York.

DE VRIES (J.) 1984: *European urbanization 1500-1800.* Methuen and Co. London.

DOETSCH (G.) 1950: *Handbuch der Laplace-Transformation. Vol.I.* Birhhaüser. Basel.

DORFMAN (R.), SAMUELSON (P.A.), SOLOW (R.M.) 1958: *Linear programming and economic analysis.* McGraw-Hill. New York.

DRAME (S.), GONFALONE (C.), MILLER (J.A.), ROEHNER (B.) 1991: *Un siècle du commerce du blé en France: 1825-1913. Les fluctuations du champ des prix.* Economica. Paris.

DUPAQUIER (J.), LACHIVER (M.), MEUVRET (J.) 1968: *Mercuriales du Pays de France et du Vexin Français (1640-1914).* S.E.V.P.E.N. Paris.

DUPONT DE NEMOURS (P.S.) 1764,1911: *De l'exportation et de l'importation des grains.* Librairie Paul Geuthner. Paris.

DUPRIEZ (L.H.), FÉTORONYI (N.B.), SZAPARY (G.), PEEMANS (J.P.) 1966: *Diffusion du progrès technique et convergence des prix. Etudes internationales.* Vol I, Editions Nauwelaerts. Louvain.

DURLAUF (S.N.) 1993: Nonergodic economic growth. Review of Economic Studies 60,349-366.

EICHENGREEN (B.) 1990: *Elusive stability: essays in the history of international finance 1919-1939.* Cambridge University Press. Cambridge.

ENGEL (E.) 1861: Die Getreidepreise, die Ernteerträge und der Getreidehandel im preussischen Staate. Zeitschrift des Königl. Preussischen Statistischen Bureaus. 10, 11, 249-289.

ENGELBRECHT (T.H.) 1908: *Die geographische Verteilung der Getreidepreise in India von 1861 bis 1905.* Verlagsbuchhandlung Paul Darey. Berlin.

ENGLE (R.F.), GRANGER (C.W.J.) 1987: Co-integration and error correction: representation, estimation and testing. Econometrica 55, 251-276.

ENGLE (R.F.), YOO (B.F.) 1987: Forecasting and testing in co-integrated systems. Journal of Econometrics 35, 143-159.

ENKE (S.) 1951: Equilibrium among spatially separated markets: solution by electric analogue. Econometrica 19, 40-47.

ERDELEYI (A.) (Ed.) 1954: *Tables of integral transforms.* Vol I. McGraw-Hill. New York.

ETLING (J.) 1937: *L'incidence des tarifs des transports sur le prix de vente des produits agricoles en France.* Librairie Technique et Economique. Paris.

EUROPA WORLD YEAR BOOK: Europa Publications limited. London.

FADEN (A.M.) 1991: The theory of comparative advantages for many countries and many industries. Preprint, Iowa State University.

FAMA (E.F.) 1965: The behavior of stock-market prices. The Journal of Business 38,34-105.

FAMA (E.), FISHER (L.), JENSEN (M.), ROLL (R.) 1969: The adjustement of stock prices to new information. International Economic Review.

FÖLDES (B.) 1905: Die Getreidepreise im 19. Jahrhundert. Jahrbücher für Nationalökonomie und Statistik 29, 467-518.

FOSSIER (R.) 1983: *Le Moyen-Age. Vol III: Le temps des crises 1250-1520.* A.Colin. Paris.

FOVILLE (A. de) 1880: *La transformation des moyens de transport et ses conséquences économiques et sociales.* Librairie Guillaumin. Paris.

FOX (K.A.) 1953: A spatial equilibrium model of the livestock-feed economy in the United States. Econometrica 21, 547-566.

FRÊCHE (G.), FRÊCHE (G.) 1967: *Le prix des grains, des vins et des légumes à Toulouse (1486-1868).* Presses Universitaires de France. Paris.

FRIEDMAN (M.) 1953: Essays in positive economics. University of Chicago Press. Chicago.

FRIEDMAN (M.), SCHWARTZ (A.) 1963: *A monetary history of the United States 1867-1960.* Princeton University Press. Princeton.

FRIEDMAN (M.), SCHWARTZ (A.) 1982: *Monetary trends in the United States and the United Kingdom: their relation to income, price and interest rates.* The University of Chicago Press. Chicago.

FRISCH (R.) 1933: Editorial. Econometrica 1,1-4.

GABSZEWICZ (J.J.), THISSE (J.-F.) 1989: Location. Core Discussion Paper No 8928. University of Louvain.

GALLOWAY (P.R.) 1985: Annual variations in death by age, death by cause, prices and weather in London, 1670 to 1830. Population Studies, 39, 487-505.

GALLOWAY (P.R.) 1986: Differentials in demographic reponses to annual price variations in pre-revolutionary France. A comparison of rich and poor areas in Rouen, 1681 to 1787. European Journal of Population 2, 269-305.

GALLOWAY (P.R.) 1992: Changements séculaires des freins à court terme à la croissance démographique en Europe de 1640 à 1909: frein préventif, frein positif et frein de température. in: *Modèles de la démographie historique.* edited by: Blum (A.), Bonneuil (N.), Blanchet (D.). INED. PUF. Paris.

GARABEDIAN (P.R.) 1964: *Partial differential equations.* Wiley. New York.

GAVEAU (B.) 1989: Le problème de Cauchy pour une équation d'onde stochastique. C.R. Acad. Sciences. Paris I, 21-24.

GOURIÉROUX (C.), LAFFONT (J.J.), MONFORT (A.) 1982: Rational expectations in dynamic linear models: analysis of the solutions. Econometrica 50,2,409-425.

GRADSHTEYN (I.S.), RYZHIK (I.M.) 1965: *Tables of integrals, series and products.* Academic Press. New York.

GRANGER (C.W.J.), ELLIOT (C.M.) 1967: A fresh look at wheat prices and markets in the eighteenth century. Economic History Review, 20, 257-265.

GRANGER (C.W.J.) 1969a: Spatial data and time series analysis. in London Papers in Regional Science. Studies in Regional Science. pp.1-24 Ed A.J. Scott.

GRANGER (C.W.J.) 1969: Investigating causal relations by econometric models and cross-spectral methods. Econometrica 37,3,424-438.

GRANGER (C.) 1981: Some properties of time series data and their use in econometric model specification. Journal of Econometrics 16, 121-130

GRANGER (C.W.J.) 1992: Evaluating economic theory. Journal of Econometrics 51,3-5.

GRENIER (J.Y.) 1984: Quelques éléments pour une étude des liens entre conjoncture économique et conjoncture démographique aux XVIIe et XVIIIe siècle. Annales de Démographie Historique, 175-199.

GRENNES (T.), JOHNSON (P.R.), THURSBY (M.) 1978: *The economics of world grain trade.* Praeger Publishers.

GRIFFITH (D.A.) 1988: *Advanced spatial statistics.* Kluwer. Dordrecht.

GRILLI (E.R.), YANG (M.C.) 1988: Primary commodity prices, manufactured good prices and the term of trade of developing countries: what the long run shows. The World Bank Economic Review 2, 1-48.

GUERIN-PACE (F), PUMAIN (D) 1990: 150 ans de croissance urbaine. Economie et Statistique 230, 5-16

GUYON (X.) 1982: Parameter estimation for a stationary process on a d-dimensional lattice. Biometrika 69,1,95-105.

HADLEY (A.T.) 1885: *Railroad transportation, its history and its laws.* Putnam. New York.

HAGEN (J.VON) 1989: Relative commodity prices and cointegration. Journal of Business and Economic Statistics 7, 4, 497-503.

HAGGETT (P.) 1990: *The geographers' art.* Blackwell. Oxford.

HAINING (R.) 1978: *Specification and estimation problems in models of spatial dependence.* Studies in Geography No24. Evanston, Ill.

HAINING (R.P.) 1983: Modeling intra-urban price competition: an example of gasoline retailing. Journal of Regional Science 23,4,517-528.

HAINING (R.) 1984: Testing a spatial interacting-markets hypothesis. Review of Economics and Statistics, 66, 576-583.

HAINING (R.) 1990: *Spatial data analysis in the social and environmental sciences.* Cambridge University Press. Cambridge.

HANNAN (E.J.), RISSANEN (J.) 1982: Recursion estimation of mixed autoregressive-moving average order. Biometrika 69,81-94. Erratum: 1983,-70,303.

HARKNESS (J.) 1978: Factor abundance and comparative advantage. American Economic Review 68, 784-800

HARLEY (C.K.) 1980: Transportation, the world trade and the Kuznets cycle 1850-1913. Explorations in Economic History 17,218-250.

HARLEY (C.K.) 1990: North Atlantic shipping in the late nineteenth century: freight rates and the interrelationship of cargoes. in *Shipping and trade 1750-1950: Essays in international maritime economic history.* Fischer (L.R.) and Nordvik (H.W.) editors. Lofthouse Publications. pp.147-171.

HARLOW (A.A.) 1962: A recursive model of the hog industry. Agricultural Economic Research, 14.

HAUGH (L.D.) 1976: Checking the independence of two stationary time series: a univariate residue cross correlation approach. Journal of the American Statistical Association 71, 378-385.

HEADY (E.O.), KALDOR (D.R) 1954: Expectations and errors in forecasting agricultural prices. Journal of Political Economy 62, 34-47.

HEFFER (J.) 1986: Le marché du blé américain: une analyse structurale. Histoire, Economie et Société 2, 265-295.

HEINE (V.) 1955: Models for two-dimensional stationary stochastic processes. Biometrika 42, 170-178.

HERBERT (C.-J.) 1755,1910: *Essai sur la police générale des grains, sur leurs prix et sur les effets de l'agriculture.* Librairie Paul Geuthner. Paris.

HICKMANN (E.), RICKER (K.) 1936: *Statistisches Handbuch des deutschen und internationalen Aussenhandels.* Verlag für Sozialpolitik. Berlin.

HILL (B.) 1974: The rank frequency form of Zipf's law. Journal of the American Statistical Association 69, 1017-1026.

HIRSCHBERG (E.) 1893: *Beiträge zur Statistik der Brotpreise im Deutschen Reich.* Heines. Berlin.

HISTORICAL STATISTICS OF THE UNITED STATES 1975: US Dept of Commerce. Washington D.C.

HITCHCOCK (F.L.) 1941: The distribution of a product from several sources to numerous localities. Journal of Mathematics and Physics 20, 224-260.

HOBSON (E.W.) 1965: *The theory of spherical and ellipsoïdal harmonics.* Chelsea Publishing Company. New York.

HOFFMAN (L.A.) 1992: Forecasting season-average wheat prices using futures prices. Wheat Situation and Outlook. US Department of Agriculture, March, 30-37.

HOOKER (R.H.) 1907: Correlation of the weather and crops. Journal of the Royal Statistical Society 19, 1-51.

HÖRMANDER (L.) 1983: *The analysis of linear partial differential operators.* Vol I. Springer Verlag.

HOTELLING (H.) 1929: Stability in competition. Economic Journal, 36,41-57

HSIAO (C.) 1986: *Analysis of panel data.* Cambridge University Press. Cambridge.

HYMANS (S.H.) 1967: *Probability theory with application to econometric and decision making theory.* Prentice Hall.

ISARD (W.) 1952: A general location principle of an optimum space-economy. Econometrica 20, 406-430.

ISARD (W.) 1956: *Location and space economy.* The M.I.T. Press. Cambridge Mass.

ISSERLIS (L.) 1938: Tramp shipping cargoes and freights. Journal of the Royal Statistical Society p.122

JAYET (H.) forthcoming, 1994: *Analyse spatiale quantitative: une introduction.* Economica. Paris.

JACOBS (A.), RICHTER (H.) 1935: Die Getreidepreise in Deutschland seit dem Ausgang des 18. Jahrhunderts. Vierteljahrshefte zur Statistiks des Deutschen Reichs 44, 273-321.

JOHANSEN (S.) 1988: Statistical analysis of cointegration vectors. Journal of Economic Dynamics and Control 12, 231-254.

JONES (D.) 1983: Mechanisms of the geographical transmission of economic fluctuations. Annals of the Association of American Geographers 73,35-50.

JÖRBERG (L.) 1972: *A history of prices in Sweden 1732-1914. Vol.I and Vol.II.* Cleerup. Lund.

JUDGE (G.G.) 1956: A spatial equilibrium model for eggs. Storrs Agricultural Experiment Station Bulletin No 318. University of Connecticut. Storrs.

KAPLAN (S.L.) 1984: *Provisioning Paris: merchants and millers in the grain trade during the 18th century.* Ithaca.

KENDALL (M.G.) 1953: The analysis of economic time series. Part 1: Prices. Journal of the Royal Statistical Society 96,11-25

KENDALL (M.), STUART (A.), ORD(J.K.) 1987: *Advanced theory of statistics. Vol I.* Charles Griffin. London.

KINDLEBERGER (C.P.) 1978: *Manias, panics and crashes. A history of financial crisis.* Basic Books. New York.

KINDERMANN (R.), SNELL (J.L.) 1980: *Markov random fields and their applications.* American Mathematical Society. Vol.I. Rhodes Island.

KLEIN (L.R.), PRESTON (R.S.) 1969: Stochastic nonlinear models. Econometrica 37,95-106

KOOPMANS (T.C), REITER (S.) 1951: A model of transportation. Chapter 14 in *Activity analysis of production and allocation.* Cowles Commission Monograph 13, Koopmans, ed. John Wiley. New York.

KORN (G.A.), KORN (T.M.) 1961,1968: *Mathematical Handbook for scientists and engineers.* McGraw Hill. New York.

LABROUSSE (C.E.) 1932: *Esquisse du mouvement des prix et des revenus en France au XVIIIe siècle.* Thesis. Paris.

LABROUSSE (E.), ROMANO (R), DREYFUS (F.G.) 1970: Le prix du froment en France au temps de la monnaie stable (1726-1913). SEVPEN. Paris.

LABYS (W.C.), GRANGER (C.W.J.) 1970: *Speculation, hedging and commodity price forecasts.* Heath and Co. Lexington. Mass

LABYS (W.C.) 1973: *Dynamic commodity models: specification, estimation and simulation.* Lexington Books. Lexington. Mass.

LANGLEY (J.), LANGLEY (S.) 1989: State-level wheat statistics 1949-88. US Dept of Agriculture, Statistical Bulletin No 779.

LATHAM (A.J.H.), NEAL (L.) 1982: The international market in rice and wheat 1868-1914. The Economic History Review 36,2,260-275.

LEE (T.C), SEAVER (S.K.) 1972: A positive spatial equilibrium model of the broiler markets: a simultaneous equation approach. Storrs Agricultural Experiment. Station Bulletin No 417. University of Connecticut. Storrs.

LEFEBER (L.) 1958: *Allocation in space: production, transport and industrial location.* North-Holland. Amsterdam.

LÉVY-LEBOYER (M.), BOURGUIGNON (F.) 1985: *L'économie française au 19e siècle. Analyse macroéconomique.* Economica. Paris.

LIESNER (Th.) 1989: *One hundred years of economic statistics.* Facts on File. The Economist. New York.

LJUNGBERG (J.) 1993: Prices and market integration. Sweden and Britain during the 19th and 20th centuries. European Historical Economics Workshop on Market integration (Lerici).

LÖSCH (A.) 1940: *Die räumliche Ordnung der Wirtschaft.* Jena. 1954: *The economics of location.* Yale University Press. New Haven.

LOVELL (M.C.) 1986: Tests of the rational expectations hypothesis. American Economic Review 76, 110-124.

LUCIER (G.), BUDGE (A.), PLUMMER (Ch.), SPURGEON (C.) 1991: US potato statistics. US Dept of Agriculture. Statistical Bulletin No 829.

MACHALI (M.) 1931: Prévisions du rendement du blé d'après les éléments météorologiques. Thèse. Paris.

MADDOCK (R.), CARTER (M.) 1982: A child's guide to rational expectations. Journal of Economic Literature 20, 39-51.

MAGNUS (J.R.) 1982: Multivariate error component analysis of linear and nonlinear regression models by maximum likelihood. Journal of Econometrics 19,239-285.

MAGNUS (W.), OBERHETTINGER (F.), SONI (R.P.) 1966: *Formulas and theorems for the special functions of mathematical physics.* Springer-Verlag. New York.

MANDELBROT (B.) 1960: The Pareto-Lévy law and the distribution of income. International Economic Review 1 (2), 79-106.

MANDELBROT (B.) 1963: The variation of certain speculative prices. Journal of Business 36,394-419.

MANDELBROT (B.) 1982: *The fractal geometry of nature.* Freeman and Co. San Francisco.

MALECKI (E.) 1975: Examining changes in rank-size systems of cities. Professional Geographer 27,43-47.

MALINVAUD (E.) 1990: Propos de circonstance sur les orientations de la discipline économique. Annales Economie, Société, Civilisation, 1,115-121.

MASKIN (E.), TIROLE (J.) 1988: A theory of dynamic oligipoly II. Price, competition, kinked demand curves, and Edgeworth cycles. Econometrica. 56, 571-599.

McCLOSKEY (D.), NASH (J.) 1984: Corn at interest: the extent and cost of grain storage in Medieval England. The American Economic Review 74,174-187.

McCALLA (A.F.) 1966: A duopoly model of the world wheat pricing. Journal of Farm Economics 48, 3, 711-727.

McNICOL (D.L.) 1978: *Commodity agreements and price stabilization. A policy analysis.* Lexington, Mass.

MALECKI (E.) 1975: Examining changes in rank-size systems of cities. Profesional Geographer 27,43-47

MEADOWS (D.L.) 1970: *Dynamics of commodity production cycles.* Wright-Allen Press. Cambridge. Mass.

MÉMOIRES (1770-1798): Sur la cherté des grains et sur les moyens de conserver les farines et les grains. Archives Nationales, Paris D3;35,36.

MESTAYER (M.) 1963: Le prix du blé et de l'avoine de 1329 à 1793. Revue du Nord 157-176.

MEUVRET (J.) 1956: Le commerce des grains et des farines à Paris et les marchands parisiens à l'époque de Louis XIV. Revue d'Histoire Moderne et Contemporaine 3,169-203.

MEUVRET (J.) 1971: Etudes d'histoire économique. Cahier des Annales no 32.

MJELDE (J.W.), PAGGI (M.S.) 1989: An empirical analysis of interregional price linkage. Journal of Regional Science 29,2,171-180.

MINORSKY (N.) 1947: *Introduction to non-linear mechanics. Topological methods. Analytical methods. Non-linear resonance. Relaxation oscillations.* Edwards. Ann Arbor.

MITCHELL (B.R.), DEANE (P.) 1971: *Abstract of British historical statistics.* Cambridge University Press. Cambridge.

MODESTE (V.) 1862: *De la cherté des grains et des préjugés populaires qui déterminent des violences dans les temps de disette.* Guillaumin. Paris.

MITCHELL (B.R.) 1978: *European historical Statistics 1750-1970.* Macmillan, Columbia U. Press, Sijthoff and Noordhoff.

MITCHELL (B.R.) 1982: International historical Statistics: Africa and Asia. New York University Press. New York.

MODIGLIANI (F.), WEINGARTNER (H.M.) 1958: Forecasting uses of anticipatory data on investment and sales. Quarterly Journal of Economics 72,23-54.

MOREHOUSE (N.F.), STROTZ (R.H.), HORWITZ (S.J.) 1950: An electroanalog method for investigating problems in economic dynamics: inventory oscillations. Econometrica 18,313-328.

MORSE (P.M.), FESHBACH (H.) 1953: *Methods of theoretical physics.* McGraw-Hill, New York.

MURRAY (J.D.) 1989: *Mathematical biology.* Springer. New York.

MUTH (J.F.) 1961: Rational expectations and the theory of price movements. Econometrica, 29, 3, 315-335.

NASH (V.) 1900: *The great famine and its causes.* Longmans. London.

NEAL (L.) 1990: *Rise of financial capitalism. International capital in the age of reason.* Cambridge University Press. Cambridge.

NERLOVE (M.) 1958: Adaptative expectations and cobweb phenomena. Quarterly Journal of Economics 72,227-240.

NEWBERY (D.M.G.), STIGLITZ (J.E.) 1981: *The theory of commodity price stabilization. A study in the economics of risk.* Clarendon Press. Oxford.

NORTH (D.) 1958: Ocean freight rates and economic development 1750-1913. Journal of Economic History 18,537-555.

ORD (K.) 1975: Estimation methods for models of spatial interaction. Journal of the American Statistical Association 70, 120-126.

O'ROURKE (K.), WILLIAMSON (J.G.) 1992: Were Heckscher and Ohlin right? Putting history back into the factor-price-equalization theorem. Discussion paper number 1593. Harvard Institute of Economic Research.

PAELINCK (J.H.P.), KLAASSEN (L.H.) 1979: *Spatial econometrics.* Gower. Aldershot.

PALMER (E.M.) 1985: *Graphical evolution.* John Wiley. New York.

PAPOULIS (A.) 1962: *The Fourier integral and its applications.* McGraw-Hill. New York.

PAPOULIS (A.) 1965: *Probability, random variables and stochastic processes.* McGraw Hill. Tokyo.

PAQUETTE (A.), ROEHNER (B.) 1991: *Science in english.* Belin. Paris.

PARR (J.B.) 1985: A note on the size distribution of cities over time. Journal of Urban Economics, 18,195-212.

PERSSON (K.G.) 1993: Grain price stabilization in Europe 1500-1900: theory and evidence. Paper presented at the European Economics Wokshop on Market Integration (Lerici).

PESARAN (M.H.) 1987: *The limits to rational expectations.* Basil Blackwell. Oxford.

PFISTER (C.) 1988: Fluctuations climatiques et prix céréaliers en Europe du XVIe au XXe siècle. Annales E.S.C. 41,1,25-54.

PITCHER (B.L.), HAMBLIN (R.L.), MILLER (J.L.) 1978: Diffusion of collective violence. American Sociological Review 43,23-35.

PREBISCH (R.) 1950: The economic development in Latin America and its principal problems. United Nations. Lake Sucess.

PRICE (R.) 1983: *The modernization of rural France. Communications networks and agricultural market structure in nineteenth-century France.* Hutchinson. London.

PRIESTLEY (M.B.) 1981: *Spectral analysis and time series.* Academic Press. New York.

QUAH (D.) 1993: Empirical cross-section dynamics in economic growth. European Economic Review, April 1993.

QUAH (D.) 1993: Aggregate and regional disaggregate income distribution fluctuations. London School of Economics; preprint.

RAVALLION (M.) 1986: Testing market integration. American Journal of Agricultural Economy 68, 102-109.

RAVALLION (M.) 1987: *Markets and famine.* Oxford University Press. Oxford.

REBUFFET (P.) 1945: *Aérodynamique expérimentale. Librairie Polytechnique Ch. Bérenger. Paris.*

REDMAN (D.A.) 1992: *A reader's guide to rational expectations. A survey and comprehensive annoted bibliography.* Edward Elgar. Aldershot.

RICHARDS (T.) 1983: Weather, nutrition and the economy: short run fluctuations in births, deaths and marriages, France: 1740-1909. Demography 20,2,197-212.

ROBSON (B.J.) 1973: *Urban growth: an approach.* Methuen, Andover, Hants.

ROEHNER (B.), WIESE (K.E.) 1982: A dynamic generalization of Zipf's rang-size rule. Environment and Planning A 14, 1449-1467

ROEHNER (B.) 1983: Time evolution of a system of two valued interacting elements: a microscopic interpretation of birth and death equations. International Journal of Systems Science. 14,10,1191-1216.

ROEHNER (B.) 1984: Macroeconomic regularities in the growth of nations: an empirical inquiry. International Journal of Systems Science 15, 9,

917-936.

ROEHNER (B.), WINIWARTER (P.) 1985: Aggregation of independent Paretian random variables. Advances in Applied Probability 17,465-469.

ROEHNER (B.) 1989a: How should spatial price interactions between interdependent markets be measured? Environment and Planning A, 21, 161-173.

ROEHNER (B.) 1989b: The decrease of price correlation with distance and the concept of correlation length. Environment and Planning A, 21, 289-298.

ROEHNER (B.M.) 1990a: Corrélations entre fluctuations des prix et fluctuations démographiques. France, XIXe siècle. Population 2, 299-326.

ROEHNER (B.M.) 1990b: Invariant patterns of wheat price series. Economies et Sociétés 11, 5-27.

ROEHNER (B.) 1991a: Liaison entre les conjonctures des prix des produits de base. Le cas de l'Allemagne au XIXe siècle. Histoire et Mesure 6, 31-49.

ROEHNER (B.) 1991b: Market prices and market integration: the case of nineteenth century France. Proceedings of the 31st Annual Cliometrics Conference. May 1991. Indiana University

ROEHNER (B.) 1991c: The long-term trend toward increased dispersion in the distribution of city-sizes. Environment and Planning A, 23, 1725-1740.

ROEHNER (B.) 1991d: On the direction of spatial interactions between markets. in: Spatial Analysis and Population Dynamics, D.Pumain editor. John Libbey Eurotext, INED. London.

ROEHNER (B.M.) 1995: Evolution of urban systems in the Pareto plane. Journal of Regional Science (to appear).

RUSSEL (J.C.) 1972: *Medieval regions and their cities.* David and Charles.

SAMUELSON (P.A.) 1948: International trade and the equalization of factor prices. The Economic Journal 58, 163-184.

SAMUELSON (P.A.) 1949: International factor-price equalization once again. The Economic Journal 59, 181-197.

SAMUELSON (P.A.) 1952: Spatial price equilibrium and linear programming. American Economic Review 42, 283-303.

SAMUELSON (P.A.) 1954: Prices of factors and goods in general equilibrium. The Review of Economic Studies 21, 1-20.

SAMUELSON (P.A.) 1957: Intertemporal price equilibrium: a prologue to the theory of speculation. Welwirtschaftliches Archiv 79,181-219. Reedited in Collected Papers of Paul A.Samuelson Vol 2 (1966) pp.946-984

SCHMITZ (C.J.) 1979: *World non-ferrous metal production and prices, 1700-1976.* Frank Cases and Company. London.

SCHULTZ (H.) 1938: *The theory and measurement of demand.* University of Chicago Press. Chicago.

SCHUMPETER (J.) 1933: The common sense of econometrics. Econometrica 1,5-12.

SCHWARTZ (L.) 1961: *Méthodes mathématiques pour les sciences physiques.* Hermann. Paris.

SEUFFERT (G.K.L.) 1857: *Statistik des Getreide und Viktualien-Handels im Königreiche Bayern mit Berücksichtigung des Auslandes.* Weisz. München.

SHEPPARD (E.), HAINING (R.P.), PLUMMER (P.) 1992: Spatial pricing in interdependent markets. Journal of Regional Science 32,1,55-75.

SIMON (H.) 1955: On a class of skew distributions. Biometrika 42,425-440.

SIMON (H.) 1978: Rationality as process and as product of thought. American Economic Review 68,1-16.

SINGER (H.) 1950: The distribution of gains between investing and borrowing countries. American Economic Review. Papers and Proceedings 40, 473-485.

SLICHER VAN BATH (B.H.) 1967: *The yields of different crops (mainly cereals) in relation to the seed c.810-1820.* Acta Historiae Neerlandica 2, 26-106.

SLICHER VAN BATH (B.H.) 1977: *Agriculture and the vital revolution* in The Cambridge Economic History of Europe edited by Rich (E.E.), Wilson (C.H.) Vol.5. Cambridge University Press.

SMITH (V.L.) 1963: Minimization of economic rent in spatial price equilibrium. The Review of Economic Studies 30, 24-31.

SPIEGEL (M.R.) 1978: *Formules et tables de mathématiques.* Série Schaum. McGraw-Hill. Ediscience.

STATISTIQUE DE LA FRANCE 1837: Ministère des Travaux Publics, de l'Agriculture et du Commerce. Imprimerie Nationale. Paris.

STATISTICHES JAHRBUCH FÜR DAS GROßHERZOGTUM BADEN 1915: Großherzoglichen Statistischen Landesamt. Karslruhe.

STEINDL (J.) 1965: Random processes and the growth of firms. Charles Griffin, High Wycombe.

STEWART (C.T.) 1958: The size and spacing of cities. Geographical Review 48, 222-245.

STRANG (G.) 1986: *Introduction to applied mathematics.* Wellesley-Cambridge Press. Wellesley. Mass.

TAKAYAMA (T.) 1964: Spatial equilibrium and quadratic programming. Journal of Farm Economics 46, 67-93.

TAKAYAMA (T.), JUDGE (G.G.) 1964: Equilibrium among spatially separated markets: a reformulation. Econometrica 32, 510-524.

TAKAYAMA (T.), JUDGE (G.G.) 1971: *Spatial and temporal price and allocation models.* North Holland. Amsterdam.

TIJMS (W.) 1983: *Prijzen van granen en peulvruchten Vol.II.* Historia Agriculturea XI. Nederlands Agronomisch Historisch Institut. Groningen.

TIMOSHENKO (V.P.) 1944: Interregional correlations in wheat yields and outputs. Wheat Studies of the Food Research Institute. Stanford University 20,6,213-259.

TIROLE (J.) 1985: *Concurrence imparfaite.* Economica. Paris.

TOBIN (J.) 1950: A statistical demand function for food in the U.S.A.. Journal of the Royal Statistical Society, 113, 93, 113-149.

TOUTAIN (J.C.) 1967: *Les transports en France de 1830 à 1965.* Série Histoire Quantitative de l'Economie Française No 8. Presses Universitaires de France. Paris.

TRITTON (D.J.) 1977: *Physical fluid dynamics.* Van Nostrand Reinhold Company. New York.

TYCHONOV (A.N.), SAMARSKI (A.A.) 1964: *Partial differential equations of mathematical physics.* Vol I. Holden-Day. San Francisco.

UPTON (G.), FINGLETON (B.) 1985: *Spatial data analysis by example.* Vol I,II. Wiley. New York.

USHER (A.P.) 1913: *The history of the grain trade in France.* Harvard University Press. Cambridge.

VAN DER POL (B.), BREMMER (H.) 1950: *Operational calculus based on the two-sided Laplace Integral.* Cambridge University Press. New York.

VINING (D.R.) 1976: Autocorrelated growth rates and the Pareto law; a further analysis. Journal of Political Economy. 84, 369-380.

VINING (D.R.) 1977: The rank-size rule in the absence of growth. Journal of Urban Economics 4,15-29

WEBER (A.) 1929: *Theory of the location of industries.* University of Chicago Press. Chicago.

WEIR (D.R.) 1989: Markets and mortality in France 1600-1789. in Famine, disease and the social order in early modern society, edited by: Walker(J.) and Schofield (R.S.). Cambridge Studies in Population, Economy and Society in Past Time.

WEYMAR (F.H.) 1988: *The dynamics of the world cocoa market.* MIT Press. Cambridge, Mass.

WHITTLE (P.) 1954: On stationary processes in the plane. Biometrika 41, 434-449.

WILLIAMSON (J.G.) 1980: Greasing the wheels of the sputtering export engines: midwestern grains and american growth. Explorations in Economic

History 17, 189-217.

WILLIAMSON (J.G.) 1991: Productivity and American leadership: a review article. Journal of Economic Literature 29,51-68.

WORKING (H.) 1922: Factors determining the price of potatoes in St Paul and Minneapolis. University of Minnesota Agricultural Experiment Station. Technical Bulletin No 10. St Paul.

WORKING (H.) 1925: Factors influencing price differentials between potato markets. Journal of the Farm Economics 7, 377-379.

YADRENKO (M.I.) 1983: *Spectral theory of random fields.* Optimization Software Inc. New York.

ZAPOLEON (L.B.) 1918a: Geography of wheat prices. US Departement of Agriculture. Bulletin No 594. See also Bulletin No755 (1919)

ZAPOLEON (L.B.) 1918b: Geographical phases of farm prices: corn. US Department of Agriculture. Bulletin No 696.

ZELLNER (A.) 1988: Causality and causality laws in economics. Journal of Econometrics 39,7-21.

ZIPF (G.K.) 1949: *Human behavior and the principle of least effort.* Addison-Wesley. Cambridge, Mass.

Index

MIX
Papier aus verantwortungsvollen Quellen
Paper from responsible sources
FSC® C105338

If you have any concerns about our products,
you can contact us on
ProductSafety@springernature.com

In case Publisher is established outside the EU,
the EU authorized representative is:
Springer Nature Customer Service Center GmbH
Europaplatz 3, 69115 Heidelberg, Germany

Printed by Libri Plureos GmbH
in Hamburg, Germany